Parador 12/6/93

INTRODUCTION TO REFERENCE WORK

Volume I

Basic Information Sources

McGRAW-HILL SERIES IN LIBRARY EDUCATION

Jean Key Gates, Consulting Editor
University of South Florida

INTRODUCTION
TO REFERENCE WORK

Volume I

Basic Information Sources

SECOND EDITION

William A. Katz

*Professor, School of Library
and Information Science
State University of New York at Albany*

McGraw-Hill Book Company

New York   St. Louis   San Francisco   Düsseldorf   Johannesburg
Kuala Lumpur   London   Mexico   Montreal   New Delhi
Panama   Rio de Janeiro   Singapore   Sydney   Toronto

INTRODUCTION TO REFERENCE WORK,
Volume I: Basic Information Sources

1 2 3 4 5 6 7 8 9 0   KPKP   7 9 8 7 6 5 4 3

Library of Congress Cataloging in Publication Data

Katz, William Armstrong, date
    Introduction to reference work.

    (McGraw-Hill series in library education)
    CONTENTS: v. 1.   Basic information sources.
    1.   Reference services (Libraries)
2.   Reference books.   I.   Title.
Z711.K32   1974   011'.02   73-8658
ISBN 0-07-033353-X (Vol. I)
ISBN 0-07-033354-8 (Vol. II)

This book was set in Elegante by Rocappi, Inc.
The editors were Janis Yates and David Dunham;
the designer was J. E. O'Connor;
and the production supervisor was Sam Ratkewitch.
The printer and binder was Kingsport Press, Inc.

For Janet and Linda

CONTENTS

PART III   SOURCES OF INFORMATION

PREFACE

This second edition serves the same general purpose as the first edition of 1969. Nevertheless, the revision has been extensively rewritten, updated, and, hopefully, improved over the initial effort. Some chapters have been deleted, others added, and many totally reorganized—thanks to suggestions of students and fellow teachers who seem to have found the first edition of some assistance.

The purpose of this volume is to discuss various information sources and how they are employed in reference work. It is the first of a two-volume set; and while it may be used independently by the student or the layman, the second volume, *Reference Services and Reference Processes,* is considerably more suggestive of what actual reference work is about. Consequently, the serious student of reference work should not consider that this first volume presents the total picture. It is only the beginning and, admittedly, gives a one-sided view of a most important profession.

Basic Information Sources introduces basic publications that will help the student and the layman to use the library in a more meaningful fashion. Although it is written with the reference librarian in mind, anyone who uses the library may benefit. Since it is impossible to cover the whole field and to meet everyone's needs, only foundation or basic works are considered. Nor is any effort made to cover the vast and growing area of subject specialization and bibliography. This is left to other texts and other courses. Some major subject forms are noted, but these are primarily illustrative and are not intended to be in any way exhaustive.

After a brief introduction on reference work and information sources, the text is divided into chapters on traditional forms such as bibliographies, indexes, and encyclopedias. Each chapter considers various common attributes of the form and how they relate to answering questions. While it is pointless for the student to memorize details about specific reference sources, he should at least grasp the essential areas of agreement and difference among the various forms. To this end, every effort is made to compare rather than to detail. Not all so-called basic titles are included or annotated because (1) there is no consensus on what constitutes "basic"; (2) more important, the object of this text is to discuss various forms and the titles used are primarily illustrative of those forms; and (3) finally, the annotations for a specific title are duplicated over and over again in everything from Winchell and Walford to the numerous subject bibliographies.

Suggested readings are found (1) at the end of each chapter and (2) in the footnotes. Where a footnote citation is used, it is rarely duplicated in the suggested readings at the end of the chapter. For the most part, the readings are limited to publications since 1968—thus updating the citations in the first edition and making it easier for the student to find the readings. [Note: A number of the readings will be found in the author's *Library Lit: The Best of* . . . (Metuchen, New Jersey, 1970 to date, annual). This consists of the thirty best library science articles of the year published in various magazines.]

Prices are noted for the majority of basic titles to indicate the relative expense of each work. This was suggested by several readers of the first edition who pointed out that budgetary considerations are sometimes equally as important as selection, particularly in terms of peripheral titles. Prices are of early 1973 and, obviously, are subject to change.

Bibliographic details are based on publisher's catalogs, *Books in Print,* and the latest edition of Winchell. The information is applicable as of early 1973 and, again, is subject to change.

Finally, despite the traditional arrangement and presentation of materials, this is not a vote per se for the traditional methods of teaching beginning reference courses. The material is presented in such a way that the more imaginative teacher will find himself free to use this textbook as a base for launching and developing his own style and techniques of teaching. It should serve as background material so as to release him for any type of presentation or methodology he deems necessary for his particular situation.

I am grateful to many teachers of reference and bibliography for their advice and help, particularly Frances N. Cheney of Peabody whose wit, humor, and scholarship remains an ever present inspiration. Also, special thanks to Charles Bunge of the University of Wisconsin library school and Joe Morehead of the State University of New York at Albany library school who dutifully suggested major changes for both volumes. Thanks, too, to the numerous students and teachers who so kindly made other suggestions, and particularly to the women (and not a few men) who pointed out a basically male chauvinistic slant in the first edition. Such references have been carefully deleted. For those who complained that there was a lack of piety in the first edition, fie on you. Hopefully, even the computer can occasionally laugh at itself.

The complete manuscript was read and improved by my student assistant Janet Klaessig. And to dig out an old cliché, words can not express my gratitude to Ms. Klaessig for her assistance. I realize this is a traditional thanks; but in her case, it goes quite beyond that to pure, unadulterated gratitude. It is because of her and students of her type that the future of libraries looks bright and fresh.

William A. Katz

PART ONE
INTRODUCTION

CHAPTER ONE
THE REFERENCE PROCESS

When the layman thinks of reference work, it is in terms of questions and answers. He has a question. He expects the librarian to give him an answer or, at a minimum, show him where or how the answer may be found. Disengaged from necessary quantitative and qualitative variables, reference work may be defined simply as the process of answering questions.

The ability of the librarian to translate the query into terms that can be met by a given reference source is known as reference service. A consideration of the communication process between the librarian and the person posing the question moves the definition to the broader context of the total reference process. It is a type of hierarchical scheme with reference process encompassing reference service, reference work, and, of course, the reference sources.[1] This analytical approach is not simply restating the phrase, "a rose is a rose is a rose." It serves a purpose. Until such time as the intricacies of the reference process are understood, it will be difficult to intelligently plan and organize methods of service. The definitions, or lack of definitions, mean little in themselves. Yet, in order to properly define any process it must be understood. It is suggested

---

[1] For a clear, intelligent discussion of various definitions of the reference process *see* Alan M. Rees, *The Present State and Future Prospects of Reference/Information Service* (Chicago: American Library Association, 1967), pp. 57–58.

here, as throughout the history of the reference process, that it is all too little understood.[2] For example, consider the interaction between the librarian and the person posing a question.

This is the familiar communications process, literally learned from childhood. The child asks, Why? He looks to his mother or father for a satisfactory answer. The parent, in turn, draws upon experience, knowledge, or intuition to give the proper reply. The communication elements remain the same from a parent's knee to a scientist scanning a computer print-out. First, someone has to ask the question. Second, there has to be a question or inquiry stemming from a simple Why? to How do I get special care for my aged parents? Third, there has to be someone to respond. And, finally, the person responding must have some resources with which to answer the query.

The four steps suffice to explain the operational aspects of the reference process. Still, if the parts are analyzed there are some startling variables. Someone must ask a question; but what is to explain the reluctance of millions who ask no questions—at least of a librarian? We have established that there must be a question; but once stated, how is it translated into terms the resources of the library will accept? The third element seems simple enough. There has to be someone to respond to the query. But should it necessarily be a trained librarian, a clerk, a documentalist? Fourth, there has to be resources. Yes, but what resources? Will they be adequate for the type of questions asked (and those yet to be asked)?

The problem is to try to understand and isolate the various elements of not only the reference process but the whole communications process. It is important to recognize that there is considerably more to answering questions than simply turning to the *World Almanac* or a favored encyclopedia. For example, the child and the scholar who both ask Why? pose numerous problems of communication.

Shera suggests the library is an agency of communication. "But what is the act of communication? How do we communicate? . . . We tend to assume that this is a simple act, when, as a matter of fact, it is very far from being simple." He then illustrates his point with the experience of the reference librarian and the individual posing a question.

---

[2] "Reference service is so greatly a matter of variables and intangibles that attempts to evaluate the department and its operations are rather baffling." Joseph L. Wheeler and Herbert Goldhor, *Practical Administration of Public Libraries* (New York: Harper & Row, 1962), p. 334. "No schematic rationalization of the reference function in libraries can truly correspond to the realities of day to day work with the library's public." "Reference Standards," *RQ*, June 1961, p. 2. The importance of a definition of reference work is stated succinctly by Samuel Rothstein: "Reference librarians, in failing to provide the means for accurate judgment of their place and contribution in library service, run the serious risk of having their work undervalued or ignored." Rothstein, "The Measurement and Evaluation of Reference Service," *Library Trends*, January 1964, p. 1,167.

The individual's first problem is to express the question, "to put it in terms that either the organization of the library will reveal it or the intelligence of the reference librarian can comprehend it." This problem and other communication factors "points up the very great need to analyze far more thoroughly than we have ever done, what the (reference) process is, and interpret that . . . process in psychological, neurological, and organizational terms."[3]

Charles Bunge reiterates and expands upon the communication process in an outline of what the reference librarian must consider when someone asks a question: (1) making sure the question, as understood by the librarian, coincides with the actual information needs of the patron; (2) analyzing, categorizing, or classifying the question on a number of dimensions in order to formulate a search strategy; (3) translating the terms of the question into the language of relevant parts of the reference system (for example, catalog subject headings, bibliography entries, and index terms); (4) making various decisions involved in conducting the search itself; and (5) evaluating the information, in terms of the patron and his needs.[4]

Shera, in more than one place, has pointed out that the function of the reference librarian is to serve as a mediator or middle man between the inquirer and the reference sources. This implies that the librarian not only know the sources, but be able to work closely with people who ask the questions. It is primarily a matter of communication and translation, i.e., communication between the librarian and the public, and translation of the public's questions into terms the various reference sources will accept in order to provide an answer.

In the dialogue between a questioner and the librarian, the question must first be clarified. The woman who wants something about gardening may want just that, a general book on the subject; or, more likely, a specific bit of information to assist her in checking the disease of a given plant, or in deciding what type of plants to put in a shade area. The possible real questions as opposed to the general questions are almost as numerous as the users of a library.

As Bunge says, once "the actual information needs of the patron" are recognized, the next step is to formulate a search strategy. This requires, to quote Bunge again, "translating the terms of the question in the language of relevant parts of the reference system." If a basic book on gardening is required, the librarian would find it readily enough in the card catalog under a suitable subject heading. At the other specific extreme, the question may involve searching indexes such as the *Biologi-*

[3] J. H. Shera, *Sociological Foundations of Librarianship* (New York: Asia Publishing House, 1970), pp. 32, 47, 48, 50.
[4] Charles A. Bunge, *Professional Education and Reference Efficiency*, Research Series No. 11 (Springfield, Illinois: State Library, 1967), p. 4.

cal and Agricultural Index to find the latest information on elm blight; or perhaps checking out various bibliographies such as *Subject Guide to Books in Print* or a union catalog to find what may be available on elm blight in general and in other libraries. (Note, too, that the subject "elm blight" must be translated into terms used as subject headings in the various indexes and bibliographies to cover works on elm blight.) Once the information is found, it then has to be evaluated, i.e., is it really the kind and at the level that the woman wants; is it too technical or too simple; is it applicable in this area?

Of course, all searches need not be complicated. Much of the reference work in libraries is of the simple fact type which requires direct answers: How high is the Empire State Building? What is the world record for long distance swimming? Who is my Congressman? Here, experience and knowledge of reference sources makes it relatively easy for the librarian to find the needed fact in a moment or two. Still, even at this simplistic level, the librarian must be sure that the man asking about long distance swimming is not really looking for a book on the general subject of swimming or that the question about the Empire State Building is not really one about architecture.

These few examples indicate that searching is not only a matter of finding the right reference form. There are numerous variables which make it a challenging, exciting, and often intellectually satisfying experience.

REFERENCE SERVICE AND THE PUBLIC

Whereas the theory of the reference process is difficult to isolate, it does have elemental factors easily understood. For example, on a day by day level reference entertains and, to a degree, enlightens millions of magazine and newspaper readers. Is it true that drinking milk after eating lobster will poison us? a nervous reader asks. "The Doctor Answers" in his daily column: There's no truth in that old wheeze. On another page, "Dear Abby," everyone's friendly reference librarian, copes with problems of mind, heart, and state. "Household Hints by Heloise" solves the difficulty of a woman who "had a nasty fat fire in her broiler." The Sunday supplement newspaper "Parade" features a page given over to answering queries: How much did it cost Father Daniel Berrigan and the other defendants at Harrisburg to defend themselves against the United States? and Did Marcello Mastroianni ever leave his wife for an airline hostess? (The answers: $600,000 and "yes.") *New York Magazine* periodically runs special sections to answer more pressing queries, e.g., a 10-page guide for parents seeking special care for their children. A twist of the radio or television dial offers local or national quiz and talk shows based on the question–answer syndrome. It has taken librarians a long time to realize what the mass media recognized long ago—there is a large audience in the general public with questions.

This is not to say the library should overnight become a substitute for the popular media. It is to suggest that the reference librarian is not necessarily working in a vacuum or in a mystical relationship with the public. The average man or woman understands reference work in one context, the librarian in another. The librarian may learn equally from the public and from a textbook or a classroom about reference work.

Lacking any totally satisfactory definition of the reference process, it may still be approached in understandable terms of functions. What does a reference librarian do?

It has been well over a decade since the American Library Association, Reference Services Division, Committee on Standards, reviewed the nature of reference service. Its findings are still valid and, in broad outline, will remain so for many years to come. The Committee divides reference services into two large categories—direct and indirect.[5]

The direct category includes:

Information service "This service may range from answering an apparently simple question, through recourse to an obvious reference source, to supplying information based on search in the collections of the library, combining competence in bibliothecal techniques with competence in the subject of inquiry." The depth and the character of such service varies with the type of library and the kind of patron it is designed to serve. But "the central feature of information service, irrespective of its level or its intensity, is to provide an end product in terms of information sought by the library's patron." Thus, the first duty of the reference librarian, quite simply, is to answer questions. Questions normally are answered at the reference desk or in the library. In recent years, however, there has been a marked trend toward the use of the telephone, particularly for quick fact-type questions. The mails also bring requests, both from individuals and from other libraries.

Instruction in the use of the library "The central feature of this instruction, irrespective of its level or its intensity, is to provide guidance and direction in the pursuit of information, rather than providing the

[5] "Reference Standards," *RQ,* June 1961, pp. 1-2. Since the late 1960s, the Standards Committee has tried to develop a revised set of standards "which could be applied to reference services in all libraries." A report on the activities of the Committee as relates to one study will be found in Ruth W. White's "Measuring the Immeasurable: Reference Standards," *RQ,* Summer 1972, p. 308. Other useful articles which pertain to what reference librarians do or do not do are: Mary Jo Lynch, "Academic Library Reference Policy Statements," *RQ,* Spring 1972, pp. 222+; Florence Blakely, "Perceiving Patterns of Reference Service: A Survey," RQ, Fall 1971, pp. 30+.

information itself." The paradox between this and the first service has bothered many librarians and will be discussed elsewhere.

Indirect services may be outlined:

Selection of materials This consists of the recognition of the various types of materials needed for adequate reference service—not only books, but periodicals, manuscripts, newspapers, and anything which can conceivably assist the librarian in direct service. The acquisition of reference works is a major part of reference work, as is building the total library collection. Another aspect of selection is the weeding of book collections and files.

Organization of references The organization and administration of reference is a matter of staff, coordination of reference service with other services in the library, and recognition of the importance of drawing upon all resources in libraries throughout the country and the world. In this latter respect, interlibrary loan procedures are particularly important in the day-to-day effectiveness of reference work.

Access to materials Unfortunately there is never enough access to materials. In order to develop this access, the librarian may spend some time preparing special bibliographies and homemade files. Also, interlibrary loan may be categorized as an access activity. In recent years, it has become one of the biggest elements in reference service—in fact, so large that some libraries are now divorcing it from reference and establishing it as a separate division. The division, by the way, is one over which there is considerable debate—particularly since interlibrary loan is such an integral part of the network system of reference service.

Evaluation of reference section How well is the reference section serving the public? What has been done and what can be done to improve service? This presupposes a method of evaluating not only the collection, but the organization of the reference section and the library as a whole.

Miscellaneous tasks There are a variety of "housekeeping" duties which consist of such tasks as assisting with photocopying, filing, checking in materials, keeping a wary eye on reading rooms, maintaining records, plus all the chores that are the responsibility of any library department—from budgeting to preparing reports and publicity releases. The extent of this kind of "busy work" depends to a great degree on the size of the library and the philosophy and the financial support of the reference section. However, even in the largest libraries, the professional librarian will be called upon to do a given amount of necessary routine work.

Reference questions

There are numerous methods of categorizing types of reference questions, and these are considered fully in the second volume. By the way of introduction to a rather complex situation, questions may be divided into four general categories.

Directional Where is the card catalog, the reference section, the restrooms? This is a common type of query which most libraries do not consider evaluating, and it obviously requires only a good sense of direction and a familiarity with the library. (Note: the term "directional question" is sometimes used to refer to bibliographical queries, but these may be divided among the three following types.)

Ready reference What is the name of the governor of Illinois? How long is the Mississippi River? The ready reference or fact category accounts for 85 to 95 percent of the questions asked in libraries. Answers are found primarily in the fact type of reference books, including such sources as encyclopedias, almanacs, and yearbooks. Average time to answer: one to five minutes. Average difficulty: nil, although there are times when a question of this type takes hours to answer and requires the skills of the best librarian.

Specific search I have to write a paper (or deliver a speech) on gun control. What do you have? Where can I find background information on the polar bear? This type of question normally involves a variety and number of reference sources which tend to explain things in a concise, easy-to-understand fashion. It is the query heard most often from the student or curious layman.

Research What are the causes for the current rate of inflation in Great Britain? How does a computer function in the library reference situation? The research question may come from anyone. It is usually directed to the librarian by an adult who is a specialist or who is on her way to becoming a specialist. There are no easy one line or two paragraph answers. Instead, the librarian must often call upon the total resources of the library, and often on resources of other libraries.

The four types of questions move from the simple to the complex, from a single source to multiple sources. One query might include at least three of the major categories; that is, the user may move from a simple fact to a short explanation to an involved study of a given topic.

Classification is not as important as recognizing that each question is different, each person posing the question has a singular problem. Since categorization of queries sometimes helps find answers, the divisions are of interest. Otherwise they tend to be more academic than real.[6]

REFERENCE SERVICE AND THE LIBRARY

The reference librarian does not function alone in a library but is part of a larger unit. Briefly, how do reference services fit into the library?

The specific purpose of any library is to obtain, preserve, and make available the recorded knowledge of man. It is a system which can be as intricate and involved as the table of organization for The Library of Congress or General Motors. At the other extreme, it may be as simple as the one-man small-town library or the corner barber shop.

Regardless of organizational patterns or complexities, the parts of the system are interrelated and common to all sizes and types of libraries. They consist of administrative work, technical services (acquisition and cataloging), and reader's services (circulation and reference). These broad categories cover a multiple of subsections, not to mention challenges and problems. Still, they are not independent units but part of larger units; all are closely related. They form a unity essential for library service in general, reference in particular. Let one fail and the whole system will suffer.

Administrative work

The administration is concerned with library organization and communication. The better the administration functions, the less obvious it appears—at least to the user. The reference librarian must be aware of and often participate in administrative decisions ranging from budget to automation. Precisely how administration functions effectively is the subject of countless texts and coffee conversations. It is not the topic of this text, although specific administration of reference sections and departments is discussed elsewhere.

---

[6] There are many ways to classify reference questions. For example, B. C. Vickery, "Scientific Information Problems," *Techniques of Information Retrieval*, Chapter 2, (Hamden, Connecticut: Archon Books, The Shoe String Press, Inc., 1970) divides them into three types: (1) *Current awareness* This means keeping up to date with a given field. Scientists tend to: read technical papers, scan contents of journals and offprints of articles, or (most likely) converse with colleagues. Some abstracts and indexes are used. (2) *Everyday information* This is the ready-reference type query where a specific bit of information is needed. For this type of information, scientists again tend to depend on: conversation with their peers, indexes and abstracts, and the usual quick reference aids from handbooks to encyclopedias and standard monographs. (3) *Exhaustive survey* This is another word for research in depth where every resource is called into use. Here particular reliance is on indexes and abstracts and other bibliographical aids.

Technical services—acquisitions

The selection and acquisition of materials is governed by the type of library and its users. Policies, of course, vary; but the rallying cry of the nineteenth-century activist librarians, "The right book for the right reader at the right time," is still applicable to any library. It presents many challenges. For the general collection, it presupposes a knowledge of the clientele as well as personal knowledge of the material acquired and its applicability to the reader. The librarian must cope with publishers, sources, and reviews and show an appreciation for cooperation with other libraries. The unparalleled production of library materials over the past 50 years makes the process of selection and acquisition a primary intellectual responsibility.

While reference librarians are responsible for the reference collection, their responsibility extends to the development of the library's entire collection—a collection which may serve to help them answer questions.

Technical services—cataloging

Once a piece of information is acquired, the primary dilemma is how to retrieve it from the hundreds, thousands, or millions of bits of information in the library. There are a number of avenues open, from oral communication to abstracts; but when dealing with larger information units—books, recordings, films, periodicals, or reports—the normal finding device is the card catalog. The catalog is the library's main bibliographical instrument. When properly used, it (1) enables a person to find a book for which he has the author, title, or the subject area; (2) shows what the library has by any given author, on a given subject, and in a given kind of literature; (3) assists in the choice of a book as to its form (e.g., handbook, literature, or text) or edition; (4) assists in finding other materials from government documents to films; and (5) often most important, specifically locates the item in the library. It is obviously a primary resource for reference librarians; and it is essential they understand not only the general aspects of the card catalog, but its many peculiarities.

Reader's services—circulation

Circulation is one of two primary public service points in the library. The other is reference.

After the book has been acquired and prepared for easy access, the circulation department is concerned with (1) charging out the material to the reader, (2) receiving it on return, and (3) returning it to its proper location. Other activities of the circulation department include registration of prospective borrowers, record-keeping of the number of books and patrons, and maintaining other statistics pertinent to charting the operation of the library. Depending upon the size and the type of the library, circulation can be a relatively simple or complex matter. Large public and university libraries, for example, are constantly seeking new and more efficient charging systems and methods of record-keeping of what is in or out of the library.

At the other extreme, particularly in small public libraries, up to 50 percent or more of the reference work may be centered at the circulation desk. This is normally a library with one or two professionals who must pinch-hit in almost every capacity from administration to cataloging. Also, there simply may be no space for a separate reference desk and the circulation point is a logical center where people come not only to check out books, but to ask questions. Needless to add, this is at best a stopgap type of reference.

Reader's services—reference

Reference service is part of the library and draws upon all the resources of the library to answer questions. At one time, the availability of material was fairly limited to individual libraries. If a question was beyond the resources of the library (or, for that matter, the abilities of the librarian), the user had no choice but to move on to a larger or different type library. Accessibility to information was, in a word, provincial. Today, accessibility is considerably more sophisticated. Thanks to technological innovations, from microfilm to computer tapes, it is possible to bring the holdings of almost any library to the individual, instead of the individual traveling to the library. The implications of this evolutionary process are extremely important. It is imperative to recognize that when one speaks of reference service it should in no way be limited to the parameters of a single reference collection or the holdings of a single library.

INFORMATION SOURCES

Many unexperienced reference librarians fear the moment someone stands before them and asks: who, what, when, where, how, or why? Hopefully, no single reference question will incorporate all six of the question categories. One can sometimes be quite enough, or too much. Still, it does not require an expert to know there is usually an answer, even if it is that no answer exists. The secret is to find a reference source with the correct answer. This requires education, experience, and a sense of media.

Traditionally, information sources are primarily books, magazines, and newspapers. Today, the number of forms is continuously increasing in number, variety, and sophistication. The familiar *Readers' Guide to Periodical Literature*, for example, indexes some 180 magazines. The recent *Science Citation Index* analyzes 3,000 journals, reports, patents, monographs, and books. Given the new reference aids, the possibilities of finding an answer are considerably more likely than they were 20 or 50 years ago. There is not only better access to materials, but there is enough duplication of possible reference sources to ensure that an answer will be found not in one, but in two, three, or even a dozen different places.

The majority of reference questions are of the ready-reference type. They may be answered by short, factual bits of information. Consequently, most answers come from a relatively small collection of reference works. (The reader will notice an obvious paradox. On the one hand, there are more and more sophisticated reference aids and, on the other, the majority of questions may be answered via a small number of traditional sources. The obvious conclusion, which will be discussed at length in the second volume, is that the reference librarian is not functioning at her maximum capacity, certainly not at her maximum intellectual capacity.)

What is a reference source? A reference source is usually meant as a form of a book. The real question, then, is what is a reference book? The experienced library user will snap back: "Any book which can't be taken from the library." That used to be the case, and still is in many libraries, but it hardly is a sufficient answer.[7] A reference book may be so designated when it is "designed by its arrangement and treatment to be consulted for definite items of information rather than to be read consecutively."[8] The *World Almanac* or any dictionary illustrates the definition well enough.

Excluding the specific reference book, a reference source is anything which is used to answer questions. This may be a pamphlet, a picture, a recording, an unpublished report, a magazine article, a monograph, a slide, even an individual with specialized knowledge who is available to answer the query. A telephone call may clear up a problem as may a fast look at the table of contents of a history book in the general collection.

---

[7] Most libraries now have policies of limited circulation of some reference books. For example, *see* Peter Hernon and Maureen Pastine, "Faculty Loan Policies for Reference Collections," *PLA Bulletin*, July 1972, pp. 175+. A survey of college library loan policies of reference books shows that more than one-half those surveyed permit circulation of some reference materials.

[8] *A.L.A. Glossary of Library Terms* (Chicago: American Library Association, 1943).

REFERENCE FORMS

The rigid concept of a reference source being a reference book (labeled as such and isolated in a special collection) is demonstrably false. Any experienced reference librarian will tell the beginner that the whole library, the community, the network of libraries in the area, in fact, the national and international resources available constitute the real reference sources. The obvious secret to success in reference work is coming to terms with the forms into which questions may be readily channeled for possible answers. And to begin this sometimes arduous process, it is obviously necessary to understand basics—in this case, the basic reference book forms.

In the information chain, the library comes into the picture at about the same time the scientist or researcher leaves, i.e., when the work is finished, reported, published, and dutifully indexed or abstracted. At this juncture, specific knowledge or information tends to take on a number of different forms:

Primary sources   This is original material which has not been filtered through interpretation, condensation, or evaluation by a second party. The scientist's final report in a journal is primary material. Other forms of primary or first hand material include what is found in sources such as daily newspaper reporting, monographs, dissertations, patents, manufacturer's literature, and manuscripts. The forms of reference work which allow access and control to primary sources are indexes and abstracts and bibliographies.

Secondary sources   This is material which has been modified, selected, or rearranged for a particular purpose or audience. Most of it is based upon primary source material. Secondary sources in reference work include encyclopedias; fact-type books such as almanacs, handbooks, directories; and biographical sources.

Tertiary sources   This is material which is thrice removed from the primary sources. It is the usual province of textbooks not generally considered reference sources.

The definitions of primary, secondary, and tertiary sources are useful only in that they indicate (1) relative currency (primary sources tend to be more current than secondary sources) and (2) the relative accuracy of materials (the primary sources will generally be more accurate than secondary sources, only because it represents unfiltered, original ideas; conversely, a secondary source may correct errors in the primary source).

The terms are not always that clearcut. Scientists tend to consider primary sources as journals, reports, and forms of informal exchange from conversations to speeches. They call bibliographies, abstracts and indexes, and monographs secondary sources.

When the librarian understands what a reference source will do, or will not do, it is a relatively simple matter to categorize questions in terms of those sources. The librarian may not remember the title of a source, but she will know an index, a bibliography, or a fact book is the form required for the answer. The process, familiar to everyone, involves a mastery of matching the particular question with the source and using the source to obtain an answer. It is not necessary to know the name of a cookbook, almanac, dictionary, or the like to match an everyday question with its logical form. If someone is seeking an apartment to rent, she uses an access or directional reference source—usually the classified ad section of a newspaper. Fact forms are all around us; and no one thinks twice about turning to a cookbook for a recipe or a telephone book for a number. Many homes have at least one almanac, often an encyclopedia and a dictionary. Road maps and travel guides make every American an expert on geographical sources; and the annual income tax form may drive him to another government document which explains how to fill it out. Other common reference sources which many of us use without much thought are store directories, bus and airline schedules, and manuals such as how to repair a car or how to play chess.

These admittedly simple examples illustrate that whenever a reference source has become part of our experience and educational growth, it requires little thought to match a question with a probable answer form. Library reference work is more complicated; however, the basic reference process is neither foreign nor particularly difficult once the basic forms are mastered. Those forms may be divided into two large categories—the control-access-directional type and the source type.

Control-access-directional type

BIBLIOGRAPHIES
The first broad class or form of reference sources is bibliography. This form is variously defined but in its most general sense is the technique of systematically producing descriptive lists of records.

Control The bibliography serves as a control device. It inventories what is produced from day-to-day, year-to-year, in such a way to enable the compiler (and the user) to feel he has a control, via organization, of the steady flow of knowledge. This is done through research (finding the specific source), identification, description, and classification.

Access Once the items are controlled, the individual items are so organized for easy access to facilitate intellectual work. As Robinson puts it, "The aim of the bibliography . . . is to assist the enquirer in discovering the existence or determining the identity of books or other documentary material which may be of interest to him."[9]

All the access-type reference works may be broadly defined as bibliographies; but for purpose of enumeration, they are subdivided here:

1. Guides to reference sources and the literature of a field either of a general nature or of subject nature. Example: Winchell's *Guide to Reference Books*. Holler's *The Information Sources of Political Science*. Another type of guide is the bibliography of bibliographies and the index to bibliographies.

2. The library card catalog or the catalogs of numerous libraries arranged for easy access via a union list. Technically, this is not a bibliography but is often used in the same manner.

3. General systematic enumerative bibliography which includes various forms of bibliography from universal to retrospective trade bibliography. Example: *National Union Catalog*.

4. Indexes and abstracts which are usually treated separately from bibliographies, but are considered a bibliographical aid. They are a systematic listing of materials which help to identify and trace those materials. Indexes to the contents of magazines and newspapers are the most frequently used types in the reference situation. As a tool for tapping the contents of almost any work, indexes are invaluable, usually an absolute necessity, as an integral part of a reference book. Examples: *The Readers' Guide to Periodical Literature; New York Times Index*. The indexes and abstracts are particularly important because they serve to introduce the reader to the largest single source of reference materials other than books, that is, serials.

Direction The bibliography normally does not give the user a definitive answer but serves to direct him to the source of an answer. To be used effectively, most of these must presume the items listed are either in the library or available from another library system.

Source type

These works usually suffice in themselves to give the answers. Unlike the access type of reference work, they are synoptic.

Encyclopedias The most used single source are encyclopedias; and they may be defined as works containing informational articles on sub-

---

[9] A. M. Lewin Robinson, *Systematic Bibliography* (London: Clive Bingley, 1966), p. 12.

jects in every field of knowledge, usually arranged in alphabetical order. These are used to answer specific questions about X topic or X person or general queries which may begin with, "I want something about X . . . ." Examples: *Encyclopaedia Britannica, World Book Encyclopedia.*

Fact Sources Yearbooks, almanacs, handbooks, manuals, and directories are included in this category. All of these types have many different qualities, but they share one common element: they are all used to look up factual material for quick reference work. Together they cover almost every facet of human knowledge. Examples: *World Almanac, Statesman's Yearbook.*

Dictionaries Those sources which deal primarily with all aspects of words from proper definitions to spelling are dictionaries. Examples: *Webster's Third New International Dictionary; Dictionary of American Slang.*

Biographical sources Those forms which are self-evident sources of information on people distinguished in some particular field of interest are known as biographical sources. Examples: *Who's Who; Current Biography.*

Geographical sources The forms best known are the atlases, which not only may show given countries but may illustrate themes such as historical development, social development, and scientific centers. Geographical sources also include gazetteers, dictionaries of place names, and guidebooks. Examples: *The Times Atlas of the World;* Shepherd's *Historical Atlas.*

Government documents

Government documents represent official publications ordered and normally published by the federal, state, or local government. Since they may include directional and source-type works, their separation into a particular unit is more one of convenience and organization than of distinct use in a reference situation. Examples: *Monthly Catalog of U.S. Government Publications* (access type); *United States Organizational Manual* (source type).

The neat categorization of reference types by access and by source is not always as distinctive in an actual situation. A bibliography may be the only source required if the question is simply one of verification or of trying to complete a bibliographical citation. Conversely, the bibliography at the end of an encyclopedia article, or a statement in that article, may serve to direct the patron to another source. In general, the two main categories—access and source—serve to differentiate between the principal types of reference works.

General to particular

Another breakdown of reference sources may be made by considering the scope of the works. Scope is either general or particular, and the two types tend to augment and supplement one another. Almost without exception, the most widely used, popular reference books are general in scope. For example, the major encyclopedias, and such works as almanacs and dictionaries, cover every conceivable field of interest, from ants to the zodiac. The reason for this is obvious. The vast majority of users only want quick answers or brief explanations. Being aware of this, publishers tend to issue reference works which will appeal to the widest possible audience—much as television producers, magazine publishers, and automobile manufacturers compete for the largest market. Another frequent user is the student whose curriculum is varied, whose ability to use detailed works is limited, and who probably needs a generalized approach to most types of information.

Conversely, America is breeding a brand of specialists who, after a certain point, require information in depth in a narrow subject field. General works rarely meet their needs. In this case, the publisher steps back and tries it again, this time by bringing out not just general reference sources but subject sources. Thus, there are bibliographies limited to a particular period of history, indexes to a special field of science, yearbooks and almanacs to one area of political science, biographical sources to given professions, dictionaries to the jargon of a subject area, geographical sources to a thematic aspect of a subject, and government documents to almost any conceivable interest.

This two-level approach—general reference works supported by specific works in a subject area—is applicable in almost any type of library. Regardless of how specialized the information, at one time or another the expert will need an overview, not only of his field but of supporting fields. At this stage, nothing may be better for him than a general encyclopedia article or some data from a popular yearbook or almanac. Conversely, while the student and layman will normally find all that is required in one of the general reference books, he may need the specialized works when his question either requires additional search or (and this does happen on occasion) is so "far out" that it is not covered in the general works. For example, through reading, radio, or conversation a reader may come across a quote, a word, a theory which he wishes to trace. The first reaction would be to use a standard book of quotations, possibly an unabridged dictionary, and an encyclopedia. If all these fail, the quote, word, or theory would have to be searched in specialized works.

EVALUATING REFERENCE SOURCES

A thorough understanding of the day-to-day sources of answers requires some evaluation of those sources. How does the librarian know whether a reference source is good, bad, or indifferent? A detailed answer to the question will be found later in the text—and throughout each of the chapters on form. Still, the state of the art can be stated in rather simplistic terms: (1) a good reference source is one that serves to answer questions; (2) a bad reference source is one that fails to answer questions. Constant and practical use will quickly place it in one of these two categories.

Considering the expense of most reference sources, the typical practice is to read one or more book reviews before coming to a decision to buy. Given the reviews, larger libraries usually request or automatically receive examination copies before purchase. Smaller libraries may have no choice but to accept the word of the reviewer and order or not order. Ideally, though, the reference source should be examined by a trained reference librarian before it is incorporated into the collection. No review or review medium is infallible. More important, the merits praised by a reviewer may be ideal for one type or size of library, yet of limited value for another library. What does one look for?

The work should be authoritative, that is accurate and trustworthy. This is usually guaranteed by the reputation of the publisher, author, or compiler. The source should be timely and up-to-date material both in terms of fact and interpretation. The purpose and scope should be clear and should be of a nature to fit the needs of the reference collection. And it should be geared to the audience the library serves. If the source meets all these requirements, it will measure up to the general criteria for evaluating all nonfiction.

There is a major second area to consider—arrangement and what it implies. No matter how accurate, authoritative, or apparently useful a source may be for a library, it is next to worthless when the information cannot be easily and quickly extracted. This means almost all reference sources should have an index or similar aid to allow the librarian to approach the material it contains by subject, by area, by author, and often by title. Lacking an index (or even with one), there should be suitable cross references and entries which are clear, precise, and accurately related to the whole, i.e., to the intended purpose, scope, and audience. Furthermore, the arrangement and format should be such to encourage rather than to discourage use.

There are quick methods of discovering whether the source meets these basic requirements. Think of two or three questions which the source should answer. How easy is it to find the answers? Were there any answers at all? If not, the source is not meeting its purported purpose. Reverse the process. Find two or three facts. Can they be found under logical subject, author, or title headings in the index? If not, the source is probably only partially analyzed.

Another fast analytical method is to carefully read the preface or the introduction. The well designed reference source makes it immediately clear as to its scope, purpose, and audience. Limitations, if any, should be clearly stated.

A third method is to compare the source with similar sources in the same or related fields. For example, is the material as accurate, up to date, and unbiased as other accepted sources? Does it represent a new viewpoint, method, or approach; or is it merely a rehash of other material?

There is considerably more to the evaluation process than stated here, but once the basics are understood the remainder is a matter of refinement and experience. The last word may sound as cynical or as simplistic as the reader cares to interpret it, but . . . trust no one. The reviewer, publisher, and author do make mistakes, sometimes of horrendous proportions. The librarian who evaluates reference sources with the constant suspicion of the worse is less likely to be the victim of those mistakes.

SUGGESTED READING

Berman, Sanford, "Let It All Hang Out," *Library Journal,* June 15, 1971, pp. 2,054+. An unorthodox view of what librarians in general should be doing about changing the image of the library and giving better service.

Cole, William, "Turnstiles in the Library?" *The New York Times Book Review,* March 26, 1972, pp. 2+. An informative discussion of the reference questions posed at the New York Public Library.

Durnkan, M. J., "Reference Service Patterns in Academic Libraries," *Connecticut Libraries,* Fall 1970, pp. 15+. A brief overview of types of reference services in academic libraries.

Galvin, Thomas, *Current Problems in Reference Service.* New York: R. R. Bowker Company, 1971. A compilation of thirty-five case histories in reference work designed to acquaint the student with daily problems at the reference desk. This is one in a series of such "problem centered approaches to librarianship," published by Bowker. *See also:* the bibliography in Galvin's book for other case study collections—there are many, both by Bowker and by other publishers, e.g., Wilkinson, B. R., *Reference Services for Undergraduate Students: Four Case Studies.* Metuchen, New Jersey: Scarecrow Press, 1972.

Howland, Bette, "Public Facilities—A Memoir," *Commentary,* February 1972, pp. 45+. A not overly encouraging yet realistic view of what it means to work in a public library.

MacLeish, Archibald, "The Premise of Meaning," *American Scholar,* Summer 1972, pp. 357+. Reprinted *Wilson Library Bulletin,* January 1973, pp. 424+. A literate essay by a leading poet and playwright on the implication of the library in society.

Miller, Mary, "Two Days at the Reference Desk," *RQ,* Winter 1969, pp. 107+. A listing of reference questions in a typical two-day period at a typical reference desk. *See also:* Nelson Associates, *Public Library Systems in the United States.* Chicago: American Library Association, 1969. See pages 362–365 for test reference questions used by the survey teams. The questions (often found in other forms in various surveys) are typical enough of those asked at most reference desks. *See also:* "The Exchange," a regular feature in *RQ* which considers difficult-to-answer queries.

Tripp, Edward, "Man Behind the Book, The Reference Editor," *RQ,* November 1964, pp. 7+. A look at evaluating reference books from the viewpoint of the editor.

Wells, Dorothy, "How to Do It Approach to Reference," *RQ,* Summer 1971, pp. 331+. Problems and solutions to basic housekeeping reference situations— useful perspective for beginners. For other *RQ* articles on various facets of being a reference librarian *see:* Gellatly, Peter, "Reference Anyone," Winter 1966, pp. 62+. (And replies to Gellatly, Spring 1967, pp. 127+; Summer 1967, pp. 175+.) Vavrek, Bernard, "Eliminate the Reference Department," Fall 1969, pp. 33+. King, Jack, "What Future, Reference Librarians," Spring 1971, pp. 331+. Tebbetts, D. R., and Pritchard, Hugh, "Undergraduate Reference Aids," *RQ,* Spring 1973, pp. 275+. A short report on queries most often asked concerning undergraduate reference aids.

Wyer, James I., *Reference Work.* Chicago: American Library Association, 1930. Hutchins, Margaret, *Introduction to Reference Work.* Chicago: American Library Association, 1944. While both of these texts are dated, they remain the best general introduction to the theory of reference work. Both may be read today with considerable profit by the beginner.

PART TWO
CONTROL AND ACCESS TO
INFORMATION

CHAPTER TWO
BIBLIOGRAPHIES:
INTRODUCTION

A bibliography is analogous to a map or a chart. It serves to guide the librarian in the chaotic world of books and other forms of communication. Just as no sensible navigator would set out to sea without a chart, no modern library can hope to function without bibliographical guides.

From the viewpoint of the user, who may not understand the fine shades of bibliography, it serves one basic need. He may know what he wants, but he is never sure it exists or, more important, where he can find it. The bibliography gives him the answers.

A request for a book by title, author, or subject is a common question. Normally, the first logical place to find the answer is the card catalog. For most purposes this serves well enough. It fails when a part of the book is needed, when the book is not in the library, or when it is a type of material, such as an elusive government document, which may not be in the catalog. Then, too, the patron may have the incorrect title or author or may simply find it impossible to fathom the ambiguities of the cataloging system. At this point, he desperately needs the assistance of a librarian who in turn may go to other bibliographic tools to locate the needed material.

These, then, are the practical functions of bibliography which may be defined simply as a well organized list or inventory. There are numerous definitions, and champions of this or that explanation can become quite heated in their insistence on the true meaning of the word. Still, regardless of form, it is usually enumerative; that is, some selection process is carried on to determine what or what not will be listed. Also, it is generally systematic in that the material is arranged in a consistent form. Roy Stokes sums it up:

> Enumerative bibliography is the easiest of all the particular areas of the study to understand. This is largely because it meets most accurately all that is generally required by the lay public, a straightforward listing of books and without the burdening of over-much detail. Having collected the material the importance of its systematizing becomes obvious and this area of bibliography is just as happily called "systematic" as "enumerative" . . . The basic idea of enumerative bibliography . . . is clear, the listing of the salient details about a particular group of books which have some kind of coordinating factor.[1]

SYSTEMATIC ENUMERATIVE BIBLIOGRAPHY

When the average librarian speaks of bibliography, she probably means systematic enumerative bibliography, i.e., a list of books, films, or recordings. The purpose is to assist the user in access to materials, i.e., identifying, locating, or selecting. Beyond the pragmatic use of a bibliography, it is a control device. It superimposes some order on the chaotic mass of subjects and titles. The current rate of national and international publishing is so great that it is increasing approximately three times as fast as the growth of the world's population. And while the population dies, the books linger on. What has happened, and what continues to haunt the bibliographer, is that publication is extending far beyond our present ability to control it. Consider:

1. From 1950 to 1970, the number of new titles of books increased almost 400 percent.
2. All the recorded scientific and technical literature in the history of man will double to 4.6 trillion words by 1982. In terms of the individual scientist in a given field of science, the existing literature in his particular speciality is some 11,000 books on an average.
3. Whereas there were 10,000 periodicals being published in 1900, today the figure is well over 100,000.
4. The Yale University Library estimates to keep up with the current literature it will have 200 million books by the year 2040, occupying over 6,000 miles of shelves. If Yale continues to use card catalogs, it will require 80 acres of space for its collection in 2040.

[1] Roy Stokes, *The Functions of Bibliography* (London: Andre Deutsch, 1969), p. 26.

5. A specialist who 60 years ago needed 25 minutes a day to read all the current literature in his field, in a few years, will require continuous reading every hour of the day.[2]

There is a great deal of speculation and disagreement about the exact amount of information which will be produced in the years ahead; but there is a consensus that it will be literally overwhelming in quantity, if not quality. Developing a solution to this problem is the current concern of librarians and documentalists. While no adequate definition has been given for documentation, it may be called an approach to bibliographical control by specialization. If we cannot control the mass of information, let us narrow control down to a specific area, specific forms of communication for specific users. Some of the basic documentation philosophy is applicable to general bibliography. The current effort is to limit bibliographies to one specific nation, and then keep them within increasingly narrow boundaries of type or form.

An exhaustive study of bibliography and its organization and control would far exceed the limits of this text. All that can be hoped for here is to indicate the perimeters and then concentrate on some specific work most generally employed by the librarian.

If a bibliography is to adequately meet the need for control and access, several elements are presupposed.

Completeness   Either through a single bibliography or a combination of bibliographies, the librarian should have access to the complete records of all areas of interest. This is not only in terms of what is now available, but what has been published in the past and what is being published today or is proposed for publication tomorrow. Also, the net should be broad enough to include the world, not simply one nation's works.

Access to a part   Normally the librarian is apt to think of bibliographies in terms of the whole unit, book, periodical, manuscript, or the like; but an ideal bibliography should also be analytical, allowing the librarian to approach the specific unit in terms of the smallest part of a work.

Various forms   Books are considered the main element of most bibliographies, but a comprehensive bibliographical tool would include all forms of published communication from reports and documents to phonograph records and computer tapes.

[2] The data is gathered from: Ben Bagdikian, *The Information Machines* (New York: Harper & Row, 1971), pp. 191-193.

These three elusive elements are usually referred to as parts of bibliographical control or organization, i.e., effective access to sources of information. No bibliography or set of bibliographies has yet met all of these needs. At best, a bibliography is a compromise between completeness, access to parts, and various forms.

With the bibliography in front of him, how does the librarian use it on a day-to-day basis. Regardless of form, a bibliography is used primarily for three basic purposes: (1) to identify and verify, (2) to locate, and (3) to select.

Identify and verify The usual bibliography gives standard information similar to that found on most catalog cards: author, title, edition (if other than a first edition), place of publication, publisher, date of publication, a collation (i.e., number of pages, illustrations, size), and price. Since the early 1970s, a new element has been added to many bibliographies—the International Standard Book Number, abbreviated as ISBN or simply SBN. In seeking to identify or verify any of these elements, a librarian would turn to the proper bibliography: usually beginning with the general, such as *Books in Print* or the *National Union Catalog,* and moving to the particular such as a bibliography in a narrow subject area.

Locate Location may be in terms of where the book is published, where it can be found in a library, or where it may be purchased. However, from the point of view of the patron's needs, the location is more apt to be in terms of subject. What is available in this subject area, either in a book, periodical, article, report, or some other form of communication?

Select The primary aim of a library is to build a useful collection. This presupposes selection from a vast number of possibilities. In order to assist the librarian, certain bibliographies tell him what is available in a given subject area, by a given author, in a given form, or for certain groups of readers. Depending on its purpose, a bibliography may give an estimate of the value of the particular work for a given type of reader.

Forms of systematic enumerative bibliography

In considering the forms of systematic bibliography, the analogy of a sieve is often used. The universal bibliography, the largest sieve, in fact is not a sieve at all, but a sponge. It includes everything. National or trade bibliography sifts the material in terms of what is published in a given country; and subject bibliography sifts it even further in terms of a given field of interest. Other forms may sift it to a fine point—works of a single author for a given year, for example.

Working from the all to the finite, systematic enumerative bibliography is usually subdivided into rather specific large categories.

UNIVERSAL BIBLIOGRAPHY

A true universal bibliography would include everything published, issued, or pressed in the field of communications from the beginning to the present to the future. It is now an impossible dream. In practice, the term is now employed in a narrower sense. It generally means a bibliography that is not necessarily limited by time, territory, language, subject, or form. National library catalogs, some book dealers' catalogs, and auction catalogs are the nearest thing to universal bibliography.

NATIONAL AND TRADE BIBLIOGRAPHY[3]

This kind of work is limited to materials published within a given country. The sieve may be made even finer by limiting the bibliography to a section of the country, a city, or even a hamlet. For ease of use and convenience, national bibliographies normally are divided into even finer sieves.

Time This is a matter of listing works previously published, works being published, or works to be published. Such bibliographies are normally labeled as either retrospective or current.

Form This may be in terms of bibliographical form: collection of works, monographs, components (i.e., essays, periodical articles, poems); in terms of physical form: books, recordings, pamphlets, microfilm; or in terms of published works and unpublished works (i.e., manuscripts, dissertations).

A typical national bibliography will set itself limits of time, form, and obviously origin. For example, *Books in Print* is limited to books available for purchase (time); includes only printed books, albeit both hardbound and paperbacks and some monographs and series (form); and is a trade bibliography, i.e., issued by a commercial organization (origin).

There is no limit to the possible subdivisions of national bibliography. For example, within this larger area appears bibliographies (works

[3] The term "trade" bibliography is used often as synonymous with "national." Trade bibliography refers to a bibliography issued for, and usually by, the booksellers and publishers of a particular nation. Its purpose is identical to that of national bibliography, thus the confusion in terms. The emphasis on essential rather than definitive information sets it apart.

by and about a given author) and anonym and pseudonym listings. Other sieves continue to be devised as needed.

SUBJECT BIBLIOGRAPHY

The universal and the national bibliography are the base for any subject bibliography. While the two major forms tend to be used almost exclusively by generalists such as the book dealer, the librarian, and the publisher, the subject bibliography is intended for the research worker and for others in special areas.

Once a subject is chosen, the sieves common to national bibliographies may be employed—time, form, origin, and others. However, unlike most national bibliographies, a subject work may include all the sieves. For example, a definitive bibliography on railroad engines may be retrospective, current (at least at date of publishing), include all forms from individual monographs to government publications, and reflect various sources of origin.

SELECTIVE BIBLIOGRAPHIES AND GUIDES TO REFERENCE MATERIALS

Theoretically, lists which include the "best" works for a given situation or audience are not bibliographies in the accepted definition of the term. In practice, however, they are normally so considered. They include such works as guides to reference books, special reading lists issued by a library, and books devoted to the "best" works for children, adults, students, businessmen, and others.

BIBLIOGRAPHIES OF BIBLIOGRAPHIES AND INDEXES TO BIBLIOGRAPHIES

There are few of these; but they guide the user to useful bibliographies, normally by subject, by given place, or by individual.

This does not exhaust the innumerable possibilities for methods of organizing and describing bibliographies. It hardly touches on the various combinations. There is no universally accepted method of even approaching parts and divisions of bibliography. One of the problems today is to bring some order out of this chaotic, primarily free-wheeling approach to listing materials. "The variations from one bibliographical service to another—in scope, coverage, arrangement, periodicity, format, etc.—are so great they create a confusing welter rather than a perspicacious guide to published information."[4] In this statement, Clapp sums up the view of anyone who has even paid cursory attention to the development of systematic bibliography.

[4] Verner Clapp, *The Future of the Research Library* (Urbana, Illinois: The University of Illinois Press, 1964), p. 83. The problem is not only national, but international. Consequently, a major role of such organizations as UNESCO has been to provide clearing-house services in the field of bibliography and documentation.

ANALYTICAL AND TEXTUAL BIBLIOGRAPHY

While bibliography is generally understood to mean a guide to information, it has a much older definition. Analytical bibliography is concerned with the physical description of the book. Textual bibliography goes a step further and is interested in textual variations between a manuscript and the printed book or between various editions. Often the two are combined into one scientific or art form. This type of research is designed to discover everything possible about the author's ultimate intentions. The goal is to recover the exact words that the author intended to constitute his work.

In driving toward this goal, one group of bibliographers may be experts in everything from nineteenth century printing practices to bookbinding, another group in everything from paper watermarks to title pages. An example of this cooperation is the Center for Editions for American Authors—an organization dedicated on a large scale to refining and rediscovering the texts of American authors from Melville to Hemingway. The ultimate result will be definitive editions of major American writers.

There are obvious differences between analytical and textual bibliography—the most basic being that analytical bibliography is more concerned with the physical aspects of the book, textual with the author's words. The two must necessarily work together, but this does not mean they are similar disciplines. In fact, each variety has its experts as a casual reading of the annual *Studies in Bibliography,* (Charlottesville, Virginia: University Press of Virginia, 1947 to date, annual), will reveal. In the world of librarianship, analytical bibliography is best known because of its relationship to descriptive cataloging and history of the book courses.

The results of analytical bibliography serve to answer a number of questions, or as Herman Liebert puts it:

> Most users of an analytical bibliography . . . have a book in one hand and want to know from a book in the other hand what it is that they have— usually, rather grossly, what edition it is that they have . . . whether it is part of some later printing in which the differences from the first printing represent a genuine auctorial decision and not merely an accident in the printing house.[5]

This is "pure" bibliography and, hopefully, within the jurisdiction of the scholarly librarian. Its basic principles must be understood by anyone who aims at more than routine cataloging or an appreciation of the problems involved in descriptions of books. Nor is it isolated from

[5] Herman W. Liebert, "Bibliography Old and New," *Library Chronicle of the University of Texas,* February 1972, p. 13. This is an excellent analysis of analytical bibliography.

other more frequently used types of bibliography. If the average librarian or bibliographer truly understood the importance of the "other face" of bibliography, a good many problems arising from sloppy arrangement and description would disappear. Be that as it may, this is too complicated and specialized an area to be adequately discussed here.[6]

GUIDES TO REFERENCE BOOKS AND INDEXES TO BIBLIOGRAPHIES

One type of bibliography of considerable interest to all librarians, and to beginners in particular, is the guide to reference books. These guides list, and usually annotate, the basic reference titles employed by either the generalist or the specialist. In everyday reference work, they serve the practical purpose of making it unnecessary for the librarian to remember or recall exactly the name of a given title. Given a basic understanding of the reference process, the librarian may use the guides to locate not only specific titles, but titles within subject areas by form.

The beginner who may have only a vague idea of the scope of reference work titles will find the guides of invaluable help. After a few hours of careful study of one of the general guides, the student will have a better idea of reference forms; classification of reference titles; and the purpose, scope, and audience for various types of reference works within a given form.

The primary purpose of a bibliographical guide to reference material is to introduce the user to (1) general reference sources which will assist him in research in all fields and (2) specific reference sources which will help in research in particular fields. These take a number of forms, but primarily are either (1) an annotated list of titles with brief introductory remarks before each section or chapter or (2) a handbook which not only lists and annotates basic sources, but serves to introduce the user to tools of investigative study by a discursive, almost text-book like approach. There are numerous subclassifications and types of guides.

Another type of guide is more didactic and is usually limited to a broad or even a narrow subject or area, e.g., *The Literature of Political*

---

[6] An ongoing report on analytical bibliography will be found in *The Yearbook of American Bibliographical and Textual Studies* (Columbia, South Carolina: The Press, 1971 to date, annual). Fredson Bowers is the world's leading authority on analytical bibliography. Although never easy reading, Bowers should be studied by any librarian. His two principal books are: *Principles of Bibliographical Description* (Princeton, New Jersey: Princeton University Press, 1949); *Bibliography and Textual Criticism* (New York: Oxford University Press, 1965). Other less detailed books, but classics of their kind, include: A. J. K. Esdaile, *A Student's Manual of Bibliography* (London: George Allen & Unwin, Ltd., 1954); R. B. McKerrow, *An Introduction to Bibliography for Literary Students* (Oxford: Clarendon Press, 1927).

Science (broad) or *How to Find Out in Iron and Steel* (narrow). Unfortunately, these are too often overlooked by both librarians and students. They serve, as the general guides, to give a broad overview of the subject, but then go a step further and consider the core of highly specialized publications which probably are not listed in the more familiar general guides. In addition, they may list textbooks, journals, newspapers, societies, libraries, subject experts, recordings, films—in fact, just about anything which is applicable to an understanding of research and reference in the given field. Quantity is not always quality and, as a result, the reader may find the guide is more involved with listing than with describing. The result is that the reader must sometimes turn to the general works for meaningful, detailed annotations of even basic titles.

The singular contribution of the better subject guides is not so much a rote listing of materials as a discursive discussion of (1) the field as a whole; (2) peculiarities of research (and reference) in the discipline; (3) the place of the subject in the main stream of knowledge; and (4) various forms which are especially applicable for work in the field, i.e., everything from specialized abstract services to patent guides to sources of unpublished research reports.

Depending upon the purpose, audience, and scope some guides are primarily selective, others quite general. Still, they should not be confused with subject bibliographies where the purpose is to either report on ongoing studies in a field or list retrospective studies or combine both. Subject bibliographies are primarily for the researcher and the expert and are access devices of a first order. They presuppose at least some, if not considerable, knowledge of the field. Many of them are listed in the guides. For example, *The Historian's Handbook* is a guide. The *Bibliography of Historical Writing Published in Great Britain* is as the title suggests, a subject bibliography. The former is for the novice, the latter for the expert. Usually, although not always, the distinction is clear enough in the title; and if there is any doubt, it should be clarified in the preface.

GENERAL GUIDES TO REFERENCE BOOKS

Walford, Arthur John, *Guide to Reference Materials,* 3d ed. London: Library Association, 1973 (Distributed in United States by R. R. Bowker Company), 3 vols., $13.95 per vol.

Winchell, Constance M., *Guide to Reference Books,* 8th ed. Chicago: American Library Association, 1967, 768 pp., $15. First supplement 1965–1967, 132 pp., $3.50; second supplement, 1967–1968, 174 pp., $4; third supplement, 1969–1970, 208 pp., $4.50.

Wynar, Bohdan (ed.), *American Reference Books Annual.* Littleton, Colorado: Libraries Unlimited, Inc., 1970 to date, annual, $19.75.

The two basic guides which tell a reference librarian what reference books are available in all major fields of endeavor are Winchell and Walford—as the two above titles are referred to by most librarians. (The Winchell volume supplements are now being edited by Eugene P. Sheehy and one suspects in time the name will be Sheehy, not Winchell.) Winchell and Walford are household words with librarians on both sides of the Atlantic. No more important general aids exist for the reference librarian.

They are important because they list and annotate the major titles used in reference service. Winchell and its three supplements include 11,000 entries; Walford close to 12,000. Both select basic titles from the world around. Complete bibliographical information is given for each entry, and the majority—although not all entries—are annotated.

The compilers do not intend or purport to include every reference title. They are selective, choosing only the best, or what is available when selection is limited. This process helps to weed out undesirable, unnecessary, and often out-of-print titles.

Arrangement varies in each; although the basic principle is to begin with general reference works and then move into large subject areas which, in turn, are subdivided by both smaller subjects and forms. The basic Winchell volume, for example, includes political science under the social sciences. It then subdivides it by general works (guides, bibliographies, encyclopedias) and then by country with subdivisions by form again (United States—directories, biographies, tables, yearbooks). Walford follows the same procedure. In practice, the arrangement is not all that important. Each volume features excellent title, author, and subject indexes which help the reference librarian to zero in on specific titles and subject areas regardless of the arrangement. These two basic works are, in a real sense, the librarian's bibliographies and, as such, are fair to excellent examples of how to arrange a bibliography for best use.

The primary point of separation between Winchell and Walford is that the latter includes many more British titles (naturally, as it is published in England), as well as reference books published in Europe, or even in non-European countries. Conversely, Winchell (including its supplements) offers considerable more stress on the works of United States, Canada, and Latin America. Aside from national emphasis, there seems to be a constant running argument as to which is better balanced in terms of descriptive annotations and subject coverage. The argument, though, is fairly academic. Both are excellent. Both are required in all medium to large reference libraries. Winchell, to be sure, would be a first choice in smaller libraries. Parenthetically, there is a real argument about Winchell that should be settled: the publication schedule of new editions and supplements is quite beyond comprehension. The 1968–1970 supplement, for example, did not come out until two years after the last imprint listed. And would not a new edition every three or four years be preferable to one edition and three or four supplements? The annual ARBA has to a great extent solved the timeliness problem for American imprints, and the more frequent revisions of Walford help; but anyone depending on Winchell for the latest selected work in any field is doomed to frustration.[7]

Neither Winchell nor Walford are up to date, and the librarian trying to keep up with publications of the previous year will find neither of much help. Partially filling the time-lapse vacuum is the *American Reference Books Annual.* It differs from either Winchell or Walford in three important respects: (1) it is limited to reference titles published or distributed in the United States; (2) it is comprehensive for a given year and makes no effort to be selective; (3) the annotations are written by a number of subject experts and tend to be both more critical and more expository than those found in Winchell or Walford. Depending on the extent of American publishing, the annual volume analyzes some 1,800 to 2,000 separate reference titles. The work is extremely well organized and indexed, which makes it easy to use and understand. Furthermore, citations to longer reviews in standard reviewing media are given for many of the titles. Within the limits of its scope, it is difficult to fault.

In addition to these voluminous general guides, there are numerous other guides often referred to as "little Winchells." They are usually listed in the opening sections of the subject areas covered in, yes, Winchell, Walford, and the ARBA—as well as in other general guides to reference books. They are becoming increasingly important for four reasons:

1. Specialization, accompanied by overwhelming publication, requires more and more sophisticated methods of getting at particular bits of information. The guides offer such help.
2. Of equal importance, the guides offer an overview of the communications process in a given discipline—an overview which the librarian must necessarily understand before he can adequately deal with particulars.
3. The lack of adequate reference staffing requires that more and more students do their own searching. While the librarian can be of some help, the guides afford the student or layman at least a basic introduction to the reference aids in the subject being studied.
4. Finally, the better guides serve to assist the librarian who may be called upon to work in a subject area totally foreign to her training. And, of course, they serve to refresh the memory of even the experienced.

[7] Of some limited help in the updating of *Guide to Reference Books* is the biannual listing by Eugene P. Sheehy in *College and Research Libraries,* i.e., "Selected Reference Books of 1972-1973;" "1973-1974." The annotated listings usually appear in the July and January issues.

No one is more aware of the importance—and sales potential—of these guides than publishers. The number is increasing.[8] The result is duplication (particularly where so called guides do little more than list items which are readily available and better annotated in a Winchell or Walford). There is considerable need for thorough evaluation before purchase. Of particular importance is accuracy, timeliness, comprehensiveness, and style. Too many can be faulted on all or several of these points. Where there is any question, the guide should be checked by an expert in the field and certainly should not be purchased until adequate reviews are published.[9]

INDEXES TO BIBLIOGRAPHIES AND BIBLIOGRAPHY OF BIBLIOGRAPHIES

Besterman, Theodore, *A World Bibliography of Bibliographies.* 4th ed. Geneva: Societies Bibliographica, 1965–1967, 5 vols., $200.
   Bibliographic Index; A Cumulative Bibliography of Bibliographies. New York: The H. W. Wilson Company, 1937 to date, triannual with cumulations, service basis.

Another much used form of guide to reference sources is the bibliographical index. It is much more limited than the general or subject guide in that it only includes bibliographies. Still, these may lead to other forms which can be equally as helpful as anything found in the guides.
   Bibliographic Index is a basic searching tool in any library. Its primary claim to frequent use is its relative currency. Someone who asks for material on the mass media will find a number of bibliographies which are usually no more than six months to a year old. And as a good many of these are often in magazines in the library, they are usually not difficult to find. Given one or two current bibliographies on the mass media, the user then fans out to the works included in the bibliography—and the search is on. Obviously, if something is needed on the mass media that happened a few weeks ago, it is best to go directly to the original articles and books via any standard index or abstracting service.

[8] For example, a 1972 news release from Gale Research Company: "Authoritative guides to the literature and to information sources within sixteen major areas of current interest are being prepared by subject experts for a new Gale Research Bibliographic series. It is expected there will be more than 250 volumes in the series by 1975."
[9] For earlier representative guides *see* Henry L. Alsmeyer, "Guides to the literature," *RQ,* Fall 1968, pp. 22+. Again, check out the guides listed in Winchell, Walford, and the *American Reference Books Annual* as well as in the Bibliographic Index.

There are several problems with the *Bibliographic Index*. First, it is too general for the specialist. It does examine 1,900 periodicals for bibliographies, but there are over 50,000 magazines available in United States' libraries. Second, it is relatively current but not current enough if time is an important element.

The answer to both problems is the specialized index, abstracting service, or bibliography which is issued in a special subject area on a given schedule, e.g., the *American Literary Scholarship* is an annual which provides "a systematic evaluative guide to current published studies on American literature;" and the *ABC Pol Sci: Advance Bibliography of Contents, Political Science and Government* which covers contents of some 300 journals from 30 countries.

Another element to consider in this type of search is that the user is looking for a bibliography, not necessarily seeking to compile a bibliography. If compilation is the order of business—for example, a list of current books and articles on swimming—the primary reference sources would be indexes and abstracts. In one student bibliography project, "Over half the sources used (284 out of 416) consisted of the standard indexes, such as *The Readers' Guide, The Social Sciences and Humanities Index, PAIS, The National Union Catalog,* and the *Cumulative Book Index.* Monographs accounted for 74 sources, and reference books for 58."[10]

A bibliography of bibliographies differs from a straight bibliography in that it is twice removed from the subject. It answers the question: Where can I find a bibliography on X subject, about X person, or about X place? The reader would then turn to the bibliography on X subject, or X person, or X place. The bibliography might be a separately published book or, more likely, at the end of a book, or part of a periodical article, or another type of document. When he has located the bibliography, the user would then locate the specific sources therein cited.

On the whole, bibliographies of bibliographies tend to be selective. The reason is obvious. Almost any work that is original or authoritative tends to include a bibliography. Consequently, the number of bibliographies almost equals the number of separate publications. A key to all of these would be gigantic. On the whole, then, bibliographies of bibliographies are normally cut down to size by subject, language, or form.

Several efforts were made in the past to construct bibliographies of bibliographies, and the reader is referred to Winchell or Walford for the outstanding ones. Of more importance in modern use are the ones listed here.

The most general and detailed of the group is Besterman's 5-volume work. It is considered a modern classic of bibliography and is one of the

[10] Doris Dale, "One Approach to Bibliography," *RQ*, Spring 1970, p. 241.

few general bibliographies of bibliographies. The fourth edition examines 17,000 separately collated volumes of bibliography in 40 languages. Besterman only includes separately published works, not those that appear as parts of books or articles. The bibliographies range in time from the fifteenth century through 1963.

Material is arranged alphabetically under 16,000 subject headings with adequate cross references. An index of authors, editors, and translators, titles of serials and anonymous works, libraries, and patents wind up the work. While the entry information is very exact, there are no annotations and the user must make his own decision as to its applicability.

The enormity of the task is obvious when one considers that it is accomplished almost entirely by one man. Besterman has a command of almost all the world's languages and a great capacity for work.

SUGGESTED READING

Childs, James B., "Regional and Country Guides to Reference Books," *RQ*, Winter 1970, pp. 137+. A list of the "Winchells" in other countries, with some annotations.

Clapp, Verner, "Greatest Invention Since the Title Page. . .," *Wilson Library Bulletin,* December 1971. pp. 348+. A witty, revealing history of one aspect of bibliography.

Freides, Thelma, "Bibliography in the Social Sciences," *RQ*, Fall 1971, pp. 15+; and Schipplekc, Suzanne, "The Case for Retrospective Bibliography," *RQ,* Fall 1972, pp. 9+. Two complementary discussions on both a practical and a theoretical level about various aspects of bibliography and, more particularly, the questions about levels of guides in the literature.

Haro, Robert, "The Bibliographer in the Academic Library," *Library Resources & Technical Services,* Spring 1969, pp. 163+. Primarily, the qualifications Haro believes necessary to function as a bibliographer (read: reference librarian?).

Holler, Frederick, "Political Science Sources," *RQ,* Fall 1972, pp. 12+. While concerned with one field, the author gives hints and constructive suggestions about information problems in related areas; and the whole is a good introduction to guides to the literature.

Perrine, Richard, "Causes & Cures: Catalog Use Difficulties," *RQ,* Summer 1968, pp. 169+. A study of 12 colleges and the causes which result in frustration at the card catalog.

Seibert, Grant W., "The Reference Catalog," *RQ,* Summer 1969, pp. 262+; "The Reference Catalog (Part 2)," *RQ,* Spring 1971, p. 214. The author explains how one library reference desk uses its own catalog to augment the public catalog.

Whittaker, Kenneth, "Basic British," *RQ,* Fall 1972, pp. 49+. A brief discussion of basic guides to reference sources employed by British librarians.

CHAPTER THREE
BIBLIOGRAPHIES: NATIONAL
LIBRARY CATALOGS AND
TRADE BIBLIOGRAPHIES

There is no universal bibliography. No single source will give bibliographical details on all books published in the world.[1] Nor is there such a bibliography for films, periodicals, recordings, and the like. Despite the lack of this master control, there are methods whereby the serious researcher can be relatively certain the work he is undertaking has not been duplicated. Furthermore, seeking material in almost any subject area from the sciences to the humanities, the researcher is at no loss for locating more than sufficient sources. This is not to say duplication and loss of material (for lack of proper bibliographical control) is not a problem. It is, but it is far from a hopeless situation. In many ways, the various national library catalogs do serve as an interlocking type of universal bibliography. They are not absolutely complete, but they are enough for most practical situations.

As a national library catalog is not limited by time, territory, language, subject, or by many forms of communication, it does come close to the ideal universal bibliography. And while none of the national library catalogs claim to be universal in scope, collectively they do offer a relatively comprehensive record of international publishing. The Library

[1] For a discussion of what is possible in the years ahead in terms of universal bibliography *see:* Franz G. Kaltwasser, "The Quest for Universal Bibliographical Control," *Wilson Library Bulletin,* June 1972, p. 894. (Reprinted and edited from an article in *Unesco Bulletin for Libraries,* No. 5, 1971.)

of Congress, for example, catalogs materials from around the world; and a good proportion of its holdings are books, magazines, music, and the like from international publishers. The same is true for the British Museum and the French Bibliothèque. When and if the acquisitions of these and other national libraries can be controlled and cataloged in an international scheme, the dream of universal—or at least partial universal—bibliography will have been realized.

Union catalogs

A term often associated with national library catalogs is "union" catalog, e.g., the Library of Congress' *The National Union Catalog* and *Union List of Serials*. Increasing interlibrary cooperation on local, regional, national, and an international scale makes a union list of particular importance. In fact, wherever more than one library bands together with others, there is apt to be a by-product of that cooperation—a union list. The utilization of the union list and bibliography is discussed in chapters on library networks, and elsewhere; but because the term appears throughout this text, it is well to clearly define it at this point, if only briefly.

A union catalog indicates who has what. A fuller, often repeated definition is: "an inventory common to several libraries and containing some or all of their publications listed in one or more orders of arrangement."[2] It opens up the whole bibliographical apparatus for the user who may want an item which cannot be found in her particular library. She turns to a union list to locate a given book, periodical, or newspaper in another library—which may be in the same city or thousands of miles away. Given the location and the operation of an interlibrary loan or copying process, she can then have the particular book or item borrowed from the holding library for her use.

When each library in the bibliographical network or bibliographic center knows what fellow members have purchased, a union list can be helpful in acquisitions. Expensive and little used items, for example, need only be purchased by one or two of the cooperating libraries because those items are always on call for members.

Some, although not all, of the union lists will give pertinent bibliographical information to help the library trace and identify a given item. When the sole purpose of the union catalog is location, the descriptive entry is normally kept to a minimum, e.g., *New Serial Titles*. Conversely, when it serves numerous purposes as well (e.g., *The National Union Catalog*), the description will be relatively complete. Arrangement of union catalogs differs. In most cases, the user wants a specific title and

[2] Yadwiga Kuncaitis, *Union Catalogs and Bibliographic Centers* (Columbus, Ohio: State Library of Ohio, 1968), p. 9.

knowing that title or author it is quickest to have the material arranged in alphabetical form by title or author. Few catalogs of this type have a subject entry. There are various methods of compilation ranging from a large library circulating its catalog so that smaller libraries may check off what they have to each library cataloging its own holdings and forwarding entries to the union catalog headquarters.

There are numerous other uses and dimensions to the compilation and the distribution of union lists. The union approach is a basic part of any successful cooperative move to efficiently acquire, describe, and speed information from one point to another.

NATIONAL LIBRARY CATALOGS

U.S. Library of Congress. *The National Union Catalog: A Cumulative Author List.* Washington, D.C.: Library of Congress, Card Division, 1956 to date, nine monthly issues and three quarterly cumulations, $730. (Cumulated and published by private publishers: 1953-1957, 1958, 28 vols.; 1952-1953 imprints, 1961, 30 vols.; 1958-1962, 1963, 54 vols.; 1963-1967, 1969, 72 vols. Annual cumulations usually run 12 to 14 volumes and are published as much as a year after the initial monthly set.)

U.S. Library of Congress. *Books: Subjects. A Cumulated List of Works Represented by Library of Congress Printed Cards.* Washington, D.C.: Library of Congress, Card Division, 1950 to date, three quarterly issues with annual cumulations, $470.

The two ongoing book catalogs of the Library of Congress are somewhat complicated bibliographically, as the reader will soon see, but essentially they are no different from the familiar card catalog found in the local library. This is important to recognize. Sometimes the prepossessing sets—which run to many hundred volumes—confuse the novice. However, once the user has mastered the basic purpose and scope of the set, it is relatively simple to use.

First, what is the scope of *The National Union Catalog?* One will note that each page photographically reproduces catalog cards—the same familiar cards found in many libraries. Each card represents an item cataloged by the Library of Congress *or* by one of more than 750 libraries in the United States and Canada. This feature makes it a union catalog in that it shows the holdings of more than one library. Also, it represents a vast scope which makes *The National Union Catalog* the closest thing to a world or universal bibliography now available.

What is cataloged? Almost every communications media. In this case, the entries are primarily for book, maps, atlases, pamphlets, and serials, including periodicals. The magazines are listed by title; only those cataloged by the Library of Congress are included—and for this reason, *New Serial Titles* is a much better bibliographical aid for magazines. This aside, *The National Union Catalog* is a basic for working with books and pamphlets, as well as music and films.

How is it arranged and what information is given? The volumes are arranged alphabetically by author or main entry. (Generally, the heading of a main entry is an author, but lacking such information it may be a title. It is never both author and title.) Generally, one cannot get at a title unless one knows the author. There is no subject approach in the main *National Union Catalog* and cross references are minimal.

The reproduced card varies in the amount and type of information given; but in almost all cases, it includes the typical bibliographical description in this order: full name of author, dates of birth and death; full title; place, publisher, and date: collation (e.g., paging, illustrations, maps); series; edition; notes on contents, history; tracing for subject headings and added entries; and the Library of Congress and, usually, the Dewey classifications. It now, also, includes Standard Book Numbers.

How is *The National Union Catalog* used in reference work?

1. Since this is a union catalog, i.e., it shows not only the holdings of the Library of Congress, but titles in over 750 other libraries, it allows the reference librarian to quickly locate a given title(s). Hence, the user who needs a work not in his library may find the nearest location via *The National Union Catalog*. For example, the first edition of a mystery, *The Man Who Followed Women* by Hurbert Hitchens, is identified as being in eight other libraries. Location symbols for the eight are: OOxM, TxU, OCU, OCI, MnU, NIC, ViBibV, and WU. The initials stand for libraries in various parts of the country. Initials are explained in the front of cumulative volumes. Depending on policy of the holding library, the librarian may or may not be able to borrow the title on interlibrary loan. Failing a loan, he may be able to get sections copied or, at a minimum, will know where he has to go to find the title.
2. When completed in book form, *The National Union Catalog* virtually amounts to a basic, full author bibliography. Anyone wanting to know everything (magazine articles and other such items aside) X author published has only to consult the author's name under the full *National Union Catalog* set.
3. The full cataloging not only gives details on a book (e.g., when it was published, by whom, and where), but helps the reference library to verify it does exist—an important matter when there is a question as to whether X actually did publish this or that.

Verification, however, is even more important when the reference librarian is attempting to straighten out the misspelling of a title or author's name. In other words, *The National Union Catalog* sets the record straight when there is doubt about the validity of a given bit of information.

4. In terms of acquisitions, particularly of expensive or rare items, *The National Union Catalog* permits a library to concentrate in subject areas with the assurance that the less developed areas may be augmented by interlibrary loan from other libraries.

5. In terms of cataloging (which is basic to reference service), *The National Union Catalog* offers a number of advantages (and headaches). The primary asset is central cataloging, which should, although certainly does not, limit the amount of original cataloging necessary.

6. The sixth advantage of *The National Union Catalog* is as psychological as it is real. Its very existence gives the librarian (and more involved users) a sense of order and control which would otherwise be lacking in a world that cries for some type of order.

The National Union Catalog is primarily an approach via the author. What does one do when one wants to find books in a given subject area? The user turns to the *Library of Congress Catalog. Books: Subject.* Here he will find *The National Union Catalog* entries rearranged by subject. There is one important "catch." The subject approach can only be used for material published since 1945. (The set begins in 1950, but cataloging goes back to books published from 1945.) Prior to that date, there is no subject avenue to *The National Union Catalog* titles.

The subject catalog includes all works cataloged by the Library of Congress but not necessarily by members of *The National Union Catalog.* Hence, it is not a complete *National Union Catalog.* When in doubt, and the author's name is known, *The National Union Catalog* should be double checked. Also, some, but not all, *National Union Catalog* location symbols are given—again the main *National Union Catalog* set must be checked for location.

So far the discussion has only concerned ongoing copies of *The National Union Catalog,* i.e., those published monthly and cumulated annually. But how does one locate a title published, say, in 1950; or for that matter any one of 10 million retrospective entries not in the current *National Union Catalog?* Obviously, one consults back cumulations of *The National Union Catalog.* The difficulty, though, is that *The National Union Catalog* in book form only started in 1956. The answer requires a brief historical sketch of *The National Union Catalog.*

The National Union Catalog in card form began in 1901. In addition to the Library of Congress, there were four cooperating libraries. By 1926, *The National Union Catalog* had over 2 million cards—physically located at the Library of Congress. If anyone wanted to consult *The National Union Catalog,* he had to query the Library of Congress or go there himself. The problem was solved by sending duplicate cards to key, large libraries throughout the United States. This proved costly and tremendously inefficient. So, beginning in the early 1940s, work began on a printed book catalog, i.e., the individual cards were now reproduced in the familiar *National Union Catalog* book form instead of being sent to libraries card by card. However, it was not until January 1, 1956, that it was decided that the book catalogs should be expanded not only to include Library of Congress holdings (which had been the case to that point), but to include the imprints of other libraries. So, since July 1956, the book catalog bore the new name: *The National Union Catalog.* . . .

What this means is that most large libraries have several sets of book catalogs from the Library of Congress. But prior to 1956, these catalogs represent only books cataloged by the Library of Congress, not the entire *National Union Catalog.* What was to be done with *The National Union Catalog* prior to 1956, i.e., the card catalog in the Library of Congress which was not in book form, was the next question. The answer came in 1968 when *The National Union Catalog: pre-1956 Imprints* began to be published. Coming out at the rate of five volumes per month, this is expected to be completed by late 1979 or early 1980. The estimated 610 volumes will give the user and librarian information on some 10 million titles held by the Library of Congress and close to 800 North American libraries.

Meanwhile, what does one do about locating books in *The National Union Catalog* prior to 1956? One set fills the gap for 1952 to 1956—but only partially. Prior to 1952, the only solution is: (1) wait for the complete set to be printed; (2) and more likely contact the Library of Congress which will send information on the title—information found in *The National Union Catalog* prior to 1956 or 1952 which is now being printed in book form; or (3) as an interim solution consult one of the following sets which are not complete in terms of a union catalog, but do show holdings of the Library of Congress.[3] If the librarian is searching for books published prior to July 1942, the first set would be consulted;

[3] Three firms offer counter solutions. Gale Research has reprinted part of the set in alphabetical order, i.e., *Library of Congress and National Union Catalog Author Lists, 1942–1962* (152 volumes, 2,600,000 entries, $2,888). Rowman and Littlefield offer *The National Union Catalog 1956 through 1967* (120 volumes, $2,400). NCR-Microcard Editions offers the complete sets on microfiche for $699 for the 1942–1946 set to $130 for the annual cumulations of *The National Union Catalog.* The obvious sale point is convenience—one cumulation is much easier to search than three to six separate sets.

after 1942, the other two sets. But once more, a catch: while most books in these sets follow comprehensive publishing dates, some do not, i.e., a book published in 1890 might not be cataloged by the Library of Congress until 1950.

1. 1898–1942. *A Catalog of Books Represented by Library of Congress Printed Cards Issued to July 31, 1942*. Ann Arbor, 1942–1946, 167 vols.
    The first of three series containing reproductions of printed catalog cards produced by the Library of Congress from 1898 to 1952. It seems worth repeating: these sets *do not* include material found in *The National Union Catalog*, only material cataloged by the Library of Congress.
2. 1942–1947. *A Catalog of Books Represented by Library of Congress Printed Cards: Supplement: Cards Issued August 1, 1942–December 31, 1947*. Ann Arbor, 1948, 42 vols.
3. 1948–1952. *Library of Congress Author Catalog: A Cumulative List of Works Represented by Library of Congress Printed Cards, 1948–1952*. Ann Arbor, 1953, 24 vols. The last of three series which together contain reproductions of nearly 3 million catalog cards describing books held by the Library of Congress.
4. 1953+ *see National Union Catalog Series*.[4] Once the 600, or more, volume set of *The National Union Catalog* imprints prior to 1956 is complete, the average user will only have to consult that set, plus the cumulations of *The National Union Catalog* since 1956.

LIBRARY CATALOGS IN GREAT BRITAIN

British Museum. Department of Printed Books. *General Catalogue of Printed Books*. London: Trustees of the British Museum, 1965–1966, 263 vols. Price on request.

——. *General Catalogue of Printed Books. Ten Year Supplement, 1956–1965*. London: Trustees of the British Museum, 1968, 50 vols. Price on request.

——. *Subject Index of the Works Added to the Library of the British Museum in the Years 1881–1900*. London: Trustees of the British Museum, 1881–to date. (Five-year supplements have been published since the initial three-volume work in 1903.) Price on request.

[4] A relatively clear explanation of the contents of the various sets from the first to 1969 will be found in Winchell, as well as in a short article: "The National Union Catalog; We Answer Some Queries," *American Libraries*, (ALA Bulletin), January 1969, pp. 39–41. The article also tells the function of the Gale reprint.

The Library of the British Museum is roughly equivalent to our Library of Congress, and its various catalogs are similar in purpose (if not in scope) to *The National Union Catalog.* The essential differences are:

1. The British Museum is much older than the Library of Congress and has a considerably larger collection of titles, from the fifteenth century to the all out attack on world publications by the Library of Congress in the 1960s.
2. The British Museum's catalog is not a union catalog and only shows holdings of the Museum.
3. The data for titles is somewhat briefer than found in *The National Union Catalog.*
4. Conversely, there is a larger amount of analytical material and cross references. For example, subject entries are given under personal names for biographies and books about an author's work.
5. Catchword title entries are used; and, in someways, this approach is useful for the lack of a satisfactory subject catalog—the problem, of course, is that the title must reveal something of the contents.
6. Finally, the catalog is issued approximately on an annual basis; and there are no monthly or quarterly issues, although there are cumulations.

How much duplication is there between this massive catalog and *The National Union Catalog?* Walford did a sampling and found that 75 to 80 percent of the titles in the British work are not in the American equivalent. And for titles published before 1800, the percentage is 90. With increased interest in capturing world wide titles in *The National Union Catalog,* the amount of duplication is bound to increase in the years ahead. Meanwhile, though, no large research library can afford to be without the *British Museum Catalogue.*

The *Subject Index* is considerably less useful than its American counterpart. It is not issued until several years after the main entries in the *General Catalogue* and large, rather than definitive subject headings are used.

Whereas *The National Union Catalog* can very much be considered a current bibliographical aid, the *General Catalogue*—because of its approach and its infrequent publication—is more retrospective. The librarian and researcher who wishes information on other national bibliographies should consult Winchell or Walford. Most of them tend to follow, with variations on timeliness and completeness, the patterns set by *The National Union Catalog* and the *General Catalogue.*

NATIONAL AND TRADE BIBLIOGRAPHY

The vast majority of enumerative bibliographies found in libraries can be classified as national and trade bibliographies. The distinction between the types is not always that clear—if indeed there is a distinction. It has been estimated that there are 9,600 basic types of bibliography and 147,000 possible combinations. Consequently, there are innumerable possibilities for defining, categorizing, and argument. The important consideration is not so much where the bibliography falls in the sometimes esoteric scheme of things, but rather how it is used.

Beginners are often confused by the interchangeable use of "national" and "trade" bibliography for precisely the same unit. Technically, the two terms are not synonyms, but they are usually employed as such. A national bibliography is one which lists items published only in a given country. An example, with a self-explanatory title: Charles Evans' *American Bibliography. Chronological Dictionary of All Books, Pamphlets and Periodicals, Publications Printed in the United States of America. . . .* Another is the *British National Bibliography* which only includes titles published in Great Britain. A trade bibliography is published by a commercial publisher for commercial use, although it certainly is used by libraries as well. The trade bibliography may or may not include only books published in the country of origin, although normally it does limit itself to such titles. An example of this is the R. R. Bowker Company, *Books In Print.* The distinction between the two terms is not really very important, at least in everyday reference use; and, for that reason, national and trade bibliographies are simply two words for much the same thing.

The pragmatic function of a national bibliography is to tell the librarian what was, what is, and what will be available—either for purchase or (via other aids) for possible loan from another library. As noted in the previous discussions, the national bibliographies help to give necessary bibliographical information (e.g., publisher, price, author, subject area, Library of Congress or Dewey numbers), which is used for a number of things from clarifying proper spelling to locating the item in terms of the subject area. Also, of course, the national bibliography is a primary control device for bringing some order to the 35,000 or more books published in America each year—not to mention similar staggering figures for pamphlets, reports, recordings, films, and such.

The process of compiling national bibliographies differs from country to country, but there is a given basic pattern. Effort is made, first, to give a current listing of titles published the previous week, month, or quarter. After that, these data are cumulated for the annual breakdown of titles published; and beyond that are other forms to indicate what is in print, what is out-of-print, and what is going to be published. (The same process, and this bears repeating, is applicable to other forms besides books.)

All this requires a considerable degree of cooperation between the compiler of the bibliographies and the publishers, not to mention the Library of Congress which usually supplies basic classification and cataloging information for many of the listings. Even with cooperation, there are numerous human and mechanical stumbling blocks: there is the publisher who fails to report a given title; there is delay in processing the title at the Library of Congress, or at the source of the bibliography; there are mechanical breakdowns which may result in misfiling, misprints, and the like. Despite the hazards, the system in the Western world seems to function with remarkable efficiency. It is never efficient enough, though, and improving bibliographies is the subject of a considerable amount of material in library literature, particularly in the area of automation and computerization.

United States national and trade bibliography: weekly and monthly

Publishers' Weekly. New York: R. R. Bowker Company, 1872 to date, weekly, $18.50.

   American Book Publishing Record. New York: R. R. Bowker Company, 1961 to date, monthly with annual and five-year cumulation, $19, $36.50 vol.

   Cumulative Book Index. New York: The H. W. Wilson Company, 1898 to date, monthly with three-month and annual cumulations, service basis.

   Forthcoming Books. New York: R. R. Bowker Company, 1966 to date, bimonthly, $24. *Subject Guide to Forthcoming Books,* 1967 to date, bimonthly, $11.

United States: annual and biannual

All the following titles are published by the R. R. Bowker Company.

   Publishers' Trade List Annual. 1873 to date, annual, (1972; 7 vol. $32).

   Books in Print. 1948 to date, annual (1972; 2 vol., $44.50).

   Subject Guide to Books in Print. 1957 to date, annual (1972; 2 vol., $39.50).

   Children's Books in Print. 1969 to date, annual (1972; 800 pp., $16.50).

Subject Guide to Children's Books in Print. 1970 to date, annual (1972; 790 pp., $16.50).
Paperbound Books in Print. 1955 to date, biannual, $32.50.

The primary section of importance to reference librarians (and catalogers) in *Publishers' Weekly* is the 20 to 30 page "Weekly Record" in the back of each issue. This is "a conscientious listing of current American book publication" usually for the previous week. The arrangement is by author, and most of the bibliographical information comes from the Library of Congress. Each listing includes the author, title, publisher, price, and basic bibliographic information including added entries and subject headings from the Library of Congress. And where possible, the ISBN (International Standard Book Number) is given as well as the Library of Congress card order number. The record is more than complete for small and medium sized libraries; but larger libraries will note that missing are such things as "subscription books, government publications, dissertations, quarterlies and other periodicals, pamphlets under 49 pages, and specialized publications of a transitory nature or intended as advertising." Often, too, publications of lesser known societies, institutes, symposia, and the like are not recorded.

How is the information obtained for the listings? *Publishers' Weekly* receives a so-called "listing" copy from a publisher every time a title is issued. This "listing" copy is much like the one sent to the Library of Congress for either copyright or in exchange for the Library of Congress catalog card number. Most of the cataloging information comes directly from the Library of Congress. Some books sent by the publisher to *Publishers' Weekly* are not received by the Library of Congress until much later (if at all), and this accounts for original cataloging done by the *Publishers' Weekly* staff. *Publishers' Weekly* and the Library of Congress work closely together to bring accurate, speedy information to libraries. The fact that it is not always speedy is a constant problem, matched only by the fact that not all titles are immediately included by either *Publishers' Weekly* or the Library of Congress. Still, for all but the largest library, the *Publishers' Weekly* "Weekly Record" is probably more than enough.

How is the "Weekly Record" used? Primarily, it is used by catalogers who want to find information on a book which has not been covered by catalog cards received. (The information found may be used for a catalog card immediately or until such time as the printed cards, or proof slips, are received from the Library of Congress or another source.) Hence, the arrangement in alphabetical order by author rather than by subject. Catalogers prefer this main entry approach, as do searchers in acquisitions who may be looking for a given title. In order to make the

"Weekly Record" more meaningful for other librarians, and laymen, it is rearranged once a month as *The American Book Publishing Record (ABPR)*. The contents consist of four weeks of the "Weekly Record." What is essentially different, though, is the arrangement. The author entries are reshuffled by Dewey number, i.e., titles are classified by subject with an author and title index. Once a year, the monthly *ABPR* is cumulated into an annual. The net result is a running and permanent record of the majority of publications issued by American publishers for a given week, month, and year.

How is the *ABPR* used? Again, it is primarily used by catalogers and acquisitions librarians seeking information on a received book for cataloging, or to verify a title or author. In reference work, the "Weekly Record" would be of help only if a question concerned an author: What is the title of a recent book by Arthur Smith? The reference librarian who knows "recent" means this or last week could check out individual issues of the "Weekly Record" and, then, the monthly issues of *ABPR*. Conversely, if the question concerned only the title *(Top of the Green Mountain)*, the "Weekly Record" would be worthless; and only the *ABPR* could be used. Finally, if the user wanted a recent book on mountains, the "Weekly Record" would be of no value, whereas the classified scheme of *ABPR* would be helpful. What it comes down to in an everyday practical sense is that "Weekly Record" is of limited value for reference, while *ABPR* is a subject, title, author approach to current publications. It is valuable as a means of answering such queries as: What recent books has Y written? I saw a review of Y's last book somewhere, but I can't remember the title. I can't remember the author, but there is a good book reviewed recently on mountains—can you tell me the name? And, of course, standard questions about price, publisher, and spelling are easily found in the *ABPR*. The other obvious advantage to *ABPR* is that it is a cumulation; and, therefore, neither the cataloger nor reference librarian has to search 52 issues of *Publishers' Weekly*.

Another monthly source of currently published titles is issued by a competing firm, The H. W. Wilson Company. This is their *Cumulative Book Index (CBI)*, which differs from *ABPR* is several ways. First, it is important because of its age. It goes back to 1898, and a cumulation represents a basic retrospective bibliography in libraries. *(ABPR* began in 1961 and is obviously of no value for previous publications.) Second, it not only includes American titles, but most—although certainly not all—titles issued in the English language. *(ABPR* includes only American publications, plus foreign titles released by American publishers.) Again, publishers send lists of titles. Not all publishers do so; hence, the *CBI*—as other bibliographies—is not complete. And even publishers who do send books are sometimes overlooked, e.g., "if it is an unusual format—printed on cards in a box, for instance, it is apparently not eligible for inclusion." (Dick Higgins of the Something Else Press, *COSMEP Newsletter,* April 1972, p. 5.)

Does a library need both the *CBI* and *ABPR?* Yes, if there is going to be any retrospective searching before 1961. Still, one might order back cumulations of the *CBI* for this purpose and not take current issues of *CBI.* So, again, does a library need both the current *CBI* and *ABPR?* Yes, but only if the library is ordering other than non-American titles. The *CBI,* it will be recalled, has a wider scope than *ABPR* in that it includes the majority of English language titles throughout the world. Obviously, larger libraries duplicate this service with English bibliographies such as the *British National Bibliography* (or for that matter *The National Union Catalog);* but, in many libraries, the *CBI* represents the primary outreach beyond American publishers. Well, then, why take *ABPR,* too? Because *ABPR* entries include more cataloging information (i.e., Dewey classification number, Library of Congress classification number, subject headings, and added entry tracings) than *CBI.* Also, some librarians prefer the dictionary arrangement of *CBI,* i.e., subject, author, titles entries are in one alphabet, not separated into various indexes as in *ABPR.* (For example, fiction is listed separately in *ABPR,* but in alphabetical order by author in the main listing in *CBI.)* A cost accountant weighing the similarities of the two might find it difficult to justify the duplication; but librarians who are used to calling upon both aids for help are, and rightfully so, dubious about giving up either one.

So much for ongoing current keys to American (and English language) publishing. There are two other approaches—the past and the future. The future plans of American publishers is considered in *Forthcoming Books* and its companion subject guide. This is used to answer such queries as: When will Philip Roth's new book be out? Will there be any new mysteries by X and Y this year? There is a book on the Russian revolution I heard was being published, but . . . well, can you help? In addition to these typical user questions, the cataloger and acquisitions librarian will use it to verify author, title, publishing date, publisher, and price—the types of information given for each entry. Arranged by author and title, the bimonthly service covers 5 to 7,000 titles in each issue. Furthermore, there is a cumulating continuous index to books published since the summer, i.e., since the last editions of *Books in Print* (BIP) which this supplements. Some 200 broad subject areas are covered in the subject guide.

The two primary retrospective guides to American publishing are *Books in Print* and *Subject Guide to Books in Print.* Both draw their basic information from a third work, *Publisher's Trade List Annual (PTLA).* The latter is a collection of American publisher's catalogs in book form. The catalogs conform to a certain physical cut size but may be in hundreds of various type faces, arrangements, and lengths. For convenience, the 2,250 publisher's catalogs are bound in alphabetical order.[5] The entries in the catalogs are fed into a computer (a recent innovation which, after a bad start, now seems to function relatively well)[6] and rearranged in two ways: (1) alphabetically by author and by title and (2) alphabetically by subject. The first arrangement makes up *Books in Print;* the second *Subject Guide to Books in Print.* The reliability and scope of both titles depends—the workings of the computer aside—on the accuracy of information sent by the publishers. Both titles are issued in early fall and represent books in print, i.e., books which are available for purchase.

Beginning in 1973, Bowker is making an effort to keep *Books in Print* current via a supplement, *Books in Print Supplement* (1973 to date, annual), which comes out in April. This lists new and forthcoming books, changes in prices, and out-of-print titles since *Books in Print* was issued. It also supplements *Subject Guide to Books in Print* because it is an author, title, subject approach in print, i.e., books which are available for purchase.

Books in Print includes over 355,000 individual titles from children's books to paperbacks and textbooks. Information includes author, title, price, edition, binding, publisher, year of publication, illustrations, series, and the ISBN number. Almost all titles listed in the *Publisher's Trade List Annual* are similarly found in *Subject Guide to Books in Print.* In the subject approach, there are no entries for fiction or for poetry or for Bibles. (Note, though, that the guide does list books about fiction under the author's name, i.e., criticism of Hemingway is found under Hemingway.) Other exceptions are noted in the preface. If one wants to find the missing subjects, other guides must be employed, e.g., *The Fiction Catalog,* for one selective approach. Nevertheless, the subject guide has over 67,000 Library of Congress subject headings and almost as many cross references.

How are these three basic retrospective guides used in a library? *PTLA* is limited because of arrangement but is used to answer such questions as: What are the titles in the Oxford University Press series on U? (The catalog usually arranges series by title—an arrangement found nowhere else.) What are the prices of various dictionaries published by G. & C. Merriam? Again, arrangement is by form. I like mysteries published by Harper's. What other mysteries do they issue?

Of considerably more help for daily queries, *BIP* first and foremost tells the user whether he can purchase the book, from whom, and at

---

[5] Most, although not all, publishers are represented here. For the few exceptions, see the preface. Note, too, the shorter listings for smaller publishers in the beginning of the first volume.

[6] For early difficulties and a lesson in automation, *see:* Nora Camiber et al., "Books in Print 1969: An Analysis of Errors," *American Libraries,* October 1970, p. 901.

what price. It also answers other questions: What books by Hemingway are in print? Who is the publisher of *A Manual of Caterpillar Raising?* What is the price . . .? Is Peter Y's book still in print? (Of course proper answers presuppose correct information. All too often the author or the title spelling will be incorrect, and the librarians must work as much from knowledge as from a hunch.) And, sometimes, what is the address of a publisher? A full listing of addresses is given in the back of *BIP.*

The use of the subject guide is self-evident. However, it not only helps to locate a book about a given subject for a reader, it is also used to help expand the library's collection in given areas. If, for example, there is a great demand for books about television, the subject guide gives a complete list of those available from American publishers. Note one important thing: the list is inclusive, not selective. There is nothing here to differentiate the worst from the best of the 50 or so titles. One must turn to other bibliographies and reviews for that type of vital information.

Given this basic pattern of trade and national bibliographical control, the R. R. Bowker Company and other public and private firms here and abroad establish variations on the basic theme. For example, a subject approach is found in *Children's Books in Print* and *Subject Guide to Children's Books in Print.*

The basic volume is taken from the *Publisher's Trade List Annual,* with additions and corrections as needed. It includes some 45,000 children's titles (i.e., those used in kindergarten through twelfth grade). The subject guide takes the titles and breaks them down into over 7,000 different headings. Here it differs from the basic *Subject Guide To Books in Print* in that the headings are from Sears, not from the Library of Congress; and fiction is included under subject headings, as well. Sears, obviously, offers subjects closer to the needs of children than the Library of Congress. The entries in the *Children's Books in Print* can be found as readily in *Books in Print.* (Even here, though, justification for purchase may be the unique listing not found in the basic volume, i.e., illustrators are listed as well as authors and titles.) Hence, if the library needs a Sears breakdown of titles or a breakdown by illustrators, one or both volumes can be purchased without fear of duplicating other works in the library.

Other versions of the same subject approach can be found in such Bowker titles: *Bowker's Medical Books in Print, Scientific and Technical Books in Print, El-Hi Textbooks in Print.* There are other publishers, of course, who venture into the same field, e.g., *Law Books in Print* (Dobbs Ferry, New York: Oceans Publications, Inc., 1957 to date). This latter title differs in that it includes not only American law books but all law books in the English language. It is usually two to three years behind, i.e., the 3-volume edition covering titles up through December 31, 1969, did not come out until 1972. In order to keep up with current publications, the firm issues a quarterly, *Law Books Published*, a type of *American Book Publishing Record*. Other disciplines and subject areas have similar aids.

There are, also guides based on form as well as title or subject. The best known in America is *Paperbound Books in Print*. The paperbound guide is now published and updated twice a year, in March and November. The basic arrangement is by author, and there are subject and title indexes. Most titles are found in *Books in Print*—but not all, particularly current paperbacks which have come out since the last edition of *BIP*. The collection of 112,000 or so titles has the distinct advantage of telling the user immediately whether X book is available in paperback, whether there are several editions, and which editions cost more or less. Given *BIP*, *PBIP* is not essential in a library, but it certainly is helpful; and it is indispensable in any library where paperbacks are a major form.[7]

UNITED STATES RETROSPECTIVE BIBLIOGRAPHY[8]

Most daily reference work is carried on with relatively current national and trade bibliographies. There are times when retrospective bibliography is needed. The following type of questions can be answered by consulting one or more of the retrospective bibliographies listed here: What is the original price of John Jenkins' *Lives of the Governors of the State of New York*, published in 1851? Who is the author of *The Ballad of the Abolition Blunder-buss*, published in 1861? What is the correct title of a work on rattlesnakes by S. W. Mitchell, published in 1860? The person asking this type of question is likely to be a historian, literary scholar, or librarian; or, for that matter, anyone deeply involved in research of a given subject, place, or person.

In trying to fathom these aids, which is not always easy because of erratic arrangement, coverage, and purpose, the librarian is apt to overlook other approaches which are somewhat simpler. The first one is *The National Union Catalog* which, when the pre-1956 set is complete, will supply answers to all but the most elusive and esoteric titles.

Retrospective bibliography is not limited to the United States—in fact it has reached scholarly, awesome proportions in England and on the

---

[7] For a model review of the old multivolume set, which in many ways is still applicable in principle, *see:* Marvin Kitman, "Paperbound Books in Print," *New York Times Book Review*, February 15, 1970, p. 31.

[8] When discussing retrospective bibliography, it should be kept in mind that it enjoys as many divisions and subdivisions as current bibliography. What is discussed here is limited to national, general retrospective bibliography. It does not take into consideration the highly important aspect of retrospective subject bibliography which is a study in itself. For an imaginative and innovative discussion of retrospective bibliography, *see:* Thelma Freides, "Bibliographies in the Social Sciences," *RQ*, Fall 1971, p. 15.

continent. Examples of the basic foreign retrospective bibliographies will
be found in Winchell and Walford. Regardless of national origin, retrospective bibliographies tell what was published where and by whom.
They are a source of information about national, state, and local history
and, for that matter, trace the cultural and scientific development of
people in a given place and time.

In chronological order, the leading American retrospective bibliographies are:[9]

1500?-1892   Sabin, Joseph, *Dictionary of Books Relating to America
From Its Discovery to the Present Time.* New York: Sabin,
1869-1892; Bibliographical Society of America, 1928-1936,
29 vols.

1639-1800   Evans, Charles, *American Bibliography: A Chronological
Dictionary of All Books, Pamphlets and Periodical Publications Printed in the United States of America From the
Genesis of Printing in 1639 Down to and Including the Year
1800.* Chicago: Printed for the author, 1903-1959, 14 vols.
(vols. 13 and 14 published by the American Antiquarian
Society).

1801-1819   Shaw, Ralph and Shoemaker, Richard, *American Bibliography; A Preliminary Checklist.* Metuchen, New Jersey;
Scarecrow Press, 1958-1965, 22 vols., $175.50.

1820-1861   Roorbach, Orville, *Bibliotheca Americana.* New York: O. A.
Roorbach, 1852-1861, 4 vols.

1820-1861   Shoemaker, Richard H., *A Checklist of American Imprints,
1820.* Metuchen, New Jersey: Scarecrow Press, 1964—to
date. (As of 1973, 10 vol. issued covering back to 1829. The
plan is to continue coverage up to 1861.)

1861-1870   Kelly, James, *American Catalogue of Books, Published in
the United States from January 1861 to January 1871, with
Date of Publication, Size, Price, and Publisher's Name.* New
York: John Wiley & Sons Inc., 1866-1871, 2 vols.

1872-   *Publishers' Trade List Annual.*

1876-1910   *American Catalogue of Books, 1876-1910.* New York: *Publishers' Weekly,* 1876-1910, 9 vols. in 13.

1899-1927   *United States Catalog; Books in Print.* 4th ed. New York:
The H. W. Wilson Company, 1928, 3,164 pp.

The following titles are still being published and are discussed elsewhere. They are listed here by the beginning publishing date as an

[9] Original publishers are given for these titles, but most have been reprinted by one or
more publishers and a number are available on microform.

indication of what can be used for retrospective searching from 1928 to the present.

1872-	*Publishers' Weekly*
1873-	*Publishers' Trade List Annual*
1898-	*Cumulative Book Index*
1948-	*Books in Print*
1957-	*Subject Guide to Books in Print*

Sabin differs from all the other bibliographies listed here in that he includes books, pamphlets, and periodicals printed in America *and* works printed about America in other countries. The others are limited to titles published in this country. An Oxford scholar, Sabin was an authority on rare books about America. He began his ambitious project (often called *Bibliotheca Americana*) in the early 1860s, lived long enough to see 13 volumes published by 1881. The next seven volumes were by Wilberforce Eaames. R. W. G. Vail finally called a halt to the proceedings with the final volumes in 1936. Arrangement is by author, with some title entries and other entries by names of places. Entries include collation, usually location of a copy, and a note on contents. There is no title or subject index. Each volume contains entries for one section of the alphabet up to the date of publication; hence, it is uneven in chronological coverage, particularly since cutoff dates of acceptable publications moved further and further back as the work continued. There is no guarantee that a work published in 1870, say, is apt to be found here. The author must be known or the set is virtually worthless. However, once the author is identified, the information found is enough to warrant searching.

A work of love and considerable hardship for Charles Evans, *American Bibliography* is a classic. It is considered the keystone upon which all retrospective American bibliography is built and is basic to any large collection. Arrangement is not alphabetical by author. It is chronological by dates of publication. If one does not know the date, or approximate date, there is an author, subject, and printer and publisher index to help. For each entry, there is the author's full name with birth and death dates, a full title, place, publisher, date, paging, size, and usually the location of one or more copies in American libraries.

The *Shipton National Index* is a required addition for anyone using Evans. It serves to eliminate nonexistent titles, or ghosts which Evans dutifully recorded without seeing a copy of the actual item. Furthermore, it adds over 10,000 titles discovered since Evans' set was published. The 49,197 entries are arranged alphabetically by author and short title, and there is reference to the original entry in Evans—if it is listed there. (*The National Index* is particularly valuable for use with the microcard reproduction of all nonserial titles listed in Evans, and elsewhere, and published in America before 1801. It is virtually an index to the tremendous set of nearly 50,000 individual books on microform.)

Shaw and Shoemaker continued Evans' initial efforts to 1820 and the gap between Evans and Roorbach is filled only partially. Each volume covers one year and gives the briefest author citation, along with a location for some copies. Addenda volumes include a title and author index for the full series.

Another, in the same series, is *A Checklist of American Imprints* which was to carry the same type of listing down to 1861 and the beginning of Kelly. From the 1821 volume on, this differs from the 1801-1819 set in that locations are given for the majority of copies and the compiler did check out the books listed. (In the earlier compilation, titles were primarily from secondary sources with little attention given to checking the accuracy of those sources.) Since Shoemaker's death in 1969, the series has been carried on by Gayle Cooper, Rutgers, and the publisher; ... and there is a title and author index to the 1820-1829 series.

Until the *Checklist of American Imprints* is taken down to 1861, the Roorbach bibliography is a necessity. This is a contemporary bibliography similar in its intent to *Books in Print,* but done with considerably less care. The arrangement is alphabetical by author and title with information on the publisher, size, and usually, but not always, the price and date. Entries are frequently incomplete. From 1861 to 1870, Kelly serves the same purpose as Roorbach and succeeds in giving the same type of incomplete information. Both Roorbach and Kelly, for example, list less than one-half as many titles per year as Evans who was recording a much less productive period in American publishing. Although inaccurate and incomplete, the two bibliographies are the only reference aids of their kind.

In terms of retrospective searching, then, there is something less than a blank period from the time of the last Shoemaker volume to the beginning of the *American Catalog of Books* in 1876, i.e., from 1830 to 1876. Begun by Frederick Leypoldt as a trade bibliography of books in print, the *American Catalog* was published annually and later cumulated. Arrangement is by author and title with subject supplements. The information is generally reliable and comprehensive—but no more so than the publisher's catalogs from which the information came.

Competition from The H. W. Wilson Company's *United States Catalog* caused cessation of the *American Catalog* in 1910 which did not begin publishing again until 1948 as *Books in Print.* The *United States Catalog* is really a cumulation of the *Cumulative Book Index* which began in 1898 as a type of *Books in Print* in competition with the *American Catalog.* There are four editions of the *United States Catalog,* but the most often used is the last, which lists all the books in print published in

English in the United States and Canada in 1928. (Earlier volumes must be consulted for finding books out-of-print by 1928 and for fuller information on other titles.) By 1928, the increase in the number of titles published forced Wilson to abandon the *United States Catalog* in favor of cumulative issues of the *CBI*. Until *BIP* was first issued in 1948, there was nothing equivalent to the *United States Catalog*. From 1928 to the advent of *Books in Print* in 1948 and the *American Book Publishing Record* in 1960, the librarian could consult the various cumulations of the *CBI* for retrospective titles.

From Evans to the *United States Catalog*, emphasis was on publications of the eastern United States. There was little or no record of early publishing in any Western territories or of work in large cities outside of New York; and, in fact, there were no imprint records for most regions of the United States. With this in mind, the American Imprints Inventory was launched in the latter part of the 1930s. When World War II broke out, most of the work halted. In the meantime, workers had recorded imprints from Arizona to Washington. Many of these were publications. Usually arrangement is by state, then chronologically for a given number of years. Where possible, various libraries that hold the given work are cited. A complete list will be found in Winchell under AA358.

An overview of the whole, sometimes confusing, aspect of American imprints will be found in the scholarly two-volume work by Thomas C. Tanselle: *Guide to the Study of United States Imprints* (Cambridge: Harvard University Press, 1972). This is a type of "Winchell" for the study of both enumerative and analytical bibliography and is a model of its kind for the librarian or researcher.

Subject bibliography

While the national library catalogs and the national and trade bibliographies try to be inclusive within their various scopes, a subject bibliography is exclusive. It limits itself to a single subject, area, or individual, for example: Gertrude Forrester, *Occupational Literature: An Annotated Bibliography* (New York: The H. W. Wilson Company, 1971); and *Bibliography of Wheat* (Metuchen, New Jersey: Scarecrow Press, 1971).

Given its limitation, the subject bibliography can take many paths. Some try to be comprehensive within the area, others are selective and evaluative. Some include all forms from books to recordings, others limit themselves to a single form. Some are mere lists, others are annotated. Some are current, others are retrospective, and some may be both. The variations on a theme are literally infinite.

There are thousands of subject bibliographies; and, for this reason, their study has developed into a separate discipline or course in most library schools. No effort is made here to do more than acknowledge the field. This is not to imply subject bibliography is not important. It is of major importance. It is to say that the present text must limit itself to a basic overview of all reference work, and any attempt to include subject bibliography would be quite beyond the scope of this effort.[10]

Special bibliography: types of materials

The main bibliographical effort of the world has primarily centered on the keeping of a comprehensive record of both current and retrospective publications of books. Given some control of this, the usual procedure is to expand. Next comes an effort to list serials, maps, recordings, films, dissertations, and all other forms of communication. This is usually done in one of two ways: (1) a general bibliography by form or (2) using the various forms in specialized subject bibliographies. For example, a general bibliography would list all the periodicals available for purchase in the United States or would locate the world's periodicals in a given number of libraries. A subject bibliography would limit itself to periodicals in the subject area, for example, the history of printing or some aspect of physics. The same pattern is repeated in varying degrees for each form and for each country. As a consequence, there are many bibliographies for material forms.

SUGGESTED READING

Cole, John, "Of Copyright, Men, and A National Library," *The Quarterly Journal of the Library of Congress,* April 1971, pp. 114+. A history of the copyright procedure, and, more particularly, as applicable to the deposit of copies in the Library of Congress.

Kimball, John W., *The National Union Catalog: Reference and Related Services.* Washington, D.C.: Library of Congress, 1973, 33 pp. A clear, brief explanation of the *NUC,* and how it is to be used by reference librarians.

Perreault, J. M., "Reflections on the Idea of a Universal Bibliography," *Herald of Library Science,* July 1971, pp. 214+. The author suggests some of the problems and possible solutions for a universal bibliography.

[10] Two useful introductions to subject bibliography are: Barbara M. Hale, *The Subject Bibliography of the Social Sciences and Humanities* (New York: Pergamon Press, 1970), 149 pp.; it includes a study of the history and theory of subject bibliography applicable to all fields. Robert L. Collison, *Bibliographies Subject and National.* 3d ed. (London: Crosby Lockwood & Son, 1968), 203 pp.; this is primarily an annotated listing by subject of basic subject bibliographies.

CHAPTER FOUR
INDEXING AND ABSTRACTING
SERVICES[1]

There is no more familiar reference form than the index. It is used daily by all librarians and numerous laymen; it is truly the heart of any information retrieval system. The index, whether it be a separate guide to periodical articles or part of a book, is used to locate specific pieces or bits of information in a larger unit. The majority of indexes are easy enough to understand, and the beginner's primary challenge is to isolate and identify those most commonly used in the reference process. Beyond that, the operation by which an index is created presents a number of problems of considerable interest.

Aside from the individual book index, a reference librarian is most likely to be concerned with the following types of traditional indexes:

1. Periodicals
    a. General indexes, covering many periodicals in a wide or specific subject field. *The Readers' Guide to Periodical Literature* is the most widely known of this type of index.
    b. Subject index, covering not only several periodicals, but also other material found in new books, pamphlets, reports, or government documents. The purpose is to index material

---

[1] This chapter is primarily confined to traditional indexing and abstracts. *See* Volume 2, Chapter 10, for a discussion of indexing principles and problems as related to the mechanization and analysis of the indexing process via such services as *Medlars* and *Science Citation Index*.

in a narrow subject field. Examples of this type of index are the *Applied Science & Technology Index* and *Index Medicus*.

c.   Indexes to single magazines, either at the end of a volume or as separately published works. *The Geographic Magazine Cumulative Index* is an example.

2.   Newspapers
There is limited newspaper indexing in the United States. Normally this lack of indexing is made up for by individual libraries indexing local papers.

3.   Material in collections
This includes indexes to collections of poems, plays, fiction, songs, and so on. The *Speech Index* and *Granger's Index to Poetry* are examples.

PERIODICAL INDEXES

General indexes

The Readers' Guide to Periodical Literature. New York: The H. W. Wilson Company, 1905 to date, semimonthly (September–June), monthly (July and August), service.

Social Sciences and Humanities Index. New York: The H. W. Wilson Company, 1916 to date, quarterly, service.

British Humanities Index. London: Library Association, 1962 to date, quarterly and annual cumulations, $37.50.

Canadian Periodical Index. Ottawa, Ontario: Canadian Library Association, 1948 to date, monthly, rates on request.

The vast majority of general and subject periodical indexes used in small and medium-sized American libraries—as well as the largest research library, but on a more limited scale—originate from The H. W. Wilson Company. The Wilson indexes are celebrated for their ease of use and have become a model of the best in indexing. Many of the company's publications are sold on a service basis. There is no set fee, but libraries pay in the amount of service used. This usually means the larger, better financed libraries pay more than the smaller libraries for the same index.[2]

Since 1952, the selection of works to be indexed has been determined by a group of librarians, The Committee on Wilson Indexes. In addition to deciding what should or should not be included in an index, the Committee also advises on needs for new indexes or approaches to

[2] For a complete explanation of this system, *see* the latest Wilson Company catalog of publications.

materials. How the committee operates is explained in full by Edwin B. Colburn in an article in the *ALA Bulletin* (January 1965, pp. 35 +). The committee, whose membership is rotated periodically, draws upon advice and suggestions from subscribers to the Wilson indexes.

While this formalized approach is employed by the Wilson Company, variations on the method are used by any publisher of continuous indexes who wishes to stay in business. He, of course, must satisfy the needs of his customers (i.e., librarians) and to this end will frequently consult with users as to what should or should not be included in an index. The service basis approach is not unique, although the scale on which it is carried on by Wilson is peculiar to that firm.

Discussion of general periodical indexes becomes more and more a fiction. Emphasis is now on specialized indexes; and with the exception of the *Readers' Guide* and a few more limited indexes abroad, the day of attempting to cover a general field is about past. Because of its wide scope, the *Readers' Guide* is by far the most popular general index in America, followed only by its smaller brother, the *Abridged Readers' Guide*. Some 160 magazines of general interest are indexed in the larger work, approximately 44 in the junior edition. Subjectwise they range from the *American Libraries* to *Esquire* to the *Yale Review*. The assumption is that the wide coverage will ensure that most users will find something about a subject.

The main work is issued twice a month and is one of the most recent guides to literature. It frequently is the only guide to current material on some out-of-the-way point raised at a reference desk. Cumulations serve the retrospective needs of many patrons.

The abridged version, issued monthly from September to June, is geared to smaller libraries and schools. There is some debate as to the wisdom of more than halving the coverage, particularly if it is possible to secure indexed material from a larger library. Its low price (less than half that of the regular work) and its selection of periodicals primarily for students seem to ensure its popularity.

The great advantage of the indexes for general use is the arrangement. Author and subject entries are in a single alphabet. The subject headings, as in all the Wilson indexes, are consistent and easy to locate. Furthermore, there are numerous cross references and *see* and *see also* references which make the indexes a model for rapid use. Each entry contains all necessary information to find the article. There is a minimum of abbreviations, and these are clearly explained in the front of the index.

Having suffered a division, the *British Humanities Index* is somewhat less ambitious than *The Readers' Guide to Periodical Literature*. From 1915, it was the *Subject Index to Periodicals*, but after 1962, it omitted titles in the fields of education (taken up by *British Educational*

Index) and technology *(British Technology Index)*. Medical sciences and business were also cut out. What remains is a serviceable and relatively general guide to British journals covering such subjects as politics, economics, history, and literature. Unlike *The Readers' Guide*, it is of limited use in the area of current materials because it is published only quarterly with annual cumulations. By the time the index and the corresponding periodicals reach America, the timeliness factor is nil.

The *Canadian Periodical Index* is an approximate equivalent to *The Readers' Guide*. It is an author–subject index to about 90 Canadian general magazines, 15 in French. It has a checkered history of names and scope, but the present work is as valuable as it is useful for all Canadian libraries, and for many American ones as well. Published monthly, there are annual cumulations.

Closer to home, the *Social Sciences and Humanities Index*, issued quarterly, covers much the same American areas as its British counterpart, the *British Humanities Index*. It, too, started under a different name (*The Readers' Guide* to *Periodical Literature Supplement*, and from 1920 through March 1965 was the *International Index*). Some 210 titles are analyzed; and as a back-up for *The Readers' Guide*, it is the second most important general index in any library.

Subject indexes

All the following titles are published by The H. W. Wilson Company:

Applied Science and Technology Index. 1958 to date, monthly, service.

Art Index. 1929 to date, quarterly, service.

Biological and Agricultural Index. 1964 to date, monthly, service.

Business Periodicals Index. 1958 to date, monthly, service.

Education Index. 1929 to date, monthly, service.

Index to Legal Periodicals. 1908 to date, monthly, service.

Library Literature. 1933 to date, bimonthly, service.

Not all subject indexes are published by The H. W. Wilson Company. There are scores of indexes from *The Catholic Periodical and Literature Index* (Haverford, Pennsylvania: Catholic Library Assn., 1930 to date, bimonthly) and *Ekistic Index* (Athens, Greece: Athens Technological Organization, 1968 to date, semiannual) to *Index to Little Magazines* (Chicago: The Swallow Press, Inc., annual) and the *Music Index* (Detroit: Information Service, 1949 to date, monthly).[3] Still, for day-to-day use

---

[3] See the author's *Magazines for Libraries*, "Abstracts and Indexes" section for an annotated list of the major subject indexes. Equally helpful: Jean Kujoth, *Subject Guide to Periodical Indexes and Review Indexes* (Metuchen, New Jersey: Scarecrow Press, 1969), 129 pp. This includes 210 indexes grouped by subject in the first section, and a description of the indexes in the second section.

over a broad area of subjects and periodicals, the Wilson indexes have become fairly standard and, for the most part, equally satisfactory. The other subject indexes are most often found in larger or specialized collections.

When considering subject indexes, two important facts must be kept in mind:

1. Despite the titles of indexes, many of them are considerably more broad in coverage than would be indicated by such key title works as "art" or "education." While emphasis is on works in these areas, related fields are often considered. Therefore, anyone doing a subject analysis in depth often should consult indexes which take in fringe area topics.
2. The majority of the subject indexes are not confined solely to magazines. Many include books, monographs, bulletins, and even government documents.

What is more, the majority are not parochial, but tend to be international in scope. True, not many foreign-language works are listed, but anything in English is usually noted, even if issued abroad.

Because of this wider base of coverage, many libraries are doubtful about including such indexes. What good is it to find a particular article in a specialized journal and then not be able to obtain the journal? This has been discussed earlier, but it bears repeating. The library should be in a position either to borrow the journal or have a copy made of the article. If it is not, it had better look to improving its services. Also, to repeat another consideration: Even without the pertinent items indexed, the indexes do serve to give the reader a broader view of the topic than he might get simply from a general index.

There is little point in describing each of the Wilson subject indexes. For the most part, their titles are explanatory of scope and purpose. The audience can be either the specialist or the generalist—journals and periodicals for both are indexed. Most indexed titles are American, but there are representative selections from other countries in other languages. The number indexed ranges from 180 to over 300. Also, as noted, many of the indexes include such forms as monographic series, annuals, yearbooks.

The approach is fairly the same, i.e., the author and subject entries are in a single alphabet and there are the usual excellent cross references. Each has its peculiarities, but a reading of the prefatory material for each index will clarify the finer points.

One non-Wilson subject-type index which is to be found in most libraries is the *Public Affairs Information Service, Bulletin* (New York: Public Affairs Information Service, 1915 to date, weekly.) This has the noteworthy advantage of currency, and it is the major source of information in the social sciences. As such, it is a close rival to *The Readers' Guide* as a good general index.

The *Bulletin* (or *PAIS* as it is usually called) is issued weekly and cumulated five times a year, with a final annual volume which may be purchased separately. Libraries with limited budgets may want the annual as the best source of information on periodicals, government documents, reports, and some books in such areas as government, public administration, international affairs, and economics. A valuable addition is a "key to periodical references" and a list of "publications analyzed." Both serve as a handy check list and buying guide for the library.

While works analyzed are limited to those in English, coverage is international. Arrangement is alphabetical, primarily by subject. A few of the entries have brief descriptive notes on both contents and purpose. Beginning in 1972, *PAIS* issued a second index—*Foreign Language Index*—which does much the same service as the *Bulletin*. The essential difference is that the quarterly index considers the same material in a number of foreign language journals, books, reports, pamphlets, and the like. For all but the largest research library, the basic *Bulletin* will probably be quite enough.

Retrospective periodical indexes

Poole's Index to Periodical Literature, 1802–1906. vol. 1, 1802–1881, Boston: Osgood, 1882; vols. 2–6 (supplements 1–5), Boston: Houghton Mifflin Company, 1888–1908) (reprinted 6 vols. in 7 vols., Gloucester, Mass.: Peter Smith Publisher, 1938).

This was the first general magazine index, and the forerunner of *The Readers' Guide.* It was the imagination of William Frederick Poole, a pioneer in both bibliography and library science, that made the index possible. Recognizing that many older periodicals were not being used for lack of proper indexing, he set out, after one or two preliminary starts, to index 470 American and English periodicals covering the period 1802 to 1881. Having completed this work, he issued five supplements which brought the indexing up to 1908.

The modern user is sometimes frustrated when he realizes that the total approach is by subject of an article. The author index to some 300,000 references in the main set and the supplements are supplied by C. Edward Wall's *Cumulative Author Index for Poole's Index . . .* (Ann Arbor, Michigan: Pierian Press, 1971, 488 pp.). The index is computer produced and not entirely easy to follow, but it is a great help to anyone seeking an author entry in Poole.

With all its faults, Poole's work is still a considerable achievement and an invaluable tool for the man or woman seeking some key to nineteenth-century periodicals. The last decade of the century is better treated in *Nineteenth Century Readers' Guide to Periodical Literature, 1890-1899* with supplementary indexing 1900-1922. New York: The H. W. Wilson Company, 1944, 2 vols.

Limited to 51 periodicals (as contrasted with Poole's 470), this thoroughly indexes by author and subject magazines for the years 1890 to 1899. Some 14 are indexed beyond 1900 to 1922. At one time, it was planned to rework the nineteenth-century guide' in its entirety, but apparently the plans have been dropped for the present. In effect, it is hoped to apply modern indexing techniques to at least 51 nineteenth-century periodicals that are more readily available and most frequently used in libraries.

NEWSPAPER INDEXES

The New York Times Index. New York: The New York Times, 1851 to date, semimonthly, $87.50; annual cumulation, $87.50; combines, $150.

Newspaper Index. Wooster, Ohio: Bell & Howell, 1972 to date, monthly, $695. (Individual sections for individual papers, $225.)

Christian Science Monitor Index. Ann Arbor, Michigan: University Microfilms, 1960 to date, monthly, $20.

Wall Street Journal Index. Princeton, New Jersey: Dow Jones Books, Inc., 1958 to date, monthly, $75, annual vol. $75. Combined monthly and annual $125.

National Observer Index. Princeton, New Jersey: Dow Jones Books, Inc., 1969 to date, annual, $18.

The Times. London: The Times, 1906 to date, bimonthly, $73.

For the reference librarian, newspapers primarily serve as sources of information about current events and personalities. When the library has a relatively complete run of national or local newspapers, they are an excellent source for retrospective historical searching. Reference value increases with the age and the completeness of the run. Recognition of this was long in coming to libraries; and as a consequence, many early newspapers are missing either in entirety or for important years. Failure of libraries to keep early newspapers was primarily the old argument of space. Today, the problem has been overcome to a great extent by availability of microfilm copies and cooperative storage arrangements, whereby at least one library in a state will be responsible for runs of the original copies.

Most large newspapers such as *The New York Times* now have a microfilm edition. The microfilm is normally prepared from the final edition, which is the one indexed. Libraries usually subscribe to both the microfilm and the printed edition, discarding the latter after daily use. The Library of Congress regularly updates a bibliography, *Newspapers on Microfilm,* which includes entries by state and by country.

Selection of newspapers depends upon the size of the library and the type of patrons. A minimal selection will include the local newspapers, city, county, and state, and *The New York Times.* On an international level, selection is usually made on the basis of ethnic language groups in the community.

Since the last edition of this text, there have been several new indexes to newspapers, but there are still too few. The burden of indexing local papers now, as in the past, rests primarily upon the state and large city and university libraries. Some progress has been made and if the Bell & Howell project succeeds in attracting subscribers, it is possible the net of newspaper indexing will be broadened.

The major difficulty remains: while there are too few indexes, the indexes themselves are not prompt. *The New York Times Index* comes out twice a month, but may not reach the library until another month or more has elapsed. The other indexes are primarily monthly. As a consequence, when one discusses recency of newspaper indexes, it is a relative matter.

A distinct advantage of *The New York Times Index* is its wide scope and relative completeness. While the United States does not have a daily national newspaper, the *Times* in its effort to cover all major news events, both national and international, comes close to being a national paper. The index itself affords a wealth of information and frequently is used even without reference to the individual papers. Each entry includes a brief abstract of the news story. Consequently, someone seeking a single fact, such as the name of an official, date of an event, or title of a play, may often find all he needs in the index. Also, since all material is dated, the index serves as an entry into other unindexed newspapers and magazines. For example, if the user is uncertain as to the day X ship sank and wishes to see how it was covered in his own newspaper or in a magazine, the *Times Index* will narrow the search by giving him the day the event occurred.

The New York Times Index is arranged in dictionary form with sufficient cross references to names and related topics. Events under each of the main headings are arranged chronologically. Book and theatre reviews are listed under those respective headings.

Some libraries subscribe only to the cumulated volume. This serves not only as an index but also as a type of guide to the activities of the previous year. Thanks to the rather full abstracts, maps, and charts, one may use the cumulated volume as a reference source in itself. One problem: The cumulation rarely appears until four or five months after the first of the next year.

Beginning in 1972, *The New York Times Index* became part of a much larger system for retrieving data from the *Times* clipping morgue. The *Times* is on microfiche which may be recalled in a semiautomatic fashion when someone in the *Times* building finds reference to an item in the automated index.[4]

The *Bell & Howell Newspaper Index* is really four indexes to four geographically important newspapers—*Chicago Tribune, Los Angeles Times, The New Orleans Times Picayune,* and *The Washington Post.* Libraries may purchase the complete index, or at a reduced price only one or two of the indexes of individual newspapers. The obvious advantage of the index is that it affords a wide scope of coverage as seen from four different viewpoints. There are two approaches. The first section is divided by subject with subdivisions by newspapers. There are no abstracts, but the entries are descriptive enough to give the drift of the article. The reader can soon see how four newspapers view everything from a story on the President to a story on the winning chances of a tennis star. The second section is an alphabetical arrangement of personal names in the news—again arranged under each of the newspapers. The format, in either the "four in one" index or the individual indexes, is clear and the subject approach is easy to follow.

Issued since 1958, the index to *The Wall Street Journal* comes but monthly and is cumulated annually. While of primary interest in business and economic studies, the paper is more general in its news coverage than the title or its previous history would indicate. It has, for example, excellent book reviews and frequently carries articles in depth about national problems other than those linked to economics.

A monthly newspaper index, the *Christian Science Monitor Index* has been issued since 1960. Although the newspaper is biased on its editorial page, the general news which it reports is considered to be extremely objective. In fact, many libraries which draw the line at subscribing to any religious-supported newspapers make an exception of the *Monitor.* Consequently, the index is extremely useful as an adjunct to *The New York Times Index,* especially where a library has a group of patrons with an interest in the reporting of international and national affairs in some depth.

The *Monitor Index* cites stories found in its three editions: Eastern, Western, and Midwestern. The approach is primarily by subject, and no effort is made to annotate the items such as is found in the *Times Index.*

[4] John Rothman, "The New York Times Information Bank." *Special Libraries,* March 1972, pp. 111 + . (This is discussed in detail in vol. 2 of this text.)

It has one distinct advantage over the other indexes—a much lower price.

The National Observer annual index is in two parts: subject and personal names. There is a statement of content, the amount of text, and an indication of illustrations. The subject headings are well chosen, and there are a number of cross references. While the frequency of publication limits the index's use to retrospective searching, it is valuable enough for that—particularly since the weekly *National Observer* is a type of *Time* or *Newsweek* in its coverage of the week's events.

The Times of London index is in dictionary form with sufficient cross references to names and related topics. And while not as detailed as *The New York Times Index*, it does well enough. Again, though, its relative infrequency of appearance—coupled with mailing from abroad—severely limits its use as a current events index.

MATERIAL IN COLLECTIONS

Anthologies and collections are a peculiar blessing or curse for any reference librarian. Many of them are useless, others are on the borderline, and a few are worthwhile in that they bring the attention of readers to material which otherwise might be missed or overlooked. Regardless of merit, all collections may serve the reference librarian when he is seeking a particular speech, essay, poem, play, or other literary form. In reference, the usefulness of anthologies is dependent upon adequate indexes.

This type of material is approached by the average user in one of several ways. He may know the author and want a play, a poem, or other form by that author. He may know the name of the work, but more than likely he is uncertain. Another approach is, "I want something about X subject in a play, poem, short story. . . ."

Consequently, the most useful indexes to material in collections are organized so they may be approached by author, subject, and title of specific works. Failing to find a particular title in an anthology or collection usually means it has been published independently and has still to find its way into a collective form. The card catalog certainly should be checked; and failing this, standard bibliographical tools such as the *Cumulative Book Index* and *Books in Print* should also be checked.

Indexes to materials in collections serve two other valuable purposes. The majority include books or other materials which have been analyzed; and since the analysis tends to be selective, the librarian has a built-in buying guide to the better or outstanding books in the field. For example, the *Essay and General Literature Index* picks up selections from most of the outstanding collections of essays. The library that had the majority of these books in its collection would have a good representative group of works.

Another use, particularly in these days of close cooperation among libraries, is that the indexes can be used to locate books not found in the library. Given a specific request for an essay, and lacking the title in which the essay appears, the librarian may request the book on interlibrary loan by giving the specific and precise bibliographical information found in the index.

There are numerous such guides to materials in collections, but the most commonly used (which are typical enough of the genre) include:

Essay and General Literature Index. New York: The H. W. Wilson Company, 1900 to date, semiannual, $22, 5 year cumulations, $22.

Short Story Index. New York: The H. W. Wilson Company, 1953, 1,553 pp; supplements, issued every four years, i.e., 1950–1954, 1955–1958, 1959–1963, 1964–1968, 1969–1973, $24 plus $10 to $19 for supplements.

Granger's Index to Poetry. 6th ed. New York: Columbia University, 1973, 2,000 pp., $80.

Ottemiller's Index to Plays in Collections. 5th ed. Metuchen, New Jersey: Scarecrow Press, 1971, 452 pp., $11.

Aside from sharing a similar purpose of locating bits of information from collections and anthologies and individual books and magazines, this type of reference aid tends to center in the humanities, particularly in literature. There is little need for such assistance in the social sciences and the sciences, or where the need does exist it is usually met via an abstracting or indexing service. While the titles listed here are the better known, each year new entries appear. These range from guides to science fiction stories to information on handicrafts, costumes, photographs, and such. Once the form is recognized, the only basic change is the topic(s) covered and the thoroughness, or lack of thoroughness, in arrangement and depth of analysis.

Issued semiannually, the *Essay and General Literature Index* is the single most popular work in libraries for an entry into miscellaneous collections of articles. Every field of knowledge is covered from art to medicine, and the approach is primarily by subject and sometimes by title. An author's works as well as criticism of his individual efforts are listed under the author's name. Books to be analyzed in the index are listed monthly in the *Wilson Library Bulletin*, and the list frequently serves as a buying guide for this type of material. A major area not covered, however, is collective biography. (Since 1946 Wilson has been publishing *Biography Index*, mentioned elsewhere in this text.) The subject approach makes this work particularly useful for students seeking information for term papers or, for that matter, ideas for such papers.

Both as a finding tool and as an inspiration for students seeking material on subjects suitable for papers, the *Short Story Index* is an invaluable aid in any type of library. The main volume and the supplements list close to 100,000 stories in some 7,000 collections published up to 1973. Stories are indexed by author, title, and subject in one alphabet. The collections indexed are noted with full bibliographical information for each work.

Another helpful aid for reference librarians seeking elusive authors is the full details given for each author indexed. His name, dates of birth and death, and the title of a given story will often lead to a collection that has biographical data.

The sixth edition of Granger's follows previous editions in arrangement and approach. Close to 800 poetry anthologies are analyzed in three alphabets which cover title and first line, author, and subject. Each of the anthologies is listed with full bibliographical information. Not only is Granger's useful for tracing elusive poems, but the first line approach serves as a resource for quotations which may not be included in standard quotation books. An equally useful reference work in this area is: Brewton, John. *Index to Poetry for Children and Young People: 1965-1969* (New York: The H. W. Wilson Company, 1972), 575 pp. This offers a title, subject, author, and first line approach to 117 collections, and supplements the original 1942 index.

In its fifth edition, the Ottemiller index to plays covers the period from 1900 to the early 1970s. Some 1,047 collections are analyzed and from them come over 3,000 different plays. Analysis is by author and title. This guide points up given limitations which can be built into such works. More involved with finding where plays were anthologized and collected than the availability of the collections, the work is of limited use for libraries. Why? Because many of the titles analyzed are no longer in print. Consequently, while a good index, the volume is virtually worthless as a buying guide.

ABSTRACTING SERVICES[5]

What are the differences between the traditional indexes as exemplified by The H. W. Wilson Company group and newer models of retrieving bits of information?

[5] Harold Borko and Seymour Chatman, "Criteria for Acceptable Abstract . . ." *American Documentation*, April 1963. (Also in Tefko Saracevic, (ed.), *Introduction to Information Science* [New York: R. R. Bowker Company, 1970], p. 364. A survey of criteria and methods for abstracting.)

The first difference is really a discussion of another form. This is the abstract. As defined by Collison, an abstract: "is the terse presentation in (as far as possible) the author's own language, of all the points made, in the same order as in the original piece of primary documentary information—and that can be a book, a research report, a periodical article, a speech, the proceedings of a conference, an interview, etc."[6]

An index locates materials; an abstract goes a step further by not only locating, but briefly describing the essential points of a primary source in a given field. Usually the abstract is short—50 to 150 words—indicates primary points, methodology, arguments, essential results, and conclusions. The purpose of an abstract is twofold: (1) it saves time by elaboration on content and thus indicates to the user whether he wishes to read the full article; (2) it serves as a rapid method of surveying the retrospective literature without actually looking at the primary materials.

Abstracts increase in popularity and in necessity with the volume of material. Whereas 50 years ago a scholar might leisurely examine everything in a narrow field simply by consulting an index and picking out appropriate titles and authors, he now needs a firmer hand and a more explicit guide to the thousands of articles published each year. Abstracting services are not only signposts, but detailed maps of the territory which save the scholar needless searching.

The majority of abstracting services aim at relatively complete coverage of a narrow subject area. Coverage tends to be worldwide with abstracts of foreign-language articles in English. Format varies with abstract to abstract, although normally the issues: (1) are arranged under broad subject headings with appropriate author and some subject indexing; (2) do not cumulate, but do have an annual index which is exhaustive in that it includes author, definitive subject headings, report numbers, corporate authors, and any other items that will help the reader locate the initial abstract; (3) list titles of periodicals and other material abstracted.[7]

Representative abstracting services

Library & Information Science Abstracts. London: Library Association, 1969 to date, bimonthly, $27.

Psychological Abstracts. Washington, D.C.: American Psychological Association, Inc., 1927 to date, monthly, $130.

America: History and Life; a Guide to Periodical Literature. Santa Barbara, California: American Bibliographical Center—Clio Press, 1964 to date, quarterly, service.

[6] Robert L. Collison, *Abstracts and Abstracting Services* (Santa Barbara, California: American Bibliographical Center—Clio Press, 1971), p. 3.
[7] *See* Collison, ibid. Chapter on indexing, p. 41, for other elements often found in abstracting formats.

Historical Abstracts; Bibliography of the World's Periodical Literature, 1775 to Present. Santa Barbara, California: American Bibliographical Center—Clio Press, 1955 to date, quarterly, service.

These four abstracting services are representative of what is available in the humanities, science, and the social sciences. More technical, scientific abstracts and indexes are considered in the next section. And while they obviously differ in purpose and scope, they all tend to rely upon traditional abstracting principles.

The one most familiar to librarians is *Library and Information Science Abstracts* which supplements, but does not in anyway replace, the standard index, *Library Literature.* Whereas *Library Literature* is in the traditional alphabetical subject–author arrangement, the abstracting service depends upon a classification system for the arrangement of material. Therefore, in order to properly use this, or any of the other services, the librarian must have an understanding of the classification system employed by the publisher. Here it is rather elaborate, while in other abstracting services it may be no more complicated than the basic Dewey Decimal System. The classification method if properly explained, but thanks to an author and subject index even the novice has no real difficulty in locating material.

The English-based abstracting service does overlap with the American index; but, generally, the periodicals analyzed are different enough. More important, the English publication offers abstracts which allow the user to determine the value or lack of value of the article without going to the magazine in which it is published.

Another approach in this same field is offered by *Information Science Abstracts* (Philadelphia: Documentation Abstracts Inc., 1966 to date, bimonthly). Here the emphasis is much more technical with considerable analysis of articles dealing in all aspects of communication from computers to mathematics. Again, it is a classified arrangement with an author index and an annual subject index.

One of the more familiar, often used abstracting services in almost any medium to large library is *Psychological Abstracts.* This literally covers every major journal and many books in the world involved with psychology and related fields. Foreign language articles are abstracted in English. Again, the material is arranged by an elaborate classification which does require some understanding before it can be properly used. Of considerable help is the semiannual and annual subject index. An author index is published monthly.

Here it should be noted that *Psychological Abstracts* and *Information Science Abstracts* do have subject indexes, but they are not included with each issue. An unfortunate consequence of this is that the layman may pick up an issue without a subject index and be quite lost in attempting to fathom a procedure for entry. It is argued that the abstracting services are for the expert, not the amateur—the expert is familiar with his field or that part of the field in which he is likely to be seeking material. Therefore, the classification system works to his advantage, i.e., he can search one section and one section only without referring to other sections, unless, of course, they are related. It is properly assumed he will know the classification scheme employed. It is not so with the layman who may only be used to the alphabetical approach. Hence, these and almost all abstracting services do require that the librarian either get the information directly for the unexperienced user or, at a minimum, explain how they are used.

The two primary approaches to history are *Historical Abstracts* and *America: History and Life* (which includes American and Canadian history only).[8] *Historical Abstracts* covers articles in over 2,000 periodicals and is divided into chronological sections: Part A, modern history, 1450–1914; Part B, twentieth century, 1914 to the present. Within each section, the arrangement is classified and there are subject, geographical, and name indexes. Much the same arrangement is used in *America: History and Life.* The publisher (American Bibliographical Center) issues a number of other useful abstracting services from *Art Bibliographies* to the *ABC Political Science.*

The larger the abstracting service becomes, the more elaborate its indexing process. What tends to develop is a separate indexing system for the abstracts. This, in turn, means a two or more step process for the user. He must first locate the subject(s) of interest and then go to the abstracts—often in another volume—to find what is needed. If the abstract sounds of interest, he may then have to call for the journal, report, or book. One might argue that a one-step index might be even faster than the index-abstract-item approach.

The time factor in either process is not as important as the ease of use; and there is no question that the more elaborate the indexes to abstracts become, the more difficult they are for the layman to use. A man who might be at ease with the Wilson Company *Biological and Agricultural Index* is going to be confused and upset by *Biological* or *Chemical Abstracts.*

There are various estimates as to the number and the distribution of abstracting services. Collison thinks there are well over 1,000 which index and abstract about 50,000 English and foreign language periodicals.[9]

---

[8] Margaret and Rudolph Pasler, "U.S. History Periodical Abstracting and Indexing," *RQ,* Spring 1971, p. 232. The Paslers survey the current history indexing services and note that, while they are good, they fail to take into consideration the historian's need for retrospective indexing, i.e., indexes before the advent of the two listed here, in 1955 and 1964.
[9] The basic international guide listed 1,300 for science, 200 for the social sciences and humanities—but this was in 1969. The number, if anything, has grown. Meanwhile, the guide can be recommended for its brief descriptions of each of the indexes. It is: International Federation for Documentation. *Abstracting Services.* 2d ed. (The Hague: FID, 1969, 2 vols.).

This may sound impressive, but it only begins the necessary control of information. Furthermore, most of the emphasis has been in science and technology. Sometimes prohibitive costs, particularly for current, exhaustive service, has limited abstracting and indexing in the social sciences and humanities, which are notoriously poor in this field.

Unfortunately, the social sciences and particularly the humanities have neither the financial support nor the glamour of the sciences and have had to struggle along with minimal institutional or government aid. Whereas the majority of scientific abstracting services have and continue to receive support from industry, societies, and the national governments, few of those in the humanities are so blessed. Consequently, the number of abstracting services is limited, although still needed.

Eric

U.S. Educational Resources Information Center. *Research in Education.* Washington, D.C.: Government Printing Office, 1966 to date, monthly, $21.

So far, the discussion of indexes and abstracts has been limited to traditional approaches. This is far from the whole picture; and while the ramifications of modern indexing and abstracting is discussed in detail in the second volume of this text, the reader should not be left with the initial impression that the indexing process begins and ends with what has been considered.

An excellent example of the new trends is represented by *Research in Education,* the basic abstract journal of ERIC, i.e., the Educational Research Information Center. In 1966, ERIC instituted this monthly abstract journal to bring order out of the chaos of reports on education and related areas. These reports, often federally or state financed, tended to be ignored in indexes and abstracting services. Why? Primarily because there was an almost total lack of control. No one was sure when or by whom they were available for purchase.

As the body of reports grew,[10] it became obvious some control factor was needed. The first step was to create the Educational Research Information Center. The initial project was to collect and index some 1,750 documents on the special educational needs of the disadvantaged. From this grew a national system of 19 clearinghouses designed to gather and to deliver to ERIC reports, monographs, and the like which would be

[10] In the United States alone, at least 30,000 reports (in education) annually are put into some kind of pipeline for distribution. Based upon the experience of ERIC, only about 10,000 of these are considered sufficiently valuable, significant, and of wide enough interest to be disseminated nationally." Harvey Marron and Pat Sullivan, "Information Dissemination in Education: A Status Report," *College and Research Libraries,* July 1971, p. 287.

useful for people working in education and related fields. Thus, an information network was formed—a network which is typical enough of scores of similar projects in almost all fields of interest.

The clearinghouses, established at various universities and research centers, are designated given areas for bibliographical control. For example, all aspects of reading in education is considered by the clearinghouse at Indiana University; and the University of Minnesota turns its attention to libraries. A center is normally located where there is an existing interest and special collection in the area to be controlled. This sharing of labor differs radically from traditional indexing and abstracting where the documents to be indexed are gathered at one source and indexed by one firm or association.

Each of the clearinghouses is responsible for a number of things: (1) acquiring the reports and fugitive materials in the assigned subject area; (2) selecting those of enough importance to be circulated and indexed; (3) indexing and preparing abstracts. An elaborate system is established so that each of the centers sends to the ERIC headquarters forms which cover basic bibliographical data. However, unlike the majority of traditional indexing and abstracting services, ERIC not only offers the abstract but also gives the user access to the document. Hence, if the user finds a needed entry in *Research in Education,* he is likely to find the library has a copy of the report—usually on microform, but on hard copy if required. If not in the library, the report may be ordered through ERIC's Educational Document Reproduction Service.

The primary, although not only, control for the material gathered by the clearinghouses is *Research in Education.* The monthly abstracting service lists about 10,000 items a year. Arrangement is by document accession number, a not altogether happy form. However, the material is indexed by subject, author, and clearinghouses which prepared the abstracts. There is an annual index. The majority of entries (unlike what is found in the more familiar *Education Index*) consists of reports, speeches, and other fugitive documents. In addition to the bibliographical information, each issue gives prices and procedures for ordering copies of the reports, as well as a report on research grants awarded by the U.S. Office of Education.

Supporting this basic service are several secondary, private indexes. First, of course, is *Education Index* which concentrates on articles from some 250 journals. A relative newcomer is *Current Index to Journals in Education* (New York: CCM Information Sciences, Inc., 1969 to date, monthly, $64). This duplicates in great degree what is found in *Education Index* but differs in that some 500 periodicals are examined and there are short, not always complete, abstracts. It is by way of a luxury for all but the largest libraries.

Both the *Current Index to Journals in Education* and *Research in*

Education use subject headings from the *Thesaurus of ERIC Descriptors* which, as of 1971, included over 6,000 terms. This is worth mentioning because it is typical and confusing. Where there is a new abstracting or indexing service, and more particularly one linked to automation, a thesaurus of subject headings developed from the discipline is encountered. (The Wilson and other traditional indexes tend to rely upon the Library of Congress, Sears, and such for subject headings which are found in most card catalogs and are by far the most familiar to librarians and average users). Usually such a thesaurus is an improvement over broader subject headings, but this implies an intimate knowledge of the field by the user—an assumption which is safe enough in fields such as chemistry, medicine, and physics, but questionable when dealing with such a broad field as education and its allied areas from psychology to library science. The wide spectrum of interests requires that most users of these indexes and abstracts check for subject headings in the *Thesaurus*—otherwise they are apt to overlook related areas of interest.[11]

Taken one step further, there are now several computer-based systems which automatically will search the holdings of ERIC. The user decides which subject(s) he wishes searched and the computer base files are scanned, thus saving him the necessity of checking through the three basic indexes and abstracts.[12]

This pattern of information dissemination in education is not unqiue. And it is growing. The time will come when every major discipline has similar information centers and corresponding indexes and abstracting services. Efforts in the direction illustrated here by ERIC may one day replace the isolated index, and more particularly the general index. The time will come, hopefully, when the whole process of looking for information will be a one-step affair whereby the computer will search for the materials, offer alternatives, and then print out what is needed—and all within a matter of minutes instead of days or even weeks.

The other major aspect of reference service which ERIC illustrates is the "networking" concept. No single publisher, research center, or library is responsible for the ERIC input and output of information. It is made possible only by close cooperation and, it might be added, financial assistance from the federal government. The need for such cooperation is illustrated by ERIC's primary mission of controlling and making available heretofore unavailable information. It is inconceivable that a single publisher could accomplish the same mission.

[11] Suzanne Schippleck, "Looking for ERIC," *RQ,* Summer 1972, pp. 352+. This is a detailed discussion of the problems with subject headings in ERIC. *See also,* her brief bibliography for additional readings in this area.
[12] John M. Morgan, "Information Retrieval Systems for ERIC," *RQ,* Summer 1972, pp. 374+.

UNION LISTS AND GUIDES TO PERIODICALS AND NEWSPAPERS

Union lists: periodicals

Titus, Edna Brown (ed.), *Union List of Serials in Libraries of the United States and Canada.* 3d ed. New York: The H. W. Wilson Company, 1965, 5 vols., $120.

New Serial Titles 1950-1970. New York: R. R. Bowker Company, 1972, 5 vols, $190.

New Serial Titles. Washington, D.C.: Library of Congress, 1961 to date, 8 issues per year, cumulated quarterly and annually.

British Union Catalogue of Periodicals. London: Butterworths Scientific Publications, 1955 to 1958, 4 vols; supplement to 1960, Hamden, Conn.: Archon Books, The Shoe String Press, 1962, 991 pp., price on request.

British Union Catalogue of Periodicals. London: Butterworths Scientific Publications, 1964 to date, quarterly and annual cumulations.

A union list serves a number of purposes, but primarily it helps to identify and locate where a title may be found. The union lists here are all for periodicals, and they provide the widest general coverage of location and bibliographical information on periodicals now available.

The base of the American series of union lists is the *Union List of Serials in Libraries of the United States and Canada,* which includes titles published before 1950. It is continued by the 20-year cumulation of *New Serial Titles* (1950 to 1970) and on an eight-times-a-year basis by the same list. Given the basic volumes and the almost monthly updating, the librarian is able to: (1) locate one or more libraries that has almost any periodical published from the beginning until today; (2) discover the name and location of the publisher; (3) discover the name—and various changes in the name—of magazine; (4) discover the beginning date of publication and, where applicable, the date it ceased publication and the date it possibly began publication again. This type of information is primarily valuable for interlibrary loan purposes and for such things as determining whether a library has a complete run of a magazine, whether the magazine is still being published, whether it changed its name, and so on.

When someone finds an article through one of the library indexes in a journal or magazine which the library does not have, the librarian turns to one of the union lists to find the closest library where the magazine may be borrowed—or the articles copied. However, not all locations are given for a magazine. And this has led in part to the development of regional, state, and even citywide periodical union lists. Given a regional list which is composed of holdings of libraries in the immediate vicinity, it is obviously easier and faster to borrow from a neighbor than from a distant library possibly located via *New Serial Titles.*[13]

The basic unit for finding what American Library has what periodical is the *Union List of Serials in Libraries of the United States and Canada.* It includes the holdings of 956 libraries, 32 of which are in Canada. Entries for 156,449 serials are alphabetically arranged, and cross references overcome the problem of name changes in periodicals. Although the third edition was issued in 1965, the list includes only publications issued before 1950. For those published after 1950, one has to turn to *New Serial Titles* and its 20-year cumulation. As the name indicates, the lists include more than periodicals; but "serial" as here used does not include such items as government publications (except some periodicals and monographic series), newspapers, and law reports. And while limited to holdings in American and Canadian libraries, the serials are international in scope and subject matter. (Not every area is covered, however, and in the third edition many new Far Eastern language serials had to be deleted.)

Since the list is primarily a finding device, it does not give detailed bibliographical information, nor does it have a subject approach. In 1955, *New Serial Titles* began issuing a classified subject arrangement of the same basic list *(New Serial Titles—Classed Subject Arrangement);* but this is of limited use because limited cumulations have been published. No such approach exists for the *Union List.*

A cumulated, somewhat involved *Subject Index to New Serial Titles 1950-1965* was issued in 1968 by Pierian Press of Ann Arbor, Michigan. The necessity to refer back to *New Serial Titles* to use the subject list limits its use for all but the librarian and the patient scholar.

The *British Union Catalogue* supplements and complements the *Union List of Serials in Libraries of the United States and Canada.* It locates more than 140,000 titles in 441 libraries in the United Kingdom— many titles not included in the *Union List.* The same general types of serials are included and excluded, although for a historian it does include newspapers before 1799. Since 1964, it has been supplemented by quarterly issues and annual accumulations which are not totally successful in picking up titles after 1960.

The importance of serials in the interlibrary loan process, and thereby in the whole of cooperative library service on a regional, national, and international basis, is exemplified by these union lists.[14] They

---

[13] For a discussion of regional and local periodical union lists *see:* Dianne Ellsworth, "The Academic Library Looks at Union Lists," *College & Research Libraries,* November 1971, p. 475.

[14] There are hundreds of regional and national union lists, many of which are listed in Winchell, Walford, and the *American Reference Books Annual.* Although dated, a still useful listing of 1,200 union lists is Ruth Freitag's *Union Lists of Serials: A Bibliography* (Washington, D.C.: Library of Congress, 1964).

are obviously in need of improvement and sophistication. There is a National Serials Data Program underway which will help locate serials in all libraries and plan automation of such records.

Union lists: newspapers

American Newspapers, 1821–1936 . . . reprint, Millwood, New York: Krause Reprint Company, 1970, 791 pp., $75.

There is no continuing union list for newspapers, and the one major union list is much dated. (Although a newspaper is a serial, they are not included in *New Serials Titles*.) The lack of union lists may be accounted for:

1. In the United States, at least, the number of newspapers has tended to decrease. There were 2,461 dailies in 1916; today, there are no more than 1,750 and the number is shrinking. The control problem, therefore, is nowhere near the proportion of magazines which worldwide now number over 100,000.
2. Current newspapers are filed, often indexed and microformed by the state and larger cities; and it is usually a simple matter to locate them, or parts of them, for interlibrary loan.
3. Lacking indexes to all but the largest newspapers, access is limited and there is little demand for given newspapers of a given date on any national or international scale. (The local newspapers may be indexed and used locally or regionally, but little of this goes on nationally.) For these, and other reasons, the need for an up-to-date newspaper union list has never been pressing. It would be highly desirable, particularly for the historian, but desirability and feasability (in terms of cost) have so far not met to produce a revised union catalog of American newspapers. The 1821–1936 list gives holdings of newspapers in some 5,700 various places from libraries to courthouses. And despite its age, it is still quite useful—the newspapers which have ceased publication are probably still in the same locations, and the papers which are still being published are usually found in a continuous run in most of the locations in the union list. And, as indicated, there have not been that many new papers started since 1936 to make it a major location problem.

The location of American newspapers prior to 1821 is found in Clarence S. Brigham's *History and Bibliography of American Newspapers, 1690–1820* (Worcester, Massachusetts: American Antiquarian Society, 1947, 2 vols.). The list is not chronologically complete; and where research is being done in a given geographical area, it is wise to check with libraries for local union lists of holdings of newspapers not included in the two major union lists.

Directories: magazines and newspapers

Ulrich's International Periodical Directory. 14th ed. New York: R. R. Bowker Company, 1971, 2 vols. $42.50.

    Standard Periodical Directory. 4th ed. New York: Oxbridge Publishing Company, 1972, $60.

    N.W. Ayer & Son's Directory of Newspapers and Periodicals. Philadelphia: N. W. Ayer & Son, Inc., 1880 to date, annual, $40.

The limitation of a union list is failure to give full bibliographical description and other publishing data about a periodical. More serious, there is no methodical subject approach. Meeting these needs, directories emphasize fuller information and classification.

The fourteenth edition of *Ulrich's* lists some 50,000 periodicals from the United States and 117 other countries. *N. W. Ayer & Son's Directory of Newspapers and Periodicals* includes over 22,000 newspapers and magazines, primarily limited to the United States and Canada; and *The Standard Periodical Directory* includes 63,000 titles. There are similar lists for other countries throughout the world.

These works are particularly useful in a reference situation for three reasons:

1. They serve as a subject approach to periodicals. The man who wants a magazine on gardening, or religion, or wood carving can find what he needs under a main subject heading or through a detailed index. Librarians in a school, college, or university attempting to fill a vacuum in a curriculum area will find a nonselective list under the appropriate subject, and the subjects cover every area of human activities from the pure sciences to the comics.
2. Price, editor, and address are frequently given for the man who wants to order a periodical or has some inquiry he wishes to direct to the publisher.
3. The librarian who wishes to find out whether a periodical is indexed or abstracted, and where, can turn to *Ulrich's.*

All of these have benefits peculiar to themselves and are worth careful study, but none is a selective list of periodicals nor are annotations given. Therefore, they are only an aid indirectly to the librarian seeking to discover what periodical to order. Still, entries will often indicate importance by the size of circulation and whether or not the periodical is indexed in any standard index.

The *Standard Periodical Directory* augments but does not substitute for *Ulrich's*. The approach of the two works is essentially the same, the scope quite different. *Ulrich's* lists a wide variety of foreign periodicals; the *Standard* is limited to 63,000 publications of the United States and Canada. The Bowker publication confines itself to periodicals and journals; but the *Standard* takes in a variety of more ephemeral material such as house organs, advisory services, directories, and some government publications. Entry information is quite complete; and there is a title, but not a subject, index. Publications are classified under some 231 major subject headings in the main body of the work.[15]

A work closely related to *Ulrich's* which includes some of the titles in the *Standard* is *Irregular Serials and Annuals: An International Directory* (2d ed. New York: R. R. Bowker Company, 1972, 1,350 pp.). Under some 230 subject headings are arranged over 18,000 "serials, annuals, proceedings, supplements, yearbooks, and annual reviews, symposiums that come out on an irregular basis or not more than once a year." Both foreign and United States publications are included, and there is a full index. Titles found here are not in the companion *Ulrich's;* and it is primarily used by librarians to identify and verify frequency of publication of materials which have irregular publishing schedules or are issued annually.

Of the four, *Ayer* serves more multiple purposes than is obvious at first sight. Arrangement is geographical, rather than by the broad subject categories found in *Ulrich's,* first by state and then by city. Preceding the section on each state, and for some cities, extensive gazetteer-type information is offered (population, distance between towns, industries, and the like). Consequently, an important secondary purpose of *Ayer* is for handy, up-to-date reference material on many states, cities, and provinces. Publications (including newspapers and periodicals) are listed under city of origin with data on size, frequency, circulation, price, and notes on officers. The classified list at the back of the book divides the works into groups: Negro publications, religious publications, trade and technical publications. The work concludes with an excellent general alphabetical index which includes all publications listed except daily and weekly newspapers.

While *Ayer* does include United States territories and the Caribbean area, similar information on European and international newspapers is found in other guides. The basic ones are: (1) *Newspaper Press Directory. Benn's Guide to Newspapers and Periodicals of the World.*

---

[15] For a short discussion of subject head differences and selection policies between *Ulrich's* and the *Standard, see:* Paula M. Strain, "Ulrich's Tries Harder," *RQ,* Summer 1970, p. 317.

(London: Benn Brothers, 1846 to date, annual) and (2) *Willing's Press Guide*. (London: Willing, 1874 to date, annual. Distributed in the United States by R. R. Bowker Company).

The *Benn* guide includes, in the first section, the basic newspapers and magazines of the British Isles. The second part, "Overseas Press," is divided into sections headed by the British Commonwealth and ending with South Africa and the United States. Generally, the bibliographical information is quite complete and there is a good, detailed index. Willing's concentrates on the British press and has much fuller information for the 4,600 periodicals and 1,200 newspapers. While neither is required in smaller libraries, both would be expected in research size libraries.

Following the same distributive pattern as union lists, the directories are first international, national, and then regional and by subject. New directories of this type appear every year and a few example titles will indicate the efforts in this field. The titles are fairly well descriptive of purposes and content: *Catholic Press Directory. Official Media Reference Guide to Catholic Newspapers, Magazines* . . . (New York: Catholic Press Association, 1923, annual). *Directory of the Jewish Press in America*. (New York: Joseph Jacobs Organization, 1972). *From Radical Left to Extreme Right; A Bibliography of Current Periodicals of Protest* . . . 2d ed. (Ann Arbor, Michigan: Campus Publishers, 1970; vol. 2, Metuchen, New Jersey: Scarecrow Press, 1972). *Selected List of Periodicals Relating to Negroes* . . . (New Haven: Yale University Library, 1970). Again, these and many more are listed in Winchell, Walford, and the *American Reference Books Annual*.

Selection aids; magazines and newspapers

Katz, Bill and Berry Gargal, *Magazines for Libraries*. 2d ed. New York: R. R. Bowker Company, 1972.

Scott, Marian H., *Periodicals for School Libraries*. rev. ed. Chicago: American Library Association, 1973, 296 pp., $4.95.

When discussing various reference sources, the selection process (i.e., what is good, bad, or indifferent) is built into evaluative comments about the general reference forms and some specific titles. When the reference librarian turns to reference titles specifically geared for the selection process, she is close to acquisitions which is another discipline in library science. Still, there are some selection aids which are of use to both the acquisitions librarian and the reference librarian. Many of these are discussed in another section of this text, but any consideration of magazines and newspapers would be lacking without at least a mention of the selection process.

In terms of reference work, the selection of periodicals is primarily in support of the available indexes. All the magazines listed in the major indexes should be in the library, or readily accessible in another library. Selection, then, is usually a matter of checking what is issued in the indexes and in the abstracts.

Beyond this rather pragmatic approach, there is a need for careful selection of magazines which may not be indexed, but may be especially useful in a given reference situation. To this end, there are several selection guides. Those listed here are only representative of a more general nature. Often subject bibliographies include a section on select magazines in their particular area.

The author's *Magazines for Libraries* is an effort to offer public, school, and college librarians, as well as laymen, an up-to-date annotated guide to some 4,500 periodicals and basic newspapers. A full bibliographical description is given for each title, along with a detailed, often critical annotation. The whole is arranged by broad subject categories, with an index and a clear indication of which magazines the author and his consultants consider best for various types of libraries and readers.

The Scott work is an alphabetically arranged list of 500 magazines for kindergarten through the twelfth grades. Selection and annotations were the work of an American Library Association committee. Basic information is given for each title, with an indication of grade level. The scope of the list is determined by the content of contemporary school curricula, but many titles are useful in public libraries. On the whole, it is an intelligent and imaginative reference aid.

There are a number of more specialized selection aids, primarily for subject areas. Many of these are listed and briefly annotated by Grant Skelley in *Magazines for Libraries.*

SUGGESTED READING

"Abstracting Services," *Library Trends,* January 1968. While a good deal of the material in this issue is dedicated to the problems of scientific abstracting, there is enough general information to be of use to beginning students.

Collison, Robert L., "Current American Trends in Indexing," *The Indexer,* April 1972, pp. 20+. A brief overview. Note: this is the official journal of the Society of Indexers, and each issue contains a variety of articles of value to anyone interested in indexing and abstracting.

Katz, Bill, *Magazine Selection: How To Build A Community Oriented Collection.* New York: R. R. Bowker Company, 1971. A sometimes unorthodox view of what a magazine collection is about. Includes a chapter on "Indexes and Abstracts."

Osborn, Andrew D., *Serial Publications: Their Place and Treatment in Libraries.* 2d ed. Chicago: American Library Association, 1973. Considers all aspects of periodicals, and includes a chapter on "Reference Aspects of Serial Publications."

Quelon, F., "Encyclopedic System of General Subject Indexes to Reference Book," *Assistant Librarian,* February 1970, pp. 24 + . A general discussion of indexing as applicable to reference work.

Whatley, H. A. "On Using Library Information Science Abstracts," *Library Association Record,* March 1971, pp. 45 + . A brief discussion of a key abstracting service for librarians. (*See also* "Comments" in the same periodical, July 1971, p. 139.)

PART THREE
SOURCES OF INFORMATION

CHAPTER FIVE
GENERAL ENCYCLOPEDIAS

Living in exile hundreds or thousands of miles from any library, bookstore, or corner drugstore, it is conceivable that the reading needs of most such persons could be met by a good encyclopedia. Short on fiction, yet long on articles of diverse and recondite information, the encyclopedia affords hours of both recreational and informative reading. For libraries, though, the general encyclopedias are handy, reliable sources of answers for ready-reference questions. They also serve students and laymen seeking an uncomplicated overview or explanation of a subject, a personality, or a place.

Encyclopedias are of two basic types. The first, and most familiar, is the general work published for a given age group, e.g., *The Americana* for adults or *The World Book* for young adults. These sets contain bits of information on almost every conceivable subject. The second type is the subject encyclopedia which affords an indepth study of all aspects of a particular subject, e.g., *The Encyclopedia of Philosophy* or the *McGraw-Hill Encyclopedia of Science and Technology*. These may be edited for either the expert or the interested layman, or both.

In terms of physical format, the majority of encyclopedias are in sets. However, there are a few which are limited to one or two volumes, are lower in price, and are primarily for the home, office, or small library.

EVALUATING ENCYCLOPEDIAS

Publishers

The real as opposed to the theoretical choice between various general encylopedias is radically limited by the number of publishers. Four firms control approximately 95 percent of the encyclopedias published in the United States. They are:

1. Encyclopaedia Britannica Educational Corporation. The Chicago-based publisher is the largest of the four with sales well over $200 million a year. It publishes, among other sets: *Encyclopaedia Britannica, Compton's Encyclopedia, Britannica Junior Encyclopaedia, Great Books of the Western World, The Annals of America.* The corporation, also, controls G. & C. Merriam Company, publishers of *Webster's* dictionaries; Frederick A. Praeger, Inc.; and the Phaidon Press, Ltd. The firm has subsidiary companies throughout the world.

2. Grolier Incorporated. The New York firm publishes *Americana, The Encyclopedia International, The New Book of Knowledge, The American Peoples Encyclopedia;* and distributes a number of sets such as *Encyclopedia Canadiana.* It also has controlling interest in the library-based Scarecrow Press. Sales are close to the *Britannica* in volume, some $158 million in 1970.

3. Crowell Collier and Macmillan, Inc. Although a large publishing house, it is fourth in sales of encyclopedias. The only two major sets are *Collier's* and the *Merit Student Encyclopedia.* However, it publishes a number of related works from the *Encyclopedia of Philosophy* to the *Harvard Classics.*

4. Field Enterprises. The Chicago firm now sells more than half the encyclopedia units in the United States, and its *World Book* is by and large the most popular among the children's and young people's sets. Like Crowell Collier and Macmillan, Inc., the firm is involved in numerous other business interests from department stores to newspapers.

The librarian who comes across an encyclopedia whose publisher is not one of the four or five more reputable publishers has a built-in warning that more than average care should be taken to double-check its authority and, for that matter, everything else about the set.

As in the automobile industry, competition among the big four is fierce; although at the same time, there is a noticeable tendency to copy a success. If one automobile design captures the fancy of the public, the other manufacturers tend to copy and modify. Much the same is true of encyclopedias. For example, when one firm initiated three-dimensional color transparencies, the others for the most part immediately followed.

Aside from cost and age suitability, there is less and less difference between the products of the big four. In specific areas, one may be better this year than last; but if this proves a "salable" area, it is certain that next year the competitor will attempt to one-up his rival.

A definite result of the competition is a strong emphasis on up-to-date material. Like newspapers of yesteryear, the encyclopedias now try to scoop one another; and they make much of this in their advertising. Spot coverage of the space adventure, the latest political battle, or world conflict is announced with a great flourish. As one critic has observed, this has led the encyclopedias to become "enslaved to their own advertising . . . and are leading people to judge their products on recency rather than fundamental coverage of the past."[1]

And yet as John Tebbel pointed out in the *Saturday Review,* "What really distinguishes encyclopedia making of today . . . is the continuous revision process."[2] No major encyclopedia publisher these days can hope to completely revise his work every few years, nor can he afford to do so. Instead, firms continually make additions to and revisions in ongoing articles such as atomic energy, the presidency, and government; and they also keep a careful check on changing thoughts and ideas in areas which do not need immediate revision each year, such as philosophy or an individual biography of a historic figure. These revisions may be based on changes not only in knowledge, but also in educational curricula which will either emphasize or de-emphasize certain areas. Another phase includes the format and illustrations; and editors develop new charts, tables, and photographs to keep the appearance of the set modern.

This continuous revision accounts for the fact that there are no new editions of a work. Early works, if revised at all, were done so completely and, when ready, over a period of 10 to 50 years, would be designated as new editions. For example, the fourteenth edition of the *Encyclopaedia Britannica* issued in 1929 was the last work designated an edition. Ideally, a new edition of an encyclopedia might be issued every 10 years, but this is simply not feasible under present production costs. This may change, for as Martin points out, "I am convinced that in a few years all the encyclopedia publishers will have their text on magnetic tape, with type automatically set and pages automatically made out for each new printing, so that we can continuously get to the roots of our encyclopedias."[3]

[1] James Kilgour, "Reference and Subscription Book Publishing," *Library Trends,* July 1958, p. 144.
[2] "Keeping Up with Knowledge," *Saturday Review,* July 10, 1965, p. 52.
[3] "Forum on Encyclopedias," *RQ,* Winter 1965, p. 8.

Meanwhile, how good is continuous revision? A way to measure the process is to avoid the advertising claims and check trends in contemporary art and lesser-known areas. All the major encyclopedias are up to date in science and technology, primarily because they make so much of it in their publicity. Yet, if the diligent reader looks in the 1973 revision of any set, he will find discrepencies between advertising claims and actual presentation. The obvious news events, from the election of a president to a sensational invention, economic movement, or personality will be up to date. But in rather static areas such as the humanities and the arts, the tendency is to be less than current. Even where, for example, there is reference to the work of an artist, a modern novelist, or a playwright, it is usually considerably less stressed than a scientific achievement. The selection is understandable. The multivolume sets are aimed at a mass audience, not at the humanist.

Sales practices[4]

The dollar volume of all subscription reference books (of which encyclopedias are a good 96 percent) in 1972 was slightly over $615 million. The figure is more meaningful when one considers that the dollar value of adult trade books was only some $270 million and total textbook sales were around $900 million. The total dollar volume of encyclopedia sales, then, is roughly about one-quarter of the volume of sales of all books sold in the United States.

Translated into hard business, this means that the four major encyclopedia publishers are first and foremost sales organizations who, with a limited number of sets, capture more dollars from those sets than all the fiction and nonfiction sold in the United States.

Although libraries are relatively important for sales, they are minimal in terms of percentages. *Publishers' Weekly* reported for 1970 the breakdown of subscription-reference book sales:

> Mail order accounts for a steadily growing proportion of domestic Subscription-Reference book sales—28.4% of the total, compared with 24.2% in 1969. Home and office sales run to 66.7% of the 1970 total, compared with 70.7% in 1969. School and library sales of Subscription-Reference books dropped to 4.9% of the total in 1970 from 1969's 5.1%.[5]

Given the large sales volume and the primary dependence upon home door-to-door selling, it is understandable that the encyclopedia salesman is somewhat less than a national hero, e.g., national columnist Sylvia Porter's statement is heard often enough: "The slippery door-to-

---

[4] What it means to be an encyclopedia salesman is indicated by an Englishman in an article applicable to America. *See:* James Hamilton-Paterson, "Learning at a Price," *New Statesman,* July 25, 1969, pp. 109+.
[5] *Publishers' Weekly,* February 7, 1972, p. 63.

door pitchman who can con you into buying encyclopedias you can't afford and don't even need."[6] The general image, to be sure, is precisely that; and there are as many honorable salesmen as less than honorable. Still, the librarian should be aware of the sales practices because she is often called upon to give an opinion of a set—an opinion which must consider the pressure salesmen exert upon consumers.

During the 1970s, the Federal Trade Commission and numerous consumer organizations have paid particular attention to encyclopedia sales practices. Several bills have been proposed in Congress to protect consumers from both salesmen and deceptive advertising.

Examples of what the consumer faces were detailed by *The New York Times* (September 26, 1971, pp. 1, 58). Reporting on a study made by the City's Department of Consumer Affairs, the *Times* found:

1. The *Britannica* salesmen used language designed to instill the fear and anxiety in parents that their children will fail in school unless an encyclopedia is purchased.
2. The two Field (World Book) salesmen based their pitch on concern for your children's education. Field has more than 9,000 full-time salesmen and some 60,000 part time, many of whom are teachers.
3. The Grolier salesmen based his pitch on a special offer, a technique often cited as deceptive by consumer protection agencies.
4. Most firms offer a "package" deal which may run the basic price of a set well over $1,000. The package consists of so-called deluxe buildings and numerous other features from reference service to subsidiary sets, such as *Childcraft*. All of this is plus finance charges, which are often represented as a bargain. It is difficult, if not impossible, for the consumer to find the basic price of a set.

And hardly a month goes by that similar stories are not heard, e.g., "The Federal Trade Commission accused Crowell Collier and Macmillan, Inc., today of deceptive practices in selling the *Harvard Classics*, and in billing buyers of encyclopedias." (*The New York Times*, February 29, 1972, p. 8.)

The Britannica

has paid $100,000 in costs and agree to cease and desist from alleged deceptive and unfair sales and hiring practices. . . . Among them: claiming

6 Sylvia Porter, "Your Money's Worth," *Albany Times Union*, November 2, 1971. (The syndicated column appeared in many other newspapers on approximately the same day. It is worth reading for the basic twelve steps a consumer may use to protect himself against encyclopedia salesmen.)

that teachers and librarians qualify for a discount price and claiming that the encyclopedia is a "new" edition unless it is substantially new or revised. The settlement was the result of a three-year investigation conducted with the company's cooperation. (*Library Journal.* October 1, 1972, p. 3,108.)

In 1960, door-to-door selling accounted for 87 percent of encyclopedia sales; in 1971, the percentage was down 57 percent. Mail order, office, and library business, not to mention overseas sales, keep the firms profitable; but the life of a door-to-door salesman grows increasingly difficult. Commissions on *World Book* average $35 to $40, *Britannica* salesmen get an average commission of $120 to $200 on a sale, and Grolier's *Americana* brings $67 to $93.

Regulations for door-to-door selling, as of 1973, included provision that the salesman must notify the purchaser that he has a "cooling off" period of some three days to reconsider, and possibly void a signed contract.[7] Salesmen are instructed to give the actual price of a set and the price(s) of additional items which may be included in the sale. They should reveal affirmatively that they are selling encyclopedias before making any other statement or asking the buyer any question—this is to prevent such abuses as the salesman gaining entrance to an unsuspecting customer as someone besides a salesman.

Which set is best?

All of this adds up to a given responsibility for librarians. Hardly a week goes by without someone asking the librarian for advice about the best encyclopedia. Columnist Porter, for example, suggests that the would-be encyclopedia buyer "ask the librarian . . . about appropriate choices and prices. . . . Ask your librarian for a responsible reference work which reviews and rates the widely sold encyclopedia."[8]

The American Library Association dutifully notes that "the prospective purchaser should avoid being rushed or pressured into buying an encyclopedia." The ALA then goes on to suggest that some companies (without naming any) use unethical sales practices. In conclusion, it is recommended that "no encyclopedia be purchased without first evalu-

---

[7] Faced with the provision, the Grolier Company capitalized upon it by running advertisements which suggested Grolier and not the FTC had made the regulation, e.g., *The New York Times,* March 23, 1971: "People talk about consumer protection. Grolier does something about it," was the headline on a full page ad telling customers they had a cooling off period after signing a contract. (The FTC regulation gives the buyer a three-day "cooling-off" period; the salesman must furnish both a written and an oral notice of such rights; the seller must pay all expenses associated with the return shipment of goods. *See:* "FTC Seeks Uniform Door to Door Code," *Publishers' Weekly,* November 20, 1972, p. 43.

[8] Porter, op. cit.

ating the set." It is strongly suggested that the would-be purchaser should be able to find evaluative material in the library.[9]

In view of the history of encyclopedia sales, the librarian has several ways of meeting the request for information about a given set.

1. Give no advice. Several major public libraries, fearful of repercussions from salesmen and publishers, adamantly refuse to advise on the purchase of this or that set. This is unprofessional and highly questionable.
2. Give limited advice. Normally the procedure here is to give the inquirer several reviews of the set or sets under question, and then let him make up his own mind. Of particular assistance in this respect are the Collected *Reference and Subscription Books Reviews* (p. 97) the Walsh compilation (p. 97); and, more particularly, the sound advice given by ALA in the article "Purchasing a General Encyclopedia" (*Booklist,* March 15, 1969) and "Children's Encyclopedias and Sets" (*Booklist,* June 15, 1970).
3. Go all out with an endorsement or a condemnation. Privately, of course, many librarians do just this. This may have some nasty repercussions, particularly when the question is between sets that are approved by ALA and are more or less even in quality.

Between these relative extremes, lies a middle path. If the set is not readily recognized either by publisher or reputation, the librarian should not hesitate to point out that the chances are it is a bad buy, from the standpoint of both cost and quality. He should be prepared to support this statement with reviews; or lacking reviews (either because the set is too new or such a dog as not to have been noticed), he should not hesitate to stand on his own professional knowledge of the set. If he can find nothing about it in print (and who is familiar with many of the works which pass for encyclopedias in supermarkets and in questionable advertisements?), he should point out that the opinion may be his, but the odds are all against the quality of the set.

If it is a recognized set, he should feel free to point out the scope as to age and popular or scholarly emphasis and indicate the difference in price schedules. Beyond that he may be on questionable ground, and here the use of a printed review is advisable. A step further, of course, is to advise the prospective purchaser to examine the various sets in the library and make his own comparison by using some of the evaluative steps suggested to him by the librarian.

[9] "Purchasing a General Encyclopedia," *The Booklist,* March 15, 1969, pp. 762-763.

Parenthetically, never argue with a patron. He may haveh purchased the set and come to you for advice as an afterthought. Or he may already have made up his mind.

Is an encyclopedia necessary?

In all h ibraries, probably several, or at least one, general encyclopedias are necessary. The question "Is this set necessary?" is valid if one asks it of individual purchasers.

A set can be useful in a home:

1. If it is written for and used by the children in the home for either or both recreational and educational purposes. The inclusion of a set does not automatically mean the child will use it or, if he does, his grades will improve.
2. The use and need of a general encyclopedia decreases with the age of the user, i.e., junior high school students are more apt to use it than a senior high school student, and a high school senior is more apt to use it than a college or university freshman. Few adults really need a general encyclopedia.
3. Adults who do feel the need for reference sources might be considerably better off buying one of the subject encyclopedias and/or purchasing a number of up-to-date ready-reference sources from the *World Almanac* to a good unabridged dictionary. Furthermore, for the price of a general encyclopedia, they could build a major reference collection in paperbacks.

Bohdan S. Wynar edits *Reference Books in Paperback* (Littleton, Colorado: Libraries Unlimited, Inc., 1972). This is a 200 page, frequently revised annotated list of some 700 in-print paperback reference works which add up to a first rate reference library for the individual and/or for the small library with a limited budget.[10] Given the money spent for a general encyclopedia, the average user would be better off purchasing paperbacks in his field(s) of interest.

If a general encyclopedia is desired for adults' use in the home, money may be saved by purchasing one which is several years old and then backing it with current, less expensive paperback reference sources. Most book stores, which otherwise do not sell new encyclopedias—an arrangement worked out by the encyclopedia publishers who prefer the door-to-door approach—offer the major used sets at greatly reduced prices.

[10] *See* an abbreviated, selected list of paperbacks for reference in: Judith Higgins and August Stellwag, "A Mini Reference Library: 21 Paperbacks," *Library Journal,* January 15, 1971, p. 245.

It should be emphasized again that this advice is for the individual. The library definitely does need current, up-to-date general encyclopedias—if only for basic ready-reference work and for help with junior high and some high school students.

Encyclopedia reviews and summaries

Librarians and laymen can count themselves particularly fortunate in that the evaluation of encyclopedias is a long standing affair for the American Library Association. Operating a type of consumer protection unit, the ALA's Reference and Subscription Books Review Committee has painstakingly evaluated every major, general, and subject set and a number of one-volume encyclopedias and related works. Furthermore, every five years the standard general sets are carefully reexamined.

The reviews appear in each issue of *Booklist,* a general review medium of the ALA, and are reprinted in book form every two years as *Reference and Subscription Book Reviews 1968-1970; 1970-1972* and so on. Given the individual reviews, and the collection, the librarian has no excuse for either purchasing a bad encyclopedia or for giving equally bad advice to those who ask for information on a particular set.

Not only are the ALA reviews long, detailed, and carefully written, but they are definite in either recommending or not recommending a given title. As might be expected, the recommendations are positive for works issued by the four major encyclopedia firms but tend to be negative, or at best reserved, about titles issued by other publishers. (This, to be sure, is for sets. Acceptance or rejection of single-volume encyclopedias follows no such pattern of publishers.) For example, in the collection of reviews published from 1968 to 1970 there were six reviews of general sets. Only one, the *New Standard,* was not published by one of the four major houses, and it was not recommended. The five others were recommended.[11]

The evaluations hardly represent a conspiracy, but more a fact of publishing life. As indicated, a well thought out encyclopedia is an extremely expensive affair, and only larger publishers (with equally large sales organizations) can afford to enter the field. Those on the outskirts usually have to cut somewhere to save expenses; and the result may be a fair encyclopedia, but not one up to the higher standards rightfully expected by the ALA committee.

Considerably more lax evaluations will be found in the frequently revised guide by S. Padraig Walsh: *General Encyclopedias in Print 1973-74.* (New York: R. R. Bowker Company, 1973, 239 pp, $10.95).

[11] *See also* the summary of recommendations of children's and adult sets in *Booklist,* June 15, 1970 and March 15, 1969. Both lists are useful guides. Both lists follow the general pattern of rejecting most sets not published by the four major publishers.

Limiting himself to the thirty-three best known general American encyclopedias, Walsh analyses them individually and in group form. Numerous charts show comparative costs, number of words, illustrations, contributors, maps, and other items. If an encyclopedia can be measured almost purely on quantitative terms, this is the place to turn. For each set, he gives considerable basic information in outline form as well as sources of reviews, articles, and the like. With later editions, he has tended to expand the work to include essays on selecting a set, the comparative value of supermarket encyclopedias, and other sometimes useful material. Finally, he rates the sets in order of acceptance. The ratings fairly well follow the big four publishing company products and the recommendations of the ALA committee. While Walsh's critical remarks are often questionable, the work is valuable for the statistical comparisons and for information on lesser known sets which are rarely reviewed elsewhere.

Beginning with the 1971 *American Reference Books Annual,* (see p. 33), Bohdan S. Wynar offers succinct, thoughtful reviews of current encyclopedias. These are particularly welcome as they are descriptive, critical, and comparative. Once more, they tend to be relatively brief. Other library oriented sources include *The Library Journal, Choice, Wilson Library Bulletin,* and *RQ.* However, few of these reviews are as extensive or as descriptive as those found in the ALA's work. The popular press, from *The New York Times* to *Saturday Review,* on occasion do examine an encyclopedia; but it is so occasional as to be virtually meaningless.

Given the ALA reviews, and the Walsh summaries, as well as the *American Reference Book Annual* critical remarks, is it necessary for the student to try her hand at evaluating encyclopedias? On a practical day-to-day basis the answer is obviously no. Examined from the viewpoint of learning as much as possible about encyclopedias (both of the multiple set and one-volume variety), the answer is yes. Also, a useful byproduct of such examination is a considerably better understanding of how reference books in general should be evaluated and examined. The encyclopedia represents the ultimate effort to compress knowledge into a single source; and, in so doing, it affords the student an excellent opportunity to weigh not only the effectiveness of the effort, but to move from there to an appreciation of what reference source criticism is all about.

Purpose

The purpose of an encyclopedia varies with the reader and with its scope. For the general encyclopedia, there are two primary purposes:

1. A source of answers to fact questions, usually of a simple nature such as who, what, when, where, and how.

2. A source of background information, both for the expert and the layman. For example, intellectuals may be puzzled over C. P. Snow's insistence that they know the second law of thermodynamics. The law is relatively well explained in most encyclopedias. Conversely, a child may be just as much in the dark over what set off the Civil War as the intellectual is about physics. Again, the child will find a clear answer in an encyclopedia.

A third purpose is directional; that is, the bibliographies at the end of articles may help the reader to find additional material in a given subject area. The importance of adequate bibliographies is particularly well recognized at the juvenile level (augmented by the use of study aids) and at the specialist's level (by highly developed bibliographies in narrow subject areas).

To clear up a common misunderstanding, it should be pointed out that no general encyclopedia is a proper source for research. (This does not include specialized works.) It is only a springboard. Furthermore, in presenting material almost undifferentiatingly, the general encyclopedia is not completely accurate or up to date; and important facts must be double-checked in another source, if only in another encyclopedia.

At the child's level, another purpose is often falsely put forth. An encyclopedia, no matter how good, is not a substitute for additional reading or for a collection of supporting reference books. In their natural enthusiasm to sell the sets, some salesmen and advertising copywriters are carried away with the proposition that an encyclopedia-oriented child is an educated child. Perhaps in reaction against this false purpose, too many teachers go to the other extreme and insist that a child find information for a paper or problem anywhere but in an encyclopedia.

While any good encyclopedia offers stimulation and information for the young, there is a built-in danger recognized by many teachers. The teacher who forbids the student to use the encyclopedia for classroom assignments is fearful of what one librarian termed engendering the encyclopedia-oriented rather than the book-oriented child. When the word gets around that the whole assignment may be garnered out of one work, few students will care to explore the resources of the library.

The primary value of an encyclopedia for the student, or for anyone approaching a new subject for the first time, is the overview. It is hoped the teacher will stress this, but it would do no harm if the librarian indicated as much. Also, many encyclopedias now offer a variety of study guides which indicate related articles the student might employ to put together, with the help of other books, a truly creative paper rather than a carbon copy of an encyclopedia article.

Scope

The scope of the specialized encyclopedia is evident in name, and becomes more so with use. The scope of the general encyclopedia is dictated primarily by two considerations.

Age level The children's encyclopedias such as the *World Book* are tied to curriculum. Consequently, they include more in-depth material on subjects of general interest to grade and high schools than, say, an adult encyclopedia such as the *Britannica*. Recognizing that the strongest sales appeal is to the adult with children, most encyclopedia publishers aim their advertising at this vulnerable place in the family pocketbook. All the standard sets claim that an audience ranging from grades six to twelve can understand and use their respective works. For example, a 1972 advertisement for the *Britannica* notes one family is happy with the way the Britannica Program "has helped their children in school. Their younger son Stephen improved his social studies average more than 20 percent." This may be true of the exceptionally bright child, but the librarian is advised to check the real age compatibility of the material before purchase, not the advertised age level.

A consequence of attempting to be all things to all age levels is twofold: (1) even in many adult encyclopedias the material is shortened for easier comprehension by the child; (2) the effort at clarity frequently results in a downright oversimplified approach to rather complex questions.

Emphasis If age level dictates one approach to scope, the emphasis of the editor accounts for the other. At one time, this varied more than it does today; one set being especially good for science, another for literature. Today, the emphasis is primarily a matter of deciding what compromise is going to be made between scholarship and popularity. Why, for example, in most adult encyclopedias, is as much space given to the subject of advertising, indeed often more, as to communism? This is not to argue the merit of emphasis, but only to point out that it is a method of determining scope.

Authority

The first question to ask about any reference book is its authority. If it is authoritative, it normally follows that it will be up-to-date, accurate, and relatively objective. Contributors and publishers constitute the authority for encyclopedias.

Authority is evident primarily in the names of the scholars who sign the articles and/or are listed as contributors somewhere in the set. Considerable importance is put upon well-known personalities and prize winners, much as a newspaper will boast of its columnists. The *Encyclopaedia Britannica* boasts of "more than 70 Nobel and Pulitzer Prize winners." While not all contributors to any encyclopedia are prize winners, the majority at least are scholars. The encyclopedia that fails to clearly indicate the qualifications of its contributors is to be highly suspected.

Writing style

In compiling an encyclopedia, the publisher is faced with what Jacques Barzun[12] terms threefold opposition. He must please the subject experts and the laymen, yet be neither too difficult nor too simple. This is apparently an impossible task, although more successful articles in individual encyclopedias indicate that even the most difficult material may be presented in a scholarly fashion and still be understood by laymen. On the whole, though, general encyclopedias tend to fall between the two poles of opposition. If anything, they wish to please the layman more than the scholar. However, while the former may represent the largest market, the curse of the latter may frighten away the buyer.

Recognizing that the purchasers are laymen, who considerably outnumber the scholars, encyclopedia firms tend to operate in a relatively standard fashion. Contributors are solicited from among the authorities in the field. They are given certain topics and outlines of what is needed and expected. The manuscript is then submitted to one or more of the encyclopedia's editors (editorial staffs of the larger encyclopedias range from 100 to 200 full-time persons), who revise, cut, and query—all for the purpose of making the contributor's manuscript understandable to the average reader. The extent of editing varies with each encyclopedia, from the extreme for the children's works (where word difficulty and length of sentence are almost as important as the content), to a limited degree for large-name contributors.

"It seems to be entirely appropriate that matter intended to be read should be as attractive as it can be made for the person who is expected to read it," claims the editorial director of Crowell Collier and Macmillan, Inc.[13] No one can argue with this assertion, unless the "package" becomes more important than the content; or, in the words of Marshall McLuhan, "The medium is the message." Critics assert that this is the

[12] Jacques Barzun, "Notes on the Making of a World Encyclopedia," *American Behavioral Scientist,* September 1963, p. 3.
[13] *RQ,* Winter 1965, p. 9.

case and rarely find the publishers these days erring on the side of too-complex material.[14]

Viewpoint

How objective and fair are encyclopedia articles? It depends where you stand. On April 11, 1972, Vice President Spiro Agnew discussed "the conversion of formerly authoritative and objective sources of encyclopedic information into vehicles of propaganda." He continued:

> The fact is that teachers and parents can no longer take it for granted that scholarly objectivity and thoroughness will be the standards in much of the material students use for basic reference.
> To discover, in Professor Hook's words, that once "reputable and time-honored" reference works have "now fallen into the hands of editors who have ideological axes to grind . . ." is indeed disquieting, not only in itself but in its symptomatic meaning to the entire American education system.[15]

Similar charges appear regularly, if not always from the Vice President, from parents, teachers, students and, in fact, anyone who takes exception to how an encyclopedia handles or fails to handle a particular article.

An outstanding example of a more justified challenge will be found in *The Treatment of Black Americans in Current Encyclopedias* (Washington, D.C.: American Federation of Teachers, 1970). Irving Sloan, a social studies teacher, carefully examined all the major sets to determine how encyclopedias handled the history and the current activities of black Americans. While all nine sets included survey articles on blacks, few of them had integrated the information into other articles. For example, if a student researched the abolitionist movement, the question is whether or not the information about the North's black abolitionists is included. If merely mentioned in a separate chapter on black history, it is likely to go unnoted.

---

[14] *Time*, November 11, 1966, p. 55. The reviewer of four children's encyclopedias made much of writing style and had a good point when he observed that one way of checking style is to compare "the books' approaches in their opening sentences on articles. . . ." Using an article on Minnesota, he noted *Compton's* "carols;" *Britannica Junior* "states" and *Book of Knowledge* "coaxes." The article tells about as much concerning *Time* style as encyclopedia style.

[15] Quoted in *Media Industry Newsletter*, April 27, 1972, p. 2. The charge is based upon the rejection by the *Encyclopaedia Britannica* of an article on civil disobedience by Ernest van den Haag which was later commented on by Sidney Hook. Professor Hook, however, was not challenging encyclopedias in general and claims the Vice President misquoted him. The editor of the *Newsletter* goes on to explore the meaning of the attack and prints some fascinating replies from publishers and educators—who, for the most part, failed to agree with Agnew's evaluation.

Thanks to the detailed study, whose methodology might be used profitably by all students and librarians to check viewpoint on other subjects, the larger firms by 1973 had made a concerted effort to better represent the blacks throughout the sets, not simply in specific articles. (Incidentally, the 1968 editions of the *Americana* and the *Encyclopedia International* were cited by Irving as being the best—then—for integrated black history.)

Except to ensure accuracy, there is little difficulty in handling facts; but when it comes to issues and ideas, another problem presents itself. How is the encyclopedia to be objective when such controversial issues are involved as capitalism and communism, civil rights and segregation, conservation or liberalism, or birth control? There are two approaches here. One is to ignore the differences entirely, depending on a chronological, historical approach. The other is an effort to balance an article by presenting two or more sides. The reader should expect at least a projection of different views, either by the contributor or the editor.

Another aspect of the question of viewpoint is what the editor chooses to include or to exclude, to emphasize or de-emphasize. Nothing dates an encyclopedia faster than antiquated articles about issues and ideas either no longer acceptable or of limited interest. An encyclopedia directed at the Western reader can hardly be expected to give as much coverage in depth, let us say, to Ghana as to New York State. Yet to exclude more than passing mention of Ghana will not be suitable either, particularly in view of the emergence of Africa as a new world force. The proportions of one article to another plague any conscientious encyclopedia editor, and there probably is no entirely satisfactory solution.

Format

A good format considers the size, type face, illustrations, and total arrangement. If components of the format are well done, it does not necessarily mean the whole is acceptable. Questions to consider here include:

Illustrations (i.e., photographs, diagrams, charts). The number of illustrations used in a single set is of some importance, for illustrations are particularly helpful at the elementary and secondary school level as well as for subjects totally unfamiliar to the reader. However, more to the point are such matters: the placing of the illustrations—are they related to the text? do they emphasize important matters or are they too general? are the illustrations functional or simply attractive? and finally are the captions adequate? The reproduction of the illustrations is another matter, and this should be checked carefully. Some illustrations have a displeasing physical quality, perhaps because too little or too much ink was employed, or the paper was a poor grade, or an inadequate cut or halftone screen was used.

Size of the type is important in that it should not be too large, even for the children's encyclopedias, or too small. Even more important is the type style, the spacing between lines, and the width of the column. All of these factors will make the work more readable when used wisely. If they are used badly, the encyclopedia will be difficult to read, especially over any length of time.

Binding should be suitable for rough wear, particularly in a library situation. Conversely, buyers should be warned that a frequent method of jacking up the price of an encyclopedia is to charge the user for a so-called deluxe binding which often is no better, in fact may be worse, than the standard library binding.

Finally, consideration should be given to the *size* of the physical volume. Is it comfortable to use; and, equally important, may it be opened readily without strain on the binding?

Arrangement and entry

General encyclopedias differ not only in terms of target audience but in the length of their articles. Some use the specific entry, such as the *Americana.* Here the information is broken down into small, specific parts. Other sets, such as the *Britannica,* employ the broader entry form which means longer, more inclusive articles. For example, under the broad entry "sun" the reader would find all the information on the sun. Under a specific entry system there would be a short article on the sun, plus separate articles on eclipses, seasons, tides, and so on.

The deceptive thing about specific and broad entries is that the specific form may appear to be offering more information, whereas the only thing it is really offering is a different approach to the same data. For example, the *Americana* has some 30 volumes and claims well over 58,000 separate articles. The *Britannica* has only 34,000 articles and is limited to 24 volumes. But in number of words, the *Britannica* has approximately 7 million more than found in the *Americana.*

Specific and broad entry forms are important to reference librarians. When reaching for a quick fact, the specific entry form is sometimes easier because the librarian rarely has to use the index volume. She simply reaches for the logical subject. Conversely, for the broad entry form, it is safer to first consult the index. The specific subject one is seeking may be part of another article. (Many encyclopedias based upon the broad entry principle compensate by using numerous cross references to related items, outline study guides, and such.)

The shift from the long to the short entry form may be explained in a number of ways, but it is primarily an effort to make the works more suitable for general, popular use. Newspapers, television, radio, and films have made many people quite literally unable to follow long, detailed explanations. The essay-type entries in the Ninth and Eleventh editions of the *Britannica,* for example, were primarily written for better than average educated adults, even scholars. Conversely, the German Brockhaus encyclopedias of the same period were prepared for a general public which was more interested in bits of factual information than in lengthy explanations. Seceding to the European tradition and the short attention span of many readers, the American publishers began to take over the European system of specific entry. Hence 21 out of 31 sets noted by Walsh are specific entry works. And of the major sets, only Collier's, Compton's and *Britannica* maintain the broad entry form.[16]

Index

All general encyclopedias are alphabetically arranged, and some have concluded that with suitable *see* and *see also* references the arrangement should serve to eliminate the index.

The argument for an index is simply that dozens of names and events occur in a single article which cannot be located unless there is a detailed index. The publishers of encyclopedias who delete the index in favor of the heavy use of cross references argue that, at least for children, this is a much less confusing, in fact easier-to-use method than a comprehensive index.

Experience indicates this is a weak argument. After many years of using just such an approach, the *World Book* gave up the struggle and in the early 1970s added an index volume.

Replacing sets

How often to replace a set depends on how extensively the set is revised, how much money is in the budget, and how many other encyclopedias the library purchases. The average American library will usually have one (or all three) of the following: *Encyclopaedia Britannica, Americana,* and *Collier's.* In the children's field, the *World Book* or *Compton's* will probably be preferred to the *Britannica Junior;* or possibly all three as well as *The New Book of Knowledge* and the *Merit Students* will be used, augmented by an adult encyclopedia. The normal procedure is to purchase a revised set every five or six years. If a library has a number of different encyclopedias, it must buy a revision of one or more each year, thus, ideally, having a current set always on hand.

In selecting an encyclopedia, there is little choice outside of the four publishers emphasized here. Costwise, there is some variation. Among

[16] Padraig J. Walsh, *General Encyclopedias in Print,* 1971-72 (New York: R. R. Bowker Company, 1971), p. 204.

adult works, the *Britannica* is the most expensive, followed by *Collier's* and then *Americana*. In the children's field, the prices cluster around $200. (Libraries receive discounts, of course, but the relative difference in cost remains the same.)

The librarian, too, must always be aware of newer sets, both those introduced by the big four and those which may be introduced by other companies. Again, the wisest move here is to wait—wait until the set is reviewed by a reliable medium.

ADULT ENCYCLOPEDIAS

Encyclopaedia Britannica. Chicago: Encyclopaedia Britannica, Inc., 24 vols., $459 ($292 for schools and libraries).

Encyclopedia Americana. New York: Grolier Incorporated, 30 vols., $375 ($262 for schools and libraries).

Britannica

William Smellie completed the first *Encyclopaedia Britannica* in 1768. The early articles were brief, almost in the dictionary form now employed by the one-volume *Columbia Encyclopedia*. For example, the article on "Woman" was but seven words, "Woman, the female of man. See Homo." Primarily, the brief entries stemmed from the method of compilation. Much like Pliny, Smellie made liberal use of pastepot and scissors, applied to books in fields covered by the encyclopedia. However, by the 1810 third edition, original contributors were employed and the 3-volume set had grown to 20 volumes. As the firm became better known, it prospered and was able to attract some of the leading scholars of the time to prepare articles; so that by the Ninth edition (1889), the publishers could boast of some 20,000 pages and over 9,000 illustrations.

The Ninth had contributions from such literary greats as Arnold and Swinburne and such noted scientists as T. H. Huxley. It, and the even more famous Eleventh, gained the name, "the scholar's edition." Many of the articles were extended essays and were so comprehensive and authoritative that they were used year after year not only in the *Encyclopaedia* but also in textbooks.

The Eleventh, published between 1910 and 1911 in 29 volumes, maintained the high intellectual standards of the Ninth, but a subtle change had taken place. Now the longer essay-type articles were divided and cut back. The argument, possibly justified, was that the shorter approach made the set easier to consult for reference purposes.

Both the Ninth and the Eleventh are landmarks, not only in the history of the *Britannica,* but in the making of the formidable legend concerning encyclopedias in general. The public came to suspect that any work that could be called an encyclopedia would be similar to the Ninth and the Eleventh, and as one writer put it: "We have all been bullied by the *Britannica* . . . since childhood, and taught to revere its contents as though they had been handed down on Mount Sinai along with the Ten Commandments."

Unfortunately, with the Ninth, the publishers priced themselves out of the popular market; and by 1900, promotional control passed from English to American hands, albeit editorial control remained with the London *Times*. With the publication of the Eleventh edition, the influence of both American and English control was evident in a landmark of scholarship.

In 1920, Sears, Roebuck and Co. acquired ownership of the work for $1,330,000. (Due in part to efforts of the American promoter Horace Hooper, who in 1915 persuaded Sears to reprint the Eleventh edition and sell it through the mails, Sears sold more than 50,000 copies of the reprint.) With the Fourteenth edition of 1929, the *Encyclopaedia* lost a good part of its British character, primarily because it was now freed from the editorial control of the London *Times*. Even with the strong American influence, the Fourteenth did not prove a financial success and, in 1941, Sears offered the work to the University of Chicago. Helping to make the financial arrangements, William Benton advanced the University $100,000 and he received a two-thirds interest in the set in 1943. Today, the *Britannica* ownership remains the same with one-third of the profits going to the University, the other two-thirds back into the company.

Americana

The *Americana* is based on the seventh edition of the German encyclopedia *Brockhaus Konversations Lexikon*. In fact, the first published set (1829 to 1833) was little more than pirated, translated articles from the German work. It was asserted in 1903 that the *Americana* was a whole new work, but still many of the articles carried over from Brockhaus. A reissue of the set was printed in 1918 with changes and additions, albeit still with material from Brockhaus. The present work, however, is totally revised. It claims to be the oldest "all American" encyclopedia in existence, although the claim is more a matter of chronology than accuracy.

As the title implies, the strength of this work is the emphasis on American history, geography, and biography. There is unquestionably a greater emphasis in this area than in any of the other sets, and it is particularly useful for out-of-the-way, little-known material about the United States. However, general coverage of America is matched with other major encyclopedias.

Americana-Britannica Compared

In a study by Dorothy Cole of the 1972 *Americana* and the *Britannica*, it was found that the two sets are quite similar in subject emphasis.[17] About one-half of the material is given over to the social sciences, and the rest is about evenly divided between the humanities and science. And of this total, from 37 to 39 percent of the articles are of a biographical nature—with scientists receiving much less attention than those in other fields. Both sets have about the same number of illustrations, with emphasis on geographical and political areas. The two sets usually have signed articles, and normally the contributors are authorities. Primarily because of the emphasis on short articles (i.e., specific entry) in *Americana*, as contrasted with articles in depth in the *Britannica*, Cole found "the incidence of unique material in *Americana* was nearly three times greater than in *Britannica*."

While both sets tend to give equal amount of space to primary subjects, *Americana* does excel in its approach to geographical areas. Not only does it give considerably more coverage of the United States and Canada, but it is almost equally as good in treating other areas of the world. And thanks to the semipopular style and emphasis on careful organization, the articles are especially suitable for work with and by older students and adults. Also, they feature a series of historical essays on each of the centuries.

The *Britannica* is equally strong in the areas of geography and history, but particularly in the latter category. Its treatment of the history of individual nations is excellent, and it also gives more attention to historical matters related to various subject areas than does the *Americana*.

Both sets have fine, detailed indexes. However, because of the shorter articles, the *Americana* is easier to use without the index; whereas the *Britannica* should, in most cases, always be used with the index—particularly for subjects treated in longer articles here, but treated separately in the *Americana*.

The essential differences between the *Americana* and the *Encyclopedia Britannica* are:

1. *Americana* tends to stress more popular treatment of materials. Complex ideas are usually presented in a way which is well within the grasp of the average educated layman. The *Britannica* can be equally popular, but most emphasis is on scholarly, detailed articles. For example, the best comparison is the material on chemistry and on physics. The *Britannica* presupposes background in both areas. Not so the *Americana*. The style of writing is considerably more scholarly, and sometimes equally

[17] Dorothy Cole, "The Characteristics of Americana & Britannica," *RQ*, Spring 1973, p. 220+.

dense, in the *Britannica* than in *Americana*. Given this difference, the *Britannica* is definitely not suited for the average high school student. The *Americana,* however, can be used effectively by more ambitious secondary school students.

2. Neither encyclopedia is entirely up to date, and neither can be trusted for current statistical data. But of the two, *Americana* puts more emphasis on modern topics with a resultant timeliness not always found in the *Britannica.* Conversely, the *Britannica* seems to be much better in historical items, particularly in the humanities. However, the real differences in timeliness are slight. One reader may find a given article or biography in *Americana* more up to date than in *Britannica,* and another reader may find quite the opposite.

3. Neither set has up-to-date bibliographies, although in recent years the *Americana* is making more effort to update. In terms of coverage, however, the *Britannica* tends to have more bibliographies than its rival. The conclusion is that as a source of bibliography neither set can be used—the exception being for retrospective searches.

Given these similarities and differences, if a choice must be made between the two sets: (1) *Americana* is better for fast, ready-reference work; (2) *Britannica* is better for scholarly, overview articles; (3) *Americana* is better for the average layman; (4) *Britannica* is better for the above-average educated layman.

HIGH SCHOOL AND POPULAR FAMILY-USE ENCYCLOPEDIAS

Collier's Encyclopedia. New York: Crowell-Collier Educational Corp., 24 vols., $329.50.

Encyclopedia International. New York: Grolier Incorporated, 20 vols., $275.

Collier's and *Encyclopedia International* share several things:

1. Audience: While *Collier's* is an adult encyclopedia, it is often used in high schools and in public libraries where *Americana* and, more particularly, the *Britannica* seem a trifle difficult for the lesser educated adult. The *International* is somewhat the same and is "designed for the broad range of high school students, and for the family of moderate educational background."

2. Style: In view of the audience, the style is popular, often almost journalistic. A concerted effort is made in both sets to make the

material as interesting as possible, and the *International* seems to stress staff writing—almost two-thirds of the articles are unsigned, i.e., by staff with an overview from consultants. Almost all articles in *Collier's* are signed, but again an obvious effort is made to simplify without insulting. Intellectually (in terms of popular topics, style, length of articles, and so on), *Collier's* is far ahead of the *International*. How important this may be for an encyclopedia used in high schools and by average adults is questionable—particularly as information in both is accurate.

3. Coverage: Both sets tend to stress topics related to high school curriculum and to popular taste. Both have good to excellent articles on the United States and major nations of the world. More detailed material is handled in easy to understand, almost outline, fashion. Of the two, the *International* intentionally puts more stress on the social sciences, humanities, and the sciences. The biographical material in the *International*, again, tends to stress more popular figures, but both are equally good in the relative amount of coverage in this area.

4. Illustrations: The two have approximately the same number of illustrations and maps, but the *International* stresses color plates which are close to 7 to 1 greater in number than in *Collier's*. Both have numerous tables and charts, although again the *International* is particularly outstanding for its tabular presentation of much information.

5. Objectivity: As both sets stress short articles, they tend to emphasize fact rather than argument. Where an issue of opinion asserts itself, a concerted effort is made to fairly balance both sides. This emphasis on data rather than on debate may or may not be an asset—depending upon the view of the reader and the librarian.

6. Bibliographies: The *International* has selected bibliographies at the end of longer articles, but these tend to be too few in number and often dated. Conversely, one of the strong points of *Collier's* is the bibliographies—in this case, in separate subject sections in the index volume. Here the books are carefully chosen, usually fairly up to date, and, according to the editors, in print for purchase. This is supposed to be a self-study aid and a type of selection tool for libraries and individuals.

A major difference seems to be timeliness, particularly of statistical data. The *International* is weak in this area, while *Collier's* (whose editors claim it is revised and reprinted three times a year) is particularly good on recent information and up-to-date statistics. In terms of library use, this may or may not be important, particularly as other standard reference aids are more likely to be used for up-to-date statistical data.

For private purchase, it may be a factor—and one worth calling attention to for those who inquire as to which set is best.

The primary difference between the two sets is in volume of coverage. *Collier's* has some 25,000 articles and over 21 million words. *International* has 11,000 more articles than found in *Collier's* (36,000), but less than one-half the total number of words (9 to 10 million). And while both indexes are excellent, *Collier's* has 400,000 entries as compared to just over 120,000 in its rival. An analysis indicates, though, that both cover an equal amount of specific material—the essential difference being that *Collier's* simply tends to give more information on any given subject.

Thanks to its more specific type entries, *International* is probably better for fast ready-reference work. Still, *Collier's* is not that far behind and it, too, can be used equally as well.

On balance, it is difficult to say one is really that much better than the other. *Collier's* does have an edge in its depth of coverage and timeliness, but may lose it when one considers that it is priced at $329 as compared to $200 for the *International*. Both the library and the layman have to ask whether the differences between the two sets are really worth the over one-third difference in price. Hopefully libraries, and more particularly high schools and public libraries, can afford them both. In this case, the library would do well to alternate purchase between one set and the other over the years.

CHILDREN'S AND YOUNG ADULTS' ENCYCLOPEDIAS

The American Educator Encyclopedia. Lake Bluff, Illinois: Tangley Oaks Educational Center, 20 vols., $130.

Compton's Encyclopedia and Fact-Index. Chicago: Encyclopaedia Britannica, Inc., 24 vols., $180.

Merit Students Encyclopedia. New York: Crowell-Collier Educational Corp., 20 vols., $319.50.

World Book Encyclopedia. Chicago: Field Enterprise Educational Corp., 22 vols., $219.50 ($134 for schools and libraries).

In terms of general excellence, price, acceptance, and sales, *World Book* unquestionably leads all the children's and young adult encyclopedias. Its only real competitor is *Compton's* with the *Merit Students Encyclopedia* a close third.[18]

---

[18] A possible fifth entry: *Young Students Encyclopedia* (Columbus, Ohio: American Education Publications, 1973, 15 vols. approximately $60). This is geared for ages 7 to 13, is edited by the staff of *My Weekly Reader*, and claims some 4,500 illustrations and 2,500 articles—a far cry from the "standard" sets in this field. But in view of the low price, it may be worth considering after it is properly reviewed.

Others in this field are too little known, e.g., *The American Educator Encyclopedia* or, for younger groups of readers, *New Book of Knowledge* and *Britannica Junior*.

All may be used with children from the fifth grade up and for many adults who want quick, easy-to-understand facts and overviews of difficult-to-understand subject matter. *World Book* and *Compton's* differ radically in that the latter takes a broad approach to subject matter with some 4,000 articles, while *World Book* takes the specific approach with 19,000 entries. Still, in number of words, the sets are almost the same; and as with the *International* and *Collier's,* the primary difference is not so much volume of material as how the material is divided and subdivided. *Merit* is similar to *World* in its specific approach, but does have almost a million more words than *Compton's*. All have indexes—*World* turning to an index only recently. *Compton's* indexing differs in that there is no single index volume, but an index and study guide at the end of each of the volumes. The advantage to this is that a single index is not tied-up by one user, but the disadvantage is obviously that one must turn to 24 instead of one index for information. *World* and *Compton's* have elaborate cross references and can be readily used without the index. The cross references in *Merit* are less evident, and there are no references to illustrations in the index.

In terms of illustrations, all three are excellent. *Compton's* has over 25,000 illustrations, with some 5,000 in color; *World* boasts 29,000 with 10,000 in color; and *Merit* has slightly over 20,000 with about one-fifth in color. In all cases, the illustrations are generally linked closely to the text and are up-to-date.

The three sets, then, have much in common. Differences, except for the specific or the broad entry form, are minimal in terms of coverage, illustrations, and, to a degree, format. The essential differences may be summed up briefly:

1. *World Book* is probably better organized than the other two, and information is easier and quicker to find.
2. The style of writing in the three is graded, i.e., the articles begin with relatively easy material and definitions and grow progressively more difficult and sophisticated. Still, the style in the *World Book* is better than its competitors. Conversely, in terms of depth of coverage *Compton's* is best; while *Merit* scores heavily in individual articles which are written specifically for given grade levels.
3. *Compton's* strong point is its "Fact" index at the end of each volume. Combining as it does an index with brief information on subjects not included in the main work, it serves as an excellent ready-reference source both for children and for adults. Conversely, *World Book's* specific arrangement and massive

cross references make it equally good for ready-reference work. *Merit* lags behind both.

4. All three are constantly being revised, but in this respect *World* has more of an active revision policy, and it shows in the more up-to-date statistical data and in the illustrations. *Compton's* is close behind, with *Merit* a third.

On balance, then, it is difficult to really say one set is all that better than the other. Thanks to its timeliness, organization, and illustrations, as well as writing style, *World Book* is usually a first choice. *Compton's* rivals *World* on almost all of these counts and is a good second. *Merit* is strong, too, but has a number of weaknesses—not to mention a considerably higher price—that puts it firmly in third place.

Having expanded from 14 to 20 volumes since 1972, *The American Educator Encyclopedia* is one of the better, low-priced children's encyclopedias. In terms of price range—under $150—it is the best. Why? There are over 13,000 articles (as compared to some 5,000 in *Britannica Junior* and close to 20,000 in *World Book*), and the over 11,000 illustrations and excellent maps are carefully placed so as to augment the articles. The material is written for the average grade school through junior high student, and some attention is given to matching length and depth of articles with curriculum. The writing style is fair to good, and the articles appear timely and authoritative. There is no index, but there are numerous cross references which relate articles. The bibliographies are fair.

Since this was rejected by The American Library Association in 1965, it has improved considerably—and in view of the reasonable price it might be suited for larger libraries where multiple encyclopedias are the order; or for families where cost, although admittedly minimal in difference between the much better *World Book,* is a factor.

This encyclopedia is an excellent example of the competition publishers face. Not only are the basic sets—from *World Book* to *Britannica Junior*—better known and better publicized, but as they have been recommended over the years by ALA, librarians can see little reason to change. And their reasoning is solid enough. Even though *The American Educator Encyclopedia* is good, it simply is not good enough (price aside) to warrant a general recommendation in a field somewhat overcrowded by even better sets.

PRE-SCHOOL AND CHILDREN'S ENCYCLOPEDIAS

Britannica Junior Encyclopaedia. Chicago: Encyclopaedia Britannica, Inc., 15 vols., $149.50 ($109 schools and libraries).

New Book of Knowledge. New York: Grolier Incorporated, 20 vols., $199.50.

Golden Book Encyclopedia. New York: Golden Press, 1969, 16 vols., $65 ($48.75, schools and libraries; $19.64, supermarkets).

Libraries and parents who wish, or can afford, encyclopedias for younger children (five to nine years of age), have a somewhat more limited choice than offered for older age groups. However, the selection problem is easier. Of the three listed here, by far the best is the *New Book of Knowledge,* followed by the *Britannica* entry, and coming in a poor third, the *Golden Book.* The *New Book of Knowledge* outweighs its competitors on all counts: it has close to 7 million words and 9,000 articles (*Britannica* close to 6 million words and slightly over 4,000 articles; *Golden Book* under a million and only a bit over 1,200 entries). The *New Book of Knowledge* has almost twice as many illustrations as in the *Britannica* and over four times as many as in the *Golden Book.* In terms of style, coverage, authority, timeliness, and the like, the *New Book of Knowledge* is far ahead of its competitors.

The major factor working for the *Britannica* is that it is aimed at a slightly lower age level, and it may be a bit more readable than the other two sets. The only thing in the *Golden Book's* favor is price, but even at the less than $20 supermarket price it is a poor set with little or no balance in subject matter, poor illustrations, and a less than happy arrangement of materials.

All the sets are by way of a luxury for most libraries, who would be better advised to first purchase the *World Book* and *Compton's.* True, the reading level in these is geared higher than in the younger children's sets; but the illustrations are an incentive, and since a good deal of material is in outline form, both sets are within the use range of the child in the third grade and up. Where a young child's set is desirable, the *New Book of Knowledge* would definitely be the first choice.

Never content to leave the field to readers, the encyclopedia firms all offer pre-school types of encyclopedias. The best known is *Childcraft—The How and Why Library* (Chicago: Field Enterprise Educational Corp., 15 vols., $77.50). The set includes stories and factual material about everything of interest to a young child from animals and art to the body. Thanks to excellent illustrations and well thought-out texts, the volumes are useful for pre-school and early grades.

A somewhat similar approach is offered by Grolier: *Our Wonderful World: An Encyclopedic Anthology for the Entire Family* (18 vols., $189.50). The thematic approach is again used here with emphasis on science, natural history, and careers. It is meant for a slightly older audience than the other sets, but is primarily for students in grades three to eight.

Another entry, this time from the Britannica, is *Compton's Precyclopedia.* This is a 16-volume set on the order of Childcraft designed to introduce the child to basic learning experiences. Libraries might want one, or all of these sets, but they would be used for casual reading, not for reference work with children. None is a substitute for a good encyclopedia.

ENCYCLOPEDIA SUPPLEMENTS—YEARBOOKS

There are two basic purposes to the encyclopedia yearbooks, annuals, or supplements. They are published annually to (1) keep the basic set up-to-date and (2) present a summary of the year's major events. A third less obvious purpose is in the field of sales—it is comforting for the buyer to realize that his set will never be outdated. (A questionable assumption, but used by almost every encyclopedia salesman.)

> All in all . . . the purchaser will find annuals mainly useful for general reading and browsing and for summaries of newsworthy events rather than for systematic updating of their respective encyclopedia sets. . . . Most encyclopedia annuals . . . are valuable enough for their independent worth to merit serious consideration for purchase."[19]

The yearbooks range in price from $5.95 *(World Book Year Book)* to $8.95 *(Britannica Book of the Year)* and are usually available only to purchasers of the initial sets. They all tend to be attractively printed and generally feature numerous illustrations.

Most of the supplements are not really related to the parent set, except in name. The arrangements are broad, with emphasis on large, current topics. Most of the material is not later incorporated into the revised basic sets—a plus and minus consideration. On the positive side, a run of the yearbooks does afford a fairly comprehensive view of the year's events. On the negative side, the library is wise to keep a run of the yearbooks because it cannot depend upon the revised parent set having the same material, at any rate in such depth. Thus, this means that someone looking for more than basic facts on a given topic should really search not only the main encyclopedia, but a number of the yearbooks.

In terms of ready reference, the most depressing element is that the index to the various yearbooks is not related to the main set. Conversely, several of the publishers *(Britannica, Compton's, World Book)* offer cumulative indexes to the yearbooks since about 1965.

The alphabetical arrangement and the scope of most of the yearbooks make them particularly useful for tracing trends in the previous year's activities. Advances in industry and sciences, sports and arts are

[19] "Reference and Subscription Book Reviews—Encyclopedia Supplements," *Booklist,* December 1, 1971, p. 298.

covered as are the national and international political scene. Aside from covering trends in major areas, the yearbooks prove most helpful for fact questions concerning biographies and obituaries, chronology of events, and current statistics. Again, scholars and specialists are responsible for the longer articles, while editors usually prepare the shorter entries.

Aside from the age of the audience for which they are prepared, it is difficult to discover significant differences between the various yearbooks. In this, they resemble the daily newspaper. One reader may prefer the slant, or emphasis, of one newspaper over another, but all are drawing from the same general materials. Nor is the analogy as farfetched as it may seem. In the annuals particularly, the predominantly newspaper-trained staffs of the larger encyclopedia firms have a holiday. Format, content, and the ever-important emphasis on up-to-date, often exciting events reveals more than a scholar behind the final book—it reveals an emphasis on what makes the daily newspaper sell, at least as seen from the viewpoint of the ex-newspaperman.

In libraries, it is sufficient to purchase yearbooks for encyclopedias not replaced that given year. If more than a single adult and children's yearbook is to be purchased, the nod will go to the work preferred by the librarian and the patrons. As long as the preference is within the standards set for encyclopedias, it is more a matter of taste than objective judgment and any one of the accepted publishers will serve as well as another.

"SUPERMARKET" ENCYCLOPEDIAS

While all the "big four" general encyclopedias are sold on a door-to-door basis, there are numerous sets which can be purchased at supermarkets, department stores, or even bookstores. As most of these cost considerably less than the major sets, the librarian is frequently asked as to their merit. For example, just how good is the *Illustrated World Encyclopedia,* a 15-volume set advertised by Boston Store for $39.95, "as one of the three best encyclopedias recommended for the elementary grades." (No indication, of course, of who says it is "best.")

ALA Walsh[20]

1. *Funk & Wagnalls New Encyclopedia.*   R
   New York: Funk & Wagnall (distributed by Crowell), 27 vols., $89.95 (supermarket prices slightly lower).
   In 1971, this set was totally revised and renamed. Up until that time, it was known as the *Funk & Wagnalls Standard Reference Encyclopedia* and, as such, was recommended by the American Library Association. (As of mid-1973, the ALA had not reviewed the new set.)

[20] NR, not recommended; R, recommended.

It is among the best buys in supermarket sets. There are 27 volumes, over 18,000 articles, 7 million words, and some 7,000 illustrations. The index has over 100,000 entries. The articles are well written and are primarily for the young adult and the average educated adult. There is considerable emphasis on history, biography, and the sciences. Thanks to the total revision, most of the material is up to date. While no substitute for one of the standard sets, it is a good buy for home purchase.

2. *Golden Book Encyclopedia* (see p. 114)   NR   R
3. *Illustrated Columbia Encyclopedia* (see p. 120)   —   R
4. *Illustrated World Encyclopedia.* Glen Cove, New York: Bobley Publishing Company, 15 vols., $42.   NR   R

A children's set (grades four through seven), the *Illustrated World* has some 15,000 short articles and over 4 million words. The material is well written but oversimplified. It, also, tends to be so brief as to be relatively worthless for reference purposes. Not a good buy.

5. *International Everyman's Encyclopedia* (see p. 118)R   R
6. *New Standard Encyclopedia.* Chicago: Standard Educational Corporation, 14 vols., $129 to $150.   NR   R

A young peoples general family set. Although Walsh recommends it, it is hard to find any justification: the price puts it well within the range of the standard sets which are so much better that any comparison is not worthwhile.

These are only representative. There are many more such encyclopedias, and a new one seems to appear every month.

If the reader is looking for an inexpensive set under $40 or so, the supermarket buys are questionable, but just passable. Anything over about $40 is no longer acceptable. The buyer might better spend the money for a good, used standard set. The evaluations indicate that Walsh is not a good source of objective criticism. The ALA is more rigorous, and rightfully so. In giving advice about the "supermarket" sets, it would be good for the librarian to point out the essential difference between Walsh and the ALA.

As a rule of thumb, it is safe to say that most sets with the Funk & Wagnall imprint (if under $50) are passable, as is the *International Everyman's.* All others should be avoided, or at best carefully checked and evaluated.

OTHER ENGLISH LANGUAGE ENCYCLOPEDIAS

Chamber's Encyclopedia. Elmsford, New York: Maxwell Science International, 15 vols., $259.

Encyclopedia Canadiana. Ottawa: Canadiana Company, Ltd. (distributed in United States by Grolier), 10 vols., $100.

International Everyman's Encyclopedia. New York: Encyclopedia Enterprises, 20 vols., $1.99 each.

Chamber's is the standard adult British encyclopedia, long ago having replaced what is essentially the Americanized *Encyclopaedia Britannica.* (However, the *Britannica* maintains sales offices in England, as in Europe, and it is sold there, too.) Unlike their American counterparts, the publishers of Chamber's do not believe in continuous revision. A completely new edition is brought out every 5 to 10 years with a loose leaf supplement issued annually to update materials. How "completely new" each edition is depends upon editorial viewpoint; and, in the past decade, the revision has not been that extensive.

In terms of coverage, it has about 30,000 entries (as compared to over 30,000 for *Britannica* and some 60,000 for *Americana*). In every other respect, from the number of illustrations to the total number of words, the British set lags well behind its two American counterparts. It seems to have undergone a number of editorial shifts in policy, but as of 1973 it remains a less than satisfactory entry for American libraries. Subjectively, and in its favor, the articles are better written and more scholarly than in most American encyclopedias. Furthermore, it does have an extensive coverage of Europe and Asia. Still, on balance, it is a long way from what should be expected from a major encyclopedia.

The Canadian entry differs from all others in that it is frankly nationalistic. It has undergone several revisions, and most of the material tends to be relatively up to date. Geared for adults and high school students, it is particularly useful for the detailed historical, geographical, and biographical information on Canada. However, it lacks the depth and breadth of a general encyclopedia and, as such, must be used with other standard sets. For what it does, it does well enough; and it should be in all larger academic and public libraries in America, certainly in all types and sizes of libraries in Canada.

The third English language encyclopedia is typical of a better-than-average supermarket product which, unlike most, can be recommended for many libraries and individuals. Why? Because it is based upon the British *Everyman's Encyclopedia,* published by Dent since 1913. (A fifth edition appeared in England in 1967, and the American work is based upon that edition.) There are nearly 50,000 unsigned articles. As the principle is specific entry instead of a broad entry, most are brief. The longer articles have rather good bibliographies, and the style of writing for all the material is excellent—not only in terms of clarity and precision, but in a manner which can be easily understood by both high school students and adults. The illustrations are fair to good, and there are helpful diagrams and charts.

The one "catch" to the set is that it does have a definite British heritage; and while an effort has been made to Americanize and update the 1967 English edition, it is primarily geared for the British reader. Still, the extensive coverage of subject matter, the editorial excellence, and the low price makes this a first among the so-called supermarket encyclopedias. As such, it is one of the few in this category recommended by the American Library Association, *Booklist* (May 1, 1972, pp. 733–734).

ONE-VOLUME ENCYCLOPEDIAS

The Columbia Encyclopedia. 3d ed. New York: Columbia University Press, 1963, 2,388 pp., $49.50.
   Lincoln Library of Essential Information. 3d ed. Columbus, Ohio: Frontier Press Co., 1972, 2 vols., 2,213 pp., $63.95 ($59.95 schools and libraries).

   Primarily in an attempt to bring an encyclopedia to the price level where it may be considered for purchase by almost anyone, several efforts have been made to issue one-volume works. From a librarian's viewpoint, they are primarily a handy source for quick reference. Entries are arranged in alphabetical order, much in the manner of the European encyclopedias. The information is stripped of almost everything except the facts. All of this adds up to a time-saver when the librarian only needs an isolated bit of data and does not require depth of coverage.
   For home purposes, the 1-volume works often are the most economical and, compared with encyclopedias in the same general price range, a considerably better buy. The information is often more exact and usually better presented than in the low-priced encyclopedias. Where cost is a factor, the librarian should always inform the user of these one-volume works and let him compare reviews, or the encyclopedias themselves.
   Although limited to one volume, the *Columbia Encyclopedia* is a good example of a case in which appearances can be deceptive. With some 7.5 million words and 75,000 brief entries, it compares favorably, verbiage-wise, with many multivolume encyclopedias. For example, it has some 15,000 more entries than the *Americana* and in words is equal to almost all the children's and young adult standard encyclopedias.
   In terms of ready reference, the *Columbia* is a valuable guide. The editors work under the assumption that the majority of subjects can be best approached via biography. Consequently, between biographical and geographical entries almost 70 percent of the entries are in these two areas. Often biographical sketches will be found for individuals not included, or at best only mentioned, in standard multivolume sets.
   The articles are unsigned, and only the longer ones have bibliographies. Most of the writing is good to excellent, and it is intentionally

written at the popular level. The authors are experts, drawn for the most part from the Columbia campus.

As the volume is only infrequently revised (every 10 to 15 years), it obviously is not the ideal aid for timely topics. Still, for basic retrospective ready-reference questions it is extremely good. (A new edition is planned for 1974–1975.)

There are a number of versions of the Columbia. The *Illustrated Columbia Encyclopedia* (New York: Rockville House, 1969, 22 vols., $1.99 each volume) is a supermarket edition which is essentially the same textually as the one-volume work. The difference is the format and the addition of rather poor illustrations. The one volume is much preferable, particularly for library work. Conversely, as the prices are about the same, the supermarket edition might be recommended where a user could not afford a larger, illustrated set for home use.

The "best buy" version of the *Columbia* is the *Columbia Viking Desk Encyclopedia* (New York: Dell, 1964, 2,016 pp., paperback, $1.95). It has close to 32,000 entries and a considerable number of cross references. In view of the low price and the amount of coverage—which is considerable for a paperback reference work—this can be highly recommended for both individuals and for the ready-reference desk of a library where the larger edition of the *Columbia* is not available. (Note: as this is based on the 1963 *Columbia,* the information on current events is dated. However, it is still extremely useful for retrospective information.)

Another one-volume paperback of some merit is the *Penguin Encyclopedia* (Baltimore: Penguin Books, 1966, 657 pp. $2.25). This has about one-half the number of entries as the *Columbia Viking;* but as the emphasis is different, it can be recommended where information is needed on Great Britain and Europe in general. In fact, it nicely complements, although in no way replaces, the *Columbia Viking.*

First issued in 1924, *The Lincoln Library of Essential Information* has the advantage over the *Columbia* of constant revision. New editions appear frequently, and each one makes an effort to update material. It appears in two volumes, with information arranged under 12 general subject fields from English language to biography and miscellany. There is a detailed index in each volume; and while the arrangement is not ideal for ready-reference work, the indexes are detailed enough to overcome the basic arrangement problem. Among its many good features are: several hundred charts and tables; updated bibliographies; quality illustrations; a good atlas of the world; and broad coverage of general knowledge. The articles are well written and can be easily understood by a junior high or high school student. As the material is arranged in a specific manner—there are some 25,000 different entries—coverage tends to be brief, factual, and unopinionated. Between this work and the *Columbia,* the *Lincoln* is a first choice in terms of revision; but when a new edition of the *Columbia* is available, the *Columbia* is preferable for ease of use.

FOREIGN-LANGUAGE ENCYCLOPEDIAS

Most reference questions can be quickly and best answered in an American encyclopedia, but there are occasions when a foreign-language work is more suitable. Obviously, the coverage of the country of origin in a foreign encyclopedia will be in considerably more depth than in an American work. This will also be true for such items as biographies of nationals, statistics, places, and events.

All of this presupposes a knowledge of a foreign language; and for this reason, the encyclopedias are not generally used except where natives of the country make up a part of the population or in college and university libraries where students and teachers may find them useful. While librarians may deplore the lack of command of one or more foreign languages on the part of the public, this is a fact and one which severely limits purchase of the foreign encyclopedia.

However, even with the most elementary knowledge of a language, several of the works are useful for their fine illustrations and maps. For example, the *Enciclopedia Italiana* boasts some of the best illustrations of any encyclopedia, particularly in the areas of the fine arts. A foreign encyclopedia is equally useful for viewpoint. It may come as a surprise to some American readers to find how the Civil War, for example, is treated in the French and the German encyclopedias; and the evaluation of various American writers and national heroes is sometimes equally revealing of how Europeans judge the United States. In more specific terms, the foreign encyclopedia is helpful for information on lesser known figures not found in American or British works; for bibliographies which emphasize a foreign language approach; for some rather detailed maps, both of cities and of regions; and for everything from plots of lesser known novels and musicals to identification of place names.

Aside from the Russians, who have only two official encyclopedias, all the Western nations have two or three firms issuing encyclopedias. On the whole, though, competition is considerably limited by the encroachment of American works and the established firms which have become synonymous with encyclopedias. In French, the *Larousse* series is usually the only one given major consideration in American schools and universities, even though there is a fair work issued by another company. Why? Probably because *Larousse* was there first and, more likely, because it continues to be an outstanding work. Need for a second French set is rarely felt except in the largest of libraries.

There is another interesting reason to explain the limitations of competition, at least with American sales. European encyclopedias tend to echo government interests, particularly when that government is a dictatorship. This serves well enough when the dictator is in power; but usually when he falls, so does the set. A good example is the German *Meyers Konversations-Lexikon.* The firm of Meyer actively supported the Nazi party, and the eighth edition of their encyclopedia was published during the Nazi reign. At the end of the war, the firm was liquidated by the Allies. This ended a publishing house which had been putting out good-to-excellent encyclopedias since 1839. While the earlier works are still found in many large libraries, a wrong guess by the publisher terminated the only major competition the other encyclopedia publisher, Brockhaus, has in Germany.

In the case of the most generally used foreign encyclopedias, albeit certainly not the only ones, the student may remember them easily in terms of who publishes what, e.g., France, *Larousse;* Germany, *Brockhaus;* Spain, *Espasa.* The Italian and Russian works do not quite fit into this formula.

French

LaGrande Encyclopédie Larousse. rev. ed. Paris: Larousse, 1972 in progress, 20 vols.

The name Larousse is as familiar to France as the *Encyclopaedia Britannica* is to the United States. Pierre Larousse was the founder of a publishing house which continues to flourish and is responsible for the basic French encyclopedias.

One problem, as with most European encyclopedias, is the alphabetical arrangement. Any student who has had a brush with a foreign language realizes that while the latin alphabet is employed, there are variations in letters—Spanish, for example, has two letters not found in English, *Ch* and *Ll.* There are also marked differences in common names. John turns up as Giovanni, Jan, Johannes, or Jehan. Consequently, before abandoning a foreign encyclopedia for lack of an entry be certain to have looked for it in terms of the language employed.

The *Grand Larousse* continues with the policy of short specific entries, but it does give some rather extensive treatment of major subjects. For example, the length of articles for countries and leading personalities often equals those found in American works.

Working on the old subscription books principle of issuing a given number of volumes per year, the new edition of *La Grande Encyclopédie* began appearing in 1972 and will eventually comprise 20 volumes—at the rate of four volumes per year. There will be a 400,000-item reference index. Over the years, the French have learned from the Americans, i.e., this edition will not only include lengthy articles, but where there is a long piece, it will be preceded by a type of study guide or precis which provides the reader with a broad outline of the subject.

The Larousse titles are particularly renown for the excellent illustrations, often in full color. And each page of this work includes photographs, charts, maps, diagrams, and the like. Regardless of one's command of French, everyone will enjoy the illustrations—even the smaller ones which are noteworthy for their sharp register.

As might be expected, the *Grand Larousse* has its forebears.[21] Scholars who fondly recall the Ninth and Eleventh editions of the *Britannica* tend to play the same game with Larousse. Another publisher, Lamirault, between 1886 and 1902, issued the 31-volume *La Grande Encyclopédie*. It has some long and some short articles and the majority are signed by the leading authorities of the time. It is found in many larger libraries where there is any interest in French history or philosophy. As an academic source, it is still unrivaled. In fact, happy the scholar who could have this set along with the Ninth of the *Britannica* and the earlier editions of the German *Brockhaus*.

German

Brockhaus Enzyklopädie. rev. ed. Weisbaden: Brockhaus, 1966 in progress, 20 vols.

Lexikothek. Gütersloh: Lexikon-Institut Bertelsmann, 1972 in progress; Part I, 10 vols.; Part II, 14 vols.; Part III, films and pictures.

First issued as *Frauenzimmer Lexikon* (between 1796 and 1808) primarily as an encyclopedia for women, Brockhaus got off to a bad start. The original publisher, possibly because of his audience, gave up the financial ghost; and in 1808, Friedrich Brockhaus purchased the set and issued the last volume. A wise man, Brockhaus continued to use his volumes not as scholarly works but as books guaranteed to give the average man (or woman) a solid education. In this respect, he was years ahead of the times; in fact so far ahead of his American and English counterparts that they freely borrowed his text, if not his sales techniques. As earlier noted, the Brockhaus works served as the basis for the early *Americana* and *Chamber's*.

Brockhaus extended his popular formula to cutting back articles to little more than dictionary length. In this respect, he followed the Euro-

---

[21] Among them is the famous Diderot *Encyclopédie,* the subject of a full length book: John Lough, *The Encyclopedie* (New York: David McKay Company, Inc., 1971). The work is not only fascinating for the specific history of the French set, but offers an excellent background for the history of the genre.

pean form of specific entry. Consequently, all the Brockhaus encyclopedias—and there is a family of them—are an admixture of dictionary and encyclopedia.

As might be expected, the longer articles are on European countries and Germany, some of which are over 100 pages. In many respects, this encyclopedia is considerably more provincial than the *Larousse;* and while it is an excellent source of material on German history and personalities, it can be passed up for other items.

In view of the scope of the *Brockhaus,* it serves a useful purpose in large research libraries or where there is a German-speaking populace, but it is probably near the bottom for choices of all the foreign-language encyclopedias.

Another well-known German publisher of encyclopedias is Bertelsmann. The firm offers a smaller version of the Brockhaus (*Das Bertelsmann Lexikon,* 7 vols.), which is excellent because of emphasis on up-to-date, timely articles and statistics. This, however, appears on the way to being replaced by a considerably more ambitious effort, the *Lexikothek.* A three-part project, it will consist (when completed) of a 10-volume alphabetically arranged encyclopedia on the order of the older *Lexikon.* There is considerable emphasis on illustrations, and in this respect the first set is similar to *La Grande Encyclopédie Larousse.* Specific entry is stressed, and there will be over 120,000 separate items in the first set (as contrasted with 75,000 entries in the one-volume American *Columbia Encyclopedia* and 60,000 in the *Americana*). The second set is primarily a subject approach which has no real counterpart in American sets. Each volume will include an outline of the subject and lengthy articles covering every aspect of geography, art, animals, science, and other subjects. One volume of the set is an atlas which has a gazeteer with 170,000 separate entries. The third section is an audio-visual supplement which will be made up of slides, films, and pictures.

It remains to be seen how valuable the *Lexikothek* will be for American libraries, although the heavily illustrated dictionary approach of the first set should be of value for ready-reference work. In any case, it will complement, rather than replace the long lived Brockhaus.

Italian

Enciclopedia Italiana di Scienze Lettere ed Arti. Rome: Instituto della Enciclopedia Italiana, 1929 to 1939, 36 vols., appendices I–III, 1938 to 1962, 5 vols.

Lavishly illustrated with black and white and superb color plates, the Italian encyclopedia is best known for its artwork. As such, it can be used profitably by anyone; and somewhat like the *National Geographic,* it will afford hours of browsing time even for the person who does not understand a word of Italian.

At perhaps a more important level, it has an outstanding reputation for detailed articles in the humanities. All the articles are signed, and there are a number of bibliographies. One good example is the article on Rome. This runs to almost 300 pages and has close to 200 photogravure plates illustrating almost every aspect of the city, present and past.

The basic set is updated continually by the various appendixes which are equally well written and illustrated. The index to the complete set is excellent and there is an index to the appendix.

Russian

Bol'shaya Sovetskaya Entskklopediya. 3d ed. Moscow: "Sovetskaya Entskklospediya," 1970 in progress, 30 vols. plus index. (*The Great Soviet Encyclopedia.* New York: Crowell Collier and Macmillan, Inc., 1974 in progress, 30 vols. plus index.)

The third edition of the *BSE* replaces the heavily doctrinaire second, issued shortly after the death of Stalin. And while it still reflects the "party" line, it is said to be considerably more objective than the previous two editions.

> The first edition, which came out in the 1920s contained so much propaganda that it is believed to have provided George Orwell with some of the inspiration for *1984* in which the hero, Winston Smith, who works for the Ministry of Truth, must rewrite history daily in order to conform with the constantly shifting party line.[22]

A comparison with the second edition offers evidence of how official Soviet thinking has relaxed since Stalin died in 1953. While Soviet bias on purely political topics is still strongly evident, there is a new team of scholars preparing the third; and they display a factual approach to such things as the U.S. Apollo moon mission, Soviet cultural figures who suffered in Stalin's purge, and current Soviet leaders.

The *BSE* is the basic encyclopedia for Soviet schools and families. Entries tend to be somewhat like American works in that they range from short, specific type items to many page articles on history, geography, social sciences, and the sciences.

Beginning in 1974, and ending in about 1980, Crowell Collier & Macmillan will publish the officially approved English translation of this set. The English edition will cost somewhere between $500 and $1,000 when complete.

[22] "Crowell Collier to Publish Soviet Encyclopedia," *Publishers' Weekly,* April 19, 1972, p. 32.

A second Russian encyclopedia is primarily a regional item. The importance of the set as an indication of an intellectual thaw in the Soviet is given in considerable detail in *The Times Literary Supplement* (June 30, 1972, p. 743). The set is: *Byelaruskaya Savietskaya Entsyklapedya* (Minsk: Academy of Sciences of the Byelorussian Soviet Socialist Republic, 4 vols., 1972).

Spanish

Enciclopedia universal ilustrada Europeo-Americana (Espasa). Barcelona: Espasa, 1905 to 1933, 80 vols. in 81, annual supplements, 1935 to date.

Usually cited simply as *Espasa,* this is a remarkable work in many respects. In the first place, it never seems to end. Obviously unaware of the techniques of continuous revision or of new editions, the publishers continue to augment the 80 volumes (actually 70 basic volumes with 10 appendixes) with annual supplements which are arranged in large subject categories and include an index. (The term "annual" must be taken advisedly, as these generally are not issued until three to five years after the period covered. For example, the 1961 to 1962 volume came out in 1966.)

Second, the publishers win hands down for the largest number of entries—they claim over 1 million. Since they are unaware, too, of "authority," none of the articles is signed. Again, as in the German and French encyclopedias the emphasis is on short, dictionary-type entries. Still, there are a number of rather long articles, particularly those dealing with Spain, Latin America, prominent writers, scientists, artists, and so on who claim Spanish as a native tongue.

There are some extensive bibliographies accompanying the longer articles, and these can be used profitably to find definitive studies usually not listed in most sources. The illustrations are poor, and even the colored plates of paintings leave much to be desired.

Like the *Brockhaus* this has a limited audience. It is one, however, that every librarian should know primarily because of its wide use in Latin America. How long this will continue is a matter of conjecture. Several American firms are now issuing essentially the same encyclopedia as those sold here, translated into Spanish.

SUGGESTED READING

"Blitzing Supermarkets' Customers With Books," *Publishers' Weekly,* August 23, 1971, pp. 71+. A short article on what is behind the effort to sell encyclopedias and other books in supermarkets.

Coren, Alan, "Some Organization Calling Itself the Encyclopaedia Britannica . . . ." *Punch,* November 24, 1971, pp. 712 +. A humorous review of the 24-volume set based on key letters on the back of the spine, e.g., A (to) Anstey and Impatiens (to) Jinotega.

Cranston, R., "Encyclopedias: Theory and Practice," *Encounter,* September 1968, pp. 81 +. By way of a review of what is theoretically expected of an encyclopedia and what is usually found in such a set.

Diderot, Denis, "The Encyclopedia," *Rameau's Nephew and Other Works,* translated by Jacques Barzun. Garden City, N.Y.: Doubleday Anchor Books, 1956, pp. 291 +. In this essay the most famous of all encyclopedia compilers explains in considerable detail the frustrations and the joys of editing a set of historical importance.

"Encyclopedia Experts Pick the Best of the Latest," *Changing Times,* August 1971, pp. 6 +. A typical layman's guide article to the "best" in encyclopedias, but of limited use to libraries. The popular consumer magazine updates this list from time to time.

"Encyclopedia Sales Fraud," *Consumer's Report,* March 1971, p. 72. Noted here because of the impact of the magazine on the American buying public, this is a short piece on sales practices.

Wall Street Journal, May 22, 1972, p. 20. An editorial on Vice President Agnew and his quest for "fairness" in encyclopedias.

Walsh, S. Padraig, *Anglo-American General Encyclopedias, 1703-1967.* New York: R. R. Bowker Company, 1968. An annotated title-by-title approach to the history of encyclopedias.

CHAPTER SIX
SUBJECT ENCYCLOPEDIAS

The subject encyclopedia differs from the general encyclopedia in several ways. The first, obvious difference is scope. The general work touches on all points of knowledge, whereas the subject encyclopedia limits itself to exploring in depth a particular area of interest. In terms of purpose, one gets the distinct impression that the American general encyclopedia is becoming more and more an extension of a sales conference aimed at a mass public and less and less an extension of editorial excellence. Not so the average subject encyclopedia. Here sales are primarily dependent upon libraries and the specialized audiences to whom the sets are directed. Given this different audience and purpose, most of the subject encyclopedias are still controlled primarily by the editorial office. Some subject sets of the big four encyclopedia firms are sometimes treated as "package" sales elements, in that they are offered along with the standard sets. Still, this is more the exception than the rule.

In an editorial sense, today's subject encyclopedia holds the position the major encyclopedias held in the nineteenth century, i.e., it is more dependent upon thorough scholarship and depth of coverage than popularity and a large sales force. Many subject encyclopedias are almost miraculous examples of what can be done in the synthesis and the presentation of knowledge in a clear, understandable, and intelligent fashion. Admittedly stretching an analogy, the subject encyclopedia is the Rolls Royce of the library reference collection compared with the Ford and Chevy general encyclopedia.

The analogy may be carried a step further in terms of cost. The majority of general encyclopedias hover between $200 and $400, but the larger subject sets usually are between $500 and $600, sometimes more. The difference in cost may be explained by the larger volume and sales of the general encyclopedias as contrasted with the lesser sales of the subject sets.

Given both these generalizations, i.e., quality and higher cost, there are notable exceptions. Just because an encyclopedia is classified as a subject work, this does not necessarily guarantee excellence. Furthermore, some sets are quite reasonably priced and well within the reach of the average library budget.

Purpose and types

The Reference and Subscription Books Committee of the American Library Association offers some sound advice on subject encyclopedias:

> The prospective purchaser should realize that numerous specialized encyclopedias are available which might serve his needs better than a general encyclopedia. Special purpose encyclopedias can be divided into three categories: (1) those which cover special fields of knowledge (e.g., *International Encyclopedia of the Social Sciences*); (2) those which cover special subjects (e.g., the *Encyclopedia of the American Revolution*); (3) those which cover special viewpoints (e.g., *The New Catholic Encyclopedia*.)[1]

The primary use of a subject or specialized encyclopedia in a library is much the same as the general set. It will be used for both ready-reference queries and for overviews of a given topic. The essential difference is the amount of emphasis on the second use. The scholarly subject set offers not one or two paragraphs on X matter (as does the more general set), but several pages, along with illustrations, and usually an extensive and, hopefully, more up-to-date bibliography. Hence, it is particularly suited for the student or layman who is doing search or research work and wants a relatively exhaustive, rather than a quick, survey of a given topic.

The subject encyclopedia may suffer from too much detail for the average user, particularly for the layman or student. Also, it may be considerably more technical than the inexperienced user is apt to appreciate. Both of these are plus points when the set is used by someone with experience or knowledge of the field.

What usually happens is that the subject set is used as a support for the more general works. Where a user expresses dissatisfaction with, or is obviously far ahead of, the general encyclopedia's efforts, the subject volumes are called into use. Also, many general encyclopedias simply

[1] "Purchasing a General Encyclopedia," *Booklist*, March 15, 1969, p. 761.

exclude details which will be found in subject works—particularly lesser known facts, biographies, and developments in rather esoteric areas of study.

From the viewpoint of the reference librarian, the subject encyclopedia offers peculiar benefits. It may be used to find ready-reference information on almost all topics from biography to geography. As a considerable amount of the information in general encyclopedias is based on the premise of popularity, the subject works are useful for filling some rather distressing gaps in lesser known, certainly less popular fields of knowledge.

As for the type of subject set, this may be approached as the ALA committee did by breaking it down into three areas, or by format. In most libraries, the latter point is of equal interest. When the average librarian thinks of encyclopedias, she envisions multiple volumes. This is true of subject encyclopedias; but, conversely, in most areas there are equally good encyclopedias of a one or two-volume nature. Also, there are numerous paperbacks which may not equal the quality of the larger sets, but serve well enough for many ready-reference purposes, as well as for home use.

Given this wide choice of formats, the librarian has the more important choice of price. Obviously, the 1- or 2-volume works are going to be less (usually considerably less) in price than the larger sets. And while they are not always the best substitutes, they certainly do well enough where a library cannot afford the multiple volumes. Furthermore, often because of arrangement and necessity for brevity, they are much easier to use for ready-reference purposes.

Encyclopedias and handbooks

"Handbooks" is another name publishers choose for these specialized works. *The New Cambridge Modern History* is very much encyclopedic in purpose and is often used as such in reference situations. *The Encyclopedia of Associations,* on the other hand, is a directory. Neither in purpose or in scope is it anywhere equivalent to the normal concept of an encyclopedia. Obviously, the librarian should always look beyond the title before deciding whether to purchase or how to classify the given work.

There is, also, a thin line between the subject or specialized encyclopedia and the traditional handbook. The handbook, as discussed in a later section, is a collection of a miscellaneous group of facts centered around one central theme or subject area, e.g., *Handbook of Physics, Handbook of Insurance.* An encyclopedia tends to be more discursive, although the dictionary, specific entry type may simply list brief facts. A handbook is usually a means of checking for bits of data to assist the user in work in progress. Also, a handbook presupposes a given degree of knowledge in the field. A subject encyclopedia normally assumes that interest, more than knowledge, is the point of departure. If one must draw distinctions, a handbook is a working tool whereas a subject encyclopedia is more of a source of background information which eventually may help to form the project or the work.

The differences between the traditional encyclopedia and the handbook are not always that evident. The title, as noted, is not necessarily a clue. What it seems to come down to is that a handbook is usually conceived in the old German *Handbuch* sense of being a compendious book or treatise for guidance in any art, occupation, or study. The encyclopedia may provide equal guidance, but the information therein tends to be more general, less directly involved with use in an actual working situation. The encyclopedia, then, is primarily for retrospective research. The handbook is primarily for ongoing help or guidance.

There are other problems, too, in grouping certain titles under subject encyclopedias. For example, the collection of historical documents in *The Annals of America* does not constitute an encyclopedia, albeit there is prefatory and explanatory material throughout the set. Conversely, it fails to meet the definition of a handbook. Then there is the *Cambridge History of English Literature* which might just as well be found in the general reading section as in the reference collection. Again, though, it probably will have more use as a subject encyclopedia.

Although all of these distinctions are fascinating in themselves (particularly to anyone who must catalog and classify the work), for everyday reference purposes they mean little. The working reference librarian soon learns that X title, whether it is called an encyclopedia or a handbook, is a fine source of information for Y type questions. And the distinction seems less important as one gets to know a subject field well.[2]

To purchase or not to purchase

The emphasis of the subject encyclopedias on narrow areas of interest make them extremely useful in all libraries, but more particularly in libraries with limited reference collections. The average small to medium-sized library neither can afford nor necessarily wants an extensive collection of reference titles in the social sciences, art, or science, for example. Some 20 or 30 years ago, the void was filled by the general encyclopedias and by limited use of periodical articles. Why? Because there simply was nothing else available. Since World War II, the phenomenon of a country becoming more and more specialized, better educated, more affluent, and weary of general solutions and approaches to

---

[2] In the first edition of this text, many of the titles listed here were included in the section on handbooks and manuals. The present arrangement seems more logical, definitely more in keeping with trends in the teaching of reference.

topics has fostered the growth of the specialized, subject encyclopedia. This is not to say they did not exist before. It is to say, the number of subject encyclopedias has increased considerably, and has continued to grow since World War II.

The public, and too many libraries, has been slow to recognize this development. While once it was thought an investment in a general encyclopedia was the basic approach to ready-reference and search questions, this is no longer true.

The wise librarian would do better to invest in one or two encyclopedias and use the moneys normally employed for additional general encyclopedias in subject works. (Larger libraries, if for no other reason than to allow multiple use of encyclopedias, will continue to want all the major sets.) The moneys saved would be sufficient to purchase: (1) at least one of the more special field encyclopedias such as the *International Encyclopedia of the Social Sciences;* (2) a number of 1- and 2-volume encyclopedias in subject areas.

Which one of the subject sets should a library purchase? This depends upon:

1. The overall quality of the work. The same general principles are used to evaluate subject sets as to check general encyclopedias. In many ways, though, it is much simpler. As the subject work is limited in scope, it may be checked quickly for depth of coverage, timeliness, illustrations, authority, ease of reading, and indexing, if not by the librarian, by one or two subject experts in the community (i.e., the town, or school or academic community). The recommendations of the American Library Association helps. The basic subject sets are reviewed by the ALA Reference and Subscription Books Committee, just as are the general sets. The reviews tend to be a bit more prompt. In addition, the librarian is apt to find lengthy reviews in scholarly journals of the subject sets. For example, an encyclopedia of education, art, science, or philosophy will inevitably be reviewed in corresponding subject journals. If the librarian is uncertain which journal is apt to have such reviews, she should check the author's *Magazines for Libraries* or *Ulrich's International Periodical Directory* for likely journals in the subject category.
2. The usefulness of the set in the library. Even the best subject encyclopedia is of limited use when the community reference questions are not likely to be involved with its particular subject matter. An extreme example: in an all Protestant community, it is unlikely that the otherwise superior *Encyclopedia Judaica* would be of much use. Conversely, the librarian might remem-

ber that sometimes subjects are not called for in a library simply because the history of the library service indicates nothing is readily available. Individuals think answers to certain types of questions unobtainable or unsatisfactory. A library with a limited collection of material on art, for example, is not likely to receive many questions in this area. At this point, the librarian might have to decide whether the purchase of a good art encyclopedia might change matters—or simply be a waste of money. There is, to be sure, no totally satisfactory answer to the prospective usefulness of any reference work in a library; but when the librarian is investing several hundred dollars, it would obviously pay to consider possible use most carefully.

3. Beyond checking out the basic merits of the set, and attempting to guess how it might be applied in a particular reference situation, the librarian will want to compare it with previous efforts in the field. This may be done by checking standard bibliographies such as Winchell and Walford; and, of course, by checking it against what may already be in the library—not only with comparable encyclopedias, but with titles in the general collection. A number of the 1- and 2-volume subject encyclopedias may simply be repetitious of material found in other works; and, in a few cases, even of material found in a good general encyclopedia. (A worthwhile review will usually point this out, but sometimes even the best reviewers slip.)

Examples

Although this textbook in no way covers subject areas, in the case of specialized encyclopedias some effort is made to show the range of possibilities. This seems important because given a number of basic subject encyclopedias, a small to medium-sized library may be able to do considerably more reference work than with multiple general sets. Furthermore, the subject encyclopedias do offer a relatively time saving, even money saving, method for building reference subject areas which otherwise might be quite beyond the library.

This is not to say larger libraries will not find the subject encyclopedias equally valuable, particularly for a quick overview or for ready-reference work; but in terms of size of collections, number of personnel, and budget, the subject encyclopedia is particularly suited for smaller libraries. All this adds up to the considered opinion that smaller libraries which consider a subject set to be a luxury are really not facing the facts. When one sees a subject set recommended only for larger libraries, it is suggested the librarian might just take a second look to see whether it might be even more valuable in smaller, more limited reference collections.

The examples given are an effort to cover major, although certainly not all, subject areas. Where possible, or feasible, each subject area is divided into: multiple sets; 1-volume works; and, sometimes, paperbacks. Again, this is only representative. Librarians and students should carefully check out the possibilities not mentioned here in Winchell, Walford, and the *American Reference Books Annual,* and, of course, weekly or monthly reviews in the literature.

ART

Encyclopedia of World Art. New York: McGraw-Hill Book Company, 1959–1968, 15 vols., $597 ($497 schools and libraries).

McGraw-Hill Dictionary of Art. New York: McGraw-Hill Book Company, 1968, 5 vols., $115.

Praeger Encyclopedia of Art. Chicago: Encyclopaedia Britannica, Inc., 1971, 5 vols. ($150 to schools and libraries).

The *Encyclopedia of World Art* is the finest set available devoted entirely to the world of art. It includes art of all periods and has exhaustive studies of art forms, history, artists, and allied subject interests. Arranged alphabetically, there are many shorter articles which answer every conceivable question in the field.

An outstanding feature is the illustrations. At the end of each volume, there are 400 to 600 black-and-white and colored reproductions. They are nicely tied to the articles by suitable cross references and identification numbers and letters.

The writing is uniformly excellent, and the work can boast that almost every scholar in the field has made at least one, if not several, contributions to the set. There are detailed bibliographies at the end of the longer articles.

The last volume is the index which not only includes the articles in alphabetical order, but also, lists the close to 9,000 illustrations. This feature is useful, since there are very few indexes to paintings. The index includes a number of cross references which, unfortunately, are not always clear.

The plan of this work was conceived in Italy. There is both an Italian version *(Enciclopedia Universale Dell'arte)* and an English translation. There is some variation, primarily in what is emphasized, between the two editions.

The other encyclopedias in this area do not compare with the *Encyclopedia of World Art* because none are as ambitious in scope. Still, within limits, the Praeger work and the *McGraw-Hill Dictionary* are certainly worth considering.

The Praeger set is based on the French *Dictionnaire Universel de l'art et des Artistes,* first issued in 1967. It includes over 4,000 alphabetically arranged entries with well-integrated illustrations—about 1,000 per volume. There is a good index. The primary value of the encyclopedia is the readable articles on both individual artists and on various aspects of art. All periods and countries are adequately covered.

The McGraw-Hill entry offers a greater amount of material—some 15,000 entries with over 2,000 rather long articles. There are over 2,300 good-to-excellent illustrations. The difference between the two sets is primarily a difference of purpose. The Praeger volumes stress the discursive approach, while the McGraw-Hill set is literally a dictionary with emphasis on short, concise entries. It serves to define terms and to identify artistic works. It is helpful, too, for biographies. A major part of the 15,000 entries are biographical sketches. As a ready-reference aid, the McGraw-Hill entry would be preferable; but for longer background pieces the Praeger set would be a first choice. Hopefully, libraries will be able to buy both. If a choice is necessary, the Praeger would be better suited to junior and senior high school libraries, the McGraw-Hill to colleges and universities.

One-volume encyclopedias of art

Oxford Companion to Art. New York: Oxford University Press, 1970, 1,277 pp., $25.

Baigell, Matthew, *A History of American Painting.* New York: Praeger, 1971, 288 pp., $9.95.

Somewhat similar to the *McGraw-Hill Dictionary of Art,* the Oxford work differs in price, in illustrations (very few), and in length of entries (shorter). Still, it serves fairly much the same purpose in that it can be used as a handy source of definitions, biographies, and background information on various periods and types of art. There are bibliographies, but these are in a separate section and are generally inadequate. As a 1-volume encyclopedia or handbook, the Oxford title will serve well enough; but for most libraries, it should be augmented by one of the fuller encyclopedia sets.

For the more discursive approach to art, and more particularly American painters, the Baigell title is typical of many in this field. It represents a survey of more than 300 years of painting, includes 200 good illustrations, and has a useful index.

Paperback art encyclopedias are generally not too satisfactory because of the poor illustrations—necessary to keep costs within limits. Penguin Books does issue a number of handbook-dictionary-encyclopedia-type works which can be useful for ready reference, if not always for visual impact. Among the better ones: Murray, Peter, *A Dictionary of Art and Artists* (1971, 455 pp., $1.75); and Fleming, John, *The Penguin Dictionary of Architecture* (1969, 247 pp., $1.95). Both give short definitions and explanations of artistic movements, and include biographical sketches.

EDUCATION

The Encyclopedia of Education. New York: Free Press, The Macmillan Company, 1971, 10 vols., $395. (Also available as 10 vols. in 5 vols. at $199.)

Hopke, William E. (ed.), *The Encyclopedia of Careers and Vocational Guidance.* rev. ed. Chicago: J. G. Ferguson, 1972, 2 vols., $39.50.

In view of the number of bibliographies, indexes, and abstracting services, not to mention individual monographs and books given over to education, it is surprising that there is only one really basic encyclopedia in the field. And this comes rather late—a good 50 years after the classic Monroe's *Cyclopedia of Education.* The encyclopedia was almost worth the wait. It provides basic material in every area of education (biographies excepted).

The encyclopedia has more than 1,000 articles which examine the history, theory, and philosophy of education. All are written by subject experts and are not only authoritative but clear and literate—no mean achievement in this field. There are usually detailed bibliographies which will assist any library in building collections.

While most emphasis is on American education, and more particularly American curriculum, there are comparative articles which take in the world scene. There is an excellent index which gives it a ready-reference value.

At a considerably less-ambitious level, the Hopke encyclopedia is primarily a source of basic vocational information for young adults and their advisors. The first volume includes background articles and then goes on, as does the whole of the second volume, to opportunities in over 600 occupations. The information is concise, yet accurate—it not only includes the advantages of certain careers, but points out their disadvantages. *See also, Occupational Outlook Handbook.*

HISTORY

The New Cambridge Modern History. New York: Cambridge University Press, 1957–1970, 13 vols., $225.

Adams, James T. (ed.), *Dictionary of American History.* New York: Charles Scribner's Sons, 1940–1963, 6 vols. and index, $120.

Makers of America. Chicago: Encyclopaedia Britannica, Inc., 1971, 10 vols., ($79.50 to schools and libraries).

Annals of America. Chicago: Encyclopaedia Britannica, Inc., 1969, 20 vols. and supplements, $164.

Adler, Mortimer J. (ed.), *The Negro in American History.* Chicago: Encyclopaedia Britannica Education Corporation, 1969, 3 vols., $24.50.

Commager, Henry S., *Documents of American History.* 9th ed. New York: Appleton-Century-Crofts, Inc., 1973.

Worldmark Encyclopedia of the Nations. 4th ed. New York: Worldmark Press and Harper & Row Publishers, Incorporated, 1971, 5 vols., $69.95.

The Cambridge University Press histories are widely known and respected. No medium-to-large library can afford not to have one of these sets, although the most frequently used by the average reader will be the work devoted to modern history. This begins with the Renaissance and closes shortly after World War II. Each volume is edited by a scholar of the period and individual articles are by various experts.

Most of the series can be read as straight history, although it is obviously useful as a reference aid. The revised modern history has been criticized for a number of failures, from too much emphasis on political history to a lack of bibliographies. The latter fault is remedied in part by a separate bibliographical volume, *A Bibliography of Modern History* (New York: Cambridge University Press, 1968). Of particular value is the atlas which can be purchased separately. All the historical maps are clear and excellent for detail.

In addition to modern history, the same press has issued: *Cambridge Ancient History, Cambridge Economic History of Europe, Cambridge History of the Bible, Cambridge Medieval History,* and a number of other multiple-volume sets which are standard reference aids in larger research libraries. All enjoy a scholarly reputation; and while each can be criticized for this or that, they are basic and among the most authoritative in the field.

There is nothing quite like the Cambridge volumes for American history. Probably the closest thing is the *American Nation* series issued in 28 volumes from 1904 to 1918 by Harper. The same publisher began a similar series in 1954, but this has not proven to be up to the quality of the original.

The standard overview of American history for the layman and the expert is the *Dictionary of American History* which must be supplemented by later works as it only carries the study to the 1950s. The title derives from the fact that the vast majority of articles are brief, but this is more a matter of editing than depth of scope. Actually, major periods are simply broken down into much smaller parts than normally found in an encyclopedia and then treated as separate, specific entries. This is ideal for reference work and tends to make the index a useful, albeit redundant tool. Cross references tie similar articles together.

A supplemental volume was issued in 1961, which brings the story up through 1960. A 1-volume abridgment was achieved by dropping a number of articles and virtually eliminating all the bibliographies. This is a handy item for the home, but in no way can replace the full set.

A useful companion to the *Dictionary,* and a reference work that can stand on its own, is: *Album of American History,* edited by James T. Adams (New York: Charles Scribner's Sons, rev. ed., 1969, 6 vols.). Using some 6,000 contemporary drawings and cartoons, the editor gives a *Life* approach to American history up through 1968. Fortunately, there is an excellent index which makes it possible to find material both by subject and by event or individual.

The purpose of the Britannica *Makers of America* is to show the contribution of ethnic pluralism to the American scene. In this sense, it is considerably narrower in scope than other titles listed here; but, at the same time, it performs a valuable service. Each volume has introductory material, and there is a long essay in the initial volume which discusses the melting pot and the cultural pluralism concepts. Arranged chronologically, the set moves from 1536 through 1970. It is primarily made up of original contemporary documents (e.g., newspaper stories, letters, diaries) quoted in part or in full. Each item is fully illustrated. The final volume contains various subject indexes which makes it relatively easy to locate specific material. The depth of coverage and scholarship is somewhat superficial, but the set will be useful for public and school libraries.

At a more sophisticated and more general level, the same firm's *Annals of America* would probably be a first choice in college and university libraries. The 20-volume set is a chronological record of American life from 1492 to 1968 and comprises more than 2,200 original documents by some 1,200 authors. Organized chronologically, the set boasts over 5,000 illustrations with an alphabetical index for ready-reference work. The work follows the same general pattern of the familiar 54-volume *Great Books of the Western World.* The publisher plans to keep the volumes up to date with supplements.

A more limited collection is *The Negro in American History.* Each of the three volumes contains about 100 selections which tell the story of the black in America from 1493 to 1968. The entries are preceded by brief headnotes and there are introductory essays for each of the main sections. The publisher fails to make much of the fact that most of the documents are taken directly from his *Annals of America*—and only about one-fifth are new to the three-volume work. Despite the duplication, the set belongs in almost every library; and certainly in any library serving blacks—whether that be a high school; public, or college or university library.

It will be noted that all of these works, e.g., *Album of American History* and *Makers of America*, are basically collections or anthologies of documents, pictures, and the like. They all have necessary introductory and connective editorial material, but none is on the same order as a well-constructed, original encyclopedia.

The best known work in this field, which has undergone numerous updatings and revisions, is the Commager collection of American documents. Each of the documents is prefaced by short explanatory notes; and it has the advantage over the sets of being more selective, in a single volume, and generally more useful in smaller library reference situations.

The *Worldmark Encyclopedia* is closer to a handbook than an encyclopedia or a history of any particular nation or area. It is cited here to remind students that modern historical events and related subject areas are usually found in handbooks and yearbooks. Unlike the other sets, it is primarily for the high school student and the layman. Revised periodically, it has been criticized as being somewhat simplistic and not always up to date. Still, the brief treatment is useful in schools; and the timeliness, where necessary, can be checked against other works.

As the title indicates, the scope of this work is international. It has one outstanding feature—rather than considering countries in general fashion, it approaches all of them via some 50 subjects and topics. Thus, when the student wants an overall view of law, religion, language, topography, he finds it easy to compare one country with another.

The set is particularly helpful for comparison and for newer countries which are not so fully treated in the general encyclopedias. There are bibliographies for each of the nations, a special section on the United Nations, and some biographical material.

Much of the material may be found in a regular encyclopedia, so why bother? This is an example of a case where it is worth the bother because a good editor and a publisher decided a new approach to information was needed. The approach, not to mention the *relative* recency of materials, makes it well worth considering, especially for a ready-reference situation.

LITERATURE AND DRAMA

Encyclopedia of World Literature in the 20th Century. New York: Frederick Ungar Publishing Co., 1967–1971, 3 vols., $98.

McGraw-Hill Encyclopedia of World Drama. New York: McGraw-Hill Book Company, 1972, 4 vols., $120.

Cambridge History of English Literature. New York: Cambridge University Press, 1907 to 1932, 15 vols., $105.

Literature and World Civilization. ed. by David Daiches and Anthony Thorley. London: Aldus, 1972, 6 vols. in progress, $20 each volume.

A number of subject encyclopedias represent translations into English from other languages. When this is the case, the publisher should clearly state what, if any, updating has been done; and what, if any, revisions have been made in view of a different audience. In the *Encyclopedia of World Literature,* both provisions have been met. The encyclopedia represents a translation of the German *Lexikon der Weltliteratur im 20 Jahrhundert* (Freiberg: Herder, 1960–1961, 2 vols.). Published some 10 years before the translated version, the original work features articles on authors, national literature, literary forms, and the like. Most emphasis was on European writing and writers. With the 3-volume translated version, the material was updated and expanded to include some 1,300 articles of various length. About 50 percent of the revised work is new . . . particularly in the last volume which carries literature up to 1970.

Another useful general set is the 3-volume *Cassell's Encyclopedia of Literature* (London: Cassell & Co., Ltd.) which in 1973 was undergoing a major revision from the 2-volume 1953 edition. This is somewhat similar in approach to the German-based title; it differs though in that there are considerably more, although briefer, entries of a biographical nature. The library with *Cassell's* and the *Encyclopedia of World Literature* would be more than adequately served for both relatively up-to-date and retrospective materials. Libraries with smaller budgets and lesser research needs will be able to get by with material found in general encyclopedias and in the numerous, less expensive 1-volume works.

The publisher of the drama encyclopedia rightfully claims it "is the most comprehensive reference work ever published on drama as literature." The four volumes cover all types of drama, national theatre, and playwrights. It is particularly useful for the synopses of plays and for the detailed biographies which cover about 300 major dramatists. The scope is international and the set is geared for both the layman and the expert. Of particular use for ready reference is the index of plays which lists some 30,000 entries.

The *Cambridge History of English Literature* is the basic set in its field. It certainly is the most extensive. The first volume opens with the earliest of literature and closes with cycles of romances. The twelfth and fourteenth volumes carry the history through the nineteenth century and the fifteenth volume is an extensive index. Each chapter is written by an expert and ends with an extensive bibliography.

For libraries who can neither afford nor find the larger set, the *Con-*

cise *Cambridge History of English Literature* (New York: Cambridge University Press, 1969, 976 pp.) is helpful. Now in its third edition—it is revised about every 10 years—the volume represents a trustworthy abridgment of the original set.

The bibliographies were published (1940–1957) separately but are now largely superceded by *The New Cambridge Bibliography of English Literature* (New York: Cambridge University Press, 1970 in progress, 5 vols., $49.50 each volume). The five-volume work contains about 25 to 30 percent more material than the original work; but the scope remains the same: it attempts to list and classify both primary and secondary materials in English studies, i.e., as related to the British Isles. One essential difference: with the fourth volume, the bibliography for the first time is extended into the twentieth century, i.e., volume 4 covers 1900–1950. Each volume has its own index, but the fifth has a cumulated index for the set. The bibliography is considered by almost everyone the basic one in its field and, as such, should be found in all larger libraries.

The purpose of the *Literature and Western Civilization* set is to provide a survey—primarily for well-educated laymen—of Western culture as reflected in the literature. Each of the volumes includes various essays by scholars and experts on facets of the arts and the civilizations which produced them, e.g., Lattimore on "Legend in Greek Tragedy," and Dover on "Classical Greek Oratory." Eventually there is to be an index volume. In the meantime, as with many sets of this type, it may be enjoyed for itself as good reading and will serve to augment such reference works as the *Cambridge Ancient History* and the various other Cambridge Histories of the world.

Probably no other field offers so many diverse and excellent multiple-set and single-volume encyclopedias. Each serves a different purpose, and for larger libraries most can be recommended. Still, given an adequate set of general encyclopedias and two or three of the more moderately priced literature sets, most libraries will have enough materials for ready-reference and search questions. Those seeking broader coverage are referred to such works as *The Oxford History of English Literature* (Oxford: Clarendon Press, 1945–1963, 12 vols.). This set begins with Chaucer and goes up through the twentieth century.

MUSIC

Grove's Dictionary of Music and Musicians. 5th ed. New York: St. Martin's Press, Inc., 1954, 9 vols. and supplement, 1961, $60.

Although by now dated, and badly in need of a new edition, the standard multiset encyclopedia of music is unquestionably Grove's.

(Note: The publisher says a new edition is planned for sometime in the mid 1970s.) It is particularly useful for scholarly articles on various schools, musicians, and composers—at least prior to the early 1950s. Originally published in 1878 to 1889, it retains a bit of its conservative, Victorian attitudes and is weak on trends in modern music. As such, it is often the butt of criticism by more liberal scholars.

Given this fault, it is customary then to point out that it has an English bias, primarily because Sir George Grove wrote many of the longer entries himself. This may be, but it will not bother anyone except the scholar. For most purposes, it serves well enough to answer questions concerning every conceivable aspect of traditional music.

Arrangement is alphabetical; and there is no index, but an abundance of cross references. One disturbing lack is any reference to opera plots, although there is enough material on the composers and the theory of opera.

There are a number of excellent, scholarly sets similar to Grove in foreign languages, e.g., *Encyclopedie de la Musique* (1958–61), *Die Musik in Geschichte und Gegenwart* (1948–1968), and *La Musica* (1966 in progress). A brief critical summary of the latter set, with reference to Grove, is given in the December 24, 1971 *Times Literary Supplement* (p. 1,609).

One volume references on music

Scholes, Percy A., *The Oxford Companion to Music*. 10th rev. ed. New York: Oxford University Press, 1970, 1,189 pp., $25.

Fuld, James J., *The Book of World Famous Music*. New York: Crown Publishers, Inc., 1971, 688 pp., $15.

There are numerous 1-volume music encyclopedias, and these two are representative of the group. Probably the best known is the Scholes entry which has undergone many editions and revisions. It follows the usual Oxford Companion format and style, with a dictionary approach to entries. However, as more than one critic points out, the work is much dated and extremely erratic in its presentation of material. Despite its rather long life, it is far from a first choice for any reference library—it is noted here as much to warn off the librarian, as anything else. This, by the way, is an excellent example of a title which has gained deserved fame on its past performance but is now long past retirement.

Considerably narrower in scope, but equally more satisfying for reference purposes, the Fuld volume gives full information on some 1,200 songs and compositions. It is an excellent reference source for little known facts about all types of music from classical to popular songs. The first line of each piece is given and there is complete information on its history. Fuld is, also, the author of *The Book of World-Famous Music* (New York: Crown Publishers, Inc., 1970, 604 pp., $15) which serves as a companion piece to his other work. Thanks to a full index, it can be used for many reference queries concerning such topics as compositions, composers, operas, and ballets.

Somehow, the field tends to attract works primarily geared for popular consumption rather than for reference work; e.g., David Ewen's *Complete Book of the American Musical Theatre* (New York: Holt, Rinehart and Winston, Inc., 1970, 800 pp., $15) is a pleasant enough study of the genre, but the arrangement and presentation makes it difficult, if not impossible, for reference work. Needless to say, librarians should pay careful attention to reviews, and ultimately to the books themselves, before purchasing musical enyclcopedias.

Among the better paperback entries is a work which is dated, yet still useful: Westrup, J. A., *The New College Encyclopedia of Music* (New York: W. W. Norton & Company, Inc., 1960, 739 pp., $3.95). Based on an English work, this gives brief definitions and history of music and musical terms. There are a number of biographies, and some of the entries run as long as a page. The arrangement and style make it suitable for reference work in almost any type of library. More up to date is Jacobs, Arthur, *A New Dictionary of Music* (Baltimore: Penguin Books, Inc., 1970, 424 pp., $1.75). This includes, in dictionary form, basic information on composers, scores, terms, and performers. While not as complete as Westrup, it is equally good.

RELIGION AND PHILOSOPHY

New Catholic Encyclopedia. New York: McGraw-Hill Book Company, 1967, 15 vols., $550 ($450 schools and libraries).

Encyclopaedia Judaica. New York: Crowell Collier and Macmillan, Inc., 1972, 16 vols., $500.

Encyclopedia of Philosophy. New York: Crowell Collier and Macmillan, Inc., 1967, 8 vols., $219.50.

When the librarian considers religious encyclopedias, it is necessary to emphasize that most of them, and more particularly the two listed here, are considerably broader in scope and purpose than their titles might suggest. They all provide a vast amount of accurate, generally unbiased information in related fields from philosophy to political science and the social sciences. Furthermore, they offer rather straightforward, scholarly articles on other world religions.

The situation was not always this clear-cut. Earlier efforts were much less ecumenical, tended to stress narrow religious lines of thought, and were more supportive of theology and dogma than necessarily of scholarship. For the most part, this has changed and, given enough basic information on religious oriented encyclopedias, the librarian runs little or no risk of purchasing a bad set.

By now, the *New Catholic Encyclopedia* is well enough known to be generally accepted in most libraries, and certainly in the majority of Catholic school libraries from high school through the university. Its 17,000 articles by close to 5,000 scholars (many of whom have no affiliation with the church) is a model of objectivity. The set is quite obviously strongest in the areas of religion, theology, and philosophy; but in literature and history it compares favorably to more general encyclopedias. In an average reference collection, its primary value would be for the philosophy and comparative religious articles, as well as for many biographical pieces not often found elsewhere. Furthermore, it has excellent illustrations, bibliographies, and a fine index.

Encyclopaedia Judaica is noteworthy as being the first Jewish encyclopedia of major proportions to be published in the past 100 years.[3] It has one peculiarity—the first, not the last, volume serves as the index. There are over 25,000 articles which cover close to 6,000 years of Jewish history. Unlike the Catholic set, it makes no effort to deal in non-Jewish subject areas; and its primary value is for the biographical material and the historical scholarship which points up the role Jews have played in world civilization. Nevertheless, the subject matter is diverse enough, ranging from articles on art, science, mysticism, and the Bible to modern Yiddish literature. There are over 8,000 illustrations with hundreds of maps and charts. The set represents a major contribution to Jewish history and culture. (Annual yearbooks are planned.)

In this same area, there is a somewhat more modest, less expensive set. This is the *Encyclopedia of Zionism and Israel* (New York: McGraw-Hill Book Company, 1971, 2 vols., $39.50). It is primarily limited to the Zionist movement but has over 3,000 well-written articles on every aspect of Zionism from cultural customs to architecture. And while much of the material is limited to Israel, there are well-documented pieces on interrelations between major countries and the Zionist movement. It is obviously more limited than the *Encyclopaedia Judaica,* but within its scope, an excellent choice.

Encyclopedia of Philosophy is another basic set in the field, and by now is in most medium to large American libraries. There are over 1,450

---

[3] "Encyclopaedia Judaica," *Publishers' Weekly,* February 28, 1972, pp. 46+. A history of the set.

articles by 500 contributors, and the style and the approach is primarily for the educated layman rather than the expert. Some $800,000 went into the encyclopedia, an impressive amount considering that when it was started in 1957 the editor had in mind a 3-volume work. Arrangement is alphabetical, and there is a comprehensive index in the last volume. One useful feature is the bibliographies. Many of these are annotated and graded. The editor freely admits that because this is the first major encyclopedia of philosophy in English, it represents many of his own biases. For example, John Dewey and A. N. Whitehead have been downgraded, while St. Augustine and Voltaire have received more space than might be expected.

Another standard, although much dated set, in this area is James Hastings' *Encyclopedia of Religion and Ethics* (New York: Charles Scribner's Sons 1961, 13 vols., $270; $245 schools and libraries). First published between 1908 and 1926, it represents all aspects of religion and ethics. The aim of the 886 scholar contributors was to give a universal overview of religion and philosophy. The set is now particularly useful for the comparative historical approaches to the world religions and can be used when augmented by one or more of the above encyclopedias. The 757 page index is a model of its kind.

SCIENCE

McGraw-Hill Encyclopedia of Science and Technology. 3d ed. New York: McGraw-Hill Book Company, 1971, 15 vols., $360 ($295 schools and libraries).

McGraw-Hill Yearbook of Science and Technology. New York: McGraw-Hill Book Company, approximately 500 pp., $27.50 ($15.90 to owners of main set).

Scientific American Resource Library. San Francisco: W. H. Freeman and Company, 1969–1971, 15 vols., $150.

In the field of science, the best all-around general encyclopedia is the McGraw-Hill entry. "No other multi-volume English language science encyclopedia has attained this level of excellence." (*Booklist,* December 15, 1971, p. 339.) The set is periodically revised and kept updated via the *Yearbook.* There are some 7,600 articles which move from broad survey types to specific shorter entries for specialized areas. Each volume is nicely illustrated, and there are numerous graphs and charts.

The style of writing is unusually clear, and the set may be used both by young adults (i.e., high school students) and by experts who may be seeking an overview of a field they know little about. Thanks to the arrangement and the index, it is particularly useful to the librarian for ready-reference questions, especially those which call for brief definitions of terms which may be foreign to the librarian or the user.

The *Scientific American* entry is not an encyclopedia, but a collection of previously published articles from the scientific magazine. The basic anthology approach is divided into earth science, life sciences, social sciences, psychology, and the physical sciences. Each volume has its own author and topic index, and the subject index often refers to related articles in other volumes. The set is best used for augmenting class work at the high school and college level. It is of some value as a reference aid, but the arrangement precludes the ease of use of the McGraw-Hill title. The publishers, from time to time, plan to bring out additional volumes of reprints. (As the magazine is indexed in several basic indexes, and as most libraries subscribe, the same articles are now available in libraries.)

SOCIAL SCIENCES

International Encyclopedia of the Social Sciences. New York: Crowell Collier and Macmillan, Inc., 1968, 17 vols., $495.

This is unquestionably the single-subject encyclopedia of most use and greatest interest in libraries. Its coverage includes subjects most often central to reference questions and, more particularly, those dealing with a limited amount of research, or requiring an unbiased overview of a given area. Some 1,500 scholars from 30 countries have contributed lengthy, comparative, analytical articles on all aspects of the social sciences, e.g., anthropology, economics, geography, history, law, political science, psychology, sociology, and statistics. In addition to articles on various subject matter, the set includes some 600 biographies.

The set is arranged alphabetically, and there are copious cross references and a detailed index. All of this makes it extremely easy to use for reference work. Of particular interest is the arrangement of related articles under a single heading, e.g., there are 12 contributions under the heading "Learning"; and for "Leadership," related articles on psychological aspects, sociological aspects, and political aspects are included in a group.

While this is an entirely new work, it is based upon the equally famous *Encyclopedia of the Social Sciences* (New York: Crowell Collier and Macmillan, Inc., 1937, 8 vols.) which enjoyed continuous use for some 40 years in American libraries. It is still valuable for retrospective, historical material and, more particularly, for over 4,000 biographies. In fact, the *International* is not meant to supplement, only to complement its predecessor. Hopefully, libraries will have both sets.

SUGGESTED READING

"An Encyclopedia out of Zion" (Encyclopaedia Judaica), *Times Literary Supplement,* March 23, 1973, pp. 309 +. A lengthy review of a basic set which is useful for points given on evaluation.

Einbinder, Harvey, "The International Encyclopedia of the Social Sciences," *Library Journal,* April 15, 1969, p. 1,592. The critic of *Encyclopaedia Britannica* points up the advantages (and some disadvantages) of a subject work over a general encyclopedia.

Sills, E., "Editing a Scientific Encyclopedia," *Science,* March 14, 1969, p. 1,169. A careful explanation of the problems of putting together a well-organized and meaningful subject encyclopedia.

Smith, F. Seymour, "Subject Dictionaries and Encyclopedias," *British Book News,* October, November, December 1968, pp. 723, 797, 875. A series of annotated titles. Of some help for pointing out the parameters of the field in terms of titles cited.

"The Encyclopedia of Library and Information Science," *Wilson Library Bulletin,* March 1973, pp. 598 +. A pro and con argument about the subject encyclopedia for library science—useful because of some interesting hints on how to evaluate a subject set.

CHAPTER SEVEN
GENERAL ALMANACS, YEARBOOKS, HANDBOOKS, AND CURRENT SOURCES AND STATISTICS

When someone has a ready-reference, quick fact type of question, the whole library and its resources may be needed to find a particular answer. Still, for the vast majority of queries such as What is the population of X? What is the cost of living in Y? and How high is P? there are a group of reference aids which are prepared especially for rapidly finding such answers. These include almanacs, yearbooks, handbooks, manuals, and directories. Some of these forms are of a general nature, but the majority are published in specific subject fields or areas of interest. Obviously, ready reference is not limited to these titles—encyclopedias, dictionaries, biographical and geographical sources are used, too—but by their very purpose and scope, they are often shortcuts to quick answers.

There are problems not generally associated with the other forms. The first is that many of these titles simply do not fit into a neat form, or category. As indicated in the discussion of subject encyclopedias, the categorization of title with form sometimes may be more a fiction than a reality.

For the beginning reference librarian, this very lack of categorization makes it somewhat difficult to isolate and discuss a form which may be more in the mind of the textbook writer than in active duty in a library. The titles, as Fetros rightfully claims, "are too often derived from traditional standardized lists which are not flexible enough to reflect changes in public interest and the newer titles being published."[1]

The point seems particularly important here; because when considering the various almanacs, handbooks, directories, and such (of which there are literally hundreds), there is little of a unifying element, little of the overriding form which governs most other types of reference materials. A manual may be a handbook, an almanac more of an encyclopedia, and a directory a first-class biographical guide. Technically, of course, it is one or the other; but in daily operations, the librarian is not about to begin such a classification scheme when faced with a pressing question. She can only deal in general parameters. And, yet, the duplication, the multi-information aspects of almost all of these titles, works to usually help her find an answer in almost any title, within the general form, she chooses.

Another problem is that all of these forms tend to duplicate, at least in part, much of the basic information found in other forms. For example, the contents of the four or five general almanacs include not only similar material, but much of the same data found in encyclopedias, biographical aids, geographical sources, and even dictionaries and bibliographical aids. Conversely, much of the information in any general encyclopedia may be duplicated in an almanac, handbook, manual, and sometimes in a directory.

It has often been said that the majority of the ready-reference questions in a library may be answered with an encyclopedia, an almanac, *Subject Guide to Books in Print,* and a good biographical source—in fact a handful of titles. There is some truth to this assumption. Duplication of material is so widespread that the librarian soon learns it is pointless to search many titles, when one or two will do not only for questions A and B but also for questions C through Z.

The duplication phenomenon explains the small collection of reference books found near every reference desk in almost every library. This is a core of perhaps 75 to 100 titles wherein most answers are found. Beyond that core collection, though, may stretch shelves and shelves of other reference titles. And why? Because just as the librarian is certain all answers are in her basic collection, along comes a query that requires going to the larger group of titles—or even beyond that to the general collection or to another library. Also, it is important to emphasize that the discussion is primarily concerned with ready-reference aids, not with equally important reference titles which are employed for more detailed search and research-type queries.

The duplication factor, or the multireference character, of many reference titles is important to grasp. In the rush to learn as much as

[1] John G. Fetros, "Useful But Little Known Reference Tools," *RQ,* Fall 1970, p. 22.

possible about forms and individual titles, the beginner may sometimes feel a surge of frustration and despair. The truth is that the vast multiplicity of information in various titles has a positive element, particularly for the beginner. Given all of these sources and the various choices, the librarian may assume there is an answer to almost any ready-reference question—not in one, but in several sources. Lacking knowledge of, or access to, X or Y almanac or handbook, she is just as likely to find the answer in P encyclopedia or R biographical aid.

Why all this duplication? Primarily because nothing breeds success in publishing like success. First there was one almanac. It sold well. Next there was a third—and so on and so on. As specific titles and forms become increasingly popular (and lucrative), they tend to spawn similar titles by other publishers. Works tend to divide and subdivide as long as the market (library and the public alike) continues to support such specialization and division. This is not to say each new title is a carbon copy of the last. It is not, but there is always the duplication, multi-information factor present. This is the factor, after all, which guaranteed the success of Y title, and it should be included and modified in P title. Sometimes the modification of a new title or a version of a form is a distinct improvement—other times it is less than a happy compromise with quality.

Another major aspect of so much duplication concerns the reference budget. Is it really necessary to buy all the titles when they may duplicate much of the same material? Yes and no—yes, if the budget is large enough to afford the luxury; no, if the budget is so small that it is pinched when an extra encyclopedia must be purchased. In any case, the wise librarian will carefully check the title or the reviews or both before purchase.[2]

Definitions

Almanac In today's library, an almanac is a compendium of useful data and statistics relating to countries, personalities, events, subjects, and the like. It may be thought of as a type of specific-entry encyclopedia stripped of adjectives and adverbs and limited to the skeleton of information.

As the majority of special subject almanacs are published on an annual or biannual schedule, they are sometimes called yearbooks and annuals. Traditionally, the almanac per se tended to be general in na-

---

[2] The enormity of duplication in reference works and some suggestions how to solve the problem in terms of purchase is given by Carl White in his excellent article: "How to Avoid Duplicated Information," *RQ*, Winter 1970, pp. 127 + . This should be required reading for every reference librarian who must determine what to buy or reject.

ture; the yearbook and annual more specific, i.e., limited to a given area or subject. No more. There are now subject almanacs and encyclopedia yearbooks which are as broad in their coverage as the general almanac.

Yearbook/Annual   A yearbook is an annual compendium of data and statistics. An almanac will inevitably cover material of the previous year, too. The essential difference is that the almanac will also include considerably retrospective material—material which may or may not be in the average yearbook. The yearbook's primary purpose is to record the year's activities by country, subject, or specialized area. There are, to be sure, general yearbooks and, most notably, the yearbooks issued by encyclopedia companies. Still, in ready-reference work, the most often used type is usually confined to special areas of interest.

Directory   The *A.L.A. Glossary of Library Terms* defines a directory as "a list of persons or organizations, systematically arranged, usually in alphabetical or classed order, giving addresses, affiliations, etc., for individuals, and address, officers, functions and similar data for organizations."

The definition is clear enough for a directory in its "pure" form; but aside from directory-type information found in biographical sources, it should be reiterated that many other ready-reference tools have sections devoted to directory information. Yearbooks and almanacs inevitably include vast amounts of directory-type material. For example, the *World Almanac* has information on art galleries, museums, historic sites, and an entire section devoted to "Associations and Societies" which gives the address, number of members, and names of chief executives. The second section of *The Bowker Annual of Library and Book Trade Information* presents directory-type information about associations.

Handbooks and Manuals   The terms "manual" and "handbook" are often used synonymously, particularly by the *A.L.A. Glossary of Library Terms* which defines a handbook as "a small reference book; a manual." A manual normally tends to be equated with how-to-do-it, whether it be preparing a dinner or repairing an automobile. As a consequence, many are found in the general collection or, in some libraries, where use is constant (as for works on etiquette); the books may be duplicated in the reference collection.

A handbook more likely is a miscellaneous group of facts centered around one central theme or subject area. The term literally comes from the German *Handbuch,* i.e., a book which could be held in the hand comfortably. The form developed in the nineteenth century, particularly with the nouveau riche and the lesser educated who sought quick, reliable information on an art, occupation, or other form of study. Publishers tended to issue them as "How-to" type works for breaking social barriers. By the twentieth century, the term became more general and is now used in all areas of human endeavor from the sciences to the humanities, and more often by people seeking information rather than instant status.

ALMANACS AND YEARBOOKS

Although almanacs and yearbooks tend to be distinctive types or forms of reference work, they are closely enough related both in terms of use and scope to be treated here as a single class of ready-reference aid. Aside from the general almanac, e.g., *World Almanac,* and the general yearbook, e.g., *Britannica Book of the Year,* the subject almanac and yearbook tend to be similar and often are used for much the same purpose in a reference situation.

PURPOSE

Recency   Regardless of form and presentation, the user turns to a yearbook or an almanac for relatively recent information on a subject or personality. The purpose of many of these works is to update standard texts which may be issued or totally revised only infrequently. An encyclopedia yearbook, for example, is a compromise, even an excuse for not rewriting major articles in the encyclopedia each year.

Brief facts   Where a single statistic or a fact is required, normally without benefit of explanation, the almanac serves a useful purpose. A yearbook will be good if the reader wishes a limited amount of background information on a recent development or seeks a fact not found in a standard almanac.

Trends   With their concern with recency, almanacs and yearbooks either directly or by implication indicate trends in the development or, if you will, the regression of man. Obvious scientific advances are chronicled, as are the events, persons, and places of importance over the previous year. One reason for maintaining a run of certain almanacs and yearbooks is to indicate such trends. For example, in the 1908 *World Almanac,* there were some 22 pages devoted to railroads. In the 1973 issue, only 3, while television performers rated close to 10 pages. The obvious shift in interest of Americans over the past 50 years is reflected in collections of yearbooks and almanacs. More important for the historian, many of these early works are convenient sources of statistical information otherwise lost.

Informal index Most of the reliable yearbooks and almanacs cite sources of information and, as such, can be used as informal indexes. For example, a patron interested in retail sales will find general information in any good almanac or yearbook. These in turn will cite sources such as *Fortune, Business Week,* or *Moody's Industrials* which will provide additional keys to information. Specific citations to government sources of statistics may quickly guide the reader to primary material otherwise difficult to locate.

Directory and biographical information Many yearbooks and almanacs include material normally found in a directory. For example, a yearbook in a special field may well include the names of the principal leaders in that field with addresses and perhaps short biographical sketches. The *World Almanac,* among others, lists associations and societies, with addresses.

Browsing Crammend into the odd corners of almost any yearbook or almanac are masses of unrelated, frequently fascinating bits of information. The true lover of facts, and America is a country of such lovers, delights simply in thumbing through many of these works. From the point of view of the dedicated reference librarian, this purpose may seem inconsequential; but it is downright fascinating for any observer of the passing social scene. The reference librarian with a good memory will discover many outstanding items in yearbooks and almanacs that may serve a useful purpose on some distant day at the reference desk. Parenthetically, it is hoped no librarian will fall victim to the "fact mania" which serves to amaze at parties, but to bore in conversation.

General Almanacs

Information Please Almanac. New York: Simon & Schuster, Inc., 1947 to date, paperback, $2.95.

   The Official Associated Press Almanac (formerly called *The New York Times Encyclopedic Almanac*). Chicago: Quadrangle Books, Inc., 1969 to date, paperback, $3.95.[3]

   Reader's Digest Almanac. New York: Funk & Wagnalls, Company, 1966 to date, paperback, $3.95.

   Whitaker's Almanack. Whitaker' New York: British Book Center, 1869 to date, $7.95.

---

[3] Note: also issued as *Family Almanac,* a publication of *Family Circle* magazine, a subsidiary of *The New York Times.* The *Family Almanac* is a somewhat revised, reduced edition which differs in price ($2.70) and inclusion of capsule television movie reviews. It is not needed in libraries which have the regular *New York Times Almanac.*

The World Almanac and Book of Facts. Garden City, New York: Newspaper Enterprise Association and Doubleday & Company, Inc., 1868 to date, paperback, $4.95.

Negro Almanac. 2d ed. New York: Bellwether Company, 1971, 1,110 pp., $27.95.

In the beginning, the almanac was a book which was arranged by months, weeks, and days with pertinent information concerning the rising and setting of the moon, times of low and high tides, a calendar of holy days, and some bits of miscellaneous information. This type dates back to some 1,200 years before Christ and was primarily employed by farmers and then in connection with holy days.

During the Middle Ages, the horae, psalters, and missals were derived in part from almanacs. Shifting from religion to astronomy and astrology, then to medicine, and finally to scraps of general information, the almanac underwent many changes from the Middle Ages down through the eighteenth century. In America, by far the most famous work of this type was Benjamin Franklin's *Poor Richard's Almanack* first published in 1732. The *Old Farmer's Almanac,* based on *Poor Richard,* has been published annually in this country since 1792. Between traditional yellow covers, the almanac includes anecdotes and pleasantries, historical dates, zodiac signs, planting tables, puzzles, recipes, and even poetry. The present editor, Robb Sagendorph, claims that while the almanac is primarily for farmers, this now includes everyone who has a garden, livestock, or even a lawn. Patent medicine companies still are fond of the almanac; and one almanac familiar to those in the South is the *Ladies' Birthday Almanac,* issued by the Chattanooga Medicine Company. As one reader explained: "I wouldn's think of doing a thing without first consulting my almanac." How useful this type of reference work is in a library may be questionable, but a study of almanacs is a microcosm of American culture.

As for the more accepted type of almanac, the pattern was first established by the *American Almanac and Repository of Useful Knowledge* published in Boston from 1830 to 1861. Subsequent almanacs were issued by newspapers and rapidly developed into compendiums of useful data and statistics on international, national, state, and local affairs.

All the titles listed here are basic, general almanacs which are to be found in most American libraries. If an order of general use and importance was to be given, they might be ranked as follows: (1) *World Almanac;* (2) *Information Please Almanac; (3) Associated Press Almanac* (4) *Negro Almanac* (which might be a second in some libraries); (5) *Whitaker's Almanac;* and (6) *Reader's Digest Almanac.* The order of preference is based upon familiarity (probably no other reference work is better known or more used in American libraries than the *World Almanac*), general usefulness, and dependability.

With the exceptions of *Whitaker*, all are American based and are primarily concerned with data of interest to American readers. In varying degree, they all tend to cover the same basic subject matters; and while there is an appreciable degree of duplication, the low cost makes it possible to have at least two or three at the reference desk. As the various almanacs cover all aspects of the current scene from education and religion to politics and the arts, they inevitably differ enough in what is added or deleted to make it impossible to always rate one better than the other. The best one is the one which answers the one specific question. Today that may be the *World Almanac*, tomorrow *Whitaker's*. In terms of searching, though, it is usually preferable to begin with the *World* and work through the order of preference stated in the previous paragraph.

The *World Almanac* was first issued by the *World*, a New York newspaper, in 1868.[4] For seven years, publication stopped until Joseph Pulitzer revived the work in 1885. The 1966 edition was erroneously listed as the eighty-first, but the mistake was corrected in 1967 when the book celebrated its centennial. *Whitaker's* is named after the founder of the publishing firm; it differs little in makeup, but certainly differs in content, from the first edition in 1869.

All almanacs have several points in common: (1) they enjoy rather healthy sales and are to be found in many homes; (2) they depend heavily upon government sources for statistics, and readers frequently will find the same sources (when given) quoted in all the almanacs; and (3) except for updating and revising, much of the same basic material is carried over year after year.

Of the six works, the English entry is by far the most extensively indexed (25,000 entries), followed closely by the *World Almanac*. It is distinctive, as might be expected, in that there is considerable emphasis upon Great Britain and European governments. For example, the 1973 edition boasts of close to 100 pages of almost a complete directory of the royalty and peerage, with another 150 pages devoted to government and public offices—right down to salaries paid to officials. Salaries came to be a feature when Whitaker started the almanac. He asked for salaries; they were not given, so Whitaker printed what he thought the employees were worth. The entire subject of Great Britain is dismissed in the American almanacs in less than a dozen pages. Where *Whitaker's* and the American books meet, however, is on standard information about

---

[4] For a whimsical appreciation of the *World Almanac, see:* "Almanac," *The New Yorker,* February 24, 1973, p. 36.

events of the year, foreign countries, and international statistics. *Whitaker's* places more emphasis on emerging nations.

If there is little real duplication between *Whitaker's* and the American works, the five almanacs published on this side of the Atlantic are similar to each other in scope if not arrangement and emphasis. The cousins of the *World Almanac* tend to feature discursive larger units on such subjects as lively arts, science, education, and medicine. *Information Please Almanac* expanded its title to include *Atlas and Yearbook* and added special features such as "Can we trust politicians?" and "How much we earn and spend" (1972 ed.). Both *Information Please* and the *Reader's Digest* tend to gravitate more to the methods of encyclopedia yearbooks than to the standard form set by traditional almanacs. Both are considerably more attractive in makeup (larger type, spacing, and illustration) than the *World*. As for binding, all almanacs come in both hard and soft covers. Libraries normally buy the hardbound editions.

The Official Associated Press Almanac is stronger on statistical data arranged under such broad categories as "The United States," "Travel/ Transportation," and "Religion." In fact, much of the information is on the order of what is found in *The New York Times Index*. The indexing is only fair and not as detailed as found in *Information Please Almanac* and the *World Almanac*. Conversely, its strongest point is the emphasis on biographical information and on current data on the world's nations—in alphabetical order by country.

A method of testing the philosophy and the coverage of these four works is to simply turn to the index and take the first 10 entries for any letter in the alphabet. For example, under "D" the user soon ascertains that *Whitaker's* favors many place names; the *World*, events and statistics; the *Information Please Almanac* and *Reader's Digest Almanac*, popular items; and *The New York Times*, names and biographical entries. For example, *Information Please Almanac* has an entry for "dance halls" (which proves to be a statistic) and *Reader's Digest* has two entries for "Dalton," one the gangster, the other, the English scientist.

The *Negro Almanac* is closer to an encyclopedia than the traditional ready-reference source. There are 32 chapters, plus a selected and useful bibliography on black materials for the library. The sections cover everything from biographical material to civil rights, legal status for blacks, income, and education. There are, to be sure, the standard statistical tables and charts; but much of the information is presented in an essay, discursive fashion. While other almanacs depend almost completely upon primary sources for their information, this work often commissions special articles. The almanac is an example of a publisher filling a much needed void. Lacking anything of this type, the library has to depend primarily upon encyclopedias and hit and miss use of other almanacs, handbooks, and yearbooks. Not all the basic information—from history to current economics—is brought together in one source.

Almanacs are inevitably not only sources of expected information, but mines of unexpected facts. For example, *The New York Times* entry gives the average travel agent's commission (7 to 20 percent) as well as a complete section on leisure time activities from antiques to photography. The *Information Please Almanac* offers a crossword puzzle guide.

In view of the diversity of data and the frequent use of almanacs in ready-reference work, it would help any beginning librarian to study the various titles. It is obviously pointless to remember organization (usually so broad as to be meaningless), but it is useful to know in a general way the types of normal and not so normal information one is likely to find in each almanac.

General yearbooks

In the sense many almanacs are general, there are really no general yearbooks or annuals other than the ubiquitous encyclopedia yearbooks. Much basic annual data will be found elsewhere—more particularly, in general encyclopedias and in the various sections of the general almanacs given over to national surveys, e.g., *The Official Associated Press Almanac* has over 250 pages devoted to "The United States" and close to 200 pages on "World Nations." The *Information Please Almanac* has large sections on "World History," "American Economy."

DIRECTORIES

The fact that this is the age of the organization will come as no surprise to anyone who even glances at the daily newspaper or books on social criticism. The number of organizations, agencies, fraternal groups, business structures, and clubs in the United States is in the hundreds of thousands. Each of these is connected in one way or another with an individual or a group of individuals. Consequently, sources of information about organizations is on two levels: (1) the structure and operational activities of the organization itself, and (2) the members and officers.

The latter level closely relates directories to biographical dictionaries and other biographical sources. Frequently, the two forms can be used to augment one another. For example, the user may want the address of the president of X firm or the address of the firm itself. Lacking or failing to find the information in a business directory, the librarian might well locate it in a current edition of *Who's Who in America.* Suppose that a student wants some information on the leading executives in the steel industry. *Thomas Register of American Manufacturers* gives the names of the presidents of several large firms which can then be researched in *Who's Who in America* or a *World's Who in Commerce and Industry* for additional personal information.

A nineteenth-century city directory may give the historian the clue he needs for supporting or starting research in some specific area such as publishing, manufacturing, music, or a variety of other occupational headings used in these directories. Given the names of individuals, he may then proceed to more fully detailed information about them and their activities in local histories. And mention has been made of the value of directories for tracing biographical questions about little-known persons.

The relation of directories to other library resources is stressed because it frequently strikes the librarian that an old directory is of little value, or a particular directory seems too limited in potential use for purchase. Historically, directories may prove as valuable as any single work in a library. Recognition of this fact can be found in a number of bibliographies of directories, such as Dorothy N. Spear's *Bibliography of American Directories Through 1860* (Worcester, Massachusetts: American Antiquarian Society, 1961, 389 pp.).

These remarks hopefully set the directory in its proper context. Unfortunately, of all reference forms, they appear to the novice to be the dullest sources in any library, regardless of their type or size.

Additional directory-type sources

As previously noted, the almanac and the yearbook often include directory-type information, e.g., *The New York Times Almanac* has a section called "The Directory" which lists major Societies and Associations; and *The Municipal Yearbook* lists many city officials. There are numerous other sources of directory information:

1. Encyclopedias frequently identify various organizations, particularly those of a general nature which deal with political or fraternal activities.
2. Gazetteers, guidebooks, and atlases will often give information on principal industries, historical sites, museums, and the like.
3. A wide variety of government publications are either entirely devoted to directory-type information or include such information as part of a given work. Also, while some works are technically directories (*Ulrich's* and *Ayer*, for example), they are so closely associated with other forms (periodicals and newspapers) that they are rarely thought of as directories per se, but rather as guides.

Purpose

The purpose of directories is self-explanatory in the definition, but among the most frequent uses are those involved with answering questions concerning: (1) an individual or firm's address or telephone number; (2) the full name of an individual, firm, or organization; (3) a description of a particular manufacturer's product or a service; or (4) the ubiquitous question that begins with, "Who is . . ." president of the firm, head of the school, responsible for advertising, in charge of buying manuscripts, and so on.

Less obvious uses of directories include: (1) limited, but up-to-date biographical information on an individual—is he still president, chairman, or with this or that company or organization; (2) historical and current data about an institution, firm, or political group—when was it founded, how many members did it have; (3) commercial use such as selecting a list of individuals or companies or organizations for a mailing in a particular area—a directory of doctors and dentists serves as the basic list for a medical supply house or a dealer in medical books; (4) basic sources of random or selective samplings in a social or commercial survey. Directories are frequently employed by social scientists to isolate certain desired groups for study. And so it goes. Because directories are intimately concerned with man and his organizations, they serve almost as many uses as the imagination can bring to bear on the data.

Scope

Directories are easier to use than any other reference tool primarily because the scope is normally indicated in the title and the type of information is limited and usually presented in an orderly, clear fashion.

There are many ways to categorize directories, but briefly they may be divided as follows.

Local directories These are primarily limited to two types: telephone books and city directories. However, in this category may also be included all other types issued only for a limited geographic audience—for example, directories of local schools, garden clubs, department stores, theaters, or social groups. The distinction is more academic than important.

Governmental directories This group includes guides to post offices, army and navy posts, and the thousand and one different services offered by federal, state, and city governments. This would also include guides to international agencies.

Institutional directories These are lists of schools, foundations, libraries, hospitals, museums, and similar organizations.

Professional directories   These are primarily lists of a professional organization such as law, medicine, librarianship, and the like.

Trade and business directories   These are primarily lists of manufacturers' information about companies, industries, and personal services.

A peculiar feature of many directories is the emphasis on advertising. The majority of city directories, for example, include large sections devoted to advertising, very much like the yellow pages of the telephone book. This in no way detracts from their reliability or use. Directories are primarily employed for a type of information which is about as objective as anything available. The inclusion or exclusion of advertisements has little or no effect on their value. Since advertising makes the city directory financially possible, few rural areas or small communities without a relatively broad base of business and industry are represented by directories.

Guides to directories[5]

Guide to American Directories. 7th ed. New York: Klein, 1968, 588 pp., $30.

Current British Directories. 6th ed. New York: International Publications Service, 1970, 270 pp., $22.50.

Current European Directories. Beckenham, England: CBD Research Ltd., 1969, 222 pp., $22.50.

International Bibliography of Directories. New York: R. R. Bowker Company, 1972, 700 pp., $28.

With these guides, the majority of libraries have the help they need in determining what is available and where. All are frequently revised and, in their way, are quite exhaustive.

The American volume describes in detail more than 3,350 directories of various kinds. The list covers institutions, individuals, and business firms. The text is arranged according to lines of business or subject, and there is a complete title index. For each entry, full bibliographical details are given, including the number of listings and, where applicable, how the directory is arranged.

Close to 2,000 directories are included in the British work, including almost 500 which are international in scope. Unlike the American volume, there is more emphasis on regional, telephone, and county directories than on business directories—hence the number of listings. A second section does include the standard type of directory by specialty with a subject index.

[5] Stanley C. Wyllie, Jr., "The Dayton Directory System," *RQ*, Winter 1965, pp. 25+.

The European directory is an annotated guide to several thousand various types of directories published in Europe, e.g., the first section includes commercial, telephone, association, research, biographical, gazetteer, and city directories. The second section is an alphabetical list of specialized industrial directories, incorporating information found in the first half.

Published in Germany, distributed in the United States by Bowker, the *International Bibliography of Directories* has one major point to recommend it: among this group, it is the most up to date. Conversely, most emphasis is on European and non-Western countries. This, to be sure, is a "plus" for large research libraries but of limited interest to smaller libraries. More than 6,000 directories are arranged under 50 subject fields, which are further subdivided by some 300 headings. Each entry gives the title of the directory, publishers, frequency of issue, number of entries, and any other pertinent information. There is, also, a geographical subject index.

The *Public Affairs Information Bulletin* bound volumes include a section "Directories" which lists selected current works. And there are numerous other sources for directories such as *Business Reference Sources* (Cambridge, Massachusetts: Baker Library, Graduate School of Business Administration, Harvard, rev. ed., 1971). The index to the *Monthly Catalog of U.S. Government Publications* separately lists directories under that head. This is particularly useful for up-to-date government directory publications on everything from zip codes to health and drugs. Furthermore, many of these are quite inexpensive. The basic directories listed in Winchell, Walford, and the *American Reference Books Annual* will suffice for most situations.

General directories

While there are numerous basic directories for various subjects and areas, there simply are no general directories. The form defines (and defies) such an application.

There are, on the other hand, literally thousands of special directories. These will be discussed in the next chapter under the various subject sections.

Local directories

The two most obvious, and probably the most used, local directories are the telephone book and the city directory. The latter is particularly valuable for locating information about an individual when only the name of a street or the approximate street address is known. Part of the city directory includes an alphabetical list of streets and roads in the area, giving names of residents (unless it is an apartment building, when names may or may not be included). The resident usually is identified by occupation and whether or not he owns his own home.

The classified section of the directory is a complete list of businesses and professions, differing from the yellow pages of the telephone book in that the latter is a paid service which may not include all firms. Like the telephone book, city directories are usually issued each year or every two years.

The majority of city directories are published by one firm, the R. L. Polk Co. of Detroit. Founded in 1870, the company issues over 800 publications. In addition to its city directories, it also publishes a directory for banks and direct-mail concerns.

Given enough telephone directories, many of the specialized directories might be short-circuited. Telephone books, however, have the limitation that information can only be gained when: (1) a name is known, that is, before I can find the address I must have the full name; (2) geographical location is known; (3) a subject is known, although here it may be argued that the yellow pages with the classified listings somewhat overcomes the handicap of not knowing the precise product area by using cross references.

HANDBOOKS AND MANUALS

The primary purpose of handbooks or manuals is to serve as a ready-reference source for a given field of knowledge. Emphasis normally is on established knowledge rather than recent advances, although in the field of science handbooks that are more than a few years old may be almost totally useless. Perhaps too much stress is placed upon their use to answer quick fact questions. True, many of them do serve this purpose, but the more specialized works also serve as background material, as keys to specific forms of knowledge.

The scientific handbook in particular presupposes a basic knowledge of the subject field. A good part of the information is given in shorthand form, freely employing tables, graphs, symbols, equations, formulas, and downright jargon which only the expert understands. Much the same, to be sure, can be said about the specialized manual. For example, a layman would find the *Handbook of Chemistry and Physics* almost meaningless if he did not at least appreciate the difference between molecular weight and specific gravity; and the *Radio Engineering Handbook* is for an experienced engineer, not for the gentleman who wants to fix his television or radio without benefit of a knowledge of circuits.

It is well to keep the purposes of the various handbooks and manuals clearly in mind when ordering them or when recommending them to patrons. Many times, an answer will be more quickly found in a general work, even though the specific title of the handbook may make it a more apparent source.

Scope

With some exceptions, the vast majority of handbooks and manuals have one thing in common—a limited scope. They tend to zero in on a specific area of interest or a subject. In fact, their particular value is the depth of information they give in a narrow field. The exceptions, such as the *Reader's Encyclopedia,* are really closer in scope to encyclopedias (as the title implies) than to handbooks, but are cited here somewhat arbitrarily as specimens of the rare catch-all type of reference books.

There are countless manuals and handbooks. New ones appear each year, old ones disappear or undergo a name change. It is obviously impossible to remember them all. What happens in practice is that due to ease of arrangement, lack of another substitute, or through use, librarians adopt favorites. Many of the answers they find might as easily be discovered in some of the works previously discussed, but manuals and handbooks have their value.

General handbooks and manuals

Benet, William Rose (ed.) *The Reader's Encyclopedia.* 2d ed. New York: Thomas Y. Crowell Company, 1965, 1,118 pp., $8.95.

Kane, Joseph N., *Famous First Facts.* 3d ed. New York: The H. W. Wilson Company, 1964, 1,165 pp., $22.

————, *Facts About the Presidents.* 2d ed. New York: The H. W. Wilson Company, 1968, 384 pp., $10.

The Guinness Book of World Records. New York: Sterling Publishing Co., Inc., 1955 to date, annual, $5.95.

Although these handbooks and manuals vary in scope and purpose, they are among the few catch-all sources of facts covering almost every area of human knowledge and interest. Much of the information can be found elsewhere, for example, in a good encyclopedia. Why then use them? Primarily because the compendium type of arrangement is such that they are easy to use to discover an isolated fact which might be buried in an encyclopedia article or in a footnote in another work.

As the title implies, *The Reader's Encyclopedia* is geared to the reader who comes across an odd fact, author, title, character, allusion, or the like in his reading. He wants a brief answer to his query and can find it here, mainly because of the alphabetical arrangement of material. Primarily, a work like this is for rapid identification. If more than a line or two is required, the reader must then turn to a fuller source—either a subject encyclopedia article or the card catalog. With its general information such as tables of rulers of England and France, the American presidents, short descriptive entries on history, religions, mythology, philosophy, science, and other fields, this has proven to be among the handiest, fastest fact-finders available in a library. Greater coverage in the second edition extending to Latin America, the Soviet Union, the Orient, and the Near East has expanded it use. Although now somewhat dated, it remains a basic source for historical and nontime oriented facts.

The essential difference in purpose between *The Reader's Encyclopedia* and the majority of other general handbooks is that the editors have tried to reach all men and generally have succeeded. Other works tend to be much more specialized, placing the emphasis or the direction of the compilation on a narrower base. Usually, this is evident from the title.

Kane's *Famous First Facts* is the joy of the librarian seeking out-of-way information on such vital issues as who invented the toothbrush or can opener, when did the first man jump off the Brooklyn Bridge, who was the first woman to ride West. Despite its obvious catering to the fact fiend, and its limitation to events in the United States, it is of value to the scholar or researcher attempting to establish a given fact. The material is arranged alphabetically by subject, with an excellent index which approaches the facts geographically, chronologically, and by personal name.

Parenthetically, as more than one experienced reference librarian knows, a good dictionary or history of language is an excellent source for "firsts." The *Oxford English Dictionary* and H. L. Mencken's *The American Language,* to cite but two, are useful for tracing the origin not only of words but of dated questions which indicate when such things as tuxedos, cigars, and candy bars first appeared.

The second Kane standby, *Facts About The Presidents,* is primarily a biographical aid; but as facts about presidents cross all reference lines, it fits into the general handbook category. The book is divided into two parts. The first section considers each of the presidents, while the second part (and the most often used) gives comparative data on the presidents. There is an excellent index which makes it possible to locate just about any outstanding fact. Much of this material is found in standard encyclopedias, but Kane's contribution is collecting the out-of-the-ordinary data and the comparative materials.

Either unaware of Kane's contribution, or seeking to broaden the fact search to an international basis, a pair of twins by the name of Norris and Ross McWhirter are responsible for *The Guinness Book of World Records.* Emphasis here is comparative and for the most part simple downright fun. As a compilation of pure statistics, it is fondly called the "Book to End Arguments." It gives data on such diverse matters as the largest spider (Theraphose blondi, 3½ inches long) and the longest simple aria (Brunnhilde's immolation scene in Wagner's Gotterdammerung). The book was born of a notion by Sir Hugh Beaver, the head of the Guinness Stout and Ale Company (Ireland) who wanted a quick reference tool for bartenders. In a letter to the author, Norris McWhirter reported that his book is now in 12 other languages, and "the annual world sales are in excess of two million copies."[6]

Another somewhat less successful title by the same authors is *The Dunlop Illustrated Encyclopedia of Facts* (New York: Doubleday & Company, Inc., 1969, 864 pp.). It includes thousands of ready facts on everything from the nations of the world to radio and television. There are numerous illustrations and an index. As a useful, relatively inexpensive supplement for other books of this type, it serves a purpose at the ready-reference desk.

While Kane and the brothers McWhirter appeal to everyone, and serve to answer a variety of general questions, it may be argued that Benet's contribution is narrower in scope. Yes and no. It is typical enough of the handbooks demanded by curious readers; and while the asking of questions is hardly limited to bookworms, they do tend to play an important part in the reference situation. In fact, the earlier general handbooks were almost exclusively directed to this audience. For example, E. C. Brewer was the editor of a compilation in 1923, since revised, that is packed with literary information. His *Dictionary of Phrase and Fable* (London: Centenary Press; New York: Harper & Row, Publishers, Incorporated, 1970, 1,175 pp.) has gone through many editions and changes. In so doing, its scope is widened to include much of the material, and then some, found in Benet. While fans claim its chief attribute is the coverage of phrases and adages (grouped under key words), it has everything from lists of giants to abbreviations and explanations of common superstitions. A glance at Walford or Winchell will indicate that Brewer is only one in an honorable line, a line which continues to grow with the number of readers.

MISCELLANEOUS REFERENCE AIDS

Time Changes in the U.S.A. Los Angeles, California: Church of Light, Inc., 1966, $5.

National Zip Code Directory. Washington, D.C.: Government Printing Office, 1965 to date, annual, $10.

[6] Numerous articles have been written on the Guinness title, e.g., William A. Krauss, "The All Purpose Cure for Bloody Disputes," *The New York Times* (Travel section), June 11, 1972, p. 35.

Butler, Audrey, *Everyman's Dictionary of Dates*. 6th ed., New York: E. P. Dutton & Co., Inc., 1971, 518 pp., $6.50.

Awards, Honors and Prizes: A Source Book & Directory, 2d ed., Detroit: Gale Research Company, 1972, 307 pp., $24.

Emily Post's *Etiquette*. New York: Doubleday & Company, Inc., 1972, 887 pp., $7.95.

When discussing various types of almanacs, yearbooks, handbooks, manuals, and directories, there are two or three basic categories: (1) general which serve many purposes; (2) subject which are limited to a given special area (and are discussed in the next chapter); and (3) those which simply fit no neat subject area and are used occasionally where everything else fails, or because there simply is nothing quite like them available.

A fourth ready-reference category is the library's own query or information file—a file which may be built of data gathered from all types of reference and nonreference aids. Of all the groups or categories, this is probably of most importance in ready-reference work.

Josel defines a query file in these terms:

> The name of our game is not Each Digs Alone, but Cooperation. When you find the cost of spectacles in eighteenth-century American, do not inform the patron and promptly forget the source. Enter it in the query file. Then the next time the question is asked it can be answered without delay. In addition to giving specific answers such a file can also give clues to help with similar questions. It is always a Good Idea to put the source of such answers as you have found, together with the date the information was entered in the file on the card.[7]

The advice of this veteran reference librarian is followed in most libraries. In addition to the query file, every reference desk has its own peculiar set of ready-reference aids which may or may not be duplicated elsewhere. They are selected and prized because they are quick methods of answering frequently asked questions. And most of these are in the almanac, yearbook, handbook, or manual class, as represented by the titles to be discussed.

John G. Fetros of the San Francisco Library has much to say about the little known *Time Changes,* as he does about other lesser known titles of this type.[8] (His article is an excellent reminder to veterans and beginners alike that the learning process about ready-reference titles never ends.) *Time Changes* serves two purposes: (1) the most obvious is that it gives by state and by local area complete daylight savings time information; (2) its less obvious purpose is that it is an aid for astrol-

---

[7] Nathan A. Josel, "Ten Reference Commandments," *RQ*, Winter 1971, pp. 146–147.
[8] John G. Fetros, "Useful But Little Known Reference Tools," *RQ*, Fall 1970, p. 23.

ogy—"Since the exact time of birth must be known in casting a horoscope it becomes important to know whether a particular place at a particular time was on daylight savings time," Fetros says.

The *National Zip Code Directory* lists the code numbers alphabetically by state. Within each state, a complete listing is given of all post offices, stations, and branches. Also, there is additional data from a numerical list of post offices by zip code to the numbers for army and air force installations. Another useful title in this area is the *Directory of Post Offices* (Washington, D.C.: Government Printing Office, 1965 to date, annual). This approach to the zip code work, lists post offices by states and names with the zip codes. Both titles are primarily used by business and mailers of large quantities of material, but they are equally valuable for the individual who wants to know this or that about a post office—an extremely common question in libraries.

Again, it is worth noting that zip code information is available in many general sources. For example, *The New York Times Almanac* lists all the codes for towns over 25,000 population—as do many other almanacs and some general encyclopedias. Is the government publication needed? For most cases, no. But for towns under 25,000, obviously yes.

In the quest of dates, parallel historical events, and "what happened when" type of information, there are certain basic shortcuts. Many of the historical encyclopedias, particularly the Cambridge series, may be useful. General encyclopedias usually outline the major histories of nations by chronological methods and can be used for most purposes. Still, for ready reference there are numerous titles which are prepared specifically for chronological, date-type queries, e.g., Morris' *Harper Encyclopedia of the Modern World*. Most of these are handbooks with encyclopedic qualities. Butler's is of British origin and includes an alphabetical listing of major world events, people, and places from the beginning until early 1970. Although in dictionary form, the entries may range from a few words to rather lengthy explanations. In all cases, crucial dates are given.[9]

Who won what? Who was the Pulitzer Prize winner for 1955 in literature? What is the Hodgkins Medal? Questions such as these are common enough; and answers to the prize winners of the more prestigious, better known awards will be found in any encyclopedia or almanac, e.g., *The New York Times Encyclopedic Almanac* devotes over 20 pages to the subject.

Awards, Honors and Prizes: A Source Book & Directory does not list winners—but does describe over 2,000 American organizations that give prizes, with details about the qualifications to be a winner. Most of the

[9] For a discussion of this title and others of its type *see* Wilson's review in *RQ*, Winter 1971, p. 164.

emphasis is on the United States, but a few of the better known international awards are included. (Where the name of a winner is required, and cannot be found in general sources, the librarian may look up the name of the award in an appropriate index—often *The New York Times Index* or *Readers' Guide to Periodical Literature*—for the given year. Failing this, he might call or write the organization which presents the prize.)

In a more limited sense, another title helps. *Literary and Library Prizes* (New York: R. R. Bowker Company, 1970, 413 pp.) gives full information on literary and library awards in the United States, Canada, and Great Britain. Unlike the Gale publication, it includes the names of winners.

A check of *Subject Guide to Books in Print*, 1973, reveals that there are close to 100 books on etiquette. Most are general; but there are particular works for children, women, men, and for use on the telephone and in church. At the reference desk, this may be the least of the librarian's worries; but he will often get requests on specific bits of etiquette: How do I address a letter to my Congressman? Where does the boss sit when he comes to dinner? Do you have anything on big, and I do mean big weddings?

Emily Post's *Etiquette* is the standard source of answers to these and countless other queries. Since 1922, her book on etiquette has been synonymous with good manners and how to get in and out of a cab. At the time of Mrs. Post's death in 1960, the work had been through 86 printings. Some notion of its popularity may be gained by a fascinating statistic offered by the Library Extension Division of the Education Department of New York State, which reports that it is the second most stolen book from the library. The first is the Bible.

The other much favored title in this category is *Amy Vanderbilt's Etiquette* (New York: Doubleday & Company, Inc, 1972, 929 pp., $7.95). The Vanderbilt scheme of things seems to be a bit more relaxed than the Post version, and it is preferable for younger people. Both of these titles should be available at the reference desk and in the general collection.

For the librarian who is interested in the history of the manuals, an excellent, sometimes biting, work is Ester B. Aresty's *The Best Behavior* (New York: Simon & Schuster, Inc., 1970, 320 pp.). And each time a new edition of either Amy or Emily comes out there is bound to be a lengthy review, e.g., C. D. B. Bryan reviews 1972 Amy in *The New York Times Book Review* (March 19, 1972, p. 27), and Doris Grumbach explores Emily in *The New Republic* (April 29, 1972, p. 25).[10]

---

[10] A history of the Post volume, which is as witty as it is informative, will be found in James L. Cate's "Keeping Posted," *University of Chicago Magazine*, May/June 1972, pp. 24+·

CURRENT REFERENCE SOURCES

In any reference library, one of the most time-consuming, sometimes futile types of searches is for current material on recent events. How is one to answer the question concerning a presidential appointment of a week or a month ago, trace current sporting records, or find information on a prominent man who died only last week?

Sources for yesterday's events

There are some specialized services such as business newsletters, daily reports of research in progress, and internal communication which attempt to keep up with daily affairs. On the whole, though, there is little or nothing that meets this need for the average reference library.

The patron who comes rushing into the library for information on an event that happened yesterday or a day or so ago must search a newspaper—either the local one or a larger newspaper such as *The New York Times* or *Washington Post*.

One source of help that varies from community to community is the local newspaper library, which can give information on immediate news events. Larger newspaper libraries have rules against giving aid to "outsiders", but in other communities, it is possible for the local librarian to make arrangements for occasional help. At any rate, it is worth investigating.

Sources for last week's events

Facts on File, a Weekly World News Digest, with Cumulative Index. New York: Facts on File, Inc., October 30, 1940 to date, weekly, $220.

Keesing's Contemporary Archives. London: Keesing's, July 1, 1931 to date, weekly (represented in the United States by Charles Scribner's Sons), $50.

Canadian News Facts. Toronto: Canadian News Facts, January 1, 1967 to date, biweekly, $95.

Congressional Quarterly Service Weekly Report, 1943 to date. Washington, D.C.: Congressional Quarterly, Inc., 1943 to date, weekly, $144.

Deadline Data on World Affairs. Greenwich, Connecticut: Deadline Data (McGraw-Hill Book Company) 1955 to date, weekly, $250.

News Bank Series. Spring Valley, New York: Arcata Microfilm Corp, 1970 to date, monthly, $996. (Smaller units available at lower prices.)

All the services except the Canadian and News Bank entries are issued weekly and cover events of the preceding week. Their up-todateness depends on two factors: (1) prompt publication after the end of the period covered and (2) the time it takes to get them through the mails. This varies from work to work, place to place. However, in general, the time lag normally is one or two or even three weeks behind the needs of the patron.

For a more current, although more time-consuming search, the librarian must resort to weekly magazines and newspapers such as *Newsweek, Time,* the *National Observer,* or the news summary in the Sunday edition of *The New York Times.*

Granted that the weekly news services are somewhat behind desired schedule, they still are sources for material of at least relative currency. They all cumulate and have cumulative indexes which also make them invaluable as retrospective research tools. They have a distinct advantage over periodical indexes in that they usually offer complete, although abridged, data and information in themselves, and the user does not have to turn from them to the primary sources (as with a periodical index) to find what he seeks.

Of all the services, *Facts on File* tends to be the most prompt (the United States mails permitting) and normally only a few days have elapsed since the last date covered. Emphasis is on news events in the United States, with international coverage related for the most part to American affairs. Material is gathered primarily from the major newspapers and condensed into objective, short, factual reports. It is arranged under broad subject headings such as "World affairs," "finance," "economics," "national affairs," and so on. This is a bit confusing; but fortunately, every two weeks, monthly, and then quarterly and annually, a detailed index is issued which covers previous issues. Sources of information are not indicated, but on the whole the material is reliable.

In *Keesing's Contemporary Archives,* emphasis differs from *Facts on File* in two important respects. The scope is primarily that of the United Kingdom, Europe, and the Commonwealth. Detailed subject reports in certain areas are frequently included (the reports are by experts and frequently delay the weekly publication by several days), as are full texts of important speeches and documents. Conversely, *Keesing's* does not cover in any detail many ephemeral events such as sports, arts, or movies which may be included in *Facts on File.* Arrangement is by country, territory, or continent with some broad subject headings such as religion, aviation, fine arts. Every second week, an index is issued which is cumulated quarterly and annually.

The obvious advantage of *Keesing's* for any research library is not its recency (coming from England it may be several weeks behind the published date), but rather its different scope. Also, because sources of information are clearly indicated for major items, it proves to be a springboard for further searching.

Following much the same procedure and format as *Facts on File*, *Canadian News Facts* differs in its scope and its frequency—every two weeks rather than weekly. Each of the news digests varies from 8 to 12 pages and is almost exclusively concerned with Canada. While it would be a first choice for Canadian libraries, it would be well down the selection scale for all but the largest American libraries.

While both *Keesing's* and *Facts on File* are sources of general news events, there are some specialized weekly services which assist the reference librarian. Among the best of those giving detailed reports on government activities is the *Congressional Quarterly*. Issued by a private firm, not by the government, it presents in condensed form all congressional and political activities of the previous week—not simply those limited to Congress. Bills, acts, names of congressmen, how they voted, committee action, major legislation, and related subjects are covered in full, competently indexed and summarized in a "fact sheet" procedure. Since the service is indexed in *Public Affairs Information Service Bulletin*, it may be approached by two indexes. As a shortcut to official publications and to avoid going through individual newspapers, the service is a major aid. Another firm, Commerce Clearing House, Chicago, issues the *Congressional Index* on a weekly basis; and it covers the same material but in a somewhat different fashion. Emphasis is placed on indexing all legislation pending in Congress; and, as such, it gives up-to-date information on where a bill or act is in Congress.

As aids to experts and to students, both of these guides should be used more. Unfortunately, they seem to be little known in the smaller libraries which may be using only *Facts on File*.

There are two rather unique services—at least in terms of format—which are used in libraries for current materials. *Deadline Data* is a weekly service in card format. The basic set consists of some 8,000 cards which are filed alphabetically by 250 countries and subjects from the "European Common Market" to "Disarmament." The initial set provides current statistical and historical data on each of the countries and subjects. Each week about 50 cards are sent to the library. These serve to update the information in the basic set, as well as report new developments (i.e., both new subjects and events of a national or international nature). There are numerous cross references and sources of information are clearly identified. Most of the material is taken from newspapers and periodicals. The emphasis is on political science and history; but it also touches on major military, economic, and social events. The set is relatively easy to use and particularly suited for larger collections that wish to augment *Facts on File* and *Keesing's*.

A similar, although monthly, service is *News Bank*. Original articles are selected from 105 American newspapers and photographed on a 4 by 6 inch microfiche. In a month's time, there are some 6,000 articles compiled on approximately 100 cards. The subscribing library receives the cards plus a monthly index to each of the news and feature articles. Also, there is a "Newsbank Newsletter" which abstracts highlights of the month's articles. Finally, there is an annual cumulative index. The service has the advantage of offering both the index and the material in a handy package form, but it is expensive—close to $1,000 for the complete unit. The company offers parts of the overall service at reduced prices (i.e., a political science library or a socioeconomic development library). While this is a unique approach, it does have the drawback of using only newspaper sources—and most of them from less than well-edited or well-written local newspapers. Conversely, it does offer the unique slant of specific, localized events, not, as the publisher says, "national media generalities." Between this and *Deadline Data,* the latter would be preferable for most libraries; the former would provide an additional service in quite large public and university situations.

What is interesting about both of these approaches is their break with the traditional index-to-source theory of information. *Facts on File* and *Keesing's* break this circle, too, but in considerably more abbreviated form. The day may come when all indexes will be published in some type of handy microform or condensation of materials on cards.

Bimonthly sources of events

While *The Reference Shelf* (New York: The H. W. Wilson Company, 1922 to date, bimonthly, $20) does not and could not cover all news topics, the work does, in a period of a year, manage to touch on current major items of interest.[11] Although ostensibly for debaters, the series can be used effectively by almost anyone from the high school student to the layman interested in well-rounded reporting. Among topics covered in the past have been justice, economic policy, youth, the People's Republic of China, airways, and culture. Each 200-page or so volume reprints articles by journalists and experts and gives the pros and cons of any debatable issue; and there is connecting editorial material, as well as a comprehensive bibliography. The sixth volume is an annual edition of *Representative American Speeches* which includes the best speeches of the year given by government officials, businessmen, teachers, and so on. Biographical notes are appended.

Sources for last year's events

Several of the aforementioned works are annually cumulated and where retrospective detail is required, the librarian may want to turn to a general encyclopedia yearbook or one of the annual news service indexes.

[11] John B. White, "The Indexing of The Reference Shelf," *Library Resources & Technical Services,* Fall 1970, pp. 553 + . Sources of indexing for the aid as well as a discussion of its checkered bibliographical history.

Among the best is *The New York Times Index* annual cumulated volume. Not only is this a specific index, but the majority of entries are in the form of brief abstracts which often suffice to give answers to questions without the need to resort to the newspaper. Events are arranged chronologically so it is easy to follow developments.

The oldest of the news-summary reference works is the *Annual Register; World Events.* (New York: St. Martin's Press, Inc.). Issued since 1758, it is primarily concerned with news events of an international nature and those pertaining to England and the Commwealth. Two of its several parts are devoted to science and literature. These normally take the form of discursive essays on various aspects of the previous year. There are also lists of public documents, obituaries, and the usual chronicle of events. An excellent index makes the work particularly easy to use.[12]

Facts on File issues the American counterpart to the *Annual Register.* This is *News Dictionary* which selects and arranges the news alphabetically under name, place, and subject. Published since 1965, it is little more than a compilation of material found in *Facts on File* which has an excellent annual index itself. It is questionable whether subscribers to the service would need the news annual, but nonsubscribers will find it a helpful compilation. A better purchase for smaller libraries is the *Facts on File Yearbook* which is the annual index and a full sequence of the 52 weekly news digests. There is also a *Facts on File 5 Year Index.*

With these various reference approaches to current materials, most libraries will have little difficulty answering ready-reference questions—particularly of a political or social nature. All include an assortment of ongoing statistical data which may be drawn in part, or in full, from government reports, private studies, and even newspapers. However, when more than "in-the-news" types of statistics are required, the librarian must turn to sources which are particularly published for statistical data. Form wise, these tend to be considered as yearbooks; but in view of the compilation of sometimes both current and retrospective data, others are equally handbooks. Regardless of the reference title form, they share the statistical umbrella and, as such, are often isolated in ready-reference collections.

STATISTICAL REFERENCE SOURCES

Statistics, by definition, are concerned "with the collection, classification, analysis, and interpretation of numerical facts or data." As such, they are of considerable importance to reference librarians. Rarely a day goes by that someone does not want a statistic. Usually, they are of a simple

---

[12] "All in a Year," *Times Literary Supplement,* August 18, 1972, p. 971. A review and discussion of the 1971 edition of *The Annual Register* which questions the reliability of such a "rapidly compiled record."

nature, e.g., What is the height of X, the population of Y, the crime rate in America, the number of lefthanded Presidents, the cost of living in New York, the profits of Y company over the past 10 years. Questions such as these may be answered in standard reference sources from the almanac and encyclopedia to a financial service to the *Statistical Abstract of the United States.* Where difficulty arises over current statistics, the librarian should keep in mind the various indexes. Of particular help is the *Business Periodicals Index* and the *Public Affairs Information Service Bulletin,* as well as *The New York Times Index.* The best source for material on business and economics is unquestionably the monthly *Wall Street Journal Index.*

Many of the queries are in the social sciences and economics and business. Questions dealing with esoteric subjects require equally specialized sources, but this moves the reference librarian into the study of subject bibliography which is beyond the present text. Nevertheless, the vast number of queries dealing with statistics are neither that difficult nor that specialized. In addition to the numerous general sources discussed throughout this text, it may be of some comfort to realize that most statistical questions may be answered in the few basic titles discussed in this section. A librarian does not necessarily have to be an expert in statistical method to find, or even to interpret, the majority of such figures. The mystique of statistical data is just that and is as often a cover for poor research and garbled thinking as it is reliable and thoughtful work in a given field. Surely the most important thing for the beginning librarian to keep in mind is that statistics are essentially no different than other reference sources, and certainly do not enjoy any exalted status.

How accurate are the statistics found in the various reference sources? In almost all cases, statistics are subject to interpretation; a point which needs little emphasis for anyone who reads the daily newspaper and sees how, by quoting the same basic sources, different reporters, politicians, or company presidents may evaluate the state of the economy, the growth of housing, the number of poor, or the number of unemployed. George Orwell summed it all nicely in 1939:

> Statistics, even when they are honestly presented, (and how often does this happen nowadays?) are almost always misleading, because one never knows what factors they leave out of account. To give a crude illustration, it would be easy to show, by stating the figures for fuel-consumption and saying nothing about the temperature, that everyone in Central Africa is suffering from the cold.[13]

A Commission on Federal Statistics, to cite an actual example, urged, in late 1971, that statistical data on crime be shifted from the

[13] *The Collected Essays, Journalism and Letters of George Orwell* (Harmondsworth, England: Penquin Books, 1970, vol. 1), pp. 417–8.

Federal Bureau of Investigation. Why? The Commission observed the FBI was tempted "to use the statistics they collect for purpose of arguing the law enforcement positions they hold. (FBI statistics are published in *Uniform Crime Reports for the United States and its Possessions* (Washington, D.C.: Government Printing Office, 1930 to date, annual). Another study charged that drug statistics of the Food and Drug Administration were "very weak" and that federal bureaucrats typically fabricated data. The Commission recommended that the Office of Management and Budget be directed "to audit statistical activities of all Government agencies and make the finds public.[14]

Even with the best of intentions, statistics may be only approximate. A census official notes, "the value of a statistic does not depend upon it being exactly true." Which is to say that the variables in collecting statistics are such that the best that can be hoped for—even in the United States census—is an approximately true value. Precisely how "true" the statistical data is depends upon the reliability of the gathering agency.

Statistical data are only as good as the original method of gathering and compilation; and, more important, how those data are interpreted. Fortunately, most of the basic reference sources simply pass on the raw data without much effort at analysis or interpretation—and where this is done, it tends to be in rather noncontroversial areas.

Most of the almanacs, handbooks, encyclopedias, and other reference sources gather statistical data from primary sources. They then rearrange, interpret (in terms of what is included, excluded, or emphasized), and present it in their various works. For the individual who wants to be absolutely sure that the original source cited was really used and not altered, he had best check with that source. Most reference works do cite the sources. Those who do not should be highly suspected.

General statistical sources

American Statistics Index. Washington, D.C.: Congressional Information Service, 1973 to date, annual, monthly and quarterly supplements, $450.

Statistical Sources. 3d ed. Detroit: Gale Research Company, 1971, 647 pp., $27.50.

The best single source for government statistics, the *American Statistics Index* covers virtually all statistical publications issued by the government, i.e., periodicals, special surveys, reports, and monographs. The first annual volume included all publications in print as of January 1, 1973. The monthly publication notes new articles as they appear in periodicals, changes made in series, new editions of statistical data, and the like.

[14] *The New York Times,* December 11, 1971, p. 18.

Material is arranged by the issuing department, i.e., Department of Commerce, Department of Health, Education and Welfare, and so on. Divisions are noted under each department and there follows: (1) detailed notes about the content, scope, and purpose of statistical series issued by the departments; (2) annotations of particular items sometimes in considerable detail; (3) full bibliographical information, e.g., date of publication, number of pages or volumes, price, the Superintendent of Documents item and classification number (as well as the number used by the issuing department).

With this amount of information, the index serves as an up-to-date source of background material on almost all government statistical data. In terms of ready-reference work, the title has a number of indexes to the material: (1) an index of subjects and authors with extensive cross references; the index is particularly valuable as it not only includes the main publications, but cites individual articles and groups of related tables in those publications; (2) an index by categories where the data is broken down by state, industry, or commodity, for example.

On a limited scale, a somewhat similar effort is made in *Statistics Sources.* (It is, however, neither as detailed nor as informative as the aforementioned index.)

Frequently revised, the Gale publication is a basic subject guide to statistical sources. Some 11,000 subject entries are arranged alphabetically with references to statistical works for the subject, e.g., periodicals, annuals, yearbooks, directories, books, pamphlets, reports, and the like. The breakdown is primarily limited to basic statistical data. There are a limited number of foreign statistics. The third edition claims to have some 16,000 citations.

Another work, with a definite British bias, is Joan M. Harvey's *Sources of Statistics* (2d rev. ed. Hamden, Connecticut: Linnet Books, 1971, 126 pp., $5.50). This describes the principal statistical publications of the United Kingdom and some United States and international titles. It is in a discursive form (i.e., chapters on justice, advertising and the like) and of limited value except for larger libraries.

Numerous other aids are published every year, but for most libraries the *American Statistics Index* will be quite adequate, particularly if it is supported by the quarterly *Predicasts* (p. 180). The high price may make it prohibitive for smaller libraries which will be able to get along in most situations with the less satisfactory *Statistics Sources.* Of course, in any case, all these services presuppose the library has most of the documents and sources indexed—or, at best, has ready access to them via interlibrary loan and other network services.

For the individual librarian who may quake at the sound of the word "statistics," the sources offer considerable moral support. They are relatively easy to use and will meet the needs of all but the most highly specialized type of libraries. Also, the librarian who is totally unfamiliar with statistics might learn considerably more about their purpose, scope, and potential audience by studying these titles—as well, of course, as some basic texts such as Paul Hoel's *Elementary Statistics* (3d ed. New York: John Wiley & Sons, Inc., 1971, 310 pp.). This is particularly suited for the beginner who may have no more than high school mathematics to support his interest.

Social and political science statistics

U.S. Bureau of the Census. *Statistical Abstract of the United States.* Washington, D.C.: Government Printing Office, 1879 to date, annual, $5.75. Supplement: *Historical Statistics of the United States, Colonial Times to 1957.* 1960, $6, continuation to 1962, $1.

———. *County and City Data Book.* Washington, D.C.: Government Printing Office, 1952 to date, irregular, $4.75.

———. *Congressional District Data Book.* Washington, D.C.: Government Printing Office, 1961 to date, biennial, $4.75.

United Nations Statistical Office. *Statistical Yearbook.* New York: UNIPUB, 1949 to date, annual, $24.

Economic Almanac. New York: Crowell Collier and Macmillan, Inc., 1940 to date, biennial, $9.95; paperback $2.95.

The *Statistical Abstract of the United States* primarily emphasizes national data, with some attention to statistics from regions and individual states. Statistics for cities and other smaller geographic units are used only infrequently. A consequence of the relatively broad scope is that it is an excellent tool for comparative national studies but limited for units smaller than a state.

Statistical Abstract of the United States is divided into approximately 34 major sections. Each is preceded by a summary which explains terminology and clearly states sources and origin of data. Broad topics include education, public lands, vital statistics, population, and almost any conceivable area likely to be of interest to either the expert or the layman. There is an excellent index which is particularly strong on the subject approach.

While the majority of statistics are from government sources, close to 75 private firms and organizations supply material. As these are designated, *Statistical Abstract* serves another worthwhile purpose as a guide to major statistical services outside of the government.

Most of the data are presented in tabular form. The text is issued annually and each of the tables is updated by one year. For purposes of comparisons, figures are usually retained for several previous years. *Historical Statistics of the United States,* however, is more useful for comparative historical research. Covering the period from 1610 to 1962, it groups materials in much the same way as *Statistical Abstract,* with statistics in time series, primarily on an annual basis. Text notes specify sources and include information on questions of reliability and definitions.

Much of the data found in general almanacs, encyclopedias, handbooks, and the like are drawn directly from the *Statistical Abstract.* For example, the *Statistical Abstract* was reprinted with some introductory material by Grosset & Dunlap, Inc., as *The American Almanac* in 1972. (Government publications generally are not copyrighted. Therefore, they are often published in a somewhat different or even exact form by private publishers. As the government titles are usually less expensive, the wise librarian should check where there is any doubt.)

The *Economic Almanac* includes from 24 to 30 separate sections such as labor, productivity, banking, and finance. Statistical data is given on activities in the United States. (There are separate sections on Canada and the international scene.) A publication of the National Industrial Conference Board, its primary value is the rearrangement of *Statistical Abstract* data in an easy-to-use fashion. There is an excellent index and a glossary.

A useful summary of the *Statistical Abstract* is offered in the *Pocket Data Book* (Washington, D.C.: Government Printing Office, 1971, 300 pp., biennial, paperback, $1.75). It contains numerous easy-to-read and easy-to-follow graphs and charts which summarize the primary data found in the larger work. Such topics as population, vital statistics, finance, and welfare are covered. Because of its effective presentation and format, it is an ideal statistical work for high schools and for adults who may be baffled by the *Statistical Abstract.*

The advantage of the county and district aids is that they break down statistics into smaller units. *The County and City Data Book* covers areas such as cities, congressional districts, metropolitan areas, regions and some small urban centers. Normally, the unit measurement is for towns of over 25,000 population. Arrangement is by this type of geographic-political unit. The statistical information is similar in purpose and type to that found in *Statistical Abstract* but at the "grass roots" level. Such categories as school systems, population characteristics, dwellings, city finance and employment, climate, and hospitals are statistically summarized. The *County and City Data Book* is based on the last census and on supplementary studies. When enough new material is collected, a new edition is issued.

The *Congressional District Data Book* is particularly valuable for the breakdown of statistics by congressional districts. Much of the same material is found in the previous work cited, but the arrangement here is useful from another viewpoint. For example, many of the districts follow county boundaries, and the work can be used for a quick summary of county statistics. Also, there are particular statistics for a good number of nonwhite population districts.

Another statistical guide is the U.S. National Vital Statistics Division's *Vital Statistics of the United States* (Washington, D.C.: Government Printing Office, 1937 to date, annual). This breaks down vital statistics—e.g., population, births and deaths, divorces and marriages—by states, large cities, and other geographical areas. Incidentally, each volume usually includes a discussion of how the statistics are gathered and indicates problems with accuracy—a useful approach to the whole statistical question.

In most general reference situations, international statistics found in almanacs, yearbooks, and encyclopedias will be sufficient. Where currency and special areas are important, the United Nations *Statistical Yearbook* is invaluable. Roughly the international equivalent of *Statistical Abstract*, it covers, in a broad form, over 150 geographical areas by agriculture, manufacturing, transportation, trade, and so on. The arrangement by subject, rather than by country, allows quick comparisons between countries. Also, it often includes statistics which can be found in no other source because the countries do not have their own statistical gathering organizations.[15] The annual volume is updated by the *Monthly Bulletin of Statistics*. The United Nations issues a number of other valuable statistical sources.

Population data are given in the United Nations' *Demographic Yearbook* (New York: UNIPUB, 1948 to date, annual). This gives statistics on population for some 250 different geographical areas—and includes such information as marriage and divorce rates, deaths, and births.

The U.S. Bureau of the Census publishes similar titles of a specialized nature. They issue a quarterly catalog, *Bureau of the Census Catalog*, which includes annotations of both published and unpublished materials. Also, from time to time the U.S. Office of Statistical Standards updates a useful bibliography: *Statistical Services of the United States Government*. This work features an explanation of the federal statistical system, outlines the primary programs, and ends with a listing of publications. A short, useful bibliography of census material will be found in William R. Thompson's "The Census—How It Can Help the Patron," *Wilson Library Bulletin*, November 1972, pp. 275 + .

Business and economic statistics

Predicasts. Cleveland, Ohio: Predicasts, Inc., quarterly, $172.

Editor and Publisher Market Guide. New York: Editor and Publisher, annual, $10.

---

[15] After 1972, Taiwan statistics, at the insistence of Peking, are no longer included. As far as the yearbook goes, Taiwan, with its 14 million people, has ceased to exist. *The New York Times*, August 7, 1972, p. 6.

Survey of Buying Power. New York: Sales Management, 1960 to date, annual, $8.

Survey of Current Business. Washington, D.C.: Government Printing Office, 1921 to date, monthly, weekly supplements, $9.

ACCRA Cost of Living Index. Chicago: American Chamber of Commerce, quarterly, $35.

There are numerous compilations of data regarding the various facets of American and international economy. These range from highly specialized titles, for the experts, to general information found in almanacs, yearbooks, and via indexes to magazine and newspaper articles. There are a few compilations which are of such a general nature that they can be used in most situations where highly specialized data are not required.

The best single source of statistical data for basic economic indicators and a number of products is *Predicasts.* Not only are the statistics given, but the exact source is noted. The service eliminates the necessity of checking an index for a source and then finding the statistics. It is all here. Furthermore, the service is increasing its scope to include statistical data on such fields as medical and health service, legal services, and education. Although expensive, it is well worth the investment because it is up to date and extremely easy to use.

Statistical up-to-date information about American cities can be found in a number of sources from almanacs to *N. W. Ayer & Son's Directory of Newspapers and Periodicals* to encyclopedias. But the best ready-reference source is the *Editor and Publisher* guide. Arranged geographically by United States and Canadian cities which have one or more daily newspapers, it gives standard data on population, climate, industries, chain stores, newspaper circulation and the like. Note, though, it is only for large cities. Many small communities do not have a daily newspaper. Another related, useful title in this same field is the *Rand McNally Commercial Atlas and Marketing Guide* (Chicago: Rand McNally & Company, 1876 to date, annual). It provides a state by state, city, and county summary of population, business, communications, and the like.

Where estimates of the growth of cities and towns is required, the best single source is not a government document but the privately published *Survey of Buying Power.* This annual collects from a number of government surveys such statistics as population estimates of growth for states, cities, metropolitan areas, and countries. Furthermore, the figures are broken down by age groups by area. Beyond these generally useful statistics, there is special data such as retail sales estimates by categories and effective buying income.

The *Survey of Current Business* is the major statistical source of information on a monthly basis about business. Among the 2,500 statistical series is information on finance, transportation, commodities, construction, real estate, and general business indicators. However, it should be noted this is a periodical, not a reference book. In the area of business and economics, periodicals play a major role in reference since they are up to date and currency is of primary importance in the field. Other well-known government serials of this type include *Monthly Labor Review* (Washington, D.C.: Government Printing Office, 1915 to date, monthly). By and large, this is one of the major economic reference aids in almost any library. It gives detailed cost of living statistics in the monthly "Consumer Price Index" and some 30 tables on all aspects of employment and labor. There are, also, summaries of research, briefs on foreign language works, and book reviews. Another much used periodical is the *Federal Reserve Bulletin* (Washington, D.C.: Board of Governors of the Federal Reserve System, 1915 to date, monthly, $6.). This is the basic source of statistical data on banking and monetary matters.

The *Cost of Living Index* supplements the *Monthly Labor Review*. It is considerably easier to use in that it is arranged to show the cost of living differences between some 150 American cities—which includes a number of smaller communities not otherwise listed in standard sources. In addition to the cost of living figures for cities, there are separate comparative figures for housing, transportation, food, and so on.[16]

Still more general works of value in this field are the various census materials and the *Statistical Abstract of the United States,* as well as *Economic Almanac.* All of these bring together a large amount of statistical data and information which is elaborated and expanded upon in the aforementioned titles.

SUGGESTED READING

Farber, M. A., "U.N. Statistical Office a Growing Success," *The New York Times,* November 4, 1972, p. 11. A brief report on the importance of United Nations statistical publications.

Grosvenor, Peter, "How Two Nuts Established the Guinness Book of Records." *Publishers' Weekly.* August 14, 1972, pp. 25+. A short, snappy history of the fabulous and fascinating ready-reference aid.

Grover, K. C., "Telephone Directories." *Library Association Record,* May 1970, pp. 200+· A short informative article on how telephone directories are used in reference work.

Jensen, Marilyn, "Selected Sources of Current Population, Vital and Health Statistics," *Bulletin of the Medical Library Association,* January 1972, pp. 14+· A useful listing of the more basic statistical sources often used by both medical and nonmedical librarians.

"Old Farmer's Almanac," *Newsweek,* December 6, 1971, p. 69. A short piece on one of the best known almanacs in America.

[16] For a good summary of various sources used to find the cost of living in various places, *see:* John G. Fetros, "Guides to the Cost of Living," *RQ,* Winter 1971, pp. 140+.

CHAPTER EIGHT
SUBJECT ALMANACS, YEARBOOKS, HANDBOOKS, MANUALS, AND DIRECTORIES

As there are so few general almanacs, yearbooks, directories, and manuals and handbooks, the majority of these forms are more applicable to specific areas and subjects. The forms tend to ¡overshadow¦one¦ another; and for the beginner, the best approach is to study a few of the basic areas of everyday library reference work and see how these forms are applied in answering reference questions. This, it should be quickly noted, is not an effort to become involved with subject bibliography or subject reference work. It is to demonstrate, if only in a cursory fashion, how the various ready-reference forms are useful in specific situations.

GOVERNMENT AND POLITICAL SCIENCE

Almanacs

Congressional Quarterly Almanac. Washington, D.C.: Congressional Quarterly, Inc., 1945 to date, annual, $47.50.

    Canadian Almanac and Directory. New York: Pitman Publishing Corporation, 1847 to date, $16.50.

    Almanac of American Politics. Boston: Gambit, 1972, biennial, 1,052 pp., $12.95; paperback $4.05.

    The Almanac of World Military Power. New York: R. R. Bowker Company, 1972, 360 pp., $22.50.

The single best retrospective source of information on congressional—and to a degree executive and judiciary—action is the annual *Congressional Quarterly Almanac*. Covering (this is based on material in the *CQ Weekly Report)* activities of the previous year, it includes information on all major legislation, how congressmen voted, highlights of the Supreme Court, basic presidential messages, and the like. There are numerous charts and graphs which speed along the ready-reference process, and the whole is brought together by a complete index.

This same publisher offers a number of related services, e.g., *America Votes* (1955 to date, biennial) which gives state-by-state, county, and ward election returns for the previous election of governors, senators, congressmen, and, where applicable, senators, and the President. *Current American Government* (in periodical form) is another of the publisher's semiannual publications which includes material of current interest about the Presidency, the Congress, the judiciary, lobbies, politics, and so on. Each issue differs in purpose and scope but generally manages to keep abreast of events of particular interest to more aware citizens.

Current information on candidates for national office is easy enough to come by, and their records can be checked in the *Congressional Quarterly Almanac*. At a local, state, or municipal level, the League of Women Voters (among other groups) publishes biographical and evaluative material on candidates. This should be available in every library, as should, of course, opposing views of other organizations.

Getting the political and governmental information down to the "nitty gritty" local scene requires some work on the part of the librarian. There simply are no national or, for that matter, state publications which entirely cover candidates and issues. The local public, school, and university libraries should provide such information from what can be obtained from the community, i.e., through the board of elections, the aforementioned League of Women Voters, and from individual candidates. A call to the local newspaper and the chamber of commerce will help beginners who are seeking methods of gathering such information in a community.

The *Canadian Almanac* is the standard ready-reference aid in Canadian libraries. However, it is in no way a general almanac. Almost total emphasis is on Canadian activities and statistics. Furthermore, it has many of the same attributes as a directory (major government officials are listed, as are agencies, insurance companies, and banks) and a biographical guide in that it contains information on members of government. The almanac is typical of national efforts elsewhere, e.g., almost every country has a similar publication. Many of these, though, are termed yearbooks, annuals, handbooks, and even directories. A few titles will be explanatory: *The Nigeria Yearbook,* the *Africa Annual, Australia Handbook, Japan Directory*. Almost all enjoy an annual or a biennial publishing schedule and in a library serve to back up and support more general works such as *The Statesman's Yearbook.*

The *Almanac of American Politics* is both encyclopedic and an almanac in nature. The first section provides background material on Washington, D.C. and the Capitol. Each senator and representative is listed with names of assistants and biographical data. Furthermore, he or she is rated by various groups and all key votes are shown. This is followed by a state-by-state, district-by-district breakdown of everything from per capita income to major defense installations. The form is familiar enough, but this has the distinct advantage of being relatively inexpensive, up to date (it is revised biennially), and fairly easy to use—there is an excellent index.

A good deal of the information found in the aforementioned almanac will be found in other sources, from an encyclopedia to a general almanac, not to mention the familiar *Congressional Quarterly Almanac.* Still, this type of almanac points up the very real fact that a reference librarian can never quite have enough current, statistical, ready-reference books.

The *World Military Power* almanac is an example of a highly specialized, carefully arranged approach to data. Two sets of information are given on a country-by-country basis: inventories of armed forces strength and summaries of the geographical, political, economic, strategic, international factors. There are numerous maps and an extensive glossary. There is a helpful index by country, regions, and international organizations. Again, some of the information is readily available elsewhere, but the arrangement and the narrow scope of the work make it ideal for not only answering questions about the military and war, but about peace, economics, politics, and so on.

Yearbooks

Statesman's Year-Book. New York: St. Martin's Press, Inc., 1864 to date, annual, $12.50.

Europa Yearbook. London: Europa Publications, Ltd. (Distributed in United States by Gale Research Company), 1946 to date, annual, 2 vols., $66.

Yearbook of the United Nations. New York: United Nations, Office of Public Information, 1947 to date, $30.

Yearbook of International Organizations. Brussels: Union of International Associations, 1948 to date (Distributed in United States by International Publications Service), biennial, $28.

Municipal Yearbook. Washington, D.C.: International City Management Association, 1934 to date, annual, $17.50.

A decided problem with government yearbooks is "recency." Most of the data in a 1973 title will be up to date in terms of 1972, or a good part of 1972, yet of little use for changes subsequent to publication of the annual. Hence, information about particular officers and government administrations—especially in areas of quick change—should be double-checked with current fact sources such as *Facts on File* or *Keesing's*.

The most popular, best known, and, in many ways, still the single best source for relatively recent information is the *Statesman's Year-Book*. Perhaps its popularity stems as much from its age as from its contents; but along with the *World Almanac* and an encyclopedia, it serves as a cornerstone for reference work in almost any type of library. As the library grows and/or becomes more specialized, there is a need for the other typical government yearbooks.

The *Statesman's Year-Book* gives detailed information on all governments of the world, although it is particularly strong for the Western nations. Information includes data and discursive discussions of constitutions, government, economic conditions, religion, agriculture, and commerce, as well as useful (although sometimes dated) lists of diplomatic representatives, heads of government, and major offices. It includes a bibliography for each country, but this is usually only perfunctory and much dated.

Information is grouped geographically, under the British Commonwealth, the United States, and the rest of the world. There is a preliminary section on international organizations. Another helpful feature is the numerous maps which show such things as time-zones and distribution of oil deposits. A reviewer observes another characteristic of the work:

> While the character of the *Year-Book* is unchanging, that of the statesman for whom it is intended is evidently not. He is now identified in the blurb as the "businessman-of-the-world." From internal evidence, his nationality is Anglo-American. Not only is the United States the only country to have a section to itself: it also shares another distinction with Britain. Details are given under every country in the world of the diplomatic representation to and from it of Britain and the United States alone. Although Ottawa, Delhi and Canberra may feel neglected—for they too have businessmen-of-the-world—there is really no alternative to such discrimination if the volume is to be kept manageable.[1]

Although it contains much of the same information found in the latter work, the first volume of *The Europa Yearbook* is particularly valuable for coverage of international organizations and individual European countries. A basic pattern is followed throughout: essential data

[1] "Briefing for Businessmen," *Times Literary Supplement,* October 6, 1972, p. 1,192. For an analysis of how back issues of the yearbook may be used *see:* James L. Becker, "The Statesman's Year-Book," *RQ,* Fall 1970, pp. 25+.

with statistical tables, information on the political and judicial systems, press and radio, publishing, finance, trade and industry, tourism, and the diplomatic corps. The second volume uses the same form for other countries of the world. Due to its prompt publication and its wide coverage, it is one of the best of all yearbooks.

Over the years, Europa publications has published a number of related annual volumes, e.g., *The Middle East and North Africa* (1948 to date); *The Far East and Australasia* (1969 to date); and *Africa South of the Sahara* (1971 to date). How much duplication is there in these sets and the parent *Europa* volumes? A good deal, but the publisher is wise enough to include just enough unique material to make them necessary for at least the larger libraries. In an analysis of the duplication, a perceptive librarian points out:

> While the librarian takes for granted the duplication of material in different reference sources, this is not so often the case within volumes from the same publisher. And although the increase of these volumes has seemed to approximate the scientific process of mitosis, I am not sure what process is illustrated by the "greater the number of volumes, the larger and more expensive they grow." But with Europa Publications, Ltd., I suspect the end is not yet quite in sight. Until then, the answer to the question whether all the volumes are necessary is still yes and no.[2]

There are numerous other reference works of a similar nature in this field, e.g., *Political Handbook and Atlas of the World* (New York: Council on Foreign Relations, distributed by Simon & Schuster, Inc., 1972). This is often rewritten and updated, and the 1972 edition covers material through 1970. It discusses some 143 countries and 95 related territories with data on everything from major newspapers to social and demographic aids. The *Worldmark Encyclopedia* is still another of this type.

The *Yearbook of the United Nations* is an example of an annual whose publishing history is always two to three years in arrears, e.g., the 1969 yearbook was issued in 1972. Be that as it may, the yearbook is an excellent source of retrospective information on all the activities of the United Nations and its related agencies. (Current information may be found via *The Statesman's Year-Book* and the *Europa Yearbook* as well as in ongoing United Nations publications.) It is usually divided into two sections. The first discusses political, economic, and social questions before the United Nations for the given year. The second section deals with international organizations related to the United Nations, e.g., International Labor Organization, International Atomic Energy Agency. There are, also, various appendices and a subject and name index. A run of the yearbooks provides an excellent summary of United Nations' activities;

[2] Elizabeth C. Hyslop, "Europa: Does 2 + 6 = 8?" *RQ,* Spring 1972, p. 212. *See also* the publisher's reply: *RQ,* Spring 1973, pp. 329 + .

but because of its tardy publishing schedule, it is of little value for questions concerning ongoing activities.

While much of the information about international organizations may be found in the aforementioned titles (as well as in general almanacs and encyclopedias), a work exclusively given over to listing and describing such groups is the *Yearbook of International Organizations.* This lists over 4,000 organizations from the Common Market to multinational business groups. It gives their purpose, structure, activities, and history. In addition, there is a directory of officials. For libraries with limited budgets, *The World of Learning* lists some 400 international organizations and, for most purposes, this would be enough.

The *Municipal Yearbook* provides specific, relatively up-to-date information on all aspects of general municipal government. It is not intended as a particular approach to individual cities other than for basic statistics and information on officeholders. There are six major sections: government setting, personnel administration, municipal finance, municipal activities, references (basic sources of information on municipal government), and directories.

A related work, although published biennially, is *The Book of States* (Lexington, Kentucky: The Council of State Governments, 1935 to date, biennial). Again this is a broad (rather than a state-by-state) approach to everything from legislative and administrative systems to natural resources and law enforcement. Of particular help in ready reference is the section "The State Pages," which are given over to a roster of state officials, state-by-state. As most of the material is based upon primary sources, it can be trusted as being authoritative and relatively current. (The publisher does issue supplements which list changes in elective officials, e.g., *State Elective Officials* and the *Legislature and State Administrative Officials Classified by Functions.*)

In addition to these two broad titles, each state and many larger municipalities issue their own annual or biennial guides, or "blue books." These vary in scope and depth of presentation, but are of major importance for all libraries, e.g., even the smallest library will want the state manual for its state. If there is any question about the title or frequency of such a manual or annual, the librarian should simply contact his state library or, for that matter, any official in the governor's office. The local manuals are invaluable for biographical information on state legislators, data on various agencies, and the like. A somewhat dated, but still useful, guide to such information is Charles Press and Oliver Williams' *State Manuals, Blue Books and Election Results* (Berkeley, California: Institute of Governmental Studies, University of California Press, 1962, 101 pp.).[3]

---

[3] An alphabetical state list of blue books, or their equivalent, will be found in: Peter Hernon, "State Publications," *Library Journal,* April 15, 1972, pp. 1,393 + .

Manuals and handbooks

U.S. National Archives and Record Service, *United States Government Organization Manual.* Washington, D.C.: Government Printing Office, 1935 to date, annual paperback, $3.

Everyman's United Nations. New York: United Nations, 1948 to date, irregular, (8th ed., 1945–1965, $6; Supplement, 1966–1970, $4).

Theis, Paul and William Steponkus. *All About Politics.* New York: R. R. Bowker Company, 1972, 300 pp., $10.95.

Civil Rights: A Guide to the People, Organizations and Events. New York: R. R. Bowker Company, 1970, 194 pp., $10.50.

Demeter, George. *Demeter's Manual of Parliamentary Law and Procedure.* Boston: Little, Brown and Company, 1969, $4.95.

The New York Times Guide to Federal Aid for Cities and Towns. Chicago: Quadrangle Books, 1972, 1,312 pp., $65.

The *Organization Manual* is one of several publications issued annually by the Government Printing Office; and by and large, it is among the most useful in any reference collection. Its basic purpose is to give in detail the organization, activities, and chief officers of all government agencies. This includes the legislative, judicial, and executive branches.

Each of the agencies is discussed separately and the units within each organizational pattern are clearly defined. Now and then, charts and diagrams are employed to make matters a bit clearer. The style is factual, yet discursive enough to hold interest of anyone remotely involved with such matters.

A useful feature of each year's work is the list of agencies which have been transferred, terminated, or abolished. Full particulars are given. This, by the way, is justification for holding several years of the manual on the shelves. All too often someone will want information on this or that agency which can only be found in earlier editions of the work.

Students, particularly those struggling through a civics or history class, find this an excellent source of factual material for papers. Adults use it for names of officials and proper addresses.

Along with the *Statistical Abstract of the United States* and the *Official Congressional Directory,* this is one of three government publications that should be in every library regardless of size or type.

The fullest and best treatment of the United Nations will be found in the frequently revised *Everyman's United Nations.* This is the official handbook which, like the *Organization Manual,* explains the structure, functions, and work of the United Nations. Usually in three parts, the first describes the various agencies; the second, and most extensive, surveys the past year's work; and the third gives information about intergovernmental agencies related to the United Nations. There is a good index. More extensive statistical and current data will be found in the *Yearbook of the United Nations* considered elsewhere.

What is the so-called "Eastern Establishment?" Where did the term "silent majority" come from? Designed specifically to answer political questions, *All About Politics* is a compendium of easy-to-use questions and answers. The authors cover hundreds of typical political questions which are apt to be asked in many library reference situations. An index brings it together. The work is particularly suited as a back-up resource item where the standard handbooks and almanacs fail to give information or information specific enough for current general reference questions dealing with the political scene.

There are a number of specialized guides and handbooks in political science. A typical, useful one is the guide to civil rights. This provides detailed information on key people, organizations, and events in the movement. The biographical information is important; but the work, also, includes a guide to acronyms and a number of appendices from congressional voting records to leading black elected officials in the United States. While much of the information in this work could be found in standard sources, it is still another example of how a compilation simply saves the reference librarian hours of time. Instead of having to search a variety of biographical titles, not to mention indexes and encyclopedias, the civil rights guide assembles all the necessary information.

On the periphery of government and political science, and equally applicable to meetings of any group, are the various rules and parliamentary regulation handbooks and manuals. The Demeter title is considerably easier to follow and to use for ready-reference work than the standard *Robert's Rules of Order*—and, of course, covers all the basic regulations established by Roberts in 1876. Material includes what to do when conducting everything from a mass meeting to how to vote and use disciplinary procedures in smaller groups. For those who prefer the standard *Robert's*, the best revised edition is: *Robert's Rules of Order, Newly Revised* (Glenview, Illinois: Scott, Foresman and Company, 1970, 594 pp., $5.95). Basic information on how to run and control a meeting is found in numerous other sources from many of the etiquette books to the encyclopedias. Usually this is enough for the average nonmeeting type, but only Robert's will satisfy the variety of meeting goers so often encountered at such gatherings as the American Library Association's annual meeting.

Representative of a growing number of books on "how to get the money," *The New York Times Guide to Federal Aid* work is designed to do just that. It lists some 656 urban aid programs, shows how to write programs to qualify for the aid, and even lists "grants often overlooked." The manual is purposefully written for the city official who may not have an office of lawyers available to interpret and analyze money available from federal agencies and foundations. It, also, is of considerable value to the layman who may be trying to find methods of improving his community. In this same category, but primarily for individual aid, *see* the *Foundations Directory*.

Biographical directories

Who's Who in American Politics. New York: R. R. Bowker Company, 1967 to date, biennial, $37.50.

U.S. Congress. *Official Congressional Directory,* Washington, D.C.: Government Printing Office, 1809 to date, annual, $7.

Congressional Staff Directory. Washington, D.C.: Congressional Staff Directory, 1959 to date, annual, $12.50.

Taylor's *Encyclopedia of Government Officials: Federal and State.* Westfield, New Jersey: Political Research, Inc., 1967 to date, annual, quarterly supplements and monthly bulletin, $60.

Among the more common reference questions are: Who is my congressman? Who are the members of the state legislature? What is the address of . . .? Almost any ready-reference type question involving a federal, state, or local government or political figure can be answered in the titles listed here.

The 1971–1972 edition of *Who's Who in American Politics* profiles nearly 16,000 prominent political figures. The data-type sketches range from the President of the United States to state legislators and mayors of major cities. It is primarily useful for information on state and city and town officials (there is a handy geographical index to facilitate use at the local level) not found in other standard sources. As noted, most states now have legislative manuals, or "bluebooks," which give limited biographical information, too, e.g., *The Illinois Blue Book,* the *Iowa Official Register* and the *Louisiana Roster of Officials,* to name but three.

There are over 20 separate sections to the *Congressional Directory,* but the principal emphasis is on short, factual biographies of congressmen and judges of the Supreme Court. The other sections are useful for such information as who is serving on what committee, votes cast for the congressmen, and foreign consular offices in the United States. A library with the Bowker publication would also need this for the additional biographical information on congressmen as well as for the handy arrangement of data on other aspects of federal government.

Where does one find information on congressmen no longer serving or those who have held office prior to 1961? If relatively famous, they will be in such sources as the *Dictionary of American Biography* (if they are deceased) or a good encyclopedia. However, for short, concise, objective sketches of all congressmen who served from 1774 to 1961 the best single source is *U.S. Congress Biographical Directory of the American Congress, 1774-1961* (Washington, D.C.: Government Printing Office, 1961, 1,863 pp.). There is a handy first section which includes officers of the executive branch of the government, i.e., the cabinets from George Washington through to the first administration of Dwight Eisenhower. There is, also, a chronological listing by state of congressmen from the First to the Eighty-sixth Congress.[4]

How does one find the name of a member of a congressional staff, a senate committee staff, or the like? Many of these are listed in the *Congressional Directory* as well as in the *United States Government Organization Manual;* but a commercial firm offers a simple, direct path to the names via the *Congressional Staff Directory.* This includes the personnel of all congressional staffs, subcommittee and committee staffs, and the like. It also lists representatives of cities with population over 1,500 and has a number of biographical sketches. The index makes it an excellent ready-reference aid for use with the other standard works.

Taylor's Encyclopedia of Government Officials is useful in that its supplements update basic directory-biographical material. The service covers close to 25,000 government officials from the state to the federal level. Useful reference information includes addresses, phone numbers, legislative districts, pictures, and charts. The book is divided into federal and state sections and is ideal for relatively current information. There is a good index, although the librarian must search through the quarterly and monthly supplements to be certain if there is any change in a given office.

There are numerous other sources of information on congress and public and political figures at all levels of government. Various departments of the federal government have their own biographical aids, e.g., U.S. Department of State's *Foreign Service List* (Washington, D.C.: Government Printing Office, 1929 to date) lists all members of the U.S. Foreign Service and other key organization staff workers abroad.

For information on government and political leaders outside the United States, there are a variety of sources from the favored *Statesman's Year-Book* to *The New York Times Index.* A handy compilation of data on foreign government leaders will be found in the *Almanac of Current World Leaders* (Pasadena, California: Marshall Crawhaw, 1958 to date, monthly except February, June, and October, $12). This is a

---

[4] Part of this is expanded and updated in Robert Sobel's *Biographical Directory of the United States Executive Branch, 1774-1971* (Westport, Connecticut: Greenwood Press, 1971, $27.50). It follows the pattern of the *Biographical Directory of the American Congress* and includes brief discursive sketches of the Presidents, heads of state, and cabinet officers. It has an excellent index. An equally excellent work of the same basic type is the *Congressional Quarterly's Guide to The Congress of the United States* (Washington, D.C.: Congressional Quarterly Service, 1971, 1 vol., $35). This follows a similar pattern to the other works and brings the history up to 1971.

pocket-sized magazine which gives up-to-date biographical information on the officials of most world states, cabinet level and above and includes current information on political events. (The subscription price includes an annual almanac which regroups and organizes the information in the monthly issues.) It is an invaluable updating service for most libraries.

BUSINESS AND ECONOMICS

Thomas Register of American Manufacturers. New York: Thomas Publishing Company, Inc., 1910 to date, annual, $39.75.

Encyclopedia of Associations. Detroit: Gale Research Company, 1964 to date, biennial, 3 vols., $111.50.

Audiovisual Market Place. New York: R. R. Bowker Company, 1964 to date, biennial, $17.50.

Poor's Register of Corporations, Directors and Executives. New York: Standard & Poor's Corporation, 1928 to date, annual, $115.

Moody's Investors Service. New York: Moody's Investors Service, 6 vols., annual, semiweekly, or weekly supplements, $150 to $250 per each service.

Standard & Poor's Corporation Records. New York: Standard & Poor's Corporation, 6 vols., 3 supplements a month, $286; *Daily News* supplement, $242 per year.

U.S. Internal Revenue Service. *Your Federal Income Tax.* Washington, D.C.: Government Printing Office, 1944 to date, annual.

The field of business, commerce, and economics is so vast as to require special courses in library science.[5] Numerous libraries serve one or more aspects of the business and economic world. They may offer basic general titles that will aid the librarian functioning in a nonspecialized situation and answering, for the most part, nontechnical, general questions about business and economics.

The most requested information falls into three categories: (1) data on various firms and businesses; (2) financial information, which includes everything from the stock market to basic facts about a corporation; and (3) general economic and business statistical data. It seems

[5] E. T. Coman, *Sources of Business Information.* rev. ed. (Berkeley: University of California Press, 1964). A dated yet still basic work which gives the best overview of the subject. A brief, annotated list of relatively up-to-date material is offered in the basic (often revised): Lorna M. Daniles, *Business Reference Sources* (Cambridge, Massachusetts: Baker Library, Graduate School of Business Administration, Harvard University, 1971), 108 pp., paperback $3). Other useful bibliographies include: *Encyclopedia of Business Information Sources* (Detroit: Gale Research Company, 1970, 2 vols., $47.50); John Fletcher, *The Use of Economic Literature* (Hamden, Connecticut: Archon Books, The Shoe String Press, Inc., 1971), 210 pp., $12.50.

worth repeating that current materials, particularly of a more specific nature, may be found in the standard indexes and bibliographies. A good deal of "how-to-buy" this or that is the subject of countless titles which many libraries will have in the general collection. And then there are the more general statistical handbooks, almanacs, and the like which are discussed throughout this section. Of limited use are encyclopedias which tend to stress the historical aspects of business and economics more than the daily activities of interest to many library patrons.

The most common type of general business question probably concerns who makes what—particularly in this day of consumer awareness when someone may wish to write a manufacturer about a faulty product or inquire about a given franchise.

There are two basic directories. The first, and by far the most important, is the *Thomas Register.* Although a trifle frightening in its size (it comes in 10 large volumes), it is relatively easy to use. More than 75,000 American firms are listed. Six of the ten volumes are alphabetically arranged by product—and under each product are the manufacturers, by state and city. Another volume is an alphabetical list of companies. The addresses, and in many cases the names of the principal officers, are listed, with size of capitalization often shown. Two more volumes are given over to manufacturers' catalogs, and a final volume is a detailed subject index with trade names and major chambers of commerce listed. The trade names are invaluable for tracing the true manufacturer of a product whose name may have little or no relation to the product itself.

Another somewhat similar work is *Kelly's Manufacturers and Merchants Directory* (London: Kelly's Directories, Ltd. 1889 to date, annual, $30). *Kelly's* is of more limited use, primarily because it is a directory of British and world manufacturers. It is mentioned here because it is so well known, so old, and often confused with the American title. It would be required only in larger libraries.

Complementing both of these directories, but more particularly *Thomas,* is the *Poor's Register.* This consists of an alphabetical list of some 34,000 American and Canadian corporations with names of officers and types of products manufactured, as well as number of employees. Both public and private companies are listed, and the directory concludes with brief biographical information on some 80,000 directors and executives. A Standard Industrial Classification index is a type of subject approach to the companies listed. *Poor's* would be used where more biographical data was needed (although prominent executives are listed in *Who's Who in America* and its various subsidiary volumes, as well as in other biographical sources), but more likely, where additional information was needed about a company.

There are numerous other directories of a more specialized variety, e.g., *Best's Insurance Reports, Broadcasting Yearbook,* and *Polk's World*

Bank Directory. Then there are regional directories such as *The Directory of New England Manufacturers.* And, as with the book industry (e.g., *Publisher's Trade List Annual*), there are numerous directories for specific industries. For example, the *Franchise Annual* (Chicago: National Franchise Reports, 1950, annual, $2.30) lists franchising companies and enough basic data about them to help anyone interested in securing a franchise.

When trying to locate information on individual firms and information about their products or equipment, it is best to start with the general, i.e., *Thomas,* and move to the particular.[6] If the information in *Thomas* is not adequate, consult the two volumes of catalogs. When the needed information is too new to be included in any of these sets, refer to the various trade magazines via indexes such as *Business Index* and the *Public Affairs Information Service Bulletin* and, of course, *The New York Times Index* and the *Wall Street Journal Index.*

A somewhat related set is the *Encyclopedia of Associations.* Here, though, the emphasis is on listing American nonprofit membership organizations—as contrasted with *Thomas* and *Kelly's* which list profit-making business organizations. Often the sets are used together because either the user or the librarian may be unaware of the status of the organization he is seeking. The organizations, which are listed alphabetically by name, are in such areas as scientific, engineering, educational, cultural, social welfare, health, and medical. It is by far the most complete directory of its type available. The second volume is a geographic executive index which lists the organizations by state and city in the first section and by executives in the second section. A third quarterly publication, *New Associations and Projects,* keeps the set up to date until the next directory is issued. Gale also publishes a somewhat similar approach in its *Research Centers Directory* and the *Directory of Special Libraries* (*see* section in this chapter, "Library Science").

Still another useful approach to businesses and associations is offered by the *Audiovisual Market Place.* It is primarily for educators seeking unevaluative directory information on sources of audio-visual materials from films to television tapes. In addition to names and addresses, it provides information on professional and trade organizations, cataloging services, a bibliography of related reference works, and even a listing of exhibitions, film festivals, and the like. There are two useful indexes. While much of this basic trade information is available in *Thomas,* this again is the case where a single, handy volume is more useful to the specialist than the bulky, larger general directory of manufacturers.

Whereas *Thomas* and similar directories give specific information

---

[6] The best basic list, which includes major examples, is to be found in James B. Woy's "Basic Trade Directories," *RQ,* Spring 1971, pp. 228 + ·

on products (and personnel), there is another set of services which give detailed corporate information. Much of this will be used by the person interested in investments and the stock market; but the services are equally valuable for current statistics, statutes, and immediate future of particular corporations and industries. The services tend to be well indexed and current.

There are numerous services of both a special and a general nature for corporate information.[7] The best, probably most used are issued by Moody's and Standard & Poor's. Moody's publishes six volumes of *Manuals*, each covering a specific field: industrials, public utilities, transportation, governments, and finance. These are updated by semiweekly reports. In the same area, Standard & Poor's publishes *Corporation Records* which gives factual information on over 7,000 major American and Canadian corporations, as well as brief data on over 5,000 smaller business concerns. This comes in a 6-volume loose leaf set which is updated with supplements. There is also a *Daily News Section* and *Daily Dividend Section*, with weekly and annual cumulations.

In addition to these standard sets, both companies issue a number of services primarily for the investor, e.g., *Standard & Poor's Industry Surveys* (the analysis of some 39 major industries with predictions of future performance, within each industry specific companies are examined), and *Standard & Poor's Stock Reports* (a total of 11 volumes which gives daily information on the American, New York, and Over-the-Counter Exchanges). Among other items, Moody's issues a weekly bond guide, *Bond Survey.* And there are other related investment aids from the *Value Line Service* to the *Wiesenberger Investment Report.*[8]

An inexpensive overview of the New York and American Stock Exchanges is offered by *Financial World Stock Factograph* (New York: Financial World, 1960 to date, annual). Some 2,300 stocks are listed with brief information about the businesses, dividend record, financial position, price range of the stock, and the like over the previous year. As the annual usually costs under $7, it is a good buy for the small library with no other service available.

The majority of libraries with a limited business collection would have one or both of the basic industrial services, e.g., *Moody's Investors Service* or *Standard & Poor's Corporation Records,* with the probable

[7] Steven Goodman, *Financial Market Place* (New York: R. R. Bowker Company, 1972). This directory indexes under 175 subjects, data on the major corporations, institutions, services, and publications in the field.

[8] Investment aids is a highly specialized area. The best overview of the subject will be found in: James B. Woy, *Investment Information: A Detailed Guide to Selected Sources* (Detroit: Gale Research Company, 1970), 231 pp. $14.50; and Sheldon Zerden's *Best Books on the Stock Market: An Analytical Bibliography* (New York: R. R. Bowker Company, 1972). A more selective list by Woy is "Loose Leaf Business Services" (*RQ,* Winter 1969, pp. 128+), a basic list of titles selected by librarians. *See also* Robert S. Burgess, "Specialized Investment Services," *Library Journal,* March 1, 1970, pp. 868+·

addition of the *Industry Surveys.* After that, the daily reports on the stock market and the various business services would be added as needed.

One section of business and economics of interest to everyman is taxes. There are countless publications in this area—for both the layman and the specialist. The basic work issued by the Internal Revenue Service is designed to help laymen understand and prepare a tax form. The language is relatively simple, there are numerous examples, and there is a detailed index. Among other general works of this type, one of the best is J. K. Lasser's *Your Income Tax* (New York: Simon & Schuster, Inc., 1937 to date, annual). An inexpensive paperback, it provides more information than found in the government publication, particularly in terms of legal ways of minimizing the amount of tax paid.

Two private publishers, Commerce Clearing House and Prentice-Hall are particularly well known for their services and texts in taxation. The majority of these are for experts, or near experts, in the field. The *CCH Federal Tax Guide* and the *CCH State Tax Guide* are loose leaf services which are designed to give up-to-date information on new tax laws. Prentice-Hall has a similar series.

Consumer services

U.S. Office of Consumer Affairs. *Guide to Federal Consumer Services.* Washington, D.C.: Government Printing Office, 1971, 151 pp., paperback $1.

There are numerous trade books which cover various aspects of consumer services; and these, along with periodical and newspaper articles, are likely to be the basis of most consumer information at a reference desk. For those who wish to do meaningful research in various aspects of the subject, there are several good government sources. *The Guide to Federal Consumer Services* is frequently revised. Material is arranged by issuing agency and there is a useful subject index. General information is given about the work of the agencies and how the interested consumer may query them for assistance. Selected publications are noted. Another useful item, again frequently updated, is the *Consumer Education: Bibliography* (Washington, D.C.: Government Printing Office, 1969, 170 pp., 65¢). This lists, but does not annotate, over 2,000 books, pamphlets, films, and other items in the field of consumer interests and education.

The government issues a number of periodicals in this area which are helpful. *The F.D.A. Papers* (Washington, D.C.: Government Printing Office, 1967 to date, monthly, $3.50) is the official magazine of the Food and Drug Administration; and each issue includes articles and field reports on investigations of consumer products.

Secretarial handbooks

Becker, Ester and Evelyn Anders, *The Successful Secretary's Handbook.* New York: Harper & Row, Publishers, Incorporated, 1971, 419 pp., $7.95.

Doris, Lillian and Bessemay Miller, *The Complete Secretary's Handbook.* 3d ed. Englewood Cliffs, New Jersey: Prentice-Hall, Inc., 1971, 224 pp., $8.50.

Webster's New World Word Book. Cleveland: The World Publishing Company, 1966, 308 pp., $2.95.

Books on secretarial practice have a multiple purpose in a reference situation. First, they do assist the professional secretary who is in need of some background information. In this respect, at least one or two of the handbooks should be duplicated in the general collection so they may be taken home and studied. Second, because of the thorough, relatively simple approach to problems of English, letter writing, style, and so on, they are helpful for the student preparing papers or the layman anxious to write the proper type of letter.

The titles listed here are standard in the field. They cover everything from office procedures and correspondence to how to get along with the boss. Probably the most helpful features of both are: (1) clear explanations of grammar, punctuation, abbreviations, capitalization, word usage, and so on; (2) detailed indexes which allow the user to find precisely what is needed when in a rush.

Either, or both, is useful in libraries; and one should be kept near the reference desk, while one or more should be available for general circulation.

In some respects, the secretarial handbooks are easier to copy with than the standard works on English considered in the section on dictionaries. However, they are no substitute for the stylist and, by all means, should be augmented by one or two good dictionaries. In this respect, a peculiar type of dictionary is represented by the *New World Word Book.* A small (about 3½ by 5 inches) book, it is primarily intended to show clearly and rapidly how words are divided by syllabication. No good typist is without this or a similar work, and it can prove a handy aid for the librarian or patron who is working on a number of letters or term papers.

EDUCATION

American Universities and Colleges. 11th ed. Washington, D.C.: American Council on Education, 1973, 1,800 pp., $22.

American Junior Colleges. 8th ed. Washington, D.C.: American Council on Education, 1971, 850 pp., $18.00.

Guide to Graduate Study. 4th ed. by Robert Quick. Washington, D.C.: American Council on Education, 1969, 637 pp., $15.

Lovejoy, C. E., *Lovejoy's College Guide.* New York: Simon & Schuster, Inc., 1952 to date, biennial, paperback, $4.95.

Sargent, Porter, ed., *The Handbook of Private Schools.* Boston: Porter Sargent, Publisher, 1915 to date, annual, $16.

The World of Learning. 1947 to date. London: Europa Publications, 1947 to date (distributed in United States by Gale Research Company), 2 vols., annual, $42.

Minerva, Jahrbuch der Gelehrten Welt. Berlin: Walter de Gruyter, 1891 to date, irregular, 4 vols. DM 672.

The Foundation Directory. New York: Columbia University Press, 1960 to date, irregular, $15.

The guides to various types and levels of schools are numerous. Each year new titles appear, others are updated. The result is necessity for careful choice by librarians.

The amount of interest in college and university education requires that almost any size library have at least a minimum of these titles. As an adjunct, there should be provision for a series of college and university catalogs or, at least, ready information about where such catalogs may be obtained. Even the best of the directories cannot give the bits of information a patential student seeks and can only find in a particular catalog.[9]

The lack of proper advisory services in some high schools makes it particularly important that at least one member of the reference department be familiar with helping teen-agers (and their parents) find information on colleges and universities. Such items as cost, entrance requirements, size of school, and strengths and weaknesses of faculty are covered in part in each of the titles listed here. There are many other popular guides, and there will be an increase in their number over the years.

Generally speaking, the most useful and authoritative directory of colleges and universities is the work issued by the American Council on Education. Revised about every four years, it is perfect for the first year of revision; but after that, the material tends to be dated and must be checked against other sources. This is particularly true for fees, but the basic information on the 1,250 accredited colleges and 2,600 professional schools is excellent and reliable. The information on accredited colleges and universities includes the history, organization, resources, staff analysis, size, degrees granted, and almost anything else a potential student would want to know. *American Junior Colleges* is revised on about the

[9] Margaret Perry, "The College Catalog Collection," *RQ,* Spring 1971, pp. 240 + · A valuable survey of how college catalogs are used in reference work.

same schedule and includes similar information for some 800 junior colleges. This includes both public and private schools.

While both the *American Universities and Colleges* and *American Junior Colleges* are geared to the beginner and the parent, the *Guide to Graduate Study* begins with a sensible essay addressed to someone who has completed, or is near finishing, his undergraduate work. The essay answers questions about who should think about graduate work and what steps he should take. This is followed by a detailed analysis of schools offering programs leading to the Ph.D., and there is a very useful index arranged by field of study.

The American Council publishes a variety of other titles in this field from *A Rating of Graduate Programs* to *Computers on Campus*. Any library with more than an average interest in education reference work would be well advised to write the Council for its catalog.

The Lovejoy directory is possibly the best known among students. It is particularly designed for high school students, and the main part of the guide consists of the same type of information given in the American Council on Education series. Listing is by state and the depth of information is less than that found in the Council books. Yet the method of presentation in a type of outline form is excellent, especially as the guide is issued every two years and its data on such items as costs and requirements are likely to be more up to date than those found in the Council directories. Another useful feature is that Lovejoy lists some junior colleges and nonaccredited schools not found in the other works. Finally, the relatively low price for the paperback edition allows most students or parents to purchase a copy for careful study at home.

Lovejoy is the author of another useful directory. This is *Lovejoy's Vocational School Guide* (New York: Simon & Schuster, Inc., 1963 to date, biennial). The arrangement is easy to follow, and it has a quantity and variety of information rarely found in the more formalized works.

One book which is especially helpful for the parent is James Cass and Max Birnbaum's *Comparative Guide to American Colleges* . . . (New York: Harper & Row, Publishers, Incorporated, 1972, 397 pp., $10.). This is a relaxed, discursive approach to 1,200 four-year colleges. While the authors claim they do not discuss the merits of each school in terms of what is "best" or "better," the data on everything from scholarships to fraternities and social life do much to help a student pick the school of his choice. The publisher updates this work regularly, and it is one that should be duplicated in the general collection.

Sargent's handbook on private schools is an annual publication that analyzes some 1,100 elementary and secondary private schools. A full description of each school is given, and all necessary data are presented in an easy-to-understand manner. There is a listing of summer camps and some advertising by the various schools, although not from all of those included. A similar title, which is equally excellent, is *Private Independent Schools* (Wallingford, Connecticut: Bunting & Lyon, 1947 to date, annual, $15). Again, it describes private elementary and secondary school programs both here and abroad. In view of interest in such schools, most libraries would do well to purchase both titles. There is enough difference between the two to justify the expense.

At the international college and university level, there are several basic directories. *The World of Learning* is arranged alphabetically by country, giving directory and bits of descriptive information about the major schools. It also includes data on libraries, societies, and other elements of culture. Consequently, it may be used for purposes other than locating a particular university or college.

Two works, both issued by associations, cover the universities and colleges of Europe. *The Commonwealth Universities Yearbook* (London: Association of the British Commonwealth, 1914 to date) is an annual which includes directory information on countries of the Commonwealth and is much more detailed than *The World of Learning*. *The International Handbook of Universities* (Paris: International Association of Universities, 1962 to date) is revised from time to time and includes that part of the world not found in the other directory. Both of these sources are modeled after the publications of the American Council on Education and tend to be quite thorough.

Minerva has been published since 1891 and enjoys the reputation of being the broadest in scope of any of the works so far noted. As the title implies, it takes in the whole of the learned world. The thirty-fifth edition (1966–1970) is in four volumes. Part one covers European institutions of higher learning, while the second part covers non-European countries, listing more than 3,000 institutions. For universities and institutions in Western Europe, the language of the country is used, with German employed for lesser countries and Russia. English is used for the United States, England, Japan, and Africa. "Institution" is interpreted broadly to include colleges, technical schools, and both private and public schools. While the *World of Learning* provides information on institutions not included in *Minerva,* i.e., museums, libraries, international organizations, and the like, the latter has considerably more information on educational institutions. Also, there are numerous indexes which make it relatively easy to locate material from biographical data on faculty to educational objectives.

Financial assistance, for both the individual and the institution, is of considerable concern and a frequent subject of questions at the reference desk. The best known work in this area is *The Foundation Directory.* The fourth edition (1971) includes in 642 pages information on 5,500 American foundations with assets of $500,000 or more which make grants of $25,000 or more. The directory is arranged by state and then by title of the organization with full information about its activities. There is a full index. Columbia also publishes *The Foundation Grants Index*. The 1970–1971 edition includes grants arranged alphabetically by foundation within seven broad subject fields: education, health, humanities, international activities, religion, sciences, and welfare. The name of the recipient and the amount received is noted for each of the grants. With both of these titles on hand, the reference librarian can give assistance to those seeking grants.

There are numerous titles in this field, and the best general compilation of guides for educational aid will be found in an annotated list by Margaret Norden ("Financial Assistance for Study and Research." *RQ*, Fall 1970, pp. 39–44). An updated service of considerable value, but equally expensive, is provided in *The Guide to Federal Assistance for Education* (New York: Appleton-Century-Crofts, Inc., 1972 to date, 2 vols., $375). The contents are updated monthly by inserts which fit into a loose-leaf notebook. The guide is valuable for a number of audiences from the head of institutions to students to scholar researchers.[10] However, this is only one of scores of titles; and because of the expense, the librarian should first investigate the numerous works listed by Norden.

These titles hardly exhaust the field. Many other publishers—both private and association—issue various guides to education and schools. For example, Barron's Educational Series has dozens of such handbooks, e.g., *Guide to College Selection* and *Guide to Two Year Colleges*. These are quite good, but the librarian at some point must ask the question concerning duplication. Is this title really necessary? Will I find the same basic information in titles on the shelf? The way out of the dilemma is to choose the half dozen to dozen titles in the area which the library finds the best for its purposes. The only reason for purchasing additional titles would be for updating, but the majority of educational handbooks and manuals and directories are frequently revised. Once a title is selected, the chances are the publisher will update it frequently enough for most purposes.

Occupations and vocations

U.S. Department of Labor, *Occupational Outlook Handbook*. Washington, D.C.: Government Printing Office, 1929 to date, biennial, $6.25.

U.S. Employment Service, *Dictionary of Occupational Titles*. 3d ed. Washington, D.C.: Government Printing Office, 1966, 2 vols., $12.00.

Forrester, Gertrude, *Occupational Literature*. New York: The H. W. Wilson Company, 1971, 619 pp., $15.

[10] For a full description of a rather complicated work see a review of the title by Joe Morehead in *RQ*, Fall 1972, pp. 81+.

Hopke, William, *The Encyclopedia of Careers and Vocational Guidance*. rev. ed. New York: Doubleday & Company, Inc., 1972, 2 vols., $39.50.

Russell, Max M., *The Blue Book of Occupational Education*. New York: CCM Information Corp., 1971, 897 pp., $29.95.

How to Pass Federal Civil Service Entrance Examinations. New York: Cowles Regnery, 1972, paperback $3.95.

Although vocational guidance in larger libraries is usually not a part of the reference situation, it is very much so in medium-sized and smaller libraries, certainly in schools. The works listed here are probably the best guides to an ever-increasing mass of publications.

When occupational and professional advice is given students by trained counselors, there inevitably is a fallout of young men and women seeking further materials—either for personal reasons or, often, for the purpose of preparing class papers. The rush has become so general that even the smallest library is likely to include a considerable amount of vocational material in the vertical file.

When working with students, or for that matter adults, a given amount of probing and patience normally is required. The user may only have a vague notion of what he needs or wants and may be quite uncertain as to his interests and the possibility of turning those interests into a channel of work. Here the *Occupational Outlook Handbook* is especially useful. Close to 700 occupations are discussed in terms likely to be understood by anyone. Each of the essays indicates what the job is likely to offer in terms of advancement, employment, location, earnings, and working conditions.

Trends and outlook are emphasized to give the reader some notion as to the growth possibilities of a given line of work. A useful chapter on methods of obtaining additional information is included. The *Handbook* frequently discusses types of employment for the noncollege graduate, especially in various industries and major types of farming.

Issued biennially, the *Handbook* is kept up to date by *Occupational Outlook Quarterly,* one of many sources listed in Forrester's *Occupational Literature*. Some 6,000 selected titles (pamphlets and books) are noted by Forrester with annotations and full bibliographic information. These are classified under 500 occupational and industrial positions. The Wilson Company publication is frequently revised.

Directed to the high school student, the first volume of the *Encyclopedia of Careers* consists of 71 articles on major fields of work and articles on how to choose a career. The second volume gives 600 detailed reports on specific occupations from poultry farmers to professional positions. In many ways, the *Encyclopedia* is little more than an elaborated *Occupational Outlook Handbook;* and the set's primary value for libraries that own the latter work is in the first volume.

A somewhat similar approach to Forrester is offered in Patricia Schuman's *Materials for Occupational Literature* (New York: R. R. Bowker Company, 1971, 201 pp., $9.95). This concentrates on technical–vocational programs—Forrester includes all major occupations and professions. Also, the emphasis is on publishers, i.e., under some 50 subject headings the author lists 600 associations and businesses which publish books, periodicals, audio-visual material, and so on.

Of a considerably more specialized nature, *Dictionary of Occupational Titles* is a compendium of every conceivable type of occupation from flagpole sitter to totem-pole carver. The first volume gives a brief description of each of the jobs listed and tells what the worker does and what skills are required. Brevity must be stressed, for it in no way equals the long essays found in the *Handbook*. Definitions are arranged alphabetically by title. The second volume presents classifications of jobs such as sales, clerical, and professional and then lists them by title. Code numbers are used in order to trace a particular job from one volume to the other.

With more emphasis on trade and technical schools, every library needs at least one directory in this area. A good choice is the Russell title. It lists more than 11,500 business, trade, and technical schools arranged by state. Some of the information is a bit scanty, but there are addresses given for those interested in additional information. There are also sections on home-study schools, nursing schools, and schools approved for veteran's training.

Many occupations, particularly at the governmental level, require that the applicant take an examination. Consequently, there are various series of manuals and they cover everything from librarian to state trooper examinations. A typical, good-to-excellent series is issued by Cowles Regnery. The paperbacks give basic details on the types of tests, how to prepare for them, and samples of test questions. Precisely how effective these manuals are for the applicant is questionable, but there is no doubt that they are in high demand. A library should have two sets— one for reference and one for circulation.

The same publisher (along with many others) issues similar titles from how to prepare for high school equivalency examinations to how to pass medical college examination tests. In fact, there is a manual for every conceivable examination a user might wish to take. Again, these should be duplicated in both the reference and the general collection.

LITERATURE

Magill, Frank N., *Masterplots*. New York: Salem Press, 1949 to date, (1972, 8 vols.), various prices.

Walker, Warren S., *Twentieth Century Short Story Explication.*

Hamden, Connecticut: The Shoe String Press, Inc., 1968, 698 pp., $10;
Supplement I, 1967-1969, 262 pp., 1970, $6.
    Combs, Richard E., *Authors: Critical and Biographical References*.
Metuchen, New Jersey: Scarecrow Press, 1971, 221 pp., $6.

Only one of the titles listed here is precisely a handbook, and that is
the Magill *Masterplots* group. The others are bibliographical guides, but
they all serve the same basic purpose—to assist the student or teacher in
compiling material about a book and or an author.

As far back as the Middle Ages, there were so-called "cribs" to
assist students studying for an examination or working on a paper.
There is nothing new about the medium and, in its place, it is a worthwhile form of publishing. Some of the works listed here can be used by
either the student or the scholar or both. Much depends upon whether,
for example, one is using *Masterplots* for a convenient means of recall-
ing a plot or for short-circuiting the need to read the book at all. A
reference librarian may have mixed views about the desirability of such
works for students, but that is a problem that students, teachers, and
parents must work out together. It is an error to deny a place on the
reference shelf to valuable sources regardless of how they may be used
or misused.

By far the most famous name in plot summaries and shortcuts to
reading is Magill. *Masterplots* is a condensation of almost every important classic in the English language. The contents consists of the works
of 232 authors and 1,200 titles. The series is revised and broadened
about every five or six years. Not only are the main characters nicely
explained, but there is also a critique of the plot which gives good, bad,
and other points about it. Due to its popularity, the publisher each year
issues an annual work which analyzes some 100 American titles published the previous year, e.g., *Magill's Literary Annual* (1954 to date).
These include both novels and nonfiction. A reprint of the annual volumes makes up the 7-volume *Contemporary Literature* set which covers
titles from 1954 through 1968.

Drawing from material collected in *Masterplots,* the compiler also
issues the following works whose titles are self-explanatory: *Cyclopedia
of Literary Characters, Cyclopedia of World Authors,* and *Masterpieces
of World Philosophy.* A glance at any of these seems to indicate that
Magill is the human answer to the computer. To be sure, he was not the
first to crank up the process in our times and many older librarians still
look to the favored Helen R. Keller's *The Reader's Digest of Books* (New
York: The Macmillan Company, 1929, 1,447 pp.) for much the same
approach. (Note: A number of these titles published in the 1960s are also
distributed by Harper & Row, Publishers, Incorporated.)

Another aspect of this growth in shortcuts is the review-book industry. Such publishers as Studymaster, Monarch Press, Barron's,

Barnes and Noble, and Crowell-Collier and Macmillan are publishing a good number of works, both in literature and other fields, which are geared to assist the student. Studymaster, for example, gives chapter notes and critical commentaries on classics *(The Aeneid)* to moderns *(Lord of the Flies)*. Each of the paperbacks includes biographical information, chapter-by-chapter notes, summary of characters, analysis of plot, and information on what may be needed by the student. Few of these should be considered for a reference situation, but they are a mixed blessing in that they do take some of the pressure off the reference librarian to help a student find an "easy approach" to an assignment.

There are numerous other approaches for refreshing the memory or gaining details about a book without actually reading or rereading the work. *The Book Review Digest* (New York: The H. W. Wilson Company, 1905 to date), for example, lists monthly reviews of the more popular fiction and nonfiction. As such, it is the basic guide to reviews and background material on current titles.

Other entrances are offered via numerous explications and bibliographies to authors and their works. The Walker title is an example of a listing which includes critical articles published in books and magazines about short stories and their authors. The user may find the name of the story or the author and, using Walker, discover more than enough information of a critical nature to help him with the preparation of a paper. Combs offers a broader approach in that he analyzes some 500 books containing literary criticism. An index provides information on the world's writers, regardless of time, period, or place. Also, for the better known writers, the obvious place to seek background information are in any of the numerous encyclopedias and encyclopedia-type handbooks.

QUOTATIONS

Stevenson, Burton E., *Home Book of Quotations. Classical and Moderns.* 10th ed. New York: Dodd, Mead & Company, Inc., 1967, 4,811 pp., $35.

Bartlett, John, *Familiar Quotations.* 14th ed. Boston: Little, Brown and Company, 1968, 1,776 pp., $15.

Brussell, Eugene E., *Dictionary of Quotable Definitions.* Englewood Cliffs, New Jersey: Prentice-Hall, Inc. 1970, 627 pp., $19.95.

What They Said In 197[-], The Yearbook of Spoken Opinion. Beverly Hills, California: Monitor Book Company, Inc., 1969 to date, annual, $17.50.

A frequent question in any library is either Who said the following? or What do you have in the way of a quote or about X subject? Any of the standard books of quotations may provide the answer. "May" is used here advisedly, for frequently the quotation is not found in any of the standard sources either because it is so unusual or, more than likely, it is garbled. When the patron is not certain about the actual wording, another approach is via subject.

By far the most famous book of quotations is Bartlett. A native of Plymouth, Massachusetts, John Bartlett was born in 1820 and at sixteen was employed by the owner of the University Bookstore in Cambridge. By the time he owned the store, he had become famous for his remarkable memory and the word around Harvard was, "Ask John Bartlett." He began a notebook which expanded into the first edition of his work in 1855. After the Civil War, he joined Little, Brown and Company, and he continued to edit his work through nine editions until his death in December 1905.

While Bartlett and the two other sources frequently contain similar material, there is need for many quotation works; often what will be found in one may not be found in the others.

Briefly the differences between Bartlett and Stevenson, aside from content, are:

1. *Arrangement.* Stevenson is arranged alphabetically under subject. Bartlett is arranged chronologically by author.
2. *Index.* Both have thorough indexes by subject, author, and key words of the quotations or verses. Stevenson does not repeat the subject words employed in the main text in the index. As more than one critic has pointed out, the indexes to these works are frequently an unconscious source of "modern" poetry. For example, from Bartlett come such immemorable lines as:
   Sleepless Eremite, nature's patient:
   nights, never so many.
   soul that perished
   to give readers sleep[11]
3. *Other features.* Stevenson has brief biographical data on authors. Bartlett features helpful historical footnotes, sometimes tracing the original quote normally associated with one individual back to another person or time.

Every year, there are a dozen or more compilations of quotations, e.g., *The Penguin Dictionary of Modern Quotations* (Baltimore: Penguin Books, Inc., 1971, 366 pp.) and Leonard Levinson *Bartlett's Unfamiliar Quotations* (New York: Cowles Book Company, 1971, 341 pp.). Larger

[11] *See also:* "New York Magazine Competition" *New York Magazine,* July 24, 1972, p. 64. Competitors were asked to submit an unexpected Bartlett pair of quotations:
Will Rogers: "I never met a man I didn't like."
Television Announcer: "Ladies and gentlemen, the President of the United States."

libraries will probably buy as many of these as the budget allows, even the questionable titles such as Levinson's nonindexed, badly chosen quote work. Smaller libraries would do well to watch for more meaningful titles such as the annual *What They Said.* Arranged by broad subject, then alphabetically by speaker, the volume includes major "quotes" spoken during the previous year by politicians, authors, teachers, criminals, and judges. A good many of these may never make their way into Bartlett, but the title is useful because it offers current thought about numerous subjects and just might be a place where the librarian could trace a pesky quote. It has a detailed index.

The Brussell title is a good source for the user who wants a quotable quote on almost any subject. Arranged in alphabetical order by subject, it contains quotes from all periods and places. Unlike the first edition, the second (1971 issued in 1972) includes indexes to subjects and to speakers. Quote sources are also clearly stated.

There is no guarantee that even with a massive set of quotation books, the librarian will be able to trace a given quote. Even the nongarbled, frequently reprinted quote may defy a source. For example, through much of 1970–1971, there appeared a statement from Adolph Hitler which was a back-handed slap at those who opposed campus "revolutionaries." Hitler was supposed to have said: "The streets of our country are in turmoil. The Universities are filled with students rebelling and rioting. . . .We need law and order. . . ." Posters flooded the campuses with these words. Then a Hitler expert, Professor Joachim Remak, spent considerable time trying to find the quotation. He could not, and his conclusion was that Hitler never said it. Who did? No one is quite certain, but Jerome Beatty, Jr., who published the quote in a column in the May 17, 1969 *Saturday Review,* traced it to the West Coast and a California liberal newsletter, the *Dixon Line.* Did the editors of the *Dixon Line* make it up? There is no answer.

How much time should a reference librarian spend on this kind of thing? There is no pat answer. If the librarian has searched the basic and not so basic sources and found nothing, she would probably be wiser to call it quits. Conversely, if she is the typical reference librarian, she may store it away in her memory and during the months or even years ahead try to find the source.

SCIENCE

Yearbook of Agriculture. Washington, D.C.: Government Printing Office, 1895 to date, annual, $3.50.

A Field Guide to the Insects of America North of Mexico. Boston: Houghton Mifflin Company, 1970, 404 pp., $5.95.

Henley's Twentieth Century Book of Formulas. New York: Books Inc., 1957, 867 pp. o.p.

Handbook of Chemistry and Physics. Cleveland, Ohio: Chemical Rubber Company, 1920 to date, annual, $56.

The *Yearbook of Agriculture* changed its approach radically in 1936. Up to that point, it was literally a report on the U.S. Department of Agriculture and its activities. After 1936, it became an annual manual or handbook approach to almost every conceivable subject related to agriculture. Each of the annuals is a work unto itself and can be treated as a definitive text—at least in terms of what the average layman or student desires about a given subject. Given its peculiar, useful scope, it is often duplicated in libraries, i.e., one copy for reference work, another for general circulation. And unlike most reference titles, it may be read from the first page through the last. Representative titles include "Good Life for Many People" (1971); "Consumers All" (1965); "Grass" (1948); "Food" (1959). The series makes an ideal, relatively inexpensive reference series for all libraries, regardless of size or type. In many ways, a "best buy" in the reference world.

For those who want statistical material on agriculture, the same department issues *Agricultural Statistics* (Washington, D.C.: Government Printing Office, 1936 to date, annual). This covers all aspects of agriculture in America from products to costs.

The excellent pocket-size Peterson *Field Guides* are added to each year, and the one on insects is representative. Each of the guides begins with background and introductory material. The bulk of the text consists of systematic descriptions, in this case of 579 insect families. The text is profusely illustrated and the descriptions are helpful in pointing up characteristics of identification. There are well over 20 titles in this series, and most libraries will want the general ones both at the reference desk and in the circulating collection. A similar series is the Nature Field Books published by Putnam, e.g., *The New Field Book of Reptiles and Amphibians* and *The New Field Book of Nature Activities and Hobbies.* These are excellent in their way, but usually not up to the Houghton Mifflin group which tends to have better illustrations.

The subtitle of Henley's fairly well sums up its scope and purpose: "book of formulas, processes and trade secrets . . . containing 10,000 selected household, workshop and scientific formulas, trade secrets, chemical recipes, processes, and money saving ideas for both the amateur and professional worker." Which is to say, formulas for almost any product from soap to perfume can be found here. How is it used? One example should suffice. In 1971, the women's liberation group at Columbia University produced at $3 an ounce a similar perfume sold by Jean Patou as "Joy" at $65 an ounce. The formula came from *Henley's.* In reporting how the women found the specific instructions, the *International Herald Tribune* (Paris, July 9, 1971, p. 7) gives some basic information on the reference work "found in just about every public library." The observant writer notes:

> The book instructs its readers in the production of mockingbird food, butter, oleomargarine, candles, casket trimmings, castor oil, chocolate, cheese, chewing gum, lozenges, ink eradicators, gun powder, nitroglycerine, dynamite, and blasting powder.
>
> A somewhat amusing—but lengthy—formula instructs amateur magicians in manufacturing a "wonderful bottle" from which can be poured, in succession, port wine, sherry, champagne, or ink "at the will of the operator."

A manual, or more precisely a handbook, of another type is the standard chemistry and physics work. This is about as basic as any title in a science library and includes all the necessary tables and physical data needed by both the student and the professional. It, as many works of this type, presupposes some basic knowledge of the fields and, unlike *Henley's,* is not for the amateur.

SUGGESTED READING

Holman, Hugh, C., "A Handbook to Literature," *The New York Times Book Review,* January 14, 1973, pp. 6+. A review of a literature handbook (not covered here) which is a model of its kind.

Stamper, Ronald, *Information in Business and Administrative Systems.* London: B. T. Batsford, 1973. While written for the business student, this book covers not only basic sources but the more important methodological problems of language and communication.

CHAPTER NINE
BIOGRAPHICAL SOURCES

Biography, as *The Oxford English Dictionary* defines it, is "the history of the lives of individual men"—and (although it may shock the male who wrote this definition) women. Addressing himself to the full-length book biography, Sir Harold Nicholson's further definition seems applicable for reference work:

> A biography must be a history, in the sense that it must be accurate and depict a person in relation to his times. It must describe an individual, with all the gradation of human character, and not merely present a type or virtue or vice. And it must be . . . written in grammatical English and with an adequate feeling for style.[1]

All these principles are not often found in reference sources, but the stress on accuracy, and honesty, is necessary for worthwhile reference aids. The form of biography in reference is not the same as found in over 1,600 biographical titles published here in 1973; although the quantitative figure is interesting because it ranks biography high among 22 divisions of American publishing—biographies are outranked only by books in sociology and economics, fiction, literature, science, juveniles, and history in that order.

[1] Sir Harold Nicholson, *Biography As An Art*, ed. by James Clifford (New York: Oxford University Press, 1962), p. 197. For a basic history of biography, consult any major encyclopedia or the cited essay.

Biography is one of the most popular forms of knowledge, entertainment, and persuasion. The reasons for this are varied, although Richard Ellmann, in speaking of biographers, probably came closer to the truth when he described the biographer (substitute reader) as "necessarily intrusive, a trespasser." Readers are anxious to be introduced to "an alien point of view, necessarily different from that mixture of self-recrimination and self-justification which the great . . . has made the subject of his lifelong conversation with himself."[2] The desire to know what everyone else is doing ranges from scholarly requests about subjects in *The Times Literary Supplement* ("Iris Tree, 1897–1968, third daughter of Sir Herbert and Lady Tree: any anecdotes, photographs, letters for a biography") to sheer gossip in the Sunday newspaper supplement, *Parade* ("I cannot believe that actress Hayley Mills has a child named Folly; is that really so?").

As biography concerns almost every aspect of human endeavor, it is a recurrent form of question in all types and sizes of libraries. The patron will want to know something about a person, and it is with this that the chapter is concerned; but he may also desire information found only indirectly in biographical sources. If, for example, the reader wants background information on the social milieu, the social motives, the social pressures on the individual in China, a biography of Mao Tse-tung may be more instructive (at least probably more palatable) than a formal history or sociological treatise. Knowledge of the leaders will tell as much about a country as the history itself—and, of course, the historian must rely on biography for any meaningful approach to his subject.

SEARCHING BIOGRAPHICAL SOURCES

Before he does anything else, a librarian has to decide what kind of source will answer a given kind of question. He obviously cannot select his source(s) until he knows just what form the answer should take. The average librarian will work from two basic, beginning queries: How much of the history of an individual life does the user require? And at what level of depth and sophistication should the answer be geared? The answer to the second, obviously, can be determined by the age, education, and the needs of the individual user. The answer to the first quantitative question will either require (1) a silhouette or simple data type of reply or (2) an answer which will require an essay form.

This data-type question is by far the most common in the ready-reference situation. Typical queries: What is the address, phone number of X? How does one spell Y's name? What is the age of R? When did

[2] Richard Ellmann, *Literary Biography* (New York: Oxford University Press, 1971), p. 1.

Beethoven die? Answers will be found in reference works particularly edited for these types of questions. They are the familiar "who's who" directory-biographical dictionary sources. Approach varies in each title, but there is a given consistency in listing names alphabetically and, at a minimum, giving the profession and position (and/or claim to fame attributes) of the individual. At a maximum, these sources will give full background on the entry from his birth and death dates to his publications, names of his children, and so on. The information is usually, although not necessarily, in outline form. It is rarely discursive or critical. The data is all.

The second major type of biographical question comes from the person who wants partial or relatively complete information on an individual. He or she may be writing a paper, preparing a speech, or seeking critical background material. Typical queries: I have to write a paper on Herman Melville. What do you have on X, a prominent American scientist? Is it about George Washington and the cherry tree?

Answers will be found in reference sources quite different from those used for the data, who's who approach. Here the emphasis is on essays (300 words to several volumes). A biographical dictionary or directory will be of little value. The reference librarian will turn to essay approaches from *Current Biography* to the *Dictionary of National Biography*.

Once this major categorization is determined, the librarian further divides the query in terms of time: (1) Is the person living or dead? (2) Did he recently come into the news? (3) If still living, was he important a few years ago, but rarely heard about now? (4) If dead, was he of enough historical importance to be included in a major retrospective biographical source? When in doubt, the best, general method of clearing for further action is to ask the user. If she does not know, then look up the same in a biographical dictionary, an index, or the like.[3]

Secondary approaches to biographical searching

In a real sense, the whole library is a source for answering biographical queries. The number of possible approaches for information is almost unlimited. A cursory glance at Slocum's "little Winchell," i.e., his *Biographical Dictionaries and Related Works*, will indicate the overwhelm-

---

[3] Another approach is by race and by sex. There are now numerous individual reference works given over to women (some of which are considered here) and minority groups, e.g., J. A. Rogers' *World's Great Men of Color* (New York: The Macmillan Company, 1973, 2 vols.). Unfortunately, there are not enough good biographical reference sources for blacks or for other minority groups. By 1973, this had promise of change, and students should attempt to keep up with developments. A useful general ap$roach is *The Emerging Minorities in America* (Santa Barbara: ABC/Clio Press, 1973) which includes some 500 biographical sketches of important American minority personalities.

ing avenues and byways to a current or historical figure. Few libraries are going to have the majority of his 4,800 possible entries to biography, yet there are sources which almost every library has in part or in whole. The student, layman, or librarian who may be unfamiliar with the more specialized works in this chapter will have no difficulty tracing a particular person through better known direct and indirect approaches.

Encyclopedias By and large encyclopedias are probably the most useful single source of biographical information, particularly for anyone of note who has died. Encyclopedia entries normally fail to include details on prominent living persons and are particularly weak in the arts and on passing political figures. Although sometimes more trouble than they are worth, various encyclopedia yearbooks can be used for current personalities.

Periodical and newspaper indexes These indexes are the most often used for the current profile lacking in the encyclopedia. First in importance are the various newspaper indexes, beginning with *The New York Times Index*. A second choice is any one of the various periodical indexes and abstracting services. Normally, the biographical subjects are listed by name, but now not always. For example, *Public Affairs Information Service Bulletin* lists biographical works under a main subject heading, "Directories, Biographical."

Almanacs Many almanacs have biographical entries, usually by subject—actors, sports, and so on. They differ from encyclopedias and indexes in that most of the sketches are of the data type, useful only for identification, sometimes address, and spelling.

Dictionaries Almost all dictionaries have biographical data-type entries in either the main section or an appendix. Again, though, most give only the briefest of information. (Note: The notable exception is *Webster's New International Dictionary*, 3d ed. There are no biographies in this basic dictionary.) In this same category are a number of specialized dictionaries which may prove helpful, i.e., everything from a dictionary of the bible to a dictionary of quotations.

Directories City directories, phone books, occupational directories, and the like are used for answering brief, sometimes vital questions about the spelling of a name, an address, or a title.

Literary handbooks and manuals Since almost every prominent personality tries his hand at writing, the vast majority of biographical subjects are, in a sense, authors. Consequently, such works as the *Cambridge History of English Literature* prove useful. Aside from literary handbooks and manuals, specialized works such as the *Government Organization Manual* will help.

Indexes to individual biographies A lesser-known figure connected with the subject of a full-length biography may be mentioned in the index. Also, footnotes and other references may lead to articles about the secondary figure. This type of approach presupposes a knowledge of the subject or the period.

Manuscripts The primary source of manuscripts is rarely used by the reference librarian but is a first choice for the serious research worker who may depend almost entirely upon original letters, diaries, documents, and the like. Some of this material is in print, but it will usually not meet the needs of the man or woman dedicated to searching out biographical material.

> Why spend years searching for original manuscripts of material already in print? The reason may be categorically stated—many of the published versions are not dependable. . . . Of course, the degree of distortion varies enormously. In some nineteenth century editions, the offense may be venial. . . . Only in our day do we begin to have complete editions, unexpurgated and unmanipulated, but the number is even now pitifully small. For the majority of subject in the past we must still use authorities which we suspect.[4]

Discussion

Some of the problems which arise in searching for biography, aside from knowledge and evaluation of what an individual work will do or not do in a given situation, are discussed below.

Two individuals with the same name For example, when the question is: "When was Alfred Smith born?" Is this in reference to a governor, an author, a poet, a banker, or a boxer? The name was, and is, the pride of all these people. And there are probably scores of other living and deceased prominent men with the name Alfred Smith, not to mention Carol Smith or John Smith. If the person asking the question knows the profession of the subject, there is little problem—although even here it may be a case of further refinement by asking whether this Alfred Smith is an American or Englishman, dead or alive, and, if dead, what

---

[4] James L. Clifford, *From Puzzles to Portraits: Problems of A Literary Biographer,* (Chapel Hill: University of North Carolina Press, 1970), p. 4.

period of history did he enlighten. Normally, there is some auxilliary clue to help separate the Smiths of the world; but it is helpful to recognize that the Smith the patron had in mind when he asked the question may not be the same Alfred Smith the librarian recognized immediately as the author of the definitive history on cannibals. In reference work, it is commendable to be certain, but never too certain—particularly when dealing with biographical queries.

Obscure or unknown persons Frequently frustration arises when the librarian has searched all the basic and secondary approaches to biography but can find little or nothing about a given individual. The first question to ask: Do I have the proper spelling of the name or even a close proximity to that spelling? A thorough search for information on E. R. Ensminger may turn up nothing, while the proper spelling of the name, E. R. Ansminger may give quite different results. If the inquirer cannot help with the spelling, one might try asking him the occupation or profession of the subject and work backwards from subject indexes or subject biographies. Still, an improper spelling may simply call a total halt to the procedure; and if there is any doubt, it would be judicious to ask the patron to try to find the correct spelling before proceeding any further.

Granted, however, if a name is accurate but cannot be identified through normal channels, what is to be done? The usual procedure is to turn to nonbiographical sources such as bibliographies (she may have written a book or an article which will give a clue). Other avenues are almost as numerous as the imagination and resources of the library, e.g., genealogical records, locally published histories, legal records, census reports, documents, and other unpublished manuscripts. And there are countless other approaches which are suggested elsewhere in this chapter and text. Parenthetically, the librarian should never forget his peers. It just may be that a phone call to a librarian, historian, or teacher will result in a satisfactory answer or lead—particularly if the person queried is an authority in the same field as the subject in question.

Time How much time and effort should the librarian spend on a search which does not immediately result in some information or keys to information? This depends upon the particular needs of the individual asking the question. For example, the historian seeking a definite bit of information about a person will require all the time the librarian can possibly give. On the other hand, a student who may be simply writing about "X person" may find it more advantageous to change his subject to "Y person" before any exhaustive search is undertaken. But even the best intentioned librarian with willingness to spend much time on a question cannot operate without resources. A lack of indexes or bibliographical guides will severely handicap a meaningful search; and even with these, if the library does not have the sources indexed, the search can be frustrating. At this point, the general procedure is to point out the problem and assist the user as much as possible with the location of other libraries or resources which will be helpful.

EVALUATION

How does the librarian know whether a biographical source—whether it be a line of data or a sketch of a prominent man or woman—is reliable? There are a number of tests.

Selection Why is a name selected (or rejected) for the various biographical sources? The population of the United States for 1972 was close to 210,000,000, but there are only some 80,000 names in the 1972-1973 edition of *Who's Who in America*. The answer is complex, but usually the selection is based on some type of outstanding achievement or excellence or eminence. The catch: who is eminent and who is not eminent? As Cedric Larson puts it:

> Standards of eminence are by no means easy to establish. Eminence, like many other human qualities, is essentially relative. Eminence is more than celebrity; the state of being publicly known is often ephemeral and, far too frequently, a synthetic marketable commodity. . . . Rarely indeed do two individuals agree as to what constitutes success, let alone eminence. . . . To be eminent is to be prominent rather than conspicuous. . . . Eminence—or at least notability—appears historically to stabilize at a proportion somewhere around 3 in every 10,000 of the population.[5]

The selection process is relatively easy to establish for biographical aids which are limited to a given subject or profession—the compiler includes as many names as qualify for his scope, e.g., *Who's Who in American Politics* or *American Authors, 1600-1900*. In both cases, the widest net is cast to include political figures and authors likely to be of interest. There are, to be sure, given limitations, but these are so broad as to cause little difficulty for the compiler. As one moves from subject and profession to the famous, eminent, or renowned on a national or international scale—or both—the choices become increasingly difficult.

While admittedly choice for other than subject and professional biographical aids is relative, all the editors of reputable works do establish some objective guidelines, e.g., *Who's Who in America* where many

[5] Cedric A. Larson, *Who; Sixty Years of American Eminence* (New York: McDowell, Obolensky, 1958, pp. 2 and 17). Note: The 1972-1973 edition does have about 3 names per 10,000 persons in the United States.

are "included arbitrarily on account of official position." This means that if you are a congressman, governor, admiral, general, Nobel Prize winner, or a foreign head of government you are automatically included; and there are numerous other categories, as well, which ensure a place in the volume. The *International Who's Who* is certain to give data on members of all reigning royal families; and the *Dictionary of American Biography* takes a more negative approach—you must first be dead to be included; after that, the editor begins his selection. At the other end of the selective scale, *Who's Who in American Politics* includes all key public officials from the federal to the local level.

Then, too, there are some automatic exclusions. *Who's Who in America* does not list anyone convicted of a crime and takes a dim view of sports figures unless they have excelled in other ways. In the case of subject biographical reference works, the exclusion is usually evident in the title, i.e., one does not look for poets in *Who's Who in American Art* or *American Men and Women of Science*—although, to be sure, the poetic skills of an artist or a scientist may be considerable.

The inclusion-exclusion process is of most interest when the reputation and fame of a work, such as *Who's Who in America,* is purposefully built upon selectivity of a high order. The natural question is one of legitimacy. Is the selection of Y based upon his desire to be included (supported by his willingness to buy the volume in question or, in a few cases, to literally pay for a place in the volume) or is it based upon the editors' notion of eminence where no amount of persuasion or cash will ensure selection? In the case of all works listed here, the answer is that they are indeed legitimate. In these works, one cannot buy his way to fame. This is not to say there is not room for argument. No one will entirely agree on all names selected or rejected, say, in *Who's Who in America.* As Larson notes: "The Marquis editors are perennially criticized for admission or exclusion of eminent Americans over the years, are quick to admit . . . sins of both omission and admission."[6]

Length of Entry   Once a name is selected, another question presents itself: How much space does the figure warrant? Should she be given five or six lines or a page? The purpose and scope of the work may dictate at least a partial answer. The *Who's Who* data approach calls for a relatively brief outline or collection of facts. The biographical dictionary may be more discursive or even briefer. And the essay type work will approach the same entry in a way peculiar to its own emphasis. Despite form, the editor still has to make decisions about balance and length.

When considering deceased persons, this may be a bit easier than with the ego-conscious living. Still, there is no satisfactory answer for

[6] Ibid, p. 9.

either. Obviously, George Washington will receive more space than, say, Mrs. Catherine Dorset, an eighteenth-century English poet. But aside from these extremes, J. O. Thorne sums it up nicely:

> . . . Fame and public esteem are constantly subject to the vagaries of fashion, and critical assessments are changed by modern research. Thus Monteverdi, whose great importance in the history of music is today more fully recognized, now receives 59 lines in place of 5 (over 1962 ed.), T. S. Eliot has 144 instead of 6, and the meagre allowance formerly given to the great impressionistic painters has been increased to match their current status. Conversely, Lord Lytton has less than half the space previously given to him. . . . Other articles, adequate in length and admirable in their time, have been refashioned because modern criticism and scholarship have modified the traditional image.[7]

And just to confuse the issue, there are those who argue it is not always possible to give space in proportion to the importance of the subject. This is particularly true of historical figures where the amount of biographical information is scant, although they may have been major figures, e.g., Shakespeare or Malory to name two.

No compiler is going to satisfy every reader with is emphasis or lack of emphasis on length. The wary librarian who finds recurrent faults in balance of treatment may conclude: (1) The work contains information received through questionnaires without due attention to editing for importance of the figure profiled. The subject may reply with due modesty in a brief manner. The not so famous may wish to puff their reputations by stretching their personal data. (2) If the source is a retrospective biography, one may assume six pages for an Idaho businessman as contrasted with one page for a Nobel Prize winner shows amazing lack of perspective by the compiler or writer. Lest these two examples seem preposterous, the student is advised to check a year of reviews of recently published titles. One of the most common complaints, aside from exclusion or inclusion, is lack of proper balance. No work will be dead center, but if tipped too precariously, the librarian is often advised to take warning.

Authority Biographical sources have several facets not considered in checking the authority for other reference books. First and foremost: who wrote the biographical entry—an editor, the subject of the biography, an authority in the field, a secretary? Obviously, in almost anything except statistical information, the person who penned the entry will have either conscious or subconscious biases. Even in a straightforward presentation of data, if the biographical subject supplied the information

---

[7] J. Thorne, "Preface," *Chamber's Biographical Dictionary* (London: Chambers, Ltd., 1969), p. 1. This is one of the few prefaces which may be read as much for entertainment as for information, and it is highly reccomended for both the beginner and the expert.

(normally the case with most current biographies), there may be slight understatements or exaggerations concerning age (men as often as women lie about this), education, or experience.[8] If the source is retrospective, was the material gathered and compiled in a historically acceptable fashion or haphazardly from secondary sources? Have sources of information, other than the biographees' own questionnaires, been cited? The preface should make all these points clear.

When the source is questionable, it should be verified in one or more other works. If there remains a serious conflict which cannot be resolved, what should be done? Depending upon how important the conflict is to the patron, the only solution is to attempt to trace the information through primary source material: newspapers, contemporary biographies, or articles about the individual or his family or his friends. This involves historical research. An excellent example may be found in the ever-recurrent arguments concerning details of Shakespeare's life and times, or the famous attempt to straighten out the facts in the life of Thomas Malory, author of the stories concerning King Arthur and his knights.[9] In many cases, even of well-known individuals, the records are uncertain or in question; and possibly the correct answers will never be known.

The date of publication of a source is particularly important when attempting to ascertain the relative truth of a given biographical sketch. Viewpoints, as noted, frequently change radically with time. For example, an entry about President Lincoln in a contemporary source may be quite different from one found in the average encyclopedia or for that matter in the *Dictionary of American Biography*.

A common question asked by laymen is whether or not a request by a publisher to include their name in this or that publication is indeed an honor, or a come-on to take part in an ego trip. And there are at least a few biographical publications of this type:

> Unscrupulous publishers will sometimes include padded or unduly eulogistic articles on comparatively unknown persons, with the expectation, or on condition, that these persons will pay for inclusion or will subscribe for the book. . . . Such books are not necessarily to be rejected if they happen

[8] Birthdates are a common headache for biographers. Nicolas Slonimsky in the preface to the fifth edition of Baker's *Biographical Dictionary of Musicians* (New York: G. Schirmer, Inc., 1958) notes: "Musicians through the centuries have altered their birthdates, invariably in the direction of the juvenation." Beethoven, for example, was eager to prove he was born in 1772 rather than 1770. Furthermore, death dates are often listed a day later, owing to delay in announcement or different time zones. Schoenberg's death is given as July 14, 1951 in most European sources, when he died on July 13, in Los Angeles.
[9] Richard D. Altick, *The Scholar Adventurers* (New York: The Macmillan Company, 1950). The chapter on Malory, "The Quest of the Knight-Prisoner," is a case history of frustration and joys in tracing biographical data.

to be the only ones in their field, but they must always be used with caution.[10]

How, then, does the librarian know if the work is truly legitimate, i.e., authoritative and based upon an accurate, relatively objective selection policy. A rule of the proverbial thumb will do in most cases: If the title is not listed (or minimally praised) in any of the basic bibliographies, i.e., Winchell, Walford, American Reference Books Annual or the current reviewing services from Reference and Subscription Book Reviews and *Choice* to *Library Journal,* the flag of warning is out.[11] Another test, based upon the librarian's knowledge of publishers, is whether or not the publisher is reputable. Even the best, to be sure, make errors in judgment about what constitutes a good biographical source, but none can be accused of trying to build a book on the gullibility of the biographees. If the book is neither reviewed nor listed, and if the publisher is a total unknown, one may safely assume that—at the very least—additional checking is in order.

Still there is no golden rule or set of standards to completely answer the question: Who can the librarian trust? It comes down to experience and knowledge:

> The catalogue of the British Museum Reading Room has a dread phrase; one comes across it written opposite certain material: "Doubtful and supposititious." Fortunately one develops, over the years of work, a sixth sense; familiarity with historical material does it. One loses one's innocence and goes about, healthily suspicious.[12]

Other points   Are there photographs? Are there bibliographies— material both by and about the subject? Is the work adequately indexed or with sufficient cross-references? (This is particularly important when one is seeking individuals connected with a major figure, but who may be mentioned only as part of a larger biographical sketch.) Is the work arranged in logical fashion? The alphabetical approach is usual, although some works may be arranged chronologically by events, birth dates, periods, or by areas of subject interest.

In practice, questions concerning biography are of such a nature that few of these evaluative tests are actually employed. If a person is

---

[10] Constance M. Winchell, *Guide to Reference Books* (Chicago: American Library Association, 1967) p. 168.
[11] One illustration will suffice. This type of review should be warning to any librarian. The *Blue Book: Leaders of the English Speaking World, 1970* (Chicago: St. James Press). Reviewed in the *1971 American Reference Books Annual* (Littleton, Colorado: Libraries Unlimited, 1971, p. 73): ". . . there is no discernible pattern for inclusion and there are some startling omissions and equally strong appearances."
[12] Catherine Drinker Bowen, *Biography: The Craft and the Calling* (Boston: Little, Brown and Company, 1969), p. 60.

well known, the problem normally is not one of locating a source but of screening out the many sources for the pertinent details. If he is an obscure personality, usually any source is welcome. Evaluation is of primary importance in considering purchase of a particular biographical source.

INDEXES AND BIBLIOGRAPHIES

General indexes and bibliographies

Biography Index: A Cumulative Index to Biographical Material in Books and Magazines. New York: The H. W. Wilson Company, 1947 to date, quarterly, bound annual and 3-year cumulations, $25.

The primary purpose of *Biography Index* is to list sources of relatively recent essay-length (sometimes shorter, sometimes longer) material about an individual. As it is a two-step reference device, that is it introduces the user to sources which in turn must be library located, it is usually not a reference work to be used by the person who is seeking (1) simple ready-reference material such as addresses or (2) material found in one step in other biographical sources such as encyclopedias and current biographies.

This index is primarily for the person who is seeking either material in depth on an individual or, more particularly, current, sometimes controversial opinion about a living or dead personality which is not found in the standard, objective biographical sources. The user dutifully begins with the latest quarterly issue and then moves back through the cumulations until he has found enough references for his purpose. The full name of the individual is given, including birth date (and death date), profession, and nationality. Some 1,900 periodicals are analyzed.

There are some secondary uses of the index: (1) Illustrations and portraits are indicated, and it can be used to find a picture of the personality. (2) An appended index lists the subjects by profession and occupation. This breakdown affords teachers an approach to biography which is useful in classrooms when studying such figures as statesmen, authors, and physicians. The subject classification approach can be of real benefit to the reference librarian, too. The librarian who is looking for something on a banker or deep-sea diver, but does not have the faintest idea as to whom might qualify, will be grateful for the subject breakdown. (3) There is a checklist of the composite books—primarily collective biographies—which are analyzed, and this does have some value for the acquisitions librarian. (4) The juvenile biographies are marked in the main index, and there is a separate heading for them in the appended index. (5) Obituary notices from *The New York Times* are included, but this is of less importance now that the *Times* has its own obituaries and biographical indexes.

Retrospective indexes and bibliographies

The New York Times Obituaries Index, 1858–1968. New York: The New York Times, 1970, 1,136 pp., $75.

    Hyamson, A. M., *A Dictionary of Universal Biography of All Ages and of All People.* 2d ed. London: Routledge & Kegan Paul, Ltd., 1951, 680 pp. (distributed in United States by E. P. Dutton Co., Inc.), $19.50.

    Slocum, Robert B., *Biographical Dictionaries and Related Works.* Detroit: Gale Research Company, 1967, 1,056 pp., $25.

The next most general, useful index to biography is *The New York Times Obituaries Index.* Its primary purpose is to locate, in the *Times,* published obituaries which are often full-length biographical essays. Thanks to the worldwide coverage of *The Times,* the list is not limited to Americans and includes almost every prominent world figure who died during the period covered by the index. Its secondary purpose, although it may be primary to many, is: (1) it does include lesser known personalities not often found in standard biographical works; (2) the obituary often presents a summation of the reputation of the figure at the time; and (3) as each entry includes not only page and issue number, but death date, it can serve as a ready-reference aid. The cutoff date is 1968, but the *Times' Biographical Edition* fills the gap from 1968 on.

    Hyamson's primary purpose is a finding list or index to 110,000 names of deceased personalities. For each of the alphabetical entries, reference is made to one of 23 biographical dictionary or encyclopedias which Hyamson indexed in his work. Not all titles listed are completely indexed, the exception being the *Dictionary of National Biography* and the *Dictionary of American Biography* which he covers in total. Each citation includes the nationality, profession, birth date, and death date, and where the primary biography is to be found.

    There are numerous versions of Hyamson, differing only in the number of entries and the types of works indexed. Where does one find these additional indexes? For works published prior to 1967, the user should check out additions to *Winchell, Walford,* and the *American Reference Books Annual.*

    Every discipline or form has it own guide, its own little "Winchell"; and in the case of biography, this is now Slocum. The purpose of Slocum's work is to lead the researcher to what he needs among the close to

5,000 collection of biographies.[13] He methodically lists other biographical indexes, who's who, genealogical works, dictionaries of anonyms and pseudonyms, portrait catalogs, government manuals, and other bibliographies. Under three main sections—Universal Biography, National or Area Biography, and Biography by Vocation—he indicates primarily nineteenth- and twentieth-century sources where the diligent researcher may find titles in his search. The user must then locate the given item(s) (assisted by excellent author, title, and subject indexes) and check it out for his particular biography.

Slocum *does not* list the million of names covered in each of the titles he has selected. How does one know a given biographical source may be of help? Some of the sources are annotated, but the majority depend upon the user grasping the fundamental scope by the broad categorization of the descriptive title. Hence, this is not for the average layman or student unless he is assisted by a librarian.

Special and subject indexes

Ireland, Norma O. (ed.), *Index to Women of the World from Ancient to Modern Times; Biographies and Portraits.* Westwood, Massachusetts: F. W. Faxon, 1970, 573 pp., $16.

Silverman, Judith, *An Index to Young Readers' Collective Biographies; Elementary and Junior High School Level.* New York: R. R. Bowker, 1970, 282 pp., $11.95.

Stanius, Ellen J., *Index to Short Biographies: For Elementary and Junior High Grades.* Metuchen, New Jersey: The Scarecrow Press, 1971, 348 pp., $7.50.

Nicholsen, Margaret, *People in Books: A Selective Guide to Biographical Literature Arranged by Vocations and Other Fields of Reader Interest.* New York: The H. W. Wilson Company, 1969, 509 pp., $12.

Publishers follow trends and try to anticipate need (and purchasing potential) of libraries. Hence, these four indexes. The first is a result of the Women's Liberation Movement's activities over the past decade. The growing recognition that women have played a role in society other than "wives of prominent men" (to note a subject entry in *Biography Index*) has resulted in a number of biographical reference aids, e.g., *Who's Who in American Women* to *Notable American Women.* Ireland provided a finding list or index to 13,000 famous women as found in 945 collective biographies and a few magazines. Arrangement is alphabetical by name with birth (and death) dates, profession, and a reference to the biogra-

[13] Reference and Subscription Book Reviews (*Booklist,* January 15, 1971) notes that a sample check indicated: "6.5 percent of the biographical entries in Winchell . . . are not included in *Biographical Dictionaries,* and that 69 percent of the entries in *Biographical Dictionary* are not in Winchell."

phy in one or more of the 945 works analyzed. As there is no index by field of activity, the user must know the name of the woman before using the index. The net is universal, but the compiler made an effort to include at least one-half of the analyzed collections published after 1950. The compiler, too, has avoided duplication of entries found in *Biography Index,* but does include sketches found in *Current Biography.* In a witty and informative introduction, she points out that the most popular category of claim to fame is "history and pioneers," the least popular, "education and athletics.")

The three other indexes noted here have one thing in common, one purpose: to direct the student, teacher, or librarian to a biography suitable for the taste, reading level, and interest of an elementary through high school student. Some of the material is duplicated in *Biography Index.* Why, then, another index, more or less three indexes? First, *Biography Index* is rarely purchased in duplicate for the children's room. Second, arrangement and, in these three indexes, names are solely for the purpose of the target audience. Third, some of the material is not analyzed in *Biography Index*—and "some" is of enough importance to warrant purchase of the additional aids.

The three reflect variables in arrangement and editing, but the primary purpose of all is to list names found in collective biographies—and, in the case of Nicholsen, in some fiction, poetry, and plays. Silverman has a main alphabetical list by names and a subject index. Stanius lists only names with identifying phrases such as "Greek poet" or "Russian spy." Nicholsen's main index is by vocation or field of activity, and she has an appended index by country and century. All, of course, give full information on the titles they have indexed, and all make an effort to include recent titles which are still in print.

CURRENT BIOGRAPHICAL SOURCES

Universal: Essay form

Current Biography. New York: The H. W. Wilson Company, 1940 to date, monthly, except August, $12, yearbook, $10.

The New York Times Biographical Edition: A Compilation of Current Biographical Information of General Interest. New York: Arno Press, 1971 to date, monthly, loose leaf, $78.

The major problem with biographical indexes is that they are two-step reference aids, i.e., the user must first find citations and then the works in which the biographical data or information appears. Unless the library has a good number of the indexed items, the frustration level of the user will be exceptionally high. A third drawback is that it takes time to index the items; and the indexes are often not current enough for the user who wants material on a person who has recently broken into the news or into the spotlight of public attention through some achievement, book, or (in these days) appearance on television, radio, or lecture platform.

There are two basic approaches to the question regarding a current figure. If the user is seeking a bit of information—address, birth date, position, education, and the like—the quickest method is to turn to one of the biographical directories, i.e., in most cases a "who's who." If the user is seeking enough information to prepare a talk, write a paper, or simply meet a need for personal background, she will need considerably more than basic data; and it is here the two titles noted are most useful.

Current Biography is by far the most popular single current essay-length biographical aid in almost any type of library. Issued monthly, it is cumulated, often with revised sketches, into annual volumes with excellent cumulative indexing. Annual emphasis is on some 320 to 350 international personalities, primarily those who are in some way influencing the American scene. Articles are long enough to include all vital information about the person and usually are relatively objective. The sketches are prepared by a special staff which draws information from other biographical sources and from the person being covered in the article. Subjects are given the opportunity to check copy before it is published and, presumably, approve the photograph which accompanies each sketch. Source references are cited. Obituary notices, with due reference to *The New York Times Obituaries Index,* are listed for those who at one time have appeared in the work. There is an index by profession which is helpful for the student who has to write something about "a plumber, scientist, artist. . ." but is not particular as to whom the individual may be. Another useful feature in the annual is a list of current "biographical references." This serves as a convenient up-to-date checklist for purchase.

The New York Times Biographical Edition serves the same purpose, and usually the same audience as *Current Biography*—it is a first choice for any medium to large library. Published each month in loose-leaf form, each sheet is a reprint of biographical material which has appeared in the *Times.* It includes obituaries, the "man in the news," and feature stories from the drama, book, sports, and Sunday magazine section. One catch: cumulative indexes are issued only every six months. Before the index is issued, the student must search for the wanted sketch.

Current Biography stresses "living leaders," takes pride in objectivity. The *Times* intersperses the biographical sketches with the daily news; these sketches are often reports on controversial, less than leader types. Most of the reporting is objective, and where there is a point of view the reader is given the reporter's byline. Profiles may be brief, or many pages, and there is no effort to revise before reprinting. There is a monthly, six-month, and annual index. The profiles are consecutively numbered and carry the date of appearance in the *Times*. And usually there is a picture of the subject.

Does the library need this and *Current Biography*, particularly as almost all figures in the Wilson publication are coverd by the *Times?* Yes, because the duplication is usually in name only. *Current Biography* has a different, purposefully, structures approach which students find easier to handle than the *Times*. Conversely, it is hard to imagine any library giving meaningful reference service in biography without the *Times*.

As both of these services are monthly and sometimes do not appear in the library for two to four weeks after publication, how does the librarian cope with a request for information on current news figures not found in either? Check the various services such as *Facts on File*, newspaper indexes, and, of course, periodical indexes. Still, the answer is too pat. All too often none of these standard aids help. It usually comes down to the "automated" memory of the librarian who, hopefully, is reading at least one or two newspapers a day and keeps up with current events well enough to recall a profile appearing here or there. Not neat, not systematic, not always an answer, but it often works. In perhaps another decade or two, the biographical sources will be computerized on a daily, hour-by-hour basis; but until then, it is the librarian who will find the ultimate answers to the difficult, sometimes impossible, biographical questions.

Universal: data form—Who's Who

International Who's Who. London: Europa Publications, 1935 to date, annual, $32 (distributed in United States by Gale Research Company).

  International Yearbook and Statesmen's Who's Who. London: Burke's Peerage, 1953 to date, annual, $31.

Other than essay-length material for student papers, the most sought after type of current biographical information is of a ready-reference type, or simple data. The questions are familiar enough: How does X spell his name? What degrees does he hold? What has X published? Is he married?

Replies to these and similar queries are found in the familiar who's who format. They vary in title, publisher, scope, and often accuracy and timeliness; but their essential purpose is the same: to present objective, usually noncontroversial facts about an individual. The approach and style is monotonously the same, i.e., most are arranged alphabetically by the name of the person and there then follows a paragraph of vital statistics.[14]

Information is normally compiled from questionnaires which have been sent to the biographee. Better publishers double- or triple-check answers—not all individuals are anxious to give away age, the college where they received (or did not receive) a degree, or past jobs which may not be a credit to their self-image. Conversely, others will forget the purpose of the reference tool and send in enough information to begin a presidential library.

One of the basic titles in this category is *The International Who's Who*. The thirty-fifth edition for 1971–1972 is typical enough; and while later annual volumes will update material and add, delete, or expand individual entries, the basic form, scope, and approach remains the same from year to year. The works open with a section of names of "reigning royal families," then move to the alphabetic listing of some 12,000 to 15,000 brief biographies "of the outstanding men and women of our time. The range is wide and takes in those who are prominent in international affairs, government, administration, diplomacy, science, medicine, law, finance, business, education, religion, literature, music, art, and entertainment."

The publisher's stated scope is accurate enough. On the first page of the main section, there are sketches of a Netherlands lawyer, a Finnish architect, two Norwegian diplomats, an Italian conductor, and an Algerian politician. The last page—prior to the annual listing of deaths since the last volume—includes four Americans, a Swiss physicist, and a Polish airline executive. The average entry runs to some 100 to 150 words which in telegraphic fashion follows a rigid pattern of covering all essential facts about the individual: birth date, nationality, career, title, honors, awards, literary works, leisure interests, home address, and, often, a phone number. This is one of the first places to look for data about living world personalities.

This, as all current universal biographical works, serves to supplement, not replace national biographical aids. A larger library with all the various national who's who on its shelves will find considerable duplication between them and the *International* books. Prominent Americans listed in *The International Who's Who* are more than likely to appear in *Who's Who in America;* and prominent Englishmen will be found in equal number in *Who's Who.* Why then purchase this, or, for that

---

[14] English novelist Simon Raven admits to the dreary style of the who's who reference book. Yet, "if one only looks a little closer there lies concealed beneath these unsightly abbreviations and dreary routine appointments—in palimpsest, as it were—such revelations of greed and falsehood, of treachery, hatred and pride, as makes the pages of the novelists seem grey by comparison." (*The Spectator,* June 20, 1970, p. 815.) This is a witty essay on the English who's who but is applicable to any of the genre.

matter, the other current universal biographical aids? There are several justifications: (1) the information is in one place; and if the librarian does not know the nationality of the individual, he is not forced to search through a number of who's who sources in hopes of hitting on the right national base; (2) not all the various who's who sources are annual, and the information in comprehensive annual works is obviously more likely to be up to date; (3) and finally, if the library is a small or medium-sized one it cannot afford, nor does it need, a bank of national who's who sources. One or two of the international works will more than suffice.

The obvious duplication between international and national biographical aids does have one definite effect—it limits publication of the general category.[15] Conversely, other directories, handbooks, and the like do have major sections devoted to international biography. An example of this is the *International Yearbook and Statesmen's Who's Who.*

The English-based annual is really a three-part work; and while more than one-half of each volume is given over to biography, there are other sections. In the 1972 edition, there are 60 pages on international organizations and 500 pages on states of the world. Much of this type of material is similar to what is found in *Statesman's Yearbook,* but the 10,000 or so biographical sketches more than justify purchase. Probably about one-quarter to one-third is duplicated in *The International Who's Who.* The remainder seem unique to this particular reference work.

National: data form—Who's Who

Who's Who in America, with World Notables. Chicago: Marquis Who's Who, Inc., 1899 to date, biennial, $69.50.

Who's Who. London: Black, 1849 to date, annual, (distributed in United States by St. Martin's Press, Inc.), $40.

If there is a necessary, publisher-imposed limitation on international who's who types of reference aids, there is no such agreement as to the number of national or regional works. Most countries have at least one, sometimes several. And they continue to be published. Despite the common titles, the majority are issued by separate firms. The title indicates the scope of the work—except the "father" of them all, the English *Who's Who,* which stops with the two key words. The publisher as-

[15] In 1973, Marquis Who's Who, Inc., published the second edition of *Who's Who in The World.* This includes much of the same information found in other titles and includes listings for 24,000 prominent men and women in all fields. While broader in coverage than the *International,* it is published rather infrequently (about every three years) and, for this reason, does not replace the *International.*

sumed the only who's who personality worth listing was English and anything beyond that in the title would be redundant.

If there are a number of national who's who sources, the number of local versions is legend. For example, Marquis issues a series of 15 titles such as *Who's Who in the East. . . in the West. . . in the South and Southeast.* The publisher asserts that the amount of duplication between any of these local works and the standard volume is less than 20 percent. Unquestionably, they are of help in a given area or for the large research or special library; but their particular claim to fame seems to be that almost anyone who avoids trouble with the law and makes some contribution to his community can find himself in at least one biographical source.[16]

The American version of *Who's Who* is the child of A. N. Marquis, a rather conservative Victorian type of figure whose earlier works were top-heavy in favor of clergymen. (Today, it is educators who make up almost one-quarter of the entries.) Even down to the mid-1940s, popular artists were given short shift, and Marquis had a habit of cutting out personalities he disliked. The architect Frank Lloyd Wright, for example, was deleted for many years. His three marriages were frowned upon by Marquis, and his contributions to the arts could in no way make up for what the editor thought to be a deplorable moral code. Since the death of its founder, the firm has become a nonprofit corporation and is considerably more liberal. (The International Telephone and Telegraph Corporation now holds controlling interest in Marquis, as it does, incidentally, in Bobbs-Merrill publishing firm as well as 400 other companies.) Today the more than 80,000 entries in two volumes include not only famed Americans from almost every walk of life, but a number of foreigners who have some influence on America. Heads of state are normally mentioned as are world-famous actors, musicians, and teachers.

One work which would be unnecessary if women were not treated as the second sex is *Who's Who of American Women* (Chicago: Marquis Who's Who, Inc., 1959 to date). A biennial dictionary of notable living American females, it follows the same general pattern as all the Marquis works. The 1970–1971 edition included 24,000 women's names. The editor's breakdown of 1,000 sketches indicates that a woman's chances to earn an entry were best as a club, civic, or religious leader (9.6 percent of all listings) and worst as a composer (0.4 percent of the entries). Librarians make up a healthy 5.2 percent of the biographies.

---

[16] Marquis, also, issues numerous other variations of who's who directory type biographical aids, e.g., *Who's Who in Government,* 1972–73, *Who's Who in the World,* etc. To have seen one is to have seen them all. The only essential difference is scope—a scope which often duplicates other efforts such as *Who's Who in American Politics* (New York: R. R. Bowker Company), and the aforementioned *International Who's Who.* Larger libraries may want all of the Marquis publications, but smaller libraries may be more selective.

While the oldest publication listing names of eminent persons is the Almanach de Gotha (Gotha: Perthes, 1763-1960), an equally venerable work is *Who's Who* first published on January 15, 1849, some 50 years, it would seem, before there were enough prominent Americans to make a volume possible here. During its first 47 years, *Who's Who* was a slim book of some 250 pages which listed the titled and official classes. In 1897, it became a biographical dictionary and the 1972-1973 edition is close to 4,000 pages. Selection is no longer based on nobility but on "personal achievement or prominence." Most entries are English, but it does include some notables from other countries. And in the past decade, it has put more and more emphasis on prominent scholars and professional people as well as political and industrial leaders.

Depending upon size and type of audience served, most American public university and college libraries will have *Who's Who in America* and possibly *Who's Who*—possibly, because the better known figures who are apt to be objects of inquiry in *Who's Who* are covered in *The International Who's Who*. Still, if the librarian works on the premise there can never be enough of such accurate, up-to-date aids, *Who's Who* will be in the library, too. Another factor is familiarity. Users expect to find *Who's Who* in the library, although many confuse it with the American version.

After the basic international and national biographical works, the library may wish to buy other national titles which range from *Who's Who in Canada* (Toronto: International Press, 1922 to date) to *Who's Who in Latin America* (Detroit: Blaine Ethridge Books, 1971, 2 vols.) and *Who's Who in Communist China* (2d ed., Hong Kong: Union Research Institute 1971, 2 vols.). The degree of reliability varies in other titles, but more particularly in those where the biographical sketches are based upon research rather than the traditional process of sending questionnaires to biographees. For example, Martin Bernal points out that:

> Throughout the twentieth century, Westerners and Japanese have been publishing *Who's Who*s in China for those doing business there. Most entries were merely lists of known appointments, but after 1949 this task became an official concern and the United States government made large and expensive efforts to catalogue Chinese communists. Projects . . . provided restricted information useful for espionage, but other more public work was also produced.[17]

A natural result of the interest in current biographies for specialists, whether they be scholars, spies, or businessmen, has been a proliferation of subject and professional types of who's who. There seems to be one

[17] Martin Bernal, "Who's Who in China," *The New York Review of Books*, March 23, 1972, p. 35. In reviewing a number of sources of Chinese biography, Bernal offers an insight into the problems of biographers in general.

for every major interest group, e.g., *Who's Who in Commercial Web Offset* to *Who's Who in Computers and Data Processing* to *Who's Who in Show Business* to *Who's Who in American Art*. Several of these types are discussed in the professional and subject chapter of this text, but the curious student will find most of them listed in current and retrospective bibliographical sources, as well as in Slocum's *Biographical Dictionaries*.

CURRENT AND RETROSPECTIVE: UNIVERSAL BIOGRAPHICAL DICTIONARIES

General

Webster's Biographical Dictionary. rev. ed. Springfield, Massachusetts: G. & C. Merriam Company, 1972, 1,697 pp., $12.95.

    Chamber's Biographical Dictionary. rev. ed., ed. by J. O. Thorne. Edinburgh and London: Chambers, Ltd., 1969, 1,432 pp., $17.50 (distributed in United States by St. Martin's Press).

    Universal biographical dictionaries are similar to the current data-type *Who's Who* in form of approach. They differ in one major respect—a good 80 percent of the entries are deceased. Also, they concentrate more on background information than items such as phone numbers and addresses. The librarian is apt to use one when he is uncertain as to the probability of the person still being alive, does not know his nationality, or, knowing both, simply wants a handy guide to birth date, pronunciation, spelling of name, profession, and the like. Then, too, the type of question is usually such that the biographical dictionary is an immediate choice. It does not take much experience to realize a governor's address is not likely to be found in a biographical dictionary, but the governor of Virginia in colonial times may be there. Precisely how universal biographical dictionaries are used depends on the habits of the reference librarians. As most entries are deceased, information on them will be found in considerably greater detail in any standard encyclopedia. If someone, for example, wants to know the birthday of Sigmund Freud; one librarian will simply flip to the F volume of an encyclopedia; another will turn to one of the biographical aids; and a third . . . well, he may have his own approach, too. Experience indicates the biographical dictionary is called into play when the librarian simply knows nothing about the requested individual other than (hopefully) an approximate spelling of the last name.

    The two titles listed here are representative of various approaches by compilers to the traditional biographical dictionary form. Webster's, which is familiar to many students and laymen, is primarily a file of 40,000 names from all periods of time and all countries. The majority of entries are short biographical sketches which give most of the data one is accustomed to finding in the who's who approach. There are more Americans, fewer English, and even fewer world figures in Webster's than the title would imply. The editors claim that at time of publication, about one-third of the entries were still alive. The major problem, though, is that while the editors scrupulously add death dates, they do little to update standing biographies. In fact, the volume has not been thoroughly revised since 1942; and as a result, it is advisable to double check any vital statistics with another source.

Chamber's claims only 15,000 names (as contrasted with Webster's 40,000 entries), but it seems to be simply another proof that quality will out do quantity. It gives the same vital information found in Webster's—although much of it is updated in a considerably better fashion—and puts particular emphasis on British and European biography. The major difference between the two is neither number nor scope, but style. Chamber's enjoys a unique position because its editors not only give facts but make a conscious effort to add some human interest and critical observations. The difference between reading the British work and Webster's is the difference between reading a phone book and a book of short, clever essays. Style does not necessarily make the difference between a good or bad reference book; but as style here is embellished with relative currency and accuracy, there simply is no comparison between the two.

The wise librarian will turn to Chamber's first; and failing to find the entry, then go to Webster's. If both fail—which is rather unlikely for average situations—there are other biographical dictionaries. Precisely how often these others are used is debatable because most are now old. Two of the more popular variety in larger reference collection are: *The New Century Cyclopedia of Names* (ed. by C. L. Barnhart, New York: Appleton-Century-Crofts, Inc., 1954, 3 vols.) and the *Universal Pronouncing Dictionary of Biography and Mythology* (5th ed., Philadelphia: J. B. Lippincott Company, 1930, 2,550 pp.). *The New Century* has over 100,000 entries for everything from mythology to place names. It even identifies plays and operas. Given this wide scope, it is considerably more than a biographical aid and is often used as a basic ready-reference tool for almost any situation when someone asks who, what, when, where, or even why. The lack of timeliness for the *Universal Pronouncing Dictionary* (usually cited as *Lippincott's Biographical Dictionary*) is a factor. Still, as neither work puts emphasis on current information, both are primarily used for locating historical names, the time element is not really all that important. *Lippincott's,* for example, is particularly useful for checking names from mythologies and classical Greek and Roman times.

Retrospective biographical sources

Dictionary of American Biography. New York: Charles Scribner's Sons, reprint, 1943, 20 vols., index and Supplements One to Three, 1944–1973. (Reprinted 1964 by publisher, 11 vols. including supplements, Vol. 11 is the index, $260.)

   Dictionary of National Biography, ed. by Leslie Stephen and Sidney Lee, 1885 to 1901; reissue, London: Oxford University Press, 1938, 21 vols. and supplement, 2d to 7th supplements, 1912 to 1971, $389.

   National Cyclopedia of American Biography. New York: James T. White Company, 1892—(in progress).

   Notable American Women 1607–1950. A Biographical Dictionary. ed. by Edward T. James, Cambridge, Massachusetts: Harvard University Press, 1971, 3 vols., $75.

   The McGraw-Hill Encyclopedia of World Biography. New York: McGraw-Hill Book Company, 1972, 12 vols., $250.

The proper use of all these national, retrospective biographical aids depends upon the librarian or user recognizing the nationality of the figure in question and that all entrants are deceased. (Where the nationality is not known, it will save time to first check: (1) one of the current, retrospective biographical dictionaries; then (2) an encyclopedia; and finally (3) *Biography Index.*

The essay-length aids are useful for someone who is preparing a paper, speech, or seeks background information in depth about an individual. Secondary, ready-reference use includes (1) reference to further sources—most of the sketches include bibliographies and location of manuscript sources; (2) portraits or photographs; (3) indexes which are often keys to information on outstanding men and women by profession, area, and so on.

The titles are particularly useful for information on lesser known figures, rarely found, or, at best, only mentioned in general sources. The famous and near famous are often written up in equal or somewhat equal length in standard encyclopedias. There is another use which is common to a few of the "classics" in reference. Catherine Drinker Bowen sums this up nicely: "Like the lover who asks, How did I live before I knew you? I myself wondered how I managed before the *DAB* was mine. Bernard De Voto persuaded me to the purchase; he said it was good for reading in bed."[18]

[18] Catherine Drinker Bowen. *Biography: The Craft and the Calling.* (Boston: Little, Brown and Company, 1969, p. 53.)

The *Dictionary of American Biography* (or the *DAB,* as it is usually called), with its supplements, covers some 15,000 figures who made a major contribution to American life. Almost all are Americans, but there are a few foreigners who significantly contributed to our history. (In this case, they have had to live in the United States for some considerable length of time.) Furthermore, no British officers "serving in America after the colonies declared their independence" are included. The distinctive elements of this basic work are best summed up in the words of the American Council of Learned Societies which sponsored the set: "The articles should be based as largely as possible on original sources; should be the product of fresh work; should eschew rhetoric, sentiment, and coloring matter generally, yet include careful characterization . . . and should be written as largely as possible by the persons most specifically qualified." This latter aspect results in some 3,000 scholarly contributors, all of whom add their distinctive styles and viewpoints to the compilation. As a consequence, most of the entries—which vary from several paragraphs to several pages—can be read as essays, rather than as a list of connected, dry facts.

There is one problem with the otherwise excellent set—timeliness. The last supplement came out in 1973, but the cutoff date of entry is 1945, i.e., only persons who died prior to 1945 can be found in the complete set. The result, of course, is that many major Americans who have died since 1945 are not included. Another supplement is underway; but as of late 1973, there was no announcement as to when it will be completed.[19] Librarians seeking essay-length information on prominent Americans who have died since 1945 should check *Current Biography, The New York Times'* two biographical contributions, and, of course, *Biography Index* and any major encyclopedia.

Thanks to a seventh supplement which appeared in 1971, the British counterpart of the *DAB* carries entries to 1960.[20] *The Dictionary of National Biography* (or *DNB*) is the model for the *DAB;* and having learned one set, the librarian can handle the other without difficulty. The *DNB* is approximately twice the size of the *DAB,* includes over 32,000 deceased "men and women of British or Irish race who have achieved any reasonable measure of distinction in any walk of life." It, also, includes early settlers in America and "persons of foreign birth who have gained eminence in this country." The original set, edited by Virginia

[19] "It is the editorial policy of the Dictionary to allow a sufficient lapse of time between the death of the subject and any attempt to write a just and considered appraisal of his life and contribution to our national history. Therefore, supplements are issued when deemed appropriate by the editorial board." Publishers statement.
[20] The seventh supplement of the *DNB* includes an index covering the years 1901-1960 in one alphabetical series. Hyamson's *A Dictionary of Universal Biography,* indexes both the *DAB* and *DNB* before 1934.

Woolf's father, includes short to long signed articles with bibliographies. Aside from the scope, it can be used in much the same way and for much the same reasons as the *DAB*.[21]

Both the *DAB* and the *DNB* are available in abridged sets.[22] Neither can be unequivocally recommended for the library able to stretch its budget to include the unabridged works. Why? Primarily because the audience and use changes. The full set is beneficial to the man or woman looking for essay-length material. The abridged set will not serve this same audience, but is geared for ready-reference questions. Most of the abridged sketches give only highlights.

Similar full-length, essay-type approaches are available from other countries. The larger the library the more likely it is to have one, or all, of these companions to the basic two. Resembling or modeled on the full *DAB* and *DNB*, for example, are such sets as the *Dictionary of Canadian Biography* (Toronto: University of Toronto Press, 1966–in progress); Australian Dictionary of Biography (Melbourne: Melbourne University Press, 1966–in progress); *Dictionnaire de Biographie Francaise* (Paris: Letouzey, 1933–in progress). All feature long, signed articles about outstanding deceased nationals. And there are many others which may be found in Slocum, Winchell, Walford, and the like.

Prior to the highly scholarly approach of the *DNB*, *DAB*, and other national works of the twentieth century, there was no dearth of essay-type biographical works. The other biographical essay-type reference titles are now much dated and are used primarily for hard-to-find retrospective biographies. In America, the most famous is *Appleton's Cyclopedia of American Biography* (New York: Appleton-Century-Crofts, Inc., 1887 to 1900, 7 vols., reprinted in 1968 by Gale Research Company, $168). Before the *DAB*, this was favored in many American libraries and still has value for biographies not found in the *DAB* and other standard sources. There are some 20,000 short to quite long signed articles dealing with Americans and foreign born who are close to the American scene. Except for the bias of the writer, the work is generally quite high in its accuracy. However, "generally" is used advisedly because Appleton's is, by way of a literary curiosity, not always that scholarly. There are, for example, some 47 sketches of people invented by the contributors. Au-

---

[21] An excellent summary, with citations to reviews and comments, of the *DNB* will be found in Walford's *Guide to Reference Material*, 2d ed., vol. 2, p. 347. For comments on who is not in the *DNB* and who some think should be included, *see* the analytical article (applicable to all such works) by Janet Adam Smith, "Viewpoint," *The Times Literary Supplement*, November 3, 1972, p. 1,314; and "To the Editor" for comments, in the *TLS*, November 10, 1972, p. 1,368.

[22] *Concise Dictionary of American Biography*, ed. by J. C. E. Hopkins. New York: Charles Scribner's Sons, 1964, 1,270 p. *Concise Dictionary of National Biography*. London: Oxford University Press, 1952, 1961, 2 vols. Of the two versions, the *DAB* is better because of its editing which maintains the flavor of the original longer sketch.

thors were paid by space and made the most of it. The nonexistent Bernhard Huhne is credited with the discovery of the California coast; and another fictitious character is a French epidemiologist who was supposed to have combated cholera in South America some 50 years before the disease reached the continent.

Parenthetically, it should be noted that *Who's Who in America* and several other current aids tend to list fictitious biographies. Samuel Hansell was given full treatment in the Marquis work for many years. Listed as a "prominent lawyer," he was a "ghost" planted by the publisher. Had the name appeared in a competitor's work, Marquis had a good case for proving plagiarism. Data about public figures are literally public, and the only way the publisher can prove violation of copyright is to plant his own imagined biographies.

Still another variety of the *DNB* or the *DAB* is *The National Cyclopedia of American Biography*. The work contains sketches of over 50,000 Americans and is particularly strong on American businessmen and industrialists. (Most, although not all, of the entrants are deceased.) This work began and continues to be more involved with the subject's ego than with his true place in history. The facts are usually correct, but there is a definite bias to make the person look as good as possible. Hence, except for extremely famous historical personages, the average entry is closer to the type of thing heard at a funeral oration than read in the *DAB*. The articles, which vary in length from one-half column to several pages, are prepared by the publisher's staff. Information is based on questionnaires, interviews, and data obtained from relatives. The gathering process, as may be imagined, leaves little latitude for criticism of the subject.

Despite the method of gathering biographical data, the *National Cyclopedia*—and other members of the genre—is still useful for locating information on lesser known Americans. A short sketch of an Ohio banker's life may prove the key to solving a historical problem; or at a more mundane level, it serves the curious who are attempting to trace roots of a family tree. Perhaps fitting to the focus, the arrangement of the *National Cyclopedia* is arbitrary and complicated.

None of the material is in alphabetical order, and the more than 55 volumes include several completed sets and sets in progress. Most of the problems before November 1971, is solved by *The National Cyclopedia of American Biography Revised Index; Permanent and Current Series* (New York: James T. White Company, 1971). This is an alphabetical index by name, subject, and topic. Apparently, the publisher will update the index from time to time.

The noticeable bias of most early essay-length biographical sources is obvious in a number of areas, e.g., emphasis is on men and on whites. A conscientious reader of these various sets might conclude her efforts by thinking most of the world has been lead down the road to civilization exclusively by white, basically middle-class men. Only in the last decade has it occurred to historians and compilers that women and minority groups had some interest in affairs. There are now a number of published and planned titles to redress the balance.

Notable American Women includes 1,359 biographies of subjects (who died prior to 1950) whose "lives and careers have had significant impact on American life in all fields of thought and action." The long, signed biographies are similar to those found in the DAB[23] and DNB, and the author of each entry has special knowledge of the subject. In explaining who was included or excluded, the editors note the usual test of inclusion—the wife of a famous man—was not considered. (The only exception is the inclusion of the wives of Presidents.) Once more, the domestic skills of a woman was seldom considered and no moral judgments as to a female being a criminal or adventuress was used to exclude. There is an excellent 33-page introduction which gives a historical survey of the role of women in American life and an index of individuals grouped by occupations. The set is commendable in every way and can be recommended for all libraries. But the division of national biography by race or sex or what you will does raise a valid question—a question posed by a Times Literary Supplement reviewer (July 7, 1972, p. 767):

> Such works as Notable American Women are not, of course, intended to be read straight through; however, to do so produces a disconcerting result. The question arises, is there truly an entity which could be described as "women's history"? Or is there not, rather, the same familiar flow of human history to which millions of women, notable and unnoticed, have contributed equally with men? Estimable as this work is (and it probably will survive into several editions as an essential reference tool), its biographies should ultimately be incorporated into the standard Dictionary of American Biography where a considerable number of notable women (?) are already to be found. If that were to occur, the historian, like history itself, could dispense with the artificalities imposed by a least one instance of really pointless adherence to discrimination by sex.

Not only are the reviewer's comments questionable, but he (or she) fails to recognize that up to this point in history neither the DAB nor any other basic source gives a correct balance between men and women,

[23] The similarity is no accident. One editor, Edward James, is editor of the DAB. Incidentally, as his co-editor Janet James points out in 1955 there were only 750 women among the 15,000 entered in the DAB. Much the same percentage seems true of the DNB; although in the seventh supplement, the editor notes in the preface that the supplement differs in three regards from past volumes: "Nobody was killed in battle; there are more scientists and engineers to be discovered here; and there are more women." How many of the 750 additional names are women he does not say.

between the majority and minority groups. That a new focus on the whole question is now being taken by publishers is much due to the various groups such as the Women's Liberation Movement.

There are now numerous books, besides biographical sources, on women's changing role in society. A useful bibliography which will lead the reader to related titles is Helen S. Astin's *Women: A Bibliography on Their Education and Careers* (Washington, D. C.: Human Service Press, 1971, 243 pp., $5.95). This includes some 350 abstracts and annotations of articles on women, primarily before 1966.

An excellent example of what the movement is attempting to achieve in way of biographical information on women will be found in a letter from Dolores and Earl Schmidt of Slippery Rock, Pennsylvania. Referring to a review of Joseph Lash's biography, *Eleanor and Franklin*, by historian Frank Freidel in *The New York Times Book Review*, the professors noted Freidel thought Eleanor Roosevelt "the most notable woman in American reform politics." They reported they chose Eleanor Roosevelt as the major woman figure to be included in textbooks, but:

Of 27 textbooks we examined, 15 did not mention her at all.

One had a picture, but no textual references.

Two mentioned only her name.

Five devoted one sentence to her.

Two had two sentences . . . and two had one whole paragraph on this "most notable woman in the history of American reform politics."

Dr. Freidel's own textbook, *A History of the United States Since 1865* had one sentence. We quote:

"Young Eleanor Roosevelt, already active in the social-justice movement, while on her honeymoon in 1905, took her husband to lunch with two prominent Fabians, Sidney and Beatrice Webb."

The reference appears on page 281. Eleanor Roosevelt never again appears in this 865-page text written by Frank Freidel, T. Harry Williams, and Richard N. Current.

The title of the above-mentioned review is *The Invisible Women: The Historian as Professional Magician.*[24]

Combining elements of all the biographical sets, the McGraw-Hill *Encyclopedia of World Biography* offers essays (articles run about 800 words) about famous, deceased figures. The scope is universal; it considers famous men and women of all periods and countries. And as the *DAB* and *DNB,* it includes famous persons from all fields—history, literature, art, science, music, and so on. Articles are by scholars and stress commentary and evaluation as much as facts. It is primarily directed to students from junior high through college, but the 5,000 biographical sketches are of obvious value for reference work with others. Further-

[24] *The New York Times Book Review,* November 14, 1971, p. 54. Apparently, Freidel never replied.

more, the set boasts 6,000 portraits, maps, and illustrations which should prove as useful as the classified index (persons, places, treaties, ideas, pictures, styles, and the like) in the final volume. All in all, this should be a basic aid for both ready-reference and essay-type queries.

National: data form—Who Was Who

Who Was Who In America. Chicago: Marquis Who's Who, Inc., 1897–1973, 6 vols., $44.50 each.

Who Was Who. London: Black, 1929 to date, decennial (Distributed in U.S. by St. Martin's Press, Inc.), $30.

The "who was who" type of retrospective biographical aid is similar in purpose, audience, and scope to the works which deal with current figures. The essential difference, of course, is that all entries are deceased. Material in both the *Who Was Who in America* and *Who Was Who* comes from the entries in the orginal current volumes. The editors update any of the material, add the death date, and revise material as needed to finish the entry. Both publishers are a bit behind. The English set covering deaths between 1961 and 1970 is to be published in 1973 or 1974, and the American set (this side of the first, historical volume goes from 1607 to 1896) is up to 1973. Current obituaries can be found as an appendix to each of the two sets.

This type of reference aid is used for ready-reference questions, e.g., birth and death dates, published works, accomplishments, and is of little value to the person seeking extensive background material. Since the bulk of reference work in this area is on the living and on essay-type materials for the dead, neither of the data-type sets is of major day-by-day importance. Their chief value is a backup device when a name cannot be found in any other source—and this type of query tends to be relatively rare.

There are varieties of this source for other countries. A single example is *Who Was Who in the U.S.S.R.* (Metuchen, New Jersey: Scarecrow Press, 1972, 687 pp.). This was compiled by the Institute for the Study of the U.S.S.R. in Munich, Germany. It consists of short entries for 5,000 prominent Soviet citizens who made some major contribution to life of the U.S.S.R. from 1917 to 1967. (Incidentally, it contains data on the persons who campaigned against the Stalin regime and were later killed or exiled.)

PROFESSIONAL AND SUBJECT BIOGRAPHIES

The importance of biography to almost everyone from the researcher to the layman has not escaped publishers. Consequently, almost every publisher's list will include works of a biographical nature from individual biographies to collective works to special listings for individuals engaged in a profession. The increase in the number of professions (almost every American considers himself a professional of sorts), coupled with the growth in education, has resulted in a proliferation of specialized biographical sources.

The reliability of some works is a trifle questionable, primarily because almost all (and sometimes all) the information is supplied directly to the editor or published by the subject. Little or no checking is involved, except in cases where there is a definite question or the biographical sketch is evaluative. Entries tend to be brief, normally giving the name, birth date, place of birth, education, particular "claim to fame," and address. There are exceptions to this brief form. The H. W. Wilson Company series on authors features rather long, discursive essays. Still, this approach is rare. Most biographical works devoted to a subject or profession have mercifully short entries.

The *primary value* of the specialized biographical work is:

1. Source of addresses
2. Source of correct spelling of names and titles
3. Source of miscellaneous information for those considering the person for employment or as an employer, as a guest speaker, or for a number of other reasons
4. And, if maintained for a number of years, the retrospective volumes may prove of invaluable aid to the historian or genealogist

What follows are examples of professional and subject sources. The examples only touch the periphery of a truly large field. Again, Slocum's *Biographical Dictionaries* should be consulted for the range of this type of biographical aid.

Education

Directory of American Scholars. 5th ed. New York: R. R. Bowker Company, 1969, 4 vols., $26.50 per vol.

Leaders in Education. 4th ed. New York: R. R. Bowker Company, 1971, 1,197 pp., $39.50.

(Note: The two titles are revised periodically, and a new edition of *Directory of American Scholars* will be published in late 1974.)

Both these data-type biographical aids are published by the same company and depend heavily upon questionnaires to the entrants for information. Both are reliable and current sources of information. As in all directories of this type, there is a given amount of duplication between this and what is found in the Marquis *Who's Who* series; but the emphasis is different enough to warrant purchase by larger libraries. As Bohdan Wynar observes:

> Who's Who in America lists a number of educators not found in this directory (Leaders in Education), primarily in the area of attainment of a position of substantial responsibility. In addition, entries we found in both Who's Who in America and this directory have a somewhat different emphasis in such catagories as publications. In our sampling, we found that Leaders in Education provides less emphasis on publications and research activities and probably more details on membership and positions held. In general, however, Leaders in Education is a carefully edited and well-balanced work. [25]

While there is a certain duplication between the two Bowker publications, the one devoted to scholars includes some 33,500 entries for college professors and research workers in all fields from history to religion and law. The Leaders volume—with 15,000 entries—is limited to education. See also, American Men and Women of Science (p. 247), which includes teachers of the sciences and social sciences not found in either title. While both of these reference works are essentially the data, who's who approach, a third title is even more refined in the amount of information given. This is The National Faculty Directory (Detroit: Gale Research Company, 1971, 2 vols.). Issued and updated annually, it gives the briefest of information (name, department, school, and address) for over 380,000 teachers, administrators, and executives at universities, colleges, and junior colleges in the United States.

Literature

The first nine of the following works are published by The H. W. Wilson Company:

American Authors: 1600–1900. 1938, 846 pp., $12.

British Authors Before 1800. 1952, 584 pp., $10.

British Authors of the Nineteenth Century. 1936, 677 pp., $12.

European Authors: 1000–1900. 1967, 1,016 pp., $24.

Twentieth Century Authors. 1942, 1,577 pp., $22. Supplement, 1955, 1,123 pp., $18.

The Junior Book of Authors. 2d ed. 1951, 309 pp.; More Junior Authors. 1963, 253 pp.; Third Book of Junior Authors. 1972, 320 pp., $8.00, $8.00, $10.50.

Contemporary Authors. Detroit: Gale Research Company, 1962 to date, annual, $25.

---

[25] American Reference Books Annual, 1972. 3d ed. (Littleton, Colorado: Libraries Unlimited, Inc., 1972), p. 251. See the 1971 edition for a negative review of Outstanding Educators of America and what to look for in evaluating such works.

Author's and Writer's Who's Who. 6th ed. London: Burke's Peerage, 1971, 887 pp. (distributed in United States by Hafner Publishing Company, Inc.), $24.95.

Commire, Anne. *Something About the Author: Facts and Pictures About Contemporary Authors and Illustrators of Books for Young People. Vol. 1.* Detroit: Gale Research Company, 1971, 233 pp., $15.

Ward, Martha E. and Dorothy A. Marquard. *Authors of Books for Young People.* 2d ed. Metuchen, New Jersey: Scarecrow Press, 1971, 579 pp., $15.

Primarily because of written reports, students use the library most often for information on specific authors. When the author is well known there is little difficulty. A good encyclopedia will give the most information, supplemented by literature handbooks and periodical articles. Where depth is required, students can turn to the card catalog and numerous bibliographies as well as standard histories of literature.

Where information is desired about lesser-known deceased writers, or for modern writers, the normal ready-reference sources rarely suffice. Here, a particular series is especially useful.

The best-known series on authors is edited by Stanley J. Kunitz, a prominent American poet, and others. All the works are issued by the Wilson Company. They are particularly useful because they not only give the essential biographical information but also include bibliographies of works by and about the author. The source of much of the material comes from the author himself, if living, or from careful research if the author is deceased. Some of the entries are printed almost verbatim as written by the author and are entertaining reading in their own right.

The Wilson author series leaves a serious gap—there is no information about authors who have made their mark since the particular volume in the series was issued. Also, the Wilson sources tend to disregard authors of more ephemeral works like romances, mysteries, popular poetry, and science fiction. Filling this vacuum, although in a considerably more abbreviated style, is *Contemporary Authors.*

The essential difference between this work and the Wilson biographies is length and depth. The 25,000 plus entries in *Contemporary Authors* rarely run more than four or five paragraphs, usually in outline form. The Wilson works feature long, descriptive articles. Issued semiannually with cumulative indexes, the Gale publication includes the majority of current American (and a few foreign) writers of juvenile stories, fiction, poetry, texts in social sciences, and nonfiction of general interest. The material is submitted by the writers. Sketches include brief biographical information and a bibliography of the author's writings, with some citations to articles about the author. The bibliographies are incomplete but do serve as a tentative check list. *Contemporary Authors* is especially useful for tracing authors who may write only one or two books. Note: Over the years this series has taken various forms. It is now issued annually as a single physical volume. The one volume is referred to as Volumes 25–28, Volumes 29–32, and so on. As of 1973, there were 8 single volumes in a complete set, but they are referred to as volumes 1–32. The bibliographical niceties are confusing, and not entirely warranted.

Still another source of information on current authors, although primarily English, is *The Author's and Writer's Who's Who*. It gives the typical "who's who" type of information on from 9,000 to 10,000 authors. Many listed here are difficult to find in almost any other source, even *Contemporary Authors*. Although the data are limited, they often will indicate other possible sources of information.

All these sources are of a general nature and include authors of all types of materials. Because of an abiding interest in writers, there are countless subdivisions. The Wilson series on junior authors, for example, is supplemented by the Commire and Ward titles. *Something About the Author* is the first of what promises to be a number of volumes. It includes 200 brief biographies in the same style as the other Gale publication, *Contemporary Authors*. The different elements, though, are: comments by the subjects about their own activities; and the illustrations, not only of the subject, but of their works. It is particularly useful for young people because the approach is directed to them and not to the adult or librarian. The interested child can make sense out of the information and, at the same time, enjoy the novel presentation.

The second edition of Ward is another matter. There are more entries—2,100 writers—but the information is brief and there is a curious lack of consistency in who is included or excluded. It is a good example of a title which would be a secondary choice after the Wilson and Gale series, and then only if there is considerable demand for such material.

The ever-present problem of currency, i.e., locating an author who has just appeared on the scene and is not recorded in any of the standard titles, can be met to a degree by consulting various indexes and the current sources mentioned in this chapter. Particularly useful is *The New York Times* services; but, in addition, there are two other excellent sources. The first is the announcement issue of the *Library Journal* three times a year. Normally each announcement number includes 30 to 60 articles, usually prepared by the author in reply to specific questions by the *Journal* staff. The second is *Publishers' Weekly*, another R. R. Bowker publication, which begins each issue with a "PW Interview," usually of an author, illustrator, or even a publisher. Additional information on contemporary figures may be found in reviews of their works in *Book Review Digest*.

Another aspect of biography and literature concerns anonyms and pseudonyms. At one time, this was a major consideration in libraries that conscientiously attempted to catalog by the real, not the assumed, name. Catalog streamlining[26] and exhaustion of the subject by literary scholars have greatly decreased the general reference interest in the area. Still, from time to time a question may be asked about the name of this or that author who employs various pennames, abbreviations, and so on.

If a relatively well-known figure such as mystery writer John Creasey (who writes under such names as Gordon Ashe and J. J. Marric) or A. E., the Irish poet (whose given name is George Russell), the information is easy to find in most literary handbooks, encyclopedias, and other biographical sources. They usually handle the matter with appropriate cross-references from the pseudonyms or initials to the given name. And, of course, from 1950 on, the information may be readily found in either the *National Union Catalog* or the *British National Bibliography,* i.e., if the person in question has been published.

Lesser-known figures—who may range from authors to politicians and scientists, not to mention actors—may be more difficult to trace. In that case, a good dictionary of anonyms and pseudonyms is useful. Many of these are listed in Winchell, Walford, and the like, but the best known is Samuel Halkett and John Laing's *Dictionary of Anonymous and Pseudonymous English Literature* (Edinburgh: Oliver & Boyd Ltd., 1926-1962, 9 vols.). This traces, by title and author, titles published in English. An example of a more current general work is Andrew Bauer's *The Hawthorn Dictionary of Pseudonyms* (New York: Hawthorn Books, Inc., 1971, 312 pp.). This provides some 10,000 entries for real names pennames, pseudonyms, and abbreviations in all fields, not just literature. There are many other titles in this area. The student need only be aware they exist and have some knowledge of the fact that a name is a name is a name is not always true.

There is no lack of reference works in the author biography area; and a glance at Winchell, Walford, or the *American Reference Books Annual* will reveal scores of new and older titles—many of which have gained favor in certain libraries.

Music

The first four of the following are published by The H. W. Wilson Company and edited by David Ewen:
   Great Composers, 1300-1900. 1966, 429 pp., $12.

---

[26] *The AngloAmerican Cataloging Rules of 1967* (rule 42) states that an author using only one pseudonym should be entered under it and, if he uses several, under the name most commonly used. The order rules advocated entry under real name when known. This, of course, is a simplified explanation of a sometimes intricate cataloging problem.

Composers Since 1900. 1969, 639 pp., $17.

Popular American Composers. 1962, 217 pp.; first supplement, 1972, 121 pp., $9.50, $6.

Baker's Biographical Dictionary of Musicians. rev. ed. by Nicholas Slonimsky. 5th ed. New York: G. Schirmer, Inc., 1958; supplement, 1971, $35 (supplement alone $7.50).

Although Baker has not been thoroughly revised since 1958, except for the various supplements (one was issued in 1965 and another in 1971), it is still the best single source of biographical information on everyone from the rock stars and opera singers to classical composers. The publisher rightly claims that the 1971 supplement's attention to popular music and musicians represents "recognition for the first time in any American music lexicon." There are now some 16,000 entries which vary from a few lines to several pages. Unfortunately, the basic edition must be checked with the supplement for new information.

The other key works in this field are Grove's Dictionary of Music and Musicians and Who's Who in Music (6th ed. New York: Hafner Publishing Company, Inc., 1972, 567 pp., $27.95). This latter work contains biographies of some 5,000 living composers, conductors, and musicians, who are internationally famous. It also includes a directory section of agents, festivals, manufacturers, opera companies, and the like, as well as brief essays. Most of the emphasis, however, is on British musical figures; and it is of limited use in many American libraries.

The user who wants an essay approach is better served by any of the Ewen titles. All, from Great Composers to Popular American Composers, follow the familiar format and approach of the Wilson series on authors, i.e., there is a long biographical sketch which is as informative as it is relaxing. Portraits and lists of principal works and bibliographies accompany each of the articles, and there is the usual thorough indexing. The series is particularly useful for public and school libraries where students do research work for papers or where people seek background information. There are numerous approaches of this type: the much praised history by the music critic of The New York Times, Harold Schonberg's The Lives of the Great Composers (New York: W. W. Norton & Company, Inc., 1970, 599 pp., $10.); not to mention other works from the prolific Ewen, e.g., David Ewen's Composers of Tomorrow's Music (New York: Dodd, Mead & Company, Inc., 1971, 176 pp., $5.)

Both Baker and Ewen have come to recognize the importance of modern pop musicians. Bob Dylan, Duke Ellington, Bobby Darin, and Henry Mancini, for example, are only a few of the modern composers included in Ewen's first supplement. There are now a number of books in print, and being published regularly, which should be considered by any reference library giving service to the younger generation—or the oldsters who follow the pop scene. One example is Irwin Stambler and Grelun Landon's *Encyclopedia of Folk, Country and Western Music* (New York: St. Martin's Press, 1969, 396 pp.). This has some 500 biographical discursive, essay-type entries for individuals as well as groups, and the appendix includes a selective discography and a bibliography.

Science and technology

American Men and Women of Science. 12th ed. New York: R. R. Bowker Company, 1972-1975, 8 vols., $37.50 per vol.

Dictionary of Scientific Biography. New York: Charles Scribner's Sons, 1970-1975, 12 vols., $35 per vol.

These titles represent the who's who approach and the essay length consideration of scientists. All are monumental in size, scope, and purpose; and no large library can afford to be without them.

The Bowker publication, when the twelfth edition is completed, will contain biographical data on over 200,000 American and Canadian scientists. The set is divided. Six volumes are devoted to the physical and biological sciences and two to three to the social and behavioral sciences. The publishing schedule varies, but each features a series of supplements which update and include new entries after the new editions are issued. Each sketch has the usual information from address to research interests. Note: The previous name of the set was simply *American Men of Science.* The recognition of women in the field accounts for the suitable change in title.

Whereas *American Men and Women of Science* is an ideal ready-reference aid, the *Dictionary of Scientific Biography* is the ideal work for critical, thoughtful essays on outstanding scientists. It is patterned after the *DAB* and, when completed, will include short to long pieces on some 5,000 deceased scientists from more than 60 countries. (The worldwide scope makes it particularly useful for even ready-reference work when dealing with scientists from non-Western countries who are not easily found in the standard sources.) Under the auspices of the American Council of Learned Societies, this set promises to be a major contribution. A final index volume will tie the whole together in terms not only of individual biographies but also of scientific concepts which will help the reader trace the history of science.

Aside from these two basic works, there are numerous other data-type and essay-length approaches. Representative titles include *Who's Who of British Scientists, 1971-1972* (Athens: Ohio University Press, 1971, 1,022 pp.; *World's Who's Who in Science* (Chicago: Marquis, Who's Who, Inc., 1968, 1,056 pp.), which is distinctive as it includes data-type biographies not only for living scientists but also for famous men and women from antiquity. The McGraw-Hill *Modern Men of Science* (New York: McGraw-Hill Book Company, 1966-1968, 2 vols.) is now a bit dated for "modern," but remains an excellent source for essay-type biographies of some 426 of the world's leading scientists. The set is updated somewhat by the McGraw-Hill *Yearbook of Science and Technology* and the McGraw-Hill *Encyclopedia of Science and Technology.*

SUGGESTED READING

Draganski, Don. "Towelbearer to the Gods," *RQ,* Spring 1971, pp. 212+. A witty essay on aspects of the vanity type biographical sketch.

"George Smith and the DNB," *The Times Literary Supplement,* December 24, 1971, pp. 1,593+. A history of the *Dictionary of National Biography,* with particular attention to the men who made it possible.

Holroyd, Michael. "Biographer's Progress," *Twentieth Century Magazine,* No. 1036, Spring 1968, pp. 9+. A short instructive account of a biographer's problems.

Review of Leon Edel's life of Henry James in *The Times Literary Supplement,* October 30, 1969, pp. 1+. A discerning review which points out many of the biographer's techniques.

Vendler, Helen. Review of *Notable American Women* in *The New York Times Book Review,* September 17, 1972, pp. 1+. A general article on the lack of biographical material on women.

CHAPTER TEN
DICTIONARIES

The general dictionary has a main mission and a secondary mission. Regardless of price, number of entries, or any other considerations, a dictionary is useless if it fails to indicate spelling, meaning, pronunciation, and syllabication (word division). Surprisingly enough, there are some that fail on one or several of these counts.

As a secondary mission, a dictionary, preferably in a single alphabet, should indicate etymology; major place names (with a clear indication of whether it is a river, a mountain, or other item); major personal names from history, mythology, and the Bible; foreign terms; phrases; synonyms and antonyms; abbreviations; and general slang terms clearly marked. Most dictionaries include other types of information, almost of an encyclopedic nature, and almost all have illustrations of varying number and quality. There is debate about whether a dictionary should be simply a dictionary and not an encyclopedia. Many American works do include considerably more information than definitions of words. Anthony Burgess surmises the reason is due to the "educative urge of the great Webster, who wanted to teach the Union all he could and to hell with delimitation of function."[1]

In view of its wide use, it is essential that the librarian thoroughly

[1] Anthony Burgess, "Speaking of Books: From A to ZZZ," *The New York Times Book Review,* September 21, 1969, p. 2.

understand what a dictionary can do, what it cannot do, and what it should do. The obvious main mission is self-evident, but there are other less apparent uses tied in with the secondary mission.

As many dictionaries include quotes to trace either the meaning or history of a word, one may use the key word of a quote to trace its source (when a book of quotations is not available or all such sources have been exhausted). For example, under "prudence" in *Webster's Dictionary of Synonyms* was recently found the source of the quote "That type of person who is conservative from prudence but revolutionary in his dreams." This is by T. S. Eliot. A good historical dictionary will also indicate the first time a word was employed, hence the source of so-called "first facts." Hutchins points out that from the *Oxford English Dictionary,* it may be established that flypapers first came into use in 1848. (*The Dictionary of American English* gives the date as 1847, but this is another matter.)

An unabridged dictionary is also a good source for finding "out what society decrees to be appropriate, though less by definition than by their choice of associations and illustrations." This point is made by two writers who examined sexism in language. They make their point with examples:

> Words associated with males—manly, virile, and masculine—are defined through a broad range of positive attributes like strength, courage, directness, and independence; and they are illustrated through such examples of contemporary usage as "a manly determination to face what comes," "a virile literary style," "a masculine love of sports." Corresponding words associated with females are defined with fewer attributes (though weakness is often one of them) and the examples given are generally negative if not clearly pejorative: "feminine wiles," "womanish tears," "a womanlike lack of promptness," "convinced that drawing was a waste of time, if not downright womanly."
>
> Male associated words are frequently applied to females to describe something that is either incongruous ("a mannish voice") or presumably commendable ("a masculine mind," "she took it like a man"), but female-associated words are unreservedly derogatory when applied to males, and are sometimes abusive to females as well.[2]

A dictionary is to be used not only for words we don't know, but for words we think we know. Usually this latter type is known imperfectly, and the chances are good that any student paper will reveal such words. For example, every cub reporter soon learns that it is dangerous to use the word "consummate" in a wedding story, and that the "past ten days" is considerably better form than the "last ten days."

---

[2] Casey Miller and Kate Swift, "One Small Step for Genkind," *The New York Times Magazine,* April 16, 1972, p. 99. *See also:* Israel Shenker, "Is it Possible for A Woman to Manhandle The King's English?" *The New York Times,* August 29, 1971, p. 58.

The primary function of a dictionary is to define words. A definition is using one set of known words to explain the unknown word. In effect, a dictionary says "this can be substituted for that in such and such circumstances." As I. A. Richards has pointed out, a dictionary can do this because it is a list of substitute symbols. With things, such as horses and cows, no substitution is involved. Here the dictionary simply enumerates properties by which a thing may be compared and distinguished from other things. Hence, both horse and cow are animals, but a good dictionary goes on to tell more about each.

Because the sciences deal primarily with "things," definitions are applicable over a large field and, knowledge of technology being equal, can be understood as well in Outer Mongolia as in Outer, Nebraska. But when one turns to the humanities (particularly religion, philosophy, and politics) and the definitions which are emotive more than enumerative, obvious problems present themselves. For example, what is the definition of a word such as "liberty," "democracy," "love," or "God" in terms of the dictionary and in terms employed by you, your neighbor, or the native of Ceylon? Consider, too, these terms chronologically. Did they mean the same 100 years ago as they do today?

> . . . words, like commanding officers and their men, can massacre innocent bystanders: and that often it is language that evokes in us a passion to embrace or reject others, to love or kill, to be free or be confined. . . . Particularly if the hand holds a gun, we value words: we do not kill, we "evacuate" or "waste"; we don't ship out bodies, we "transport remains home," and we don't fail, we "underachieve". . . . Must our attitude toward the language continue to remain that ambiguous—or that fraudulent? Too frequently language manipulates us when we are unaware of our responses to it; yet when we are conscious of these responses we conveniently dupe ourselves by ignoring the language whenever it becomes threatening.[3]

Language, which relies on emotive symbols, is a slippery beast and is insusceptible to being exactly fixed. Logicians and philosophers attempt this, of course, and with varying success, but no single dictionary is totally satisfactory. Any so-called "emotive word" requires interpretation, and this is the best a dictionary can hope for, normally by astute quotations from observations of spoken and written speech.

There are also differences in the way a word is used from one country to another; between one occupation and another; between one social class and another; and in this age, between youth and mature adults.

[3] Jerzy Kosinski, "The Reality Behind Words," *The New York Times,* October 3, 1971, p. 13. *See also:* Paul Dickson, "Demeaning of Meaning," *The New York Times,* April 13, 1972, p. 29. (A liberal's viewpoint of how government changes the meaning of words to suit its purposes.)

Scope

The public is apt to think of dictionaries in only one category, but they cover almost every aspect of language. The average library will have many of these specialized types of dictionaries. While not all are discussed here, the various types are briefly included.

GENERAL LANGUAGE

These may be subdivided:

1. *Unabridged.* The term "unabridged" is relative, as will be noted elsewhere, but generally an unabridged dictionary may be considered as one with over 250,000 entries.
2. *College or desk.* The terms "college" and "desk" are used loosely and often as synonyms by publishers. Generally, they are dictionaries with from 130,000 to 150,000 entries. Some versions run longer (up to 180,000 entries), but are not unabridged. Others are shorter and may be called "pocket" or "concise" dictionaries.
3. *Children's.* There are a number of children's dictionaries which differ not so much in number of entries, but in method of preparing simplified definitions geared to the child's educational level.

HISTORICAL OR ETYMOLOGICAL

The purpose of the historical or etymological type of dictionary is to show the history of every word from date of introduction to the present. Through the use of definitions and illustrative quotations, the changes in interpretation and meaning are traced through the years. The *Oxford English Dictionary* is by far the most famous of this type.

SLANG

The *Dictionary of American Slang* is an example of many such works which include those four-letter words, and many others, not found in some general dictionaries.

SYNONYMS AND ANTONYMS

Outside of the general and subject type, the dictionary of synonyms and antonyms is by far the most frequently used. Although not arranged in alphabetical order, Roget's *Thesaurus of English Words* is the best known, followed by Webster's *Dictionary of Synonyms*.

USAGE

Dictionaries of usage describe, often in detail, how certain words and phrases should or should not be used. They are not grammar books giving precise rules of the language; rather they trace in the usual alphabetical order the more common words and phrases. Fowler's *Dictionary of Modern English Usage* is the best known of these.

ABBREVIATIONS AND ACRONYMS

While most general dictionaries give basic abbreviations and acronyms, the library needs single sources for ready reference and to keep up with new acronyms. One of the best is the *Acronyms and Initialisms Dictionary.*

FOREIGN LANGUAGE

Normally, foreign language dictionaries are bilingual or multilingual wherein the meanings of the words of one language are given in another or in several languages. For example, *Harrap's French Standard and English Dictionary* is a typical bilingual dictionary which is self-explanatory. A multilingual, or polyglot dictionary, normally restricts itself to a specific field, otherwise the size would be overwhelming. An example is *Language of the Foreign Book Trade* which lists library and book terms and phrases in some 21 different languages, with meanings in English.

SUBJECT

There has been a tremendous proliferation of subject dictionaries over the past years, particularly in science and technology. These are primarily intended for those engaged in a particular field and give definitions of terms of a highly specialized nature. Definitions may extend, at times, to article length. Normally, the definitions are more complete and up to date than those found in a general dictionary and, because they are so new, are not to be found anywhere else. Also, they tend to be given in the jargon of the particular field, which makes many of them difficult for the layman. Librarians considering these works should decide for whom they are prepared, the specialist or the layman.

OTHER

There are dictionaries for almost every other conceivable purpose; but, for the most part, they expand on what is found in a general or subject dictionary. There are dictionaries, for example, of pronunciation, rhymes, spelling, difficult words, obsolete words, and words for crossword-puzzle fans.

Compilation

The written and spoken word is the source for the dictionary entry, but how is a dictionary put together?

In the beginning, it was primarily an individual effort. Dr. Johnson, for example, worked alone, although he did have six assistants for clerical duties. He wrote all the definitions himself, and Boswell explains:

> The words, partly taken from other dictionaries and partly supplied by himself, having been first written down with spaces left between them, he delivered in writing their etymologies, definitions, and various significations. The authorities were copied from the books themselves.[4]

Today, the smaller publishers freely copy other dictionaries. They begin by an out-and-out borrowing of words from a dictionary that is no longer copyrighted. More conscientious publishers then hire free-lance lexicographers to make a minimum number of corrections and additions. Others, and some of their handiwork is on display in some supermarkets and as low-priced pocket dictionaries, simply borrow without benefit of any editing.

A curious feature of the second edition of *Webster's Unabridged* was the inclusion of a "ghost word." The word "dord" was simply an error, on the part of an overzealous clerk, which resulted in its inclusion as a loose synonym for density. After the error was discovered it was decided to keep it in the dictionary for a few years in hopes that the type of aforementioned publisher might pick it up and be caught as a plagiarist. It later was eliminated, and there is no record of whether or not it served its purpose.

Plagiarism is not unknown, then, in the dictionary business; but a certain amount of guidance from other dictionaries is legitimate. Dr. Johnson checked previous works to ascertain what might or might not be included in his dictionary, and much the same procedure is used by all compilers today. Smaller versions of "unabridged" works, such as *Webster's New Collegiate Dictionary,* are common.

Essentially, however, a new general English dictionary or a specialized work requires the labors of many people. An unabridged dictionary costs millions of dollars and years of effort. For example, the Third edition of *Webster's Unabridged* cost $3,500,000 to produce, the 1966 *Random House Dictionary* over $3,000,000, and *The American Heritage Dictionary* over $4,000,000. (Costs go up every year—the abridged dictionary now costing more than the unabridged, which accounts for the infrequent total revision of the unabridged versions.) Work began on the new *Webster's* edition shortly after the Second was issued in 1934. A staff divided words into 109 categories (*Random House* employed 158 subject areas). Subject experts were then found (208 for the Random House work) to review old words and write definitions for new words. In addition to preparing definitions, *Webster's* collected quotations as illustrations of how the words were used (*Random House* avoided this by having editors make up their own illustrative quotes).

[4] *Boswell's Life of Johnson,* ed. by G. B. Hill (New York: Bigelow, Brown & Co., n. d.), Vol. 1, pp. 217-218.

The single greatest effort at collecting citations for a dictionary was that employed for the *Oxford English Dictionary*—at one time some 2,000,-000 quotations illustrating over 400,000 words.

Much of the cost is accounted for by the relatively recent entry of the computer into dictionary making. Both the *Random House Dictionary* and the *American Heritage Dictionary* were produced from data stored first in the computer memory bank. Ultimately, this allows cheaper production of revised editions because the quotation files and the individual words and definitions may be sorted automatically by the computer, thus eliminating thousands of hours of human labor. Another aspect of this is that when several dictionaries are entered into the computer, it is possible to rapidly consult and compare words at a computer terminal—as is being done in several research centers.

One new technique of publishing is illustrated by the miniprint *Oxford English Dictionary,* cut from 13 to 2 volumes by reducing the size of the print. This offers a cheap method of republication of larger sets and makes less demand on shelf space. Taken to the next logical step, Books for Libraries, a publisher in Freeport, Long Island, began publication of 6,000 out-of-print dictionaries in 1972. All the dictionaries will emerge in microfiche—96 or 98 pages miniaturized into a 4-by 6-inch plastic card for reading via a machine.

Subject and specialized works do not require such large staffs, or usually so much money to produce. Many of them are still essentially the work of a single person:

> Peter Glare looks up from his desk in a fairly musty room at Oxford's New Bodleian Library. . . . And he speaks with an even closer knowledge than Johnson, not having interrupted his life's work with entertaining diversions to the Hebrides or gossiping in Fleet Street coffee houses. For the past 20 years, since he graduated in Classics at Cambridge at the age of 26, Peter Glare has been working on the definitive Latin-English dictionary for the Oxford University Press. This autumn (1971) it reaches the Letter G.
>
> The reason his job is such a long one is that the *Oxford Latin Dictionary* refuses to rely on the definitions of earlier dictionaries and takes every word in its original context. Only after each section is completed, says Mr. Glare, does he allow himself a peep at what other dictionaries thought the words meant—a kind of lexicographer's treat like toffees for children who have completed good deeds. Dictionaries, it seems, tend to perpetuate error.
>
> And, although work on the *Oxford Latin Dictionary* started as long ago as 1933, Mr. Glare is racing ahead compared with other Latin-dictionary makers. The Latin dictionary, *Thesauras Linguae Latinae,* which also has its definitions in Latin is being compiled in Germany. It started in 1900 and so far, many volumes later, has reached the letter N.[5]

[5] Ian Jack, "After 20 years Mr. Glare reaches Gorgoneus-a-um," *The (London) Sunday Times,* August 1, 1971, p. 10.

A combination of computer and individual effort is illustrated in the present compilation of the *Dictionary of American Regional English (DARE)*. The purpose of the project at the University of Wisconsin is to gather all regional expressions which are rapidly disappearing. As of 1972, there were some 2,300,000 bits of information programmed into a computer.[6]

EVALUATION

In considering any dictionary, the golden rule was laid down first by Dr. Johnson who said, "Dictionaries are like watches: the worst is better than none, and the best cannot be expected to go quite true." There is no perfect dictionary and never will be until such time as the language of a country has become completely static—an event as unlikely as the discovery of a perpetual-motion mechanism. Lexicography, then, is a never-ending job. Language is always evolving, if only because of the addition of new words and the change in meaning of older words. Nor is any single dictionary sufficient. Each has its good points, each its defects.

The second rule which should be self-evident but rarely is followed: consult the preface and explanatory notes at the beginning of a dictionary. The art of using a dictionary successfully, as any reference book, is understanding how it is put together. This is particularly important in a dictionary because of the constant use of shortcuts in form of abbreviations, various methods of indicating pronunciation, and grammatical approaches.

Authority In order to discuss with any meaning how to evaluate a general English language dictionary, it should be first understood that, as in the case of encyclopedias, there are only a limited number of publishers whose works have been accepted as entirely satisfactory by any reliable authority.

In the unabridged field, there are three major publishers:

1. G. & C. Merriam Company (Encyclopaedia Britannica, Inc.), who publishes *Webster's Third New International Dictionary*.
2. Funk & Wagnalls (Reader's Digest Books, Inc.), who publishes *Funk & Wagnalls New Standard Dictionary*.
3. Random House, Inc., who publishes *The Random House Dictionary of the English Language*.

[6] Israel Shenker, "Lexicographers Find Regional English is Flourishing Despite TV," *The New York Times*, February 17, 1972, pp.35+.

The same publishers issue abridged or college or desk dictionaries, but there are a number of other reputable firms that are in this more limited field. More particularly, Houghton Mifflin's *American Heritage Dictionary* and the World Publishing Company and Doubleday are long-time publishers of quite acceptable abridged dictionaries.

In specialized fields and other areas where dictionaries are employed, there are almost as many reputable publishers as there are works. No particular monopoly of either quality or quantity exists outside of the standard unabridged and desk dictionary fields.

In terms of authority and other evaluative considerations, the librarian has several handy checkpoints. The American Library Association *Reference and Subscription Books Reviews* is the best single guide to the quality of new dictionaries; and Winchell, Walford, or standard subject bibliographies serve quite well for older works.

A comparative guide is S. Padraig Walsh's *Home Reference Books in Print* (New York: R. R. Bowker Company, 1969, 284 pp.) which analyzes and rates more than 30 well-known dictionaries published in the United States. The method is quite similar to his treatment of encyclopedias. It serves best to warn the librarian and the public about a number of really bad dictionaries that are available on a subscription basis or in the supermarkets and chain stores.

For many, the name "Webster" is the golden sign of reassurance, and it frequently is found as the principal name of a number of dictionaries. The original claim to use the name is held by G. & C. Merriam Company which bought out the unsold copies of Webster's dictionary at the time of his death. For years, the use of Webster's name was the subject of litigation. G. & C. Merriam finally lost when the copyright on the name lapsed. It is now common property and may be used by any publisher. Hence, the name "Webster's" in the title may or may not have something to do with the original work which employed the name. Unless the publisher's name is recognized, Webster per se means nothing.

Vocabulary Vocabulary may be considered in terms of the period of the language covered and the number of words or entries. Winchell notes that this may be extended to include what she terms special features such as slang, dialect, obsolete forms, and scientific or technical terms. Still, it primarily comes down to the question of how many words or definitions will be found.

In the United States, this problem is divided nicely between the "unabridged" and the "abridged" types of dictionary. The majority of dictionaries are abridged or limited to given areas. The three unabridged works vary from some 450,000 entries each for *Webster's* and *Funk &*

Wagnalls to 260,000 for *Random House.* The abridged dictionaries normally run from 130,000 to 150,000 entries.

How important is it to have a dictionary of more than, say, 100,000 words? Potentially, the number of words in the English vocabulary is infinite, but several experts have surmised that only 340,000 different graphic forms or types will exist in our language at any one time. Which is to say some 100,000 of the words found in *Webster's Third* are (1) obsolete; or, (2) unusual items extant only in isolated contexts; or, more likely, (3) many of the 100,000 words are not really different types, but simply different definitions of the same word.

What, then, constitutes a legitimate entry which may be counted as one word? Most dictionaries—at least for the advertising copywriter— count each of the definitions, not the separate entries. For example, the *Random House Dictionary of the English Language, College Edition,* claims 155,000 entries. A careful critic estimated the real number of entries, i.e., separate words at under 100,000. "Counting five random pages, I get an average of 46 separate entries per page; and this figures times 1,534 pages gives fewer than 71,000."[7]

But to return to the statistical aspects of dictionaries, how many words are really required for most users? D. R. Tallentire, who has done an extensive study of the subject, reports:

> Even our most prolific and admired writers seldom exhibit more than 30,000 different types in a lifetime of writing. Of course their latent vocabularies (the words known though not necessarily used) far exceed this number. . . . For example, Shakespeare's prodigious output comprises only 29,066 different words. . . . Shakespeare's vocabulary is less than three times larger than the 10,666 types of W. B. Yeats or the 10,097 of Matthew Arnold, though Shakespeare's total works comprise more than six times the output of either poet . . . . Though Shakespeare's revealed vocabulary represents less than 10 percent of the extant 340,000 words of English, it still accounts for more than 90 percent of the words appearing on any page of literature we care to examine . . . 10 percent of the vocabulary of English covers 90 percent of the text of all the volumes of literature in all our libraries. . . .[8]

Furthermore, Tallentire found that "about 135 words recur with sufficient frequency to constitute 50 percent of most texts." In another study, researchers excerpted 10,000 five hundred word samples from 1,000 of the most frequently used titles in grades three through nine. Overall, the survey found some 87,000 different words; but of these,

---

[7] W. V. Quine, "Letter to editor column," *The New York Review of Books,* January 1, 1970, p. 38. The letter is preceded by a letter from the editor of the Random House work. *See also:* Sidney Landau, "Dictionary Entry Count," *RQ,* September 1964, pp. 6+.

[8] D. R. Tallentire, "The Mathematics of Style," *The Times Literary Supplement,* August 13, 1971, p. 973.

35,000 appeared only once in the sample. They were typically such unusual items as "goody-goody," "Hippiesque," and "hightail." (The study also revealed that the word boy or boys appears 4,700 times versus 2,200 for girl or girls.)[9]

Thanks to the use of computers, word counts are now relatively simple. In the aforementioned studies, the computer was given the words found in the texts; and it printed out each word alphabetically by frequency. Still, all English dictionaries lack such valuable statistical information. It would be interesting and useful to know (along with a definition) how frequently the word is used and how that frequency has changed over time.

Continuous Revision The vast majority of dictionaries (unabridged and abridged) tend to be five to ten years old. Each year, a new work, or a new edition, comes along; but, on the whole, the original copyright date signifies the time when the majority of the words in the dictionary were entered. (Possible, although not necessary, revision is indicated, as in encyclopedias, by the new copyright date, i.e., on the verso of most title pages will be found "Copyright, 1966, 1967, 1970, 1972" and so on. The first date indicates the initial work.)

Somewhat like encyclopedias, the major dictionary firms employ a type of continuous revision. With each new printing, they may add or delete a given number of words. This is particularly true of the desk dictionaries which are most used by younger people and must reflect current usage and new words introduced into the language via radio, television, music, technology, and the like. On the whole, the system works rather well. No library, then, should necessarily scuttle a standard title simply because a new one comes along which claims to be entirely revised. Where a completely new approach is offered, e.g., *The American Heritage* and the *Random House* titles, the library may then want to add to its general dictionary collection. Otherwise, by simply purchasing a revised edition of a standard desk dictionary each year, the library will be able to keep up with most problems of current vocabulary.

Special Features In addition to authority and the number of words, the average layman, if not always the librarian, is most interested in the added features. Many dictionaries are encyclopedic in that they include items such as illustrations, special lists, historical data, and biographical information.

[9] Andrew H. Malcolm, "Most Common Verb in Schools. . . ." *The New York Times,* September 4, 1971, p. 22. The study was conducted by the editors of the *American Heritage Dictionary.* For a list and evaluation of such studies and published common word dictionaries, *see:* Kenneth W. Berger, "An Evaluation of the Thorndike and Lorge Word Count," *Central States Speech Journal,* Spring 1971, pp. 61 + .

The *Random House Dictionary* recognized the sales importance of these features, and almost one-fifth of the total is given over to encyclopedic information. There is a 64-page atlas, a 35-page gazetteer, a directory of colleges and universities, sections on historical documents and dates in world history, and even a concise French, Spanish, Italian, and German bilingual dictionary running to almost 200 pages.

The problem with encyclopedic type information is that where it is included it usually implies that the publisher has had to sacrifice elsewhere. If nothing else, the *Random House Dictionary* results in a massive volume, whereas other smaller works may simply solve the problem by compressing out the words in favor of the facts. By definition, a dictionary should define and not concern itself with another function. Few, however, follow this rule.

Format In evaluating the format of a dictionary, the most noticeable item is the print size and how it is affected by spacing between various words, the use of boldface type, and the differences in type families. Individual tastes will play an important part in this decision; but from the viewpoint of many users, *The American Heritage* work is the best for its typography. Here it is instructive to simply compare the typography of this single dictionary with other works.

With the exception of some colored plates, the majority of dictionary illustrations are black-and-white line drawings. Where appropriate, the actual size should be indicated, as for example in the case of an animal or plant. Numberwise, the average desk dictionary has from 600 to 1,500 illustrations, the unabridged from 7,000 to 12,000.

None of the dictionaries by major publishers can be severely criticized on grounds of format, but it is interesting to note that many questionable works frequently give themselves away for the very lack of a pleasing format. This is more often the result of using old, worn plates from another dictionary than a design of the publisher. When the paper is of a poor quality, the typography running toward gray, and the illustrations obviously dated or inconsequential, this is a good warning signal that the dictionary is possibly inferior.

Usage Although traditional titles have regularly prescribed rules for correct usage for most Americans, the ultimate authority is the dictionary. But which dictionary? Up until the publication of *Webster's Third*, it was *Webster's Second*. With the advent of the latter title, the editors broke with tradition. The Third made little or no effort to prescribe correct usage. Critics claim it opened the flood gate of permissiveness, providing no rule other than popularity. This, it is argued, not only removed Webster's as a source of proper usage, but in so doing clears the road for progressive deterioration of the language.

The editors abolished such labels as "colloquial" and "slang" and replaced them with general prescriptive terms such as "standard" and "substandard." Furthermore, many words otherwise labeled as slang in the earlier edition are now left unlabeled. Having been let down by the publishers, the ultimate authority for usage shifted to (1) standard grammars and books of usage and (2) gradually, other smaller dictionaries such as *The American Heritage Dictionary* and *The Random House Dictionary*, particularly the former which made a point in its advertising of boasting about its extensive proper usage notes.

The dissenting voices may be described as those who insist a dictionary should be an advocate of usage as contrasted with those who view a dictionary as the custodian of the language. Those who argue a dictionary should record modern language, not determine what is best or better, belong to the descriptive school. Conversely, those who assert a dictionary is the guardian of the language, protecting it from degenerating via the popular press, are in the prescriptive camp.

The *descriptive advocates* who now govern the compilation of almost every major dictionary claim:

1. The people dictate what is the proper usage of the language. Consequently when illustrating the definition of a word in a modern dictionary it is important not only to use quotes from good literature, but also from newspapers, television programs, and speeches.
2. One does not go to the dictionary to find language standards or rules for proper usage. Spelling, pronunciation, and definitions are important, but standards and usage are not.
3. A particular word used frequently enough by many people becomes acceptable usage.

The *prescriptive group* asserts that the major role of a dictionary is to set standards:

1. There is tradition and authority based upon proper historic usage.
2. Failure to support this philosophy accounts for the jargon, lingo, and fashionable verbiage driving out the pure language.
3. In a word, to believe other than this is to agree to debase the language.

The prescriptive group asserts that the major role of a dictionary is to support the precise and the exact, not the vague and the ambiguous. There are standards, there is a tradition, and there is authority. At the heart of this position is the belief that there is such a thing as universal good usage. Failure to support such a notion accounts in no small way for the jargon, lingo, and fashionable verbiage which flows from the radio and television networks and fills the popular press. In a word, the prescriptive school claims that the descriptive advocates are debasing the language.[10]

The descriptive advocates respond:

> All languages change; but they change gradually, not abruptly. This means that during the course of the development of any language, there must be periods of transition when two forms—a newer form and an older one—exist concurrently. Some speakers of the language will use one, some will use the other, and still others will use both. At such times, who can honestly judge one form or the other as being the only correct form? And if the older form was once the correct one, then at just what moment in the history of the English language did the use of you (as opposed to thou) become the correct way of addressing a single person? . . . Every language changes constantly in spite of attempts to fix it in some permanent form. . . . An accurate grammar of a given language must, therefore, be a description of the way in which the people who use that language actually speak it and write it.[11]

All of this is academic for the librarian. The point is that *Webster's Third* is essentially descriptive, whereas the only other unabridged dictionary, i.e., *Funk & Wagnall,* is prescriptive but dated. The best source is *The American Heritage Dictionary* and the majority of other desk dictionaries, always supported by a good handbook of usage. This is the fact. The argument, though, as to what is, and what should be, will continue to rage as long as there are dictionaries.

If indication of proper usage is the most debated aspect of word treatment in a dictionary, there are other elements that are of equal concern.

Spelling Where there are several forms of spelling, these should be clearly indicated. *Webster's* indicates the English spelling by the label "Brit." and other dictionaries normally indicate this by simply giving the American spelling first, e.g., "analyze, analyse" or "theater, theatre." Frequently, because of usage, two different spellings may be given, either of which is acceptable. The user must determine the form to use. For example, "addable or addible" and "lollipop or lollypop."

---

[10] This argument, pro and con, is documented for the Third by James Sledd and Wilma R. Ebbitt. The two editors gathered together articles which both praised and damned *Webster's* Third. *Dictionaries and That Dictionary* (Chicago: Scott Foresman and Company, 1962).

[11] Robert L. Allen, *English Grammars and English Grammar* (New York: Charles Scribner's Sons, 1972), pp. 58–59.

Etymologies All dictionaries, usually before or after the definition, indicate the etymology of a word by a shorthand system in brackets. The normal procedure is to show the root word in Latin, Greek, French, German, Old English, and the like. Useful as this feature is, the student of etymology will only be satisfied with historical dictionaries such as Mencken's *The American Language* to properly trace the history of a word and how it developed.

Definitions Modern American general English dictionaries give the most common meaning of the word first. *Webster's* is the only one discussed here which gives definitions in historical order. This is an important point which cannot be stressed too much, particularly when the librarian is assisting a user to find a definition. Where there are several meanings, the difference is clearly indicated by numbering each of the definitions. Parts of speech (noun, adjective, verb, and so on) are separate entries.

The wording of the definition is of primary importance, and the modern trend is to be short and employ commonly understood terms. Here, for example, are two definitions for "anthropomorphic" from two dictionaries: (1) "ascribing human form or attributes to a being or thing not human, esp. to a deity"; (2) "described or conceived in a human form or with human attributes: represented with human characteristics or under a human form: ascribing human characteristics to nonhuman things: crudely human or man-centered in character." For most purposes, not only is the first definition quite long enough, but in many ways it is clearer than the second.

Pronunciation There are different methods of indicating pronunciation, but the most common is the diacritical. Usually, a handy key to the system is given at the bottom of every other page. Acceptable pronunciation is usually indicated, not only in general, but for specific regions.

Synonyms The average user does not turn to a general dictionary for synonyms, but inclusion helps to differentiate between similar words. Some desk dictionaries indicate the differentiation and shades of meaning by short essays at the conclusion of many definitions.

Syllabication All dictionaries indicate how a word is to be divided into syllables. The method is usually a centered period or hyphen. The information is primarily for helping writers and editors, not to mention secretaries, in the division of a word at the end of a line. There are special short desk dictionaries which simply indicate syllabication of more common words without benefit of definition or pronunciation.

Grammatical Information The most generally useful grammatical help a dictionary renders is to indicate parts of speech. All single entries are classified as nouns, adjectives, verbs, and so on. Aside from this major division, dictionaries vary in method of showing adverbs, adjectives, plurals, and principal parts of a verb. Usually the method is clearly ascertainable; but, again, the prefatory remarks should be studies to explain any particular presentation.

GENERAL LANGUAGE DICTIONARIES

G. & C. Merriam Webster Company (Encyclopaedia Britannica, Inc.)

Webster's New International Dictionary of the English Language. 2d ed., 1934, 3, 195 pp. (600,000 entries) o.p.

Webster's Third New International Dictionary. 1971, 2,662 pp. (450,000 entries), $54.50.

*Webster's New Collegiate Dictionary. 8th rev. ed. 1973, 1,568 pp. (152,000 entries), $7.95.

Funk & Wagnalls Company (Reader's Digest Books, Inc.)

Funk & Wagnalls New Standard Dictionary. 1964, last totally revised in 1913, 2,816 pp. (458,000 entries), $62.50.

*Funk & Wagnalls Standard College Dictionary. rev. ed. 1969, 1,606 pp. (150,000 entries).

Houghton Mifflin

*The American Heritage Dictionary of the English Language. 1969, 1,600 pp. (155,000 entries), $9.95 to $35.

Random House

The Random House Dictionary of the English Language, ed. by Jess Stein, 1966, 2,059 pp. (260,000 entries), $30.

The American College Dictionary. 1965, 1,444 pp. (135,000 entries), $6.95.

*The Random House Dictionary of the English Language, College Edition. 1968, 1,600 pp. (155,000 entries), $7.95 and up.

The World Publishing Company (Cleveland)

Webster's New World Dictionary of the American Language. Second College Edition. 1972, 1,728 pp. (157,374 entries), $7.95 to $9.95.

    Webster's New World Dictionary. 1966, 1,724 pp. (142,000 entries), $4.95 to $5.95.

    NOTE: The asterisk indicates a smaller work, usually referred to as a desk or college dictionary. Other works listed are unabridged.

UNABRIDGED DICTIONARIES

Webster's

The single unabridged dictionary found in the majority of libraries and government agencies, *Webster's International,* was published first in 1909. A second edition came out in 1934 and the third in 1961. While the 1909 edition is rarely found in any library, it is quite common to have both the Second and Third editions. The two vary so radically from one another that many consider them to be almost two different works.

    The differences may be given as follows.

    Vocabulary   1934 ed., 600,000 entries; 1961 ed., 450,000 entries. The third was cut by eliminating some 250,000 words from the earlier work and then adding 100,000 words which have come into the language between 1934 and 1961. Because many obsolete and rare words have been deleted, the older work is absolutely necessary for historical purposes.

    Special Features   The 1934 edition had an appendix with abbreviations, arbitrary signs and symbols, forms of address, pronouncing gazetteer, biographical dictionary. A reference history edition also included a supplement "reference history of the world," which was a basic handbook on world history. The 1961 edition deleted all these features, but major abbreviations are included in the main alphabet. However, there are few proper names or geographical entries. This means that either a library must retain the earlier edition or it must purchase separate volumes for biographical and gazetteer information.

    Format   The format is primarily the same in both works. An important typographical exception is that in the Third edition all proper names and adjectives listed are in lower case. For example, "Christmas," "French," and "English" are noted in lower case, but marked, where appropriate, "use cap." The only word capitalized in the dictionary is God.

Word treatment   The treatment of words was the single most controversial point regarding the new edition. Following the descriptive school, the Third edition included many words not qualified by such terms as found in the earlier editions. The label "colloquial" was completely dropped, replacing this with "substandard" and "nonstandard." Labeling with these terms, and others such as "slang," is used cautiously. Many items were left unlabeled, e.g., "ain't" ("though disapproved by many . . . used orally by many cultivated speakers"). The new concept of acceptability is reason enough for all libraries to have the Second edition on hand to double-check the proper use of given word. The earlier work definitely was under the control of the prescriptive advocates.

Quotations   The Second tended to use classical and standard quotations; the Third's 100,000 or so quotes are primarily drawn from contemporary sources, i.e., newspapers, magazines, speeches of politicians and from writers such as P. G. Wodehouse and Mickey Spillane.

Other Elements   In both works, the historical meaning is given first; pronunciations are indicated by methods unique to Webster's and the Third edition represented a radical change in procedure from the Second; quotations in the Second are primarily from literature, but in the Third are from recent sources, many of a popular nature.

There are other differences, many of them controversial, but suffice it to say that both editions will be wanted in any library. The Second may be difficult to obtain. Booksellers report a constant demand for the earlier work. It now brings a price on the used book market of $100 and up, as compared with under $50 for the newer work.

Funk & Wagnalls

While a completely new revision of this work has not been made since 1913, it has been kept relatively up to date by inserting new words, compressing definitions of older words, and adding supplements with newer printings. It includes some 450,000 entries; but of these, over 65,000 are proper names not found in *Webster's Third.*

The essential differences between this work and Webster's are that:

1. Common, modern definitions precede the historical.
2. The pronunciation key is considerably easier to use and understand.
3. The format is more pleasing, particularly the judicious use of boldface and good spacing.

4. There are a number of illustrative phrases and quotations which differ from *Webster's* both in terms of sources and emphasis.
5. Usage is clearly indicated by standard labels, and in this respect is better than *Webster's Third*, but not up to the Second.
6. *Funk & Wagnalls* includes more encyclopedic information than *Webster's*.

There are, of course, other differences such as *Funk & Wagnalls'* preference for simplified spelling and the emphasis on illustrations; but one major drawback to the work is that it is spotty. Although the continuous revision program is well done, it must be kept within the pagination of the 1913 edition. Consequently, for everything added, something must be deleted or compressed and supplements added. Were it not for this one major drawback, it would be a real competitor in a library for *Webster's*. As it now stands, it is only a second choice.

Random House

First published in 1966, the *Random House Dictionary* is the newest contender for the label of "unabridged" dictionary. However, there is considerable debate between G. & C. (i.e., *Encyclopaedia Britannica)* and Random House as to whether the newer work is truly "unabridged." In terms of simple word count it is not. There are some 260,000 entries compared to 450,000 for *Webster's*. Still, this represents almost 100,000 more words than found in the common desk dictionary and, according to the editors, more than meets the needs of the general public, but not the needs of those who require a true unabridged dictionary.

Regardless of the merits of the debate, libraries will first want *Webster's* and then possibly consider *Random House* over *Funk & Wagnalls,* if only because of its newness.

Many critics were disenchanted with the *Random House Dictionary* because it was divided between the descriptive and prescriptive philosophy. It tends to be more liberal (with "nonstandard," "informal," "slang," and the like) than *Webster's;* but at the same time, it accepts many questionable words as acceptable. Definitions are fairly concise (some claim too brief) but usually quite clear. Quotations support the definitions, albeit the majority are made up by the editors. The results are sometimes ludicrous. For example, quotations used to support "begin," "contain," and "naked," are "Where shall I begin?" "This glass contains water." "The children swam naked in the lake." More difficult words often slip by without quotations.

A strong selling feature of the *Random House* is the amount of encyclopedic information—little of which has value for the average library. The format is generally pleasing and there are a number of excellent up-to-date illustrations.

Houghton Mifflin

Although far from an unabridged dictionary, *The American Heritage* has assumed somewhat that role in that it is an active competitor with *Random House*. In fact, the two are often compared—not so much in terms of number of entries, but rather because they represent two new approaches to American dictionaries.

Be as it may, *The American Heritage* does not replace any unabridged dictionary in the library. It does, though, serve as one of the best general home dictionaries and is a good combination of better features in the unabridged and the typical desk or college works.

It has two major claims for attention (1) Illustrations: the publisher claims there are 3,500 illustrations and more than 200 maps. These are placed at irregular intervals down the broad and otherwise blank outer margins of the pages. Most are halftones based upon great paintings and drawings. They are far better than found in any other dictionary, regardless of size. Furthermore, the typography, spacing, and so on are excellent. All of this adds up to ease of reading and explanation through illustrations. (2) Prescriptive entries: one of the major selling points of this dictionary is that it provides definite guidance on acceptable usage. The *Random House* does the same, but it tends to be more temperate; the *Heritage* more forthright.

Another valuable feature is the appendix which includes a lengthy list of the Indo-European roots and the English words that embody them. This etymology feature complements rather extensive etymologies in the body of the dictionary.[12]

OTHER UNABRIDGED DICTIONARIES

With the exception of the aforementioned dictionaries, there are no other unabridged dictionaries entirely suitable for either library or personal use. The abridged *Oxford English Dictionary* in one volume, distributed widely by a national book club, is an excellent historical dictionary, but in no way replaces the American works.

[12] John B. White, "Pictures at a Definition; A Marginal Critique," *Wilson Library Bulletin*, March 1971, pp. 674+; William Morris, "White's Time. . . ." *Wilson Library Bulletin*, March 1971, pp. 679+. A critic and the editor of the *American Heritage* discuss illustrations. A witty and perceptive dialogue.

Desk Dictionaries

The firms that issue unabridged dictionaries also publish desk dictionaries, based upon larger works. Another publisher, World, is a highly regarded source of desk dictionaries.

These works are periodically revised and all are authoritative. Differences are primarily of format, arrangement, systems of indicating pronunciation, and length of definitions. All feature synonyms, antonyms, etymologies, and limited biographical and gazetteer information. Price variations are minimal, the normal range being under $10. There are enough variations in binding, thumb indexing, and other such things that publishers' catalogs should be consulted for versions of the basic editions.

WEBSTER'S

Now in its eighth edition, *Webster's New Collegiate Dictionary* is based upon the unabridged Third. It reflects the philosophy of the larger work; and there is considerable emphasis on contemporary pronunciation, definitions, and, more important, usage. There is only a minimum of labels for illiterate or slang terminology.

The type size is quite small, at least in comparison with competitors such as the *Random House* or *American Heritage* work. Conversely, at this writing (1973) it has the advantage of being the newest of the desk dictionaries and has 22,000 new words and meanings since the last edition.

The pronunciation system is a bit difficult to follow; and as in all Webster's dictionaries, the definitions are in chronological order with the modern meaning coming last. Added features include appendixes which cover biographical data, gazetteer, forms of address, colleges and universities in the United States, vocabulary rhymes, and the like.

FUNK & WAGNALLS

Funk & Wagnall's Standard College Dictionary has one major feature—proper names, geographical names, and foreign phrases are included in one alphabet. Frequently, this is less confusing for the student, who, in *Webster's,* must consult material in the back of the dictionary.

As in the larger work upon which it is based, usage is clearly indicated, modern definitions precede the historical, and the pronunciation system is relatively clear. There are a number of added features in the appendixes.

HOUGHTON MIFFLIN

In terms of price, format, scholarship, and ease of use, the *American Heritage Dictionary* is the "best buy" in desk and college type dictionaries. It would be a first choice for all libraries, followed by the Random House *American College* or the new *Webster's Collegiate.*

RANDOM HOUSE

Although issued by Random House, *The American College Dictionary* is not based on the later, larger dictionary. Instead, it is a thoroughly modern approach to desk dictionaries. First issued in 1947, it represents the planning and philosophy of Clarence Barnhart. He was responsible for introducing new concepts, the most noteworthy (and debatable) being a systematic study of definitions. He was among the first to scientifically approach dictionary definitions in terms of their frequency of use.

With some 135,000 entries, this dictionary is particularly strong in Americanisms, modern scientific terms, and biographical data. All entries are in one alphabet and definitions are given with modern usage first. The pronunciation key is particularly easy to understand and the typography is outstanding.

In 1968, Random House issued a desk dictionary based directly on the parent work. Also called *The Random House Dictionary of the English Language*, it has the important subtitle *The College Edition.* As a desk dictionary of some 155,000 entries and 1,500 illustrations, it is essentially a cut-down version of the larger work. Although it boasts close to 20,000 more entries than the *American College Dictionary*, the latter is still preferable.

WORLD

Webster's New World Dictionary of the American Language is not a G. & C. "Webster's"; but unlikely any supermarket dictionaries that boast the same name, it is quite a legitimate desk dictionary. Published by World, it represents, like the *American College*, a new work not based upon a larger dictionary. It includes some 157,000 entries in a single alphabet but definitions are given in chronological order rather than by frequent or modern usage.

It is particularly strong on contemporary American vocabulary and the latest technological terms. Another feature is the inclusion of a considerable number of colloquialisms, slang expressions, and idiomatic expressions—all clearly labeled. Many of these are not found in other desk dictionaries, or if in *Webster's*, not always explained.

World also publishes an unabridged dictionary, *Webster's New Twentieth Century Dictionary*, which claims 400,000 entries. In coverage, it is far from comprehensive; and while recommended by *Subscription Books Bulletin* (December 1, 1957), it "is not a substitute for other standard unabridged dictionaries in the same price range." It definitely is a poor, secondary choice for libraries.

CHILDREN'S DICTIONARIES

Children's dictionaries are comprised of words based on frequency of occurrence in speech and reading encountered in school. Definitions are rewritten in simplified language, the type is usually large, there are many illustrations, and the format is generally pleasing.

The most ambitious and costly is a two-volume dictionary intended for grades four through college and suitable for the whole family: *World Book Dictionary*, ed. by Clarence L. Barnhart (Chicago: Field Enterprises Educational Corporation, 1969, 2 vols., revised annually). Although this costs slightly more than the *Third unabridged*, it has fewer entries— 190,000 compared to the *Third's* 450,000. All entries are in a single alphabet, pronunciation is simple to follow, and there are more than 2,000 pictures. Unlike the majority of dictionaries in this category, it does not include encyclopedic information, i.e., biographical and geographical type of information. And like the *World Book Encyclopedia*, it can be used advantageously by most adults. The work is generally considered by experts to be excellent, and it can be recommended without hesitation by librarians.

Some less ambitious, less costly works by the same editor of the *World Book* dictionary are based on the general principles of the more expensive work. These series are clearly printed, and all the titles are generously illustrated with meaningful thumbnail drawings. Proper nouns are included in the single alphabet. A good one-half of the definitions are complemented with examples of how the words may be used properly. There is an excellent pronunciation system. As these are considerably less expensive than the *World Book* entry, they are probably better suited for homes, although libraries will want the larger work.

The Thorndike-Barnhart Beginning Dictionary, ed. by Clarence L. Barnhart. Chicago: Scott, Foresman and Company, 1962, 720 pp. (Grades 3 to 4).

Variations on the same dictionary are to be found in two other works edited by Barnhart, with explanation of the age group in the title, e.g., *Thorndike-Barnhart Intermediate Dictionary* (Grades 5 to 8) and the *High School Dictionary*. The number of entries is increased with the grade level, 22,000 to 75,000.

G. & C. Merriam Webster; Harcourt, Brace & World, Inc.; Funk & Wagnalls; The World Publishing Company; and Doubleday & Company, Inc., all publish somewhat similar works at about the same price level. Again, individual features vary, but the overall quality of these dictionaries is uniformly high.

Further information on these and other sets may be found in The H. W. Wilson Company standard catalog series, i.e., *Children's Catalog, Junior High School Library Catalog,* and *Senior High School Catalog.*

Also, from time to time, they are reviewed in *School Library Journal* and *Top of the News*. One safe element that almost guarantees quality, though, is the name of Barnhart connected with any of the works.

HISTORICAL DICTIONARIES

Murray, Sir James et al. *New English Dictionary on Historical Principles.* Oxford: Clarendon Press, 1888 to 1933, 10 vols. and supplement; reissued in 1933 as 13 vols. under title *Oxford English Dictionary*, $300.
————*The Compact Edition of the Oxford English Dictionary.* New York: Oxford University Press, 1971, 2 vols., $75.
————*A Supplement to the Oxford English Dictionary.* ed. by R. W. Burchfield. New York: Oxford University Press, 1972, 1,356 pp., $50.

H. L. Mencken called it "the emperor of dictionaries," and *New English Dictionary on Historical Principles* (usually cited as the *OED*) is truly the English language dictionary. It took longer to prepare than almost any other book in the English language. In 1857, Dr. Richard Trench (1807 to 1886) launched the project which was to take 70 years to complete. The first of the 10 basic volumes was issued in 1884, the last supplementary volume in 1933. The work was first under the charge of Sir James Murray, then Dr. Henry Bradley, then Dr. William A. Craigie, and finally C. T. Onions. All of these men made other major contributions to historical dictionaries, and thousands of other scholars took part in the giant undertaking.

Each of the ten basic volumes weighs approximately 10 pounds, and there are about 500,000 words defined. Comparatively speaking, there are 200,000,000 characters in the basic work. The whole is supported by 2,000,000 quotations.

The *Compact Edition* includes the entire contents of the 13 volumes. This is made possible via photographically reducing the size of the type. The result is two volumes, weighing some 17 pounds and measuring almost 14 by 10 inches. The miniaturization of the type face is compensated for with the inclusion of a magnifier. Use is troublesome, particularly to locate desired words, but the reduction in price and size of the set probably compensates for the reduction in ease of use. Hopefully, most libraries may afford the printed set, but those with limited budgets (such as individuals) will find the compact work satisfactory.[13]

---

[13] The miniaturization process for printed books is not new, e.g., see the "Mini-Print" titles issued by Scarecrow Press since 1967. Precisely what future there is for this process remains to be seen, although it does offer encouragement for reprints of large sets.

As the outstanding historical dictionary in the English language, the purpose of the work is to trace the history of English words. Volunteers and the staff literally ransacked printed books, public records, manuscripts, and even private papers to come up with words and quotations. The contributions were arranged alphabetically, and each section was prepared by competent scholars.

This is not a dictionary for ready reference. But it is encyclopedic in its treatment of individual words. Under every word, anything that could be found about the historical development of the word is traced in chronological order. Meaning, origin, relations to similar words, various dialects, fashions in speaking, pronunciation, compounds, and derivatives and even more are treated in full. Every change is illustrated by an example, and each quotation is dated and the source clearly indicated.

The result is both forbidding and fascinating. For example, the word "set" is explored in 20 full pages. It has 150 main divisions. And the word "so" receives 15 columns with 50 different uses, each use illustrated with an example. Obviously, this is a work for scholars and not the gentle reader seeking a simple definition or spelling.

> What one finds in it are not cut-and-dried definitions of words resting in peace, but the lives of words—their births, maturations, fadings into feeble old age and occasional deaths. "Propaganda," for instance, has enjoyed a vigorous if well-ordered life, having been born in the seventeenth century—in the official title of the Papal "College of Propaganda," "a committee of Cardinals . . . having the care and oversight of foreign missions"—and having matured by gradual steps to its present more general meaning. Vigorous, too, if somewhat more flighty, has been the life of "Badminton": "Named from the Duke of Beaufort's country seat" and for a while the designation of a "cooling summer drink. . .of mingled claret, sugar, and soda-water," it sprang full-blown as a game played with shuttlecocks from the pages of an 1874 issue of *The Daily News*. . . .[14]

As a source of information about words, it is miraculously accurate and complete. It is weak only in one area, that of American words. However, these are treated in some fullness by Craigie and Mathews in two other works to be discussed shortly. The library will find many uses for it; and as indicated, it is an oblique source for quotations or for "first" facts when other more convenient books of quotations and ready-reference tools fail to produce results.

The *OED* abstains from any critical judgments, and there are no usage labels. The validity of some of the forms is open to question, but the editors purposefully saw their duty as recorders. Consequently, the *OED* is beloved by prescribers and describers alike.

---

[14] Christopher Lehmann-Haupt, "13 Great Volumes into Two," *The New York Times*, October 13, 1971, p. 43.

Nor is there any question that it is the most famous and most quoted dictionary in the English language. It has served everyone from sports writer A. J. Liebling to poet Robert Graves. The librarian who does not know the *OED* can be rightfully accused of plain ignorance. There are not many reference books which deserve a lasting place in a collection, but the *OED* is one of the numbered few.[15]

Beginning with the first volume in 1972, a 3-volume supplement to the main set was underway.[16] (The final volume should appear sometime in 1977-1979.) When completed, the supplement will include colloquial expressions, modern slang, and even sexual terms—all missing from the initial set.[17] The first volume, A to G, contains between 17,000 and 18,000 main words with 130,000 illustrative quotations.

There are several other smaller etymological dictionaries which nicely supplement the *OED*. Two of these are:

Onions, C. T., *The Oxford Dictionary of English Etymology.* New York: Oxford University Press, 1966, 1,025 pp., $18.

Klein, Ernest, *A Comprehensive Etymological Dictionary of the English Language.* New York: Elsevier Publishing Company, 1971, 844 pp., $29.50.

Onions' work, issued after his death, has some 24,000 main entries and 14,000 derivations. Its primary purpose is to update the *OED,* and it is a standard tool which any library with or without the *OED* should have on its shelves. As in other works of this type, Onions carefully traces the chronology of words to their origin and gives necessary quotations. Some reviewers found the book was not entirely up to date.

The Klein work is larger and more expansive than the traditional title by Onions. There are more scientific terms, proper names from mythologies and English Christian names, and a number of newer words

---

[15] There are, to be sure, some faults of omission and definition in the *OED*, and these are pointed out by Robert Graves in his essay "Best Man, Bore, Bamboozle, etc.," in the *Crowning Privilege* (London: Cassell & Co., Ltd., 1955). Graves also observes that one of the few people who were disappointed with the work was Thomas Hardy. Seeking to find a word, Hardy discovered that the authority for the word was one of his own quotations.
[16] For an informative review, *see:* William F. Buckley Jr. "The Compact Edition of the Oxford English Dictionary," *The New York Times Book Review,* December 19, 1971, pp. 1+.
[17] The event was newsworthy and appeared in many newspapers, including *The New York Times,* October 13, 1972, p. 5: "Among the new words appear ancient words once considered too gross and vulgar to be given countenance in the decent environment of a dictionary; its publicist, Elizabeth, could not bring herself to utter one of the more explicit terms. Asked what some of them were she carefully spelled out one, adding, 'You do hesitate to say it.' She said the dictionary defines the word as 'transitive verb: to copulate,' and traces its earlier written use to a sixteenth-century Scottish poet named Dunbar. 'The editors don't presume to judge,' she said. 'They recorded what appears in writing whereas the Victorian editors were inclined to act as censors.'" *See also,* the editor's comments, i.e., R. W. Burchfield, "Four Letter Words and the OED," *The Times Literary Supplement,* October 13, 1972, p. 1,233.

such as "cosmonaut" and "sputnik." Despite all of this, the earlier title remains standard, primarily because Klein is not as complete on introduction and lines of development of words.

Little, William, *Shorter Oxford English Dictionary on Historical Principles.* 3d ed. rev. New York: Oxford University Press, 1962, 2,515 pp., $35.

This is an authorized abridgment of the larger *OED,* about one-tenth its size. The page reduction from 15,000 to 2,500 gives some idea as to the extent of the cuts. Nevertheless, it does list almost two-thirds of the words found in the larger work. The abridgment was made possible by eliminating many of the quotations and the more obsolete and variant forms. Some additional entries are included.

There are two American works modeled after the *OED:*

Craigie, Sir William, and James R. Hulbert. *A Dictionary of American English on Historical Principles.* Chicago: The University of Chicago Press, 1936 to 1944, 4 vols., $100.

Mathews, Mitford, *A Dictionary of Americanisms on Historical Principles.* Chicago: The University of Chicago Press, 1951, 1,946 pp., $25.

As broad a survey as it is of the English language, the *OED* could not account for every detail in the history of English in other countries and regions. Partly for this reason, W. A. Craigie (who was one of the editors of the *OED*) developed *The Dictionary of Americanisms.*

Craigie supplements the *OED* by demonstrating changes in English words (many included in the *OED*) which took place in the American colonies and the United States. In order to trace a word used both in America and the British Isles, it is necessary to use both Craigie and the *OED.*

On the other hand, Craigie includes words which originated in the United States, giving a complete history and showing the development as in the *OED* by use of quotations. This feature makes it valuable as an aid to tracing quotations and early facts about American folklore, habits, and customs.

Mathew's work is confined to words that are peculiar to America and augments Craigie nicely. He also includes over 400 useful pen-and-ink drawings. There are approximately 50,000 words, many borrowed from other languages. Place names and names of plants and animals were drawn from Indian words, whereas the Dutch and Germans furnished us with many domestic words.

Such facts as the following may be discovered in Mathews: The term "tuxedo" is, oddly enough, an Indian word; it was the name of a minor Algonquin tribe which gave its name to a certain place in New York where a fashionable hotel was built. In addition to words, hundreds of common phrases are given with information on their origin.

In any discussion of the history of the American language, there is one outstanding work which many have enjoyed reading, literally from cover to cover. This is Henry Mencken's *The American Language* (New York: Alfred A. Knopf, Inc., 1936 to 1948). In 3 volumes, the sage of Baltimore examines the majority of American words in a style and manner that is extremely pleasing, always entertaining and informative. The initial 1-volume work of 1936 was supplemented with 2 volumes. All are easy to use as there is a detailed index in each volume.

SLANG AND DIALECT

Wentworth, Harold and Stuart Flexner. *Dictionary of American Slang.* supplemented ed. New York: Thomas Y. Crowell Company, 1960, 718 pp., $7.95.

Partridge, Eric, *A Dictionary of the Underworld*. British and American. New York: The Macmillan Company, 886 pp., 1968.

Roberts, Hermese, *The Third Ear: A Black Glossary*. Chicago: The English-Language Institute of America, 1971, paperback, 16 pp.

A culture accustomed to a dictionary providing authority on correct English usage, even to the point of overlooking and not recording substandard slang, requires some corrective measures. Corrections have been provided. (1) The change in the times now results in *The American Heritage Dictionary* (for one) clearly defining more common slang and obscene terms. This trend against the Victorian stance is gaining ground and, as seen, is even accepted by the editors of the supplement to the *Oxford English Dictionary.* (2) There are specific dictionaries which record and define particular slang and special terms from various vocations, regions, and groups. A good slang dictionary gives exhaustive definitions, provides additional quotations, and tends to be more up to date with current jargon.

The three titles listed here are representative of three approaches—general, specific, and cultural. General in scope, Wentworth and Flexner give definitions for more than 21,000 words, each supplemented by a source and one or more illustrative quotations. First published in 1960, this caused some furor among the censorious minded, particularly because of the clear definitions of vulgar words and terms. In the past decade, it has come to assume a position of acceptance in most libraries, certainly by all scholars. The particular merit of the work is a broad general approach to all aspects of the culture from the slang of space scientists and FBI men to the jargon of stripteasers and Madison Avenue advertising men. And there is an excellent preface which anyone who questions the merit of such dictionaries would do well to read.

The basic general title in the field of slang, though, remains Eric Partridge's *A Dictionary of Slang and Unconventional English* (7th ed. New York: The Macmillan Company, 1970, 1,528 pp., $18.50). This includes 50,000 entries—more than double the number found in Wentworth and Flexner. One of the first scholars to approach the subject in our time, Partridge has a fine sense of balance and appropiate quotations to illustrate his meaning. He is particularly devoted to tracing the history of given terms. As useful as this work is, the emphasis is on English terms; and for American libraries, the Wentworth and Flexner title would be preferable. Larger libraries would want them both.

A more specific emphasis is illustrated by another Partridge title. Here he is concerned only with the slang and the language of the American and British underworld of crime. Partridge is more involved with the history of words, less with currency. As a result, it is of little value to the modern crime novel reader, but of great value to the historian. There are numerous titles in this area, e.g., Eugene Landy's *The Underground Dictionary* (New York: Simon & Shuster, Inc., 1971, 20 pp.) gives up-to-date definitions of terms used by members of the counterculture. The subterranean linguist is not a scholar, but an activist on the "scene." The result is a graphic, almost how-to-do-it type definition which lacks the historical insight of many other titles in this area. And having said that, it might be noted that for the average layman, it is probably more interesting than the others. A more explicit title is Robert Wilson's *A Playboy's Book of Forbidden Words* (New York: Simon & Schuster, Inc., 1972, 320 pp.) which clearly defines taboo words and phrases in current American usage. Many of the definitions are by way of short essays with long quotations from modern authors, films, magazines, and the like. Although accurate enough, and bound to be stolen from many libraries, it does suffer from the *Playboy* syndrome of inhibited, uninhibited daring.

The language of blacks until relatively recently has been treated, where appropriate, as sections of slang dictionaries. Now, though, the blacks are quite rightfully demanding a new appraisal of the subject. Many of the expressions indigenous to black communities (as well as to other minority groups) are such inimitable parts of the culture as not to be considered slang. Furthermore, a good number of the words have become a part of the modern, standard vocabulary. Be that as it may, one of the more useful, representative lists is *The Third Ear.* Although slight in size, the definitions cover the majority of terms which many hear in relationship to music, art, and black literature. Hopefully, a more exhaustive dictionary of this type will be published soon.[18]

Another related aspect is dialect, which is a socially or regional variety of a language that differs from the standard language and, for that reason, is often treated as slang.

For example, the Southern pronunciation, "you-all" is only used to address two or more people or one person who represents a group—at least correctly. But in dialect, it may serve as a general greeting. Dialect, also, involves distinct pronunciation and phrasing. Some argue that radio, film, and television has made American dialect dead or close to static. Not so says the University of Wisconsin which in 1973 was working on a definitive work, *Dictionary of American Regional English*. This is said to be similar in scholarship to the famous 6-volume *English Dialect Dictionary* (1898-1905) which Joseph Wright compiled as the definitive list of literary and spoken language in England from 1700-1900.

SYNONYMS AND ANTONYMS DICTIONARIES

Webster's New Dictionary of Synonyms. Springfield, Massachusetts. G. & C. Merriam Company, 1968, 909 pp., $7.95.

Funk & Wagnalls' Modern Guide to Synonyms and Related Words. New York: Funk & Wagnalls, 1968, 726 pp., $8.95.

Roget's International Thesaurus. 3d ed. New York: Thomas Y. Crowell Company, 1962, 1,258 pp., $5.95.

A book of synonyms often is among the most popular in the private or public library. It offers a key to crossword puzzles, instant vocabulary, and serves almost everyone who wishes to increase or disguise his command of English. There are several dictionaries of synonyms and antonyms in English, but these appear to be more often found in libraries. Certainly, the most popular and best known is the work by Peter Mark Roget (1779 to 1869), inventor of the slide rule and a doctor in an English lunatic asylum. He began the work at age seventy-one and, by his ninetieth birthday, had seen it through 20 editions. (The term "thesaurus" means a treasury, a store, a hoard; and Roget's is precisely that.) His aim was hopefully to classify all human thought under a series of verbal

---

[18] Arthur L. Smith, *Language, Communication, and Rhetoric in Black America*. (New York: Harper & Row Publishers, Incorporated, 1972), paperback, 388 pp. This is a collection of essays on the whole matter of a "black language" and is particularly important for clearly defining the question of what is "proper" and "improper" English for blacks. For a review of other black dictionaries and the question of black English *see:* M. K. Speers, "You Makin' Sense," *New York Review of Books*, November 16, 1972, pp. 32+.

categories; and his book is so arranged. There are approximately 1,000 classifications; and within each section, headed by a key word, there are listed by parts of speech the words and phrases from which the reader selects the proper synonym. Antonyms are usually placed immediately after the main listing. Thus: possibility/impossibility; pride/humility.

Modern editions vary slightly from the first 1852 edition. The Crowell work retains the idea of grouping words according to their ideas. Editor C. O. Mawson, however, has added new categories from science and technology. An index is absolutely necessary to locate a word, and the Crowell edition has an excellent one. (Like "Webster," the term "Roget" is not copyrighted and a number of works with this name appear which are indifferent-to-good.)

The advantage of grouping is that like ideas are placed together. The distinct disadvantage is that Roget offers no guidance or annotations; and an overzealous user may select synonym or antonym which looks and sounds better, but it is far from expressing what he means. Sean O'Faolain, the Irish short-story writer, recalls he once gave a copy of *Roget's* to a Dutch-born journalist to improve his English; but the effect was appalling. For example, the journalist might wish to know the synonym for sad. He would consult the index and find four or five alternatives such as painful, gray, bad, dejected, and, surprisingly, great. When he had turned to the proper section, he would find two or three hundred synonyms. Unless the user has a clear understanding of the language, *Roget's* can be a difficult work.

Recognizing this, *Webster's* has taken another tack. Instead of arranging words by categories, words are arranged in alphabetical order. One looks up a word and finds several synonyms. More important, shades of meaning are carefully explained and then illustrated with appropriate quotations. Antonyms and contrasted words follow the main entries. The difficulty with this approach is that despite cross-references not all words can be found. Still, students find *Webster's* considerably easier to use than *Roget's*

Funk & Wagnalls' Modern Guide to Synonyms and Related Words has the advantage of being a completely new book of synonyms with current meanings of some 6,000 words. It differs from *Webster's* in a major respect—editor S. I. Hayakawa offers the main word in the margin in bold face with the synonyms and then proceeds to write clear, discriminating short essays on the variations in proper use of the words. The editor's comments are both witty and timely, particularly as he gives emphasis to standard terms used by better writers and speakers. There are a few direct quotations as found in *Webster's*. Both works serve a definite need, although the Funk & Wagnalls entry is not as useful for quick reference. Its strength lies in the marvelous essays.

An excellent explanation of the problems of synonym and antonym dictionaries, as well as a brief history, will be found in the introductory remarks to *Webster's*.

USAGE AND MANUSCRIPT STYLE DICTIONARIES

Fowler, Henry Watson, *Dictionary of Modern English Usage*. 2d ed rev. by Sir Ernest Gowers. New York: Oxford University Press, 1965, 725 pp., $7.50.

Strunk, William and E. B. White *The Elements of Style*. 2d ed. New York: The Macmillan Company, 1972, $2.95; paperback, $.95.

Turabian, Kate L. *A Manual for Writers of Term Papers, Theses, and Dissertations*. 3d ed. Chicago: The University of Chicago Press, $3.50; paperback, $1.25.

Author and critic Dwight Macdonald once observed that Fowler's dictionary is more than a book, it is an attitude toward life. Fowler and the other works are listed here for the aid and comfort of those who wish a dictionary to be prescriptive. There must be rules and regulations governing good usage, and Fowler and company lay down these rules, usually without doubt or question.

The works are invaluable for the layman who is honestly attempting to distinguish what is or is not good usage. Fowler, for example, deals extensively with grammar and syntax, analyzes how words should be used, distinguishes clichés and common errors, and settles almost any question that might arise concerning the English language. The dictionary, and the revision by Sir Ernest Gowers, has a special flavor treasured by all readers. Fowler commented on practically anything that interested him, and the hundreds of general articles can be savored for their own literary quality, aside from their instructional value.

One of the hoped for results of a faithful reading of Fowler, and others of its type, is to avoid clichés. Humorist Frank Sullivan, in an interview on his eightieth birthday, summed up the meaning of clichés with countless examples:

Q. And to what do you attribute your longevity?
A. Vice? Nothing so ill prepares a man to look down memory lane as a life of early rising, clean living and three square meals a day. It is far, far better to slumber until noon after nights on the town. . . .
Q. Have you found other virtues in vice?
A. Yes, indeed, it builds character and makes for fortitude. Many's the story I wrote for *The World* and *The New Yorker* while battling a hangover, and this has given me the ability to see the ups and downs of life in

perspective, to roll with the punches, to take adversity as it comes, to realize that there's a silver lining in the blackest cloud.[19]

Another revision of Fowler is offered by Margaret Nicholson, i.e., *A Dictionary of American English Usage Based on Fowler's Modern English Usage* (New York: Oxford University Press, 1957, 671 pp.). This is peculiarly American. While the author borrows liberally from Fowler, her entries and approach are definitely her own; and she eliminates enough of his words to allow entry of many American variations.

Having sold over 2 million copies, the first edition of the Strunk and White manual was revised in 1972. White was a pupil of Strunk, a Cornell University professor who died in 1946. The first edition followed Strunk's linguistic precision as White remembered it; but the revised work has more of White, less of Strunk. It is considerably more liberal, less prescriptive. Strunk and White set rules of good usage through hundreds of examples, and the work concludes with an essay on style by White. One example will indicate the tone of the book: "Thrust. This shown noun, suggestive of power, hinting of sex, is the darling of executives, politicos and speech writers."[20]

There are numerous other titles in this area, but a more specific, even more used work by students is the Turabian title.[21] This gives hints on style, but it is primarily a guide to the mechanics (from footnotes to bibliographies) of preparing term papers. She gives precise rules which are of considerable help to anyone working in this area. The book is based on the larger *A Manual of Style* (Chicago: The University of Chicago Press, $10). Frequently revised, this is the basic style manual for many publishers and should be found in all reference libraries.

ABBREVIATIONS AND ACRONYMS DICTIONARIES

DeSola, Ralph, *Abbreviations Dictionary*. new rev. ed. New York: Meredith Press, 1967, 298 pp., $9.95.

Acronyms and Initialisms Dictionary. 3d ed. Detroit: Gale Research Company, 1970, 484 pp., $22.50. *New Acronyms and Initialisms*, 1971 to date, annual, $15.

The majority of general dictionaries include basic abbreviations as part of the main work or as an appendix. Many acronyms (i.e., a word formed from the initial letters of syllables of the successive parts of a

---

[19] Alden Whitman, "Frank Sullivan, at 80, Finds Life is a Bowl of Cherries," *The New York Times,* September 22, 1971. p. 41.
[20] "E. B. White Rehones His Verbal Razor," *The New York Times,* May 3, 1972, pp. 41+.
[21] Robert R. Carter, "Term Paper Aids," *RQ,* Fall 1972, pp. 52+. A helpful annotated list of titles similar to Turabian.

compound term such as CARE, WAVE, NATO) are included, too. Also, most encyclopedias, almanacs, and numerous handbooks include sections for general or specific abbreviations and acronyms. Still, for ready reference, it is desirable to have at least one good, up-to-date source at hand.

One of the best is the Gale publication. Terms are in alphabetical order, by acronym or initial, and various meanings are given. There are over 80,000 entries, and each of the supplements adds some 12,000 more from all fields. (Precisely what this may be doing to the language, not to mention the sanity of the average reader, is not considered by the compilers.) If one considers that there are at least 12,000 new acronyms and initials added each year, the need for a current source is obvious. *Reverse Acronyms and Initialisms Dictionary* (Detroit: Gale Research Company, 1972, 495 pp.). A companion volume to the other Gale title, this gives the term first and then the acronym. It is, basically, a rearrangement of *Acronyms and Initialisms*. The librarian might rightfully ask is this worth another $27.50 when one has the basic set? Probably not, at least for most purposes where the user can almost guess the proper acronym without going to a backward dictionary for help.

The basic guide to abbreviations, DeSola's title is a bit dated, yet useful. In a single alphabet, he not only includes abbreviations and their definitions, but acronyms, anonyms, initials, nicknames, and the like.

For anyone who has attempted to trace a footnote reference to a magazine title and has been totally baffled by the abbreviation for the magazine's title, there is a useful guide to the full title. This is: Edward C. Wall's *Periodical Title Abbreviations* (Detroit: Gale Research Company, 1969, 210 pp.). The compiler lists abbreviations for some 10,000 periodicals in all fields. The advantage of this is that the user does not have to try to trace the title from the abbreviations given in the various periodical indexes—helpful enough when one is using the index, but frustrating when one does not know whether the abbreviation he is seeking is included in said index.

FOREIGN LANGUAGE DICTIONARIES (BILINGUAL)

Cassell's: (various paginations) *Italian Dictionary,* New York: Funk & Wagnalls, 1960; *New French Dictionary,* New York: Funk & Wagnalls, 1970; *New German Dictionary,* New York: Funk & Wagnalls, 1971; *New Latin Dictionary,* New York: Funk & Wagnalls, 1966, *Spanish Dictionary,* New York: Funk & Wagnalls, 1964.

Harrap's Standard French and English Dictionary, ed. by J. E. Mansion. rev. by Rene and Madame Ledesert. New York: Charles Scribner's Sons, 1972, 2 vols., $39.50. (English-French, 2 vols. in progress.)

PURPOSE

The primary purpose of a desk-type bilingual dictionary is to translate painlessly, quickly, and accurately. Conversely, the larger bilingual dictionaries attempt to include relevant facts, varieties of form, and other distinctions usually not found in the smaller works.

EVALUATION

The average reference librarian has difficulty in selecting foreign dictionaries. He cannot hope to be trained in all languages and, therefore, must rely on expert opinion for assistance. These experts now generally agree that the series issued by Cassell's and by Scribner's are suitable bilingual dictionaries for students and scholars.

There are many other publishers. Winchell lists close to 500 from Afrikaans to Zulu, and a number of these are available as bilingual dictionaries. However, the librarian who is planning an extensive collection of bilingual dictionaries is advised to check carefully with linguists and to study reviews.[22]

In the past, Cassell's dictionaries have been weak on idiomatic expressions and on current definitions. Since the 1950s, the problem has been solved to a great extent by careful editing and revision of the older works. Now most of the bilingual dictionaries feature many etymological notes, illustrative quotes, and, possibly more important, are relatively strong on technical terms. Where there is any doubt, the Cassell's series is a safe purchase for most libraries.

SCOPE

The primary difficulty with the desk-sized bilingual dictionary is that it attempts almost too much in a short page. *Cassell's* is a compromise between length and detail and the average user's needs for a quick word equivalent. Only the more common equivalents are noted; and no particular effort is, or can be, made to go into any exploration of other forms.

At this point, the encyclopedia type of bilingual dictionary is helpful. The work is typical. Two volumes are turned over to the foreign language and the English equivalent, the other two volumes to the English and the French equivalent. (The revision will be in 4 volumes, and the English-French 2 volumes will not be out until 1977.) The various compilers of these multivolume works have solved the problem of lack of identity between words and semantics by (1) giving long lists of

---

[22] A useful guide to both bilingual and foreign language dictionaries is the *International Bibliography of Dictionaries*, 5th ed. (New York: R. R. Bowker Company, 1972). This lists some 7,000 dictionaries from over sixty countries.

equivalents whenever possible and (2) supplementing these with use of the words in sentences to indicate proper usage.

Harrap's, and its equivalent in other languages, would be an absolute necessity for the translator, the scholar, and, in fact, anyone who was endeavoring to do more than a loose translation of a given work. Even those quite familiar with the language find the dictionary encyclopedic approach helpful.[23]

At the other extreme, between the bilingual desk dictionary and the multivolume sets are excellent paperback editions—many of them based on the larger works. For example, the *Harrap's New Pocket French and English Dictionary* (New York: Charles Scribner's Sons, 1972, 525 pp., $2.95) is a useful, handy abbreviation of the mother title. And several of the Cassell works are available in paperback as abbreviated forms of the parent titles. The better ones are listed and annotated in Bohdan S. Wynar's *Reference Books in Paperback* (Littleton, Colorado: Libraries Unlimited, 1972).

SUBJECT DICTIONARIES

Dictionaries devoted to specialized subject fields, occupations, or professions make up an important part of any reference collection. This is especially true in the sciences. General dictionaries tend to be stronger in the humanities, weaker in the fast-changing scientific fields. Consequently, there are a vast number of scientific dictionaries, but relatively few in the humanities.

The major question to ask when determining selection is: "Does this dictionary offer anything that cannot be found in a standard work now in the library?" A careful answer may result in bypassing a special dictionary. It is surprising, particularly in the humanities and social sciences, how much of the information is readily available in a general English dictionary.

While all evaluative checks to other dictionaries apply, there are also some special points to watch:

1. Are the illustrations pertinent and helpful to either the specialist or the layman? Where a technical work is directed to a lay audience, there should be a number of diagrams, photographs, or other forms of graphic art, which frequently make it easier for the uninitiated to understand the terms.

[23] "French-English Lexicon. . . ." *The New York Times,* October 8, 1972, p. 78. A short article about the revision of Harrap's which points up some of the problems involved in compiling such works.

2. Are the definitions simply brief word equivalents or is some effort made to give a real explanation of the word in context with the subject?
3. Is the dictionary international in scope or simply limited to an American audience? This is a particularly valuable question when considering the sciences. Several publishers have met the need not only of an international scope, but of translating via bilingual scientific dictionaries.
4. Are the terms up to date? Again, this is a necessity in a scientific work, somewhat less so in a social science dictionary, and may be of little relative importance in a humanistic study.

Many of the subject dictionaries are virtually encyclopedic in terms of information and presentation. They use the specific entry form, but the entry may run to considerably more than a simple definition. For example, Louise Boger's *Dictionary of World Pottery and Porcelain* (New York: Charles Scribner's Sons, 1970, 533 pp.) covers the whole history and art of porcelain and pottery. Not only are there definitions, but the author includes a large number of black-and-white illustrations, color photographs, and extensive notations. Given this scope, the dictionary is obviously more than a dictionary and might be purchased as much for its encyclopedic qualities as for its definitions.

The distinction in itself is not so important as the recognization that the use of "dictionary" in a title does not necessarily mean it is simply a conventional definition of terms. Conversely, the use of "encyclopedia" may indicate no more than a good or indifferent subject dictionary.

OTHER DICTIONARIES

NBC Handbook of Pronunciation. 3d ed. New York: Thomas Y. Crowell Company, 1964, 418 pp., $6.95.

Stillman, Frances, *The Poet's Manual and Rhyming Dictionary.* New York: Thomas Y. Crowell Company, 1965, 387 pp., $6.95.

There are numerous dictionaries covering other fields from geographical place names to personal names and surnames. Most libraries will have at least one dictionary for these various special requirements. The two titles listed here are only representative yet important additions in themselves.

Although in need of revision, the *NBC Handbook* gives the correct pronunciation of 20,000 words and proper names which are frequently mispronounced. There is a supplement on names in the news," but this is virtually worthless in the 1970s—most of the "names" have disappeared. A good many of the pronunciations are given in modern dictionaries, so why bother with such handbooks? Again, it is a matter of ease of use. Pronunciation is clearly indicated; and where there is more than one accepted pronunciation, this is given, too.

Professional poets shudder at the mention of rhyming dictionaries, but they do serve a necessary purpose in many libraries. Not all poets are pros, but there are thousands of versifiers who delight in finding words that rhyme with "love" and "dove." In addition, the manual does describe the basics of poetry, particularly the traditional forms.

SUGGESTED READING

A concise history of dictionaries will be found in most general encyclopedias, particularly in the *Americana* and *Britannica*.

"A-Z. Choosing a Dictionary," *The Times Literary Supplement,* October 13, 1972, pp. 1,209+. A lengthy discussion of major general and subject dictionaries. Many American, as well as English, titles are considered. The same issue also contains numerous reviews of foreign language dictionaries.

Allen, Robert, *English Grammars and English Grammar.* (New York: Charles Scribner's Sons, 1972, 255 pp.). A major, easy to understand survey of linguistics, including dictionaries.

Baker, John F., "Words Live at G. & C. Merriam . . ." *Publishers' Weekly,* April 9, 1973, pp. 36+. A general discussion of how the new edition of *Webster's Collegiate* series was edited, and an excellent overview of dictionary making for the student.

Collison, Robert, *Dictionaries of Foreign Languages.* New York: Hafner Publishing Company, Inc., 1965. Both a history and a bibliography.

Emblen, D. L., "Dr. Roget: His Book," *The Bookseller,* February 13, 1971, pp. 412+. An excerpt from the full study of Roget by Emblen, e.g., *Peter Mark Roget* (New York: Thomas Y. Crowell Company, 1970).

Partridge, Eric, *The Gentle Art of Lexicography.* London: Andre Deutsch, 1963. An excellent discussion of the art.

Perrin, Noel, "Before Fun City," *The New Yorker,* February 26, 1972. pp. 82+. An amusing and instructive discussion of the joy and instruction to be found in older dictionaries, i.e., John Palsgrave's *Lesclarcissement de la Langue Francoyse* (London: 1530).

Quine, V. W., "Words Enough," *The New York Review of Books,* December 4, 1969, pp. 3+. A critical article on the American Heritage and Random House college editions.

Shenker, Israel, "English, at Times, Is Just Un-American," *The New York Times,* March 8, 1972, p. 37. A revealing article on the differences in dialect (not to mention other areas) between "English English" and "American English."

CHAPTER ELEVEN
GEOGRAPHICAL SOURCES

While it is sometimes difficult to manifest excitement over reference works, geographical sources are the happy exception. On the purely imaginative level, they have the ability to transport the viewer to any part of the world and, in this day, the universe. The difference between geographical sources and other works is that they are primarily graphic representations which allow the imagination full reign. Indeed, many of them are works of art and they provide a type of satisfaction rarely found in the purely textual approach to knowledge.

Useful as this may be to the romantic, in the hard world of reference work, geographical sources are an invaluable part of any basic collection. There are as many reasons for consulting these sources as there are patrons, and most are self-evident—the location of a small town in some state or country, the nearest railroad or airline serving a village, the condition of roads in a country or state, the number of hotels in a city, and so on. More specialized or thematic sources will serve to answer everything from the location of a specific archaeological site to the name and size of a canyon on the moon.

The variety of the sources requires a basic understanding of general features shared by all.[1] Beyond that, the reference librarian must famil-

[1] For the beginner who understands little about maps and map reading, *see* the introductory material on maps and map reading in the Rand McNally *Cosmopolitan World Atlas,* as well as in most of the general atlases issued by that company and C. S. Hammond & Company.

iarize himself with the specific qualities of the individual works. Answers to geographical questions are not necessarily limited to specialized books. Geography is a component part of many other reference tools. Encyclopedias usually have individual maps or separate atlas volumes. Information about cities, towns, states, and countries frequently will be found in greater detail in an encyclopedia, yearbook, or almanac than in many of the geographical sources cited here. The distinct advantage of geographical works over more generalized reference books is that (1) they give information for smaller units not found in general works; (2) the information given often will be more precise; and (3) since they are limited to one area, they are usually easier to use.

Of course, this is not to say that geographical sources may be dispensed with if one has a good encyclopedia or other reference books. It *is* to say that the alert reference librarian will purchase works in this area that are truly contributive to the rapid and efficient answering of questions. He will avoid geographical sources which only duplicate, and rarely well, what is to be found in other reference sources.

Going beyond the general reference question, it is obvious that there is no substitute for highly specialized geographical sources—particularly individual political, physical, and thematic maps and exhaustive gazetteers and guidebooks.

Definition and scope

Geographical sources used in reference work may be subdivided into three large categories: maps and atlases, gazetteers, and guidebooks.[2]

Maps and Atlases Unlike other reference forms, geographical sources have some terms peculiar to this category. Everyone, to be sure, understands that a map is a representation of the outer boundaries of the earth on a flat surface. (These days, it may include the representation of the moon and planets as well.) An atlas is a volume containing a collection of these maps, and the nature of a globe is too self-evident to need definition. A chart is a map of water, and there are a great variety of maps designed for every purpose from indicating soil content to traffic flow. This latter type is normally referred to as a thematic map.

A physical map traces the various features of the land from the rivers and valleys to the mountains and hills. A route map shows roads,

---

[2] There is considerably more to geographical research than these arbitrary divisions. One of the best handbooks, although representing an English viewpoint, is Muriel Lock's *Geography* 2d ed. London: Clive Bingley, 1972, 529 pp., $15). The author has a pleasing style, includes not only annotated lists but some good introductory material. The arrangement, though, is not good. *See also*, Edward Taaffe's *Geography* (Englewood Cliffs, New Jersey: Prentice-Hall, Inc., 1970, 143 pp., $5.95) which provides basic information on history, methods, and research. *See also*, C. S. Minto's *How to Find Out in Geography* (New York: Pergamon Press, 1966, 99 pp.); dated, basically English, but useful.

railroads, bridges, and the like. A political map normally limits itself to political boundaries (e.g., towns, cities, counties, states) but may include topographical and route features. Either separately or as one, these three types make up the majority of maps found in general atlases.

Cartography is the art of map making, and a major headache of cartographers has been to accurately represent the features of the earth on maps. This has resulted in various projections, i.e., the effort to display the surface of a sphere upon a plane without undue distortion. Mercator or his forerunners devised a system which is still the best known today and is based upon parallel lines, that is, latitude (angular distance north or south from the equator) and longitude (angular distance east and west from the equator). This works well enough except at the polar regions which tend to be distorted. Hence, on any Mercator projection, Greenland is completely out of proportion to the United States. Since Mercator, hundreds of projections have been designed; but distortional qualities are always evident, if not in one section, in another. For example, the much praised azimuthal equidistant projection, with the North Pole at the center of the map, indicates directions and distances more accurately, but in other respects gives a peculiar stretched and pulled appearance to much of the globe.

The only relatively accurate representation of the earth is a globe. The necessity for a globe in a reference situation is probably questionable, although it is certainly desirable to have one. Reference questions per se rarely require the use of a globe. This, to be sure, is not to discount the importance of a globe, which is both a work of art and a thing of importance in specialized situations. However, the reference librarian who has had occasion to use a globe instead of a map to answer particular reference questions is rare indeed.

Gazetteers In addition to general and thematic maps, the reference librarian is most likely to use a gazetteer in answering questions regarding geographical sources. A gazetteer may be defined as a geographical dictionary, differing from the index to an atlas in that it usually is more comprehensive. A good gazetteer includes names of towns, villages, rivers, mountains, lakes and other geographical features, population, longitude and latitude, and, in some cases, brief to rather long entries tracing the history and economic and political features of the particular place.

Travel Guides Supplementing the gazetteer is the guidebook, usually limited to a single area (town, city, county, state, nation) and serving, as the title implies, to point up the highlights of travel. Generally, these books give a minimum of historical background and emphasize routes and itineraries. They usually present information on hotels, motels, museums, public buildings, restaurants, and anything else of general interest to the traveler. They are distinct from encyclopedic presentation in that they are highly pragmatic, stressing "how much," "how good," and "how long." Also, the better guidebooks are issued or revised annually.

EVALUATION[3]

Unlike other reference works, maps and atlases are fundamentally a mysterious area for the average librarian or patron. They depend primarily upon the graphic arts and mathematics for presentation and compilation. Skill in determining which is the best map or atlas draws upon a type of knowledge normally not employed in evaluating a book.

AUTHORITY

Map printing is a specialized department of the graphic arts; and while simple maps can be prepared by any artist or draftsman, more complicated works require a high degree of skill. More important, their proper reproduction necessitates expensive processes which the average printer of reference works is not equipped to handle. As with dictionaries and encyclopedias, the inherent expenses and skills of the field narrow the competent cartographic firms down to a half-dozen or so. In the United States, the leading publishers are Rand McNally & Company, C. S. Hammond & Company, and the National Geographic Society. In England, they are John G. Bartholomew (Edinburgh) and the cartographic department of the Oxford University Press.

Where the cartographic firm is not known, it is advisable to check on its reputation and integrity through other works it may have issued. It must be emphasized that the map maker may differ from the publisher and, in the case of an atlas, both should be checked most carefully. Where one or both are unknown, it is a good warning to postpone a purchase until the atlas has been reviewed in some authoritative publication.

CURRENCY

Geographical place names change frequently; and unless an atlas or map is revised frequently, it cannot hope to keep up with alterations. For example, when Bangladesh became a separate country, all map makers were still showing it as East Pakistan. The old name of the Congo remains on many maps for an area now known as Zaire.

Some of the areas which are lesser known cause equal problems. In 1971, the United Nations distributed 8,000 color maps of the self-governing British protectorate of Brunei. The maps showed a segment

---

[3] American Library Association, *Subscription Books Committee Manual* (Chicago: American Library Association, 1969), 65 pp., processed. *See:* "Guidelines for Reviewing Atlases," pp. 27-31; an outline guide to points for evaluation.

claimed by Brunei as belonging to Sarawak, which is part of Malaysia. The Brunei government refused the maps. A half-century ago, many Rand McNally maps began to show a town of "Bonzo's Grave" on maps of Australia. Many years later, a curious cartographer queried the Australian government about the town. It was not a town; it was simply the grave of a donkey called Bonzo which somehow had worked its way into maps via a prospector's sketch of the area.

Reputable map makers make up for this change by a policy somewhat similar to that of encyclopedia firms: continuous revision and reprinting. Larger firms such as Rand McNally, Hammond, and Bartholomew of Edinburgh follow this practice—a practice which normally is clearly indicated by two methods: (1) copyright date on the verso of the title page; and (2) revision date, with some indication in the preface, introduction, or jacket blurb as to the extent of the revision.

Sometimes the date of publication (usually the copyright date) and the date the maps were actually produced are quite different. The publisher that does not clearly indicate this is probably well aware of the discrepancy. The librarian foolish enough not to recognize that there may be a difference between publication date and the currency of the maps had better turn in his geography merit badge. The largest, most complete revision usually takes place the year after the census, i.e., Hammond and Rand McNally completely revised their standard atlases in 1971 and the copyright date for all their basic titles is rightfully 1971.

Revision should extend beyond the actual maps. The indexes, charts, tables, and minor aids should be updated as assiduously as the major maps. One problem with atlases and gazetteers is that they are expensive to produce and rarely can be revised each year. Consequently, even the best ones are soon dated.

There are at least four ways to escape the problem of currency for the library. First, and most obvious, one or more new acceptable atlases should be purchased annually, always, to be sure, with a clear knowledge that the purchase is really current and not simply a new printing without revision. Second, at least two publishers have methods of keeping maps current. Bartholomew of Edinburgh updates the *Times Atlas of the World* by bimonthly supplements in the *Geographical Magazine*. Rand McNally issues its *Commercial Atlas and Marketing Guide* annually with changes as needed. Third, the library may keep individual maps issued during the year by the National Geographic Society and various government agencies. Finally, current sources such as encyclopedia yearbooks, almanacs, yearbooks, and periodical indexes will sometimes serve when standard geographical sources fail.

Currency is not a major problem when one or two of these solutions are followed, particularly the first. The majority of reference questions concerning geography usually are general: Where is X town? What is the population of X country? How far is X from Y? A relatively up-to-date atlas or other geographical source will suffice.

BALANCE AND CONTENTS

The desirable atlas is one that concentrates on an integrated collection of maps and only includes other material if it contributes directly to the use of those maps. An atlas is not the encyclopedia, world almanac, and local city directory all in one nice package. Many critics of American atlases are quick to point out that publishers attempt too much and end by doing too little. In order to make their atlases competitive pricewise, they will: (1) cover the United States well, but not the remainder of the world; and (2) add encyclopedic information which fattens out the volume but is of little real worth.

The encyclopedic approach, of course, may suit the private buyer who wants to limit his personal reference collection to a few volumes. However, in a library situation, it tends to simply duplicate, and usually not too well, other materials. By crowding incomplete information into the back or the front of the volume, the editor must sacrifice the number of maps or run his price up beyond the reach of the average purchaser. Normally, the former choice is made.

Contentwise, a good atlas should include a map that shows all parts of the world equally. There should be a table of contents, a glossary of geographic terms and abbreviations, an introduction or preface explaining essentials of use, and a detailed index. Other minor additions might include such items as geographic equivalents and population comparisons. This is the ideal, rarely achieved. However, when an atlas attempts to go completely beyond the ideal into something more representative of a packaged product than a workable atlas, the librarian has every reason to exercise caution.

Within the normal atlas, regardless of content, arrangement usually follows a standard pattern. There are general maps showing the whole of the world; and then thematic maps indicating everything from population, rainfall, and wind and ocean currents to crop and industrial production. If it is an American publication, the next series is usually of the United States, and then North America and continent to continent. A good atlas will indicate the order clearly by a table of contents and, more important, world maps showing how the world is divided in the atlas with key page numbers.

QUALITY OF MAPS

The ultimate aim of a good map, whether it be a single sheet or part of an atlas, is to be accurate, easy to read, and esthetically pleasing. To achieve this aim, a map maker must consider several factors: scale, color, symbols, projections, grid systems, typography, and marginal information.

Scale The scale is the size of the map in relation to the actual area it represents. The larger the scale, that is, the less reduction, the more accurate the map will tend to be, particularly for details. The smaller the scale, the more difficult it is for the map maker to produce a truly accurate and reliable map.

The page size, or the size of an individual sheet map, will be a rapid indicator of the probable scale. Normally, the larger the page, the larger the scale. Hence the *Rand McNally Commercial Atlas,* which concentrates on large-scale reproductions of states and cities, has a map page size of 21 by 15 inches. Other large atlases will vary from 16 to 13 to 19 by 12 inches. Smaller works range from 10 by 7 to 12 by 9 inches.

Page size is not always indicative of scale. For example, an atlas may concentrate on showing only major countries and not divisions of those countries. It will have a large format, but small-scale maps. Another atlas may emphasize thematic maps of a small area and have a relatively large scale for its maps, yet may have a small to medium-sized format. Also, the page may include other material besides the map. This will increase its size while not visibly increasing the scale of the map. Conversely, another will use the full page for the map.

The format, then, is a poor guide; and in every case, the librarian needs to check the scale employed. There are two basic methods of indicating scale, and one or both should be clearly visible on each map. A bar scale is a bar divided in terms of inches representing distances. It is the only accurate method of ascertaining distances when a map has been enlarged or reduced. A natural scale, usually indicated by numerals or fractions, is a worldwide specification established in 1913 by map makers. If a map represents an area exactly one one-millionth the size of that area, it is indicated as a fraction, or 1:1,000,000 (usually noted as 1:1M). This may be divided by inches or meters to arrive at approximate distances. Hence, the aforesaid natural scale divided by 63,360—the number of inches in a statute mile—works out to approximately 16 miles per inch.

The natural scale is an excellent method of comparing the scales on various maps. In discussing maps, a base of 1:50,000 is used as the average scale of European maps. Consequently, if one wishes to ascertain how finely the nations of the world have mapped their countries, one may use the average as a comparative base. Russia, for example, is mapped at the scale of 1/100,000 while the program of topographic mapping of the whole of the United States is at the scale of 1/62,500. England, one of the best-mapped nations in the world, is at a scale of 1/2,500.

Within an atlas, the scale from map to map may vary considerably. This has the advantage of allowing larger scales where more detail is needed, the disadvantage of giving a rather peculiar notion of relative sizes. China may appear no larger than Chile or New York State, particularly if the same page size is used for all three. American atlases are often faulted for failure to maintain the same relative scales throughout their works. This is particularly true when the States and the Canadian provinces are given emphasis and the remainder of the world is pushed into a small section of the atlas. It may be argued, and justifiably in some cases, that the atlas is primarily for nationals who are more interested in particulars of North America than the remainder of the world. And European atlases frequently are guilty of the same fault with emphasis on Europe at the sacrifice of the remainder of the world.

One solution is to give each area of the world equal space and employ approximately the same scale. This is the great advantage of the *Times Atlas* over other atlases. Another solution is to concentrate almost wholly on one part of the world, as does the Rand McNally *Commercial Atlas,* or simply to abandon atlases in favor of individual maps employing the same or approximately the same scale.

WORLD ATLASES: ENGLISH LANGUAGE

The Times Atlas of the World. Comprehensive ed. Boston: Houghton Mifflin Company, 1971, 272 pp. and 123 plates, $65.

Hammond Medallion World Atlas. new census ed., Maplewood, New Jersey: C. S. Hammond & Company, 1971, 672 pp., $24.95.

Rand McNally New Cosmopolitan World Atlas. Planet Earth ed. Chicago: Rand McNally & Company, 1971, 428 pp., $19.95.

National Geographic Atlas of the World. 3d ed. Washington, D.C.: National Geographic Society, 1970, 331 pp., $18.75.

International Atlas. New York: McGraw-Hill Book Company, 1964, 400 pp., $17.85.

As previously mentioned, the two best-known American map makers are Rand McNally and C. S. Hammond, although by now *The Times* of London work (distributed here by Houghton Mifflin) is equally well known. But to be "known" is not necessarily to be best; and more than one critic has observed that only one of these, *The Times* title, "contends seriously as a top quality world atlas for general reference purposes." (The other contenders are discussed under foreign world atlases.)[4] This is by way of a purist speaking, though, and those less attuned to the fine points of maps will find the titles listed here all acceptable. This seems particularly true in terms of budget. Few are over $30, while the more widely acclaimed foreign atlases range from $80 to $90. And if the aver-

[4] Daniel A. Gomez-Ibanez, "World Atlases for General Reference," *Choice,* July/August 1969, p. 630.

age librarian is willing to accept the recommendations of the American Library Association's Reference and Subscription Book Reviews, most are approved by that group—with, to be sure, minor reservations.[5] Going considerably further in his enthusiasm, Padraig Walsh in his *General World Atlases in Print,* 4th ed. (New York: R. R. Bowker, 1973. 211 pp., $12.50), ranks them more highly.[6]

By any judgment, *The Times Atlas* is the best world atlas of all in the English language, or for that matter, any language. That it happens to be the most expensive is primarily because such loving care has been taken with emphasis on large-scale, multiple maps for several countries and an attention to detail and color rarely rivaled in American atlases. At one time, this was a 5-volume work (i.e., 1955 to 1959 edition); but since 1967, the publisher has chosen to issue it as a large (12 by 18 inches) single volume.

The volume consists of three basic parts. The first 40-page section is a conspectus of world minerals, sources of energy and food, and a variety of diagrams and star charts. The atlas proper is 123 double-page maps, the work of the English house of Bartholomew. This is the vital part, and it is typographically and color perfect. The clear typeface enables the reader to make out each of the enormous number of names. A variety of colors are used with skill and taste to show physical features, railways, rivers, political boundaries, and so on. A remarkable thing about this atlas is that it shows almost every noteworthy feature from lighthouses and tunnels to mangrove swamps—all by symbols which are carefully explained.

The Times is particularly suited for American libraries because, unlike many other atlases, it gives a large amount of space to non-European countries. No other atlas matches it for the detailed coverage of the Soviet Union, China, Africa, and Southeast Asia—lands hardly overlooked in other atlases, but usually printed in considerably less detail. No part of the world is in a scale smaller than 1:500,000 except Central America which is at 1:5,500,000. The larger land masses are supplemented with smaller, detailed maps which go from urban centers to maps of the environs of Everest.

The final section is a 200,000 name index, which for most purposes, serves as an excellent gazetteer. After each name, the country name is given with an exact reference to a map.

Late in 1972, *The New York Times* brought out a smaller edition of this title, at about one-half the price—*The New York Times Atlas of the*

[5] For an excellent summary analysis of the various Rand McNally entries, *see* "Reference and Subscription Book Reviews," *The Booklist,* December 1, 1972, pp. 310-314. Hammond Atlases are reviewed in the May 1, 1972 issue, pp. 329+.
[6] This is primarily a statistical approach to 140 English-language American atlases; it is helpful for comparisons of such things as cost, index entries, page sizes, and so on.

World (264 pp., $35)—and about one-half the details. The index includes only 90,000 entries. The overall map size is reduced, and there is considerably more encyclopedic type of information. This latter feature, as well as the price, will give it some value for home purchase; but the average library would be considerably better off purchasing the primary volume.

Between the many Rand McNally and C. S. Hammond atlases—of which only the two best titles are listed here—the choice is close. One library may prefer the Rand McNally maps, another the C. S. Hammond. Insofar as they are relatively inexpensive, accurate, and kept current by a continuous revision system, they serve general reference purposes well enough. Not only are the maps good, if uninspired, but the gazetteer information and indexing systems are excellent for ready-reference work. Timeliness can not be overstressed, because the two publishers are particularly anxious to keep up with changes—changes which are reflected in everything from population to place names and findings about the oceans and the universe. In 1971–1972, for example, the firms published a total of eleven new editions and ten revisions of atlases, primarily to catch up with the 1970 census.[7]

The *Medallion World Atlas* is the work of C. S. Hammond; and while it is frequently revised, the "New census" edition represents some basic changes from previous works in this series. The page size is smaller (9 by 12 inches) but there are more maps—some 600 including one for each of the 50 states. Among other basic features: a world index of over 100,000 place names (some 100,000 less let it be noted, than *The Times*); numerous subindexes interleaved with the maps; zip codes; sections on ecology and the Bible, as well as history; numerous diagrams and photographs; and so on. The maps are passable and the index is excellent.

One way to avoid the frills and save money is to purchase the *Ambassador* edition which sells for about $15 and is the same as the *Medallion* except for the added materials. The *Medallion* is the base for a more expensive set in two volumes (the *Hallmark* edition, $39.95, and the paperback *Headline* version, $1). The difference in each is the number and size of maps and the amount of extra material which is either added or deleted to raise or lower the price.

Rand McNally's entry follows much the same pattern of offering something in a price range for just about everyone. Still, the basic set of maps is found in its often revised *Cosmopolitan World Atlas*. This offers 400 maps with numerous map inserts in a format similar to the Hammond title. Scales range from 1:2,000,000 to 1:16,000,000 as compared with up to 1:15,000,000 for some Hammond maps. There is a 100-page

---

[7] Edward G. Burke, "U.S. Atlas Giants Update the World," *The New York Times*, September 28, 1971, p. 1, second section. *See also,* Arto Demrjian, "Making Maps at Hammond," *Publishers' Weekly*, September 1971, pp. 69+.

index which lists some 82,000 places and features. The "Planet Earth edition" means illustrations, diagrams, and brief articles on weather, geology, oceans, and the like. Various versions of the same work are found in the less expensive *Premier World Atlas* ($14.95) and the *World Atlas, Family Edition* ($12.95)—to mention only two of several.

In 1972, Rand McNally added a new dimension to its line with the $35 *The Earth and Man: A Rand McNally World Atlas* which, according to the firm's advertising, is as much an encyclopedia as an atlas. It contains encyclopedic information on the oceans, environment, and the solar system and a wealth of photographs and illustrative materials. The maps are some of the best the firm has ever published. Still, there are many other equally good, and several much more comprehensive, atlases of the world on the market.

Walsh's *General World Atlases in Print* helps here because he statistically points out the differences in the various atlases offered by the same company. Between the higher-priced and middle-priced volumes, the primary difference is one of padding. Between the middle- and the lower-priced titles, the difference is more meaningful in terms of size and number of maps.

Generally speaking, the average library would do well to purchase the medium- to high-priced titles of both C. S. Hammond and Rand McNally, i.e., the "Medallion" and the "Cosmopolitan," respectively. True, both have more encyclopedic information than possibly needed, but the cost difference between these and the lower-priced sets is minimal. Conversely, the volumes priced above the "Medallion" and the "Cosmopolitan" are too padded to warrant the extra sums.

Now in its third edition, the *National Geographic Atlas* has some 380 color maps with no particular scale. They run from 1:20,000,000 for American maps to 1:11,000,000 for Asian maps. The index provides over 139,000 entries and is one of the largest for an atlas of this price range. In itself, this is an advantage, made even more so by the fact that the maps are crowded with names but nevertheless are extremely legible. In overall quality, the maps are equal, if not better, to those found in Rand McNally and in C. S. Hammond. There is some rather inane introductory material before each of the sections but, on the whole, the padding is minimal. Important features are shown, including both roads and railroads. All in all, the National Geographic entry is as good as, if not better than, most atlases; and as it is continually appearing in new editions, it would be among the basic choices in libraries.

All of the aforementioned atlases, *The Times* aside, put considerable stress upon American maps. North America usually takes one-third to one-half of the map space. This is understandable in view of the major market, but of little value to the library where some users may not be quite so provincial or sales-minded as the publishers. A nice switch is offered by the McGraw-Hill work which reverses matters and gives about one-half of the atlas over to Europe. This is understandable because the map maker is a German (C. Bertelsmann Verlag), and the atlas is primarily a European work, i.e., *Der Grosse Bertelsmann Weltatlas*.

As in *The Times Atlas*, most of the 126 maps are double spreads; the scale is uniform, usually 1:5M; and all maps are extremely detailed and comprehensive. Political maps are given for continents, while all others are a combination of physical and political. The emphasis is on Europe, and the scale for these maps is quite large, i.e., 1:1,000,000. There are two indexes (one international and the other for central Europe) which include a total of 165,000 entries. This alone should assure the *International* a place in the reference collection. Another helpful feature is that place names are given in each country's own language, with adequate cross-references. An added feature is an excellent preface which gives a brief history of atlases and of problems faced by cartographers.

These atlases hardly exhaust the possibilities open to librarians. For example, a frequently revised title is the *Odyssey World Atlas* (New York: The Odyssey Press, Inc., 1966, 317 pp.) which consists of some 170 pages of maps (12 by 16 inches) and a good index of 105,000 place names. The thematic maps tend to be excellent, of somewhat better quality than found in other American atlases.

Literally in a class all by itself is the familiar *Goode's World Atlas* (13th ed. Chicago: Rand McNally & Company, 1970, 315 pp., $8.95). Often called, and rightfully so, "the leading American school atlas," it is familiar to anyone who went through a geography class in secondary or even primary school. First published 50 years ago, it was adopted by almost all American school systems. The maps are as good as in most Rand McNally titles; but what gives this its claim to fame are the added features, including a 30,000 name-pronouncing geographical index. There are physical, economic, and political maps as well as the standard (and highly useful) sections on how to read maps. In addition to the more than 100 special purpose maps, there is a relatively good balance— at all levels of scale, but clearly marked—of the world and the United States. Does the library need a school atlas? Obviously, "yes" if in a school; and possibly not so obviously for other types of libraries. Still an argument may be made for its inclusion because it is familiar to so many readers who might feel uncomfortable with the larger atlases.

Encyclopedia Type

Britannica Atlas. Chicago: Encyclopaedia Britannica, Inc., 1972, 556 pp., $35.

The World Book Atlas. Chicago: Field Enterprises Educational Corporation, 1972, 424 pp., $20.70.

Rand McNally supervised maps for both of these encyclopedia atlases, which may be purchased separately or at a reduced price when the encyclopedias are bought along with the atlas. Other firms, both American and foreign, have much the same practice.

The two atlases are somewhat higher in price than the general world atlases offered by Rand McNally and C. S. Hammond. Still, they do offer extra attractions. The Britannica title has 274 map pages. While supervised by Rand McNally, a good number of the maps are works of European cartographers and are of a first-rate quality, both in terms of clarity and detail. There is an extensive 160,000 place name index. A total of only eight scales are used throughout the volume and, to maintain comparability, the Soviet Union and North Africa are in 3-page foldouts. There is an extremely useful special section made up of 60 of the world's largest cities at a good scale of 1:300,000. Textual material is in four languages, and place names are translated right on the map pages. There is a minimum of padding, and the whole is an excellent atlas—in fact, so good that the library would do well to make this a first purchase among American-based works.

Libraries have a second choice in a similar atlas: *The International Atlas* (Chicago: Rand McNally & Company, 1971, 556 pp., $35). This is virtually identical to the *Britannica Atlas,* differing only in the prefatory material. There is so little difference between the two titles that the library might want to examine both first. This writer, though, opts for the Britannica.

Considerably more modest, but equally priced, the *World Book Atlas* has over 300 maps and a good, but limited, index of 80,000 place names. One of the truly outstanding features is the thematic maps which show physical features and political changes. There is, also, a most useful essay on map-reading skills which can be read profitably by most adults. While intentionally geared for younger readers, the whole is quite adequate, but far from comprehensive enough for most reference situations.

Does a library with any of the aforementioned standard atlases and the two encyclopedias (which include maps in the parent sets) need the separate encyclopedia atlases? Probably not, although it should be quickly noted that (1) the Britannica atlas is one of the best now available, and would be a first choice on its own for many collections; (2) combination sales offers make the atlases a relative bargain, i.e., when discounted below the trade price, and as such they might be seriously considered by libraries.

GOVERNMENT MAPS

In any discussion of national maps, a word must be said for a vast resource that all large libraries are aware of, but many medium-sized and small libraries often forget. This consists of federal, state, county, and, frequently, city governments. Innumerable government agencies at both the local and federal level issue general maps, thematic maps, and nautical charts.[8]

Any librarian seriously considering a more-than-average map library will use these agencies extensively. Their chief value for others is the knowledge that they issue special maps which may meet a particular need. Often these maps are at an extremely reasonable price—some of them are even available free through a judicious letter to a Congressman.

NATIONAL MAPS

U.S. Geological Survey. *The National Atlas of the United States of America.* Washington, D.C.: Government Printing Office, 1970, 417 pp., $100.

After 18 years of work and some 100 years of dreaming, the United States has its own national atlas—considerably behind some 40 other nations which have had such maps for years. The purpose of the atlas and its long history is explained in a lucid introduction.

The $3 million project is a 14-pound oversized volume with 335 pages of maps and a 41,000-entry index. It is the most expensive single volume ever produced by the United States government; and while $100 may seem comparatively high, it is well worth the price.

The volume is in two sections: "general reference maps" and "special subject maps." The first, short part consists of a general United States atlas. Most of the maps are at the scale of 1:200,000,000 with urban areas at 1:500,000 and certain other areas at 1:1,000,000. These are the basic maps familiar to the general atlas user. They show everything from national parks and wildlife refuges to 13 different varieties of water features. There are only a limited number of physical maps.

In the second section, there are some 750 thematic maps in 281 pages. These cover all topics from history, culture, climate, crime, marriages, and divorces to zip codes. In many ways, this section is the answer to almost any question likely to be asked at a reference desk about major features of the United States and its peoples. The maps are prepared at three different scales: 1:7,500,000 on two pages; 1:17,000,000; and 1:34,000,000. There is some criticism, though:

[8] Clara LeGear, *United States Atlases* (Washington, D.C.: Library of Congress, 1950), 450 pp., reprinted, 1972 by Arno Press, $18. Although dated, this gives an excellent overview of the type of national, state, county, city, and regional atlases in the Library of Congress.

The scope and magnitude of the information to be found in this section is enormous, but it is not always an easy matter to locate a subject or to determine if certain subjects are covered in the atlas. In addition to a table of contents in which each map title is listed under its major subject grouping, there is an index to map subjects which follows directly after the table of contents. Unfortunately for the user, this too is a table of contents, only in alphabetical order instead of page number order. The alphabetization is by major subject groupings. Under each major subject, each sub-group is in turn listed in alphabetical order. There is no index of individual map subjects in simple alphabetical order. Thus, if one is interested in finding a map of time zones, he must look under the major heading of "Administration," then under the sub-group, "Federal Administrative Areas," and finally, under a sub-subgroup, "Transportation," before he can find it. . . .Some subjects covered by the atlas are not indexed at all, such as drainage basins. With a little resourcefulness, the subject can be found under the major grouping, "Water," on the map entitled in the index, "Use," whose actual title is, "Water Use."[9]

The index of 41,000 place names is not overly detailed; but aside from the Rand McNally *Commercial Atlas and Marketing Guide,* it offers more names than any other work of this type. As for the quality of the maps, they are generally excellent and a challenge to many European map makers. Some 65 basic inks were used in innumerable shadings. It should be noted that the maps are the work of various individual cartographers, and they range in style according to the work of the men or women who made the map.

The thematic qualities of this atlas are of primary importance to reference librarians. Despite the poor contents approach, by searching diligently, the librarian will find answers to such queries as where there is the most thunder and lightning in the United States (Tampa, Florida).

SOURCES OF GOVERNMENT MAPS

In compiling the *National Atlas,* some 80 different government bureaus and offices supplied information and material. Many of these publish separate maps of a much more modest type, and all are available from either the departments or from the Government Printing Office. They may be located via *The United States Monthly Catalog, Monthly Checklist of State Publications, Price Lists,* and *Selected United States Government Publications,* as well as Laurence Schmeckebier's *Government Publications and Their Uses*—all discussed in Chapter 12.

[9] Review by Nathanial Abelson, Special Libraries, March 1972, p. 159. This is an excellent, detailed description as well as a critical review. A less exacting story on the history of the map will be found in *The New York Times,* February 7, 1971, p. 22.

Some of the better sources of maps include:

U.S. Geological Survey   These include a wide variety of state maps, showing drainage and political boundaries and the familiar topographic maps. A series eventually will cover the entire United States.

Coast and Geodetic Survey   These are nautical charts which cover the coastal areas, harbors, and rivers and are particularly useful for the amateur sailing fan. Large to small craft charts are available for owners of small boats. Maps differ in scale, depending on needed detail, from 1:200M to 1:20M.

Department of Agriculture   The maps issued by this department are primarily soil-survey maps, but also include highway-planning survey maps. Some of these can be extremely useful, even for the amateur gardener or farmer.

Department of Defense   The Department of Denfense maps cover everything from general charts to specialized maps of given areas. Many of them are classified, but a good number may be purchased.

Only four of the larger federal agencies are responsible for maps. Other federal maps include those issued by the Fish and Wildlife Service and the National Park Service, both under the Department of the Interior. These works are particularly useful for the weekend hunter, fisherman, or hiker who wants to follow little-known trails.

Many state agencies, quasi-public organizations, and city and county organizations also publish maps. Real estate firms and the ubiquitous gas station are good sources of local maps. Most useful of the road maps are the ones usually issued every three years by individual states. These general highway maps range in price from nothing to a small charge and should be a part of every library collection, regardless of size.

LOCAL MAPS[10]

Every library, of course, will have a suitable map of its own state, city, or town—preferably in clear view—plus maps of the county, state, and surrounding states. As noted, these are easily obtained. A problem arises when someone wants to locate a particular street in a distant city. Lacking a specific map or the Rand McNally work, the next best thing is one of the larger atlases, an encyclopedia, or a guidebook. The latter frequently includes maps of many smaller cities not found in the standard works.

[10] Jack A. Clarke, "State and Local Atlases," *RQ*, Spring 1970, pp. 232+.

Local maps may be obtained from a number of sources. Usually the chamber of commerce has city maps available for the asking. Frequently, companies issue detailed block maps, particularly if the company has a real estate interest. Also, the telephone company will often give the library a copy of their local map which shows areas where tolls are not charged. Usually this is quite large, extremely detailed, and shows considerably more than is found on most standard local maps.

OTHER NATIONAL MAPS

Almost every major nation has a national atlas or is in the process of compiling one. In addition, all nations issue individual maps, much as do the various United States agencies and departments. For a list of "National Bibliographies Containing References to Maps and Atlases," as well as other extensive references telling where and how to order all types of maps see Richard Stephenson's article.[11]

The United Nations publishes numerous maps, and most of these are available through UNIPUB (Box 433, New York, New York 10016). The distributor offers, from time to time, various catalogs such as *Scientific Maps and Atlases and Other Related Publications*, which, in themselves, are of reference value. This particular catalog, for example, not only lists the maps but also gives complete scales, descriptions, and prices.

The United States also issues maps of other countries. An excellent example is the *Atlas of China* (Washington, D.C.: Government Printing Office, 1972, 82 pp., $5.25). Compiled by the Central Intelligence Agency, it includes detailed maps of modern China. There also are thematic maps which trace the history and the economy of China.

WORLD ATLASES: FOREIGN LANGUAGE

German

Der Grosse Bertelsmann Waltatlas. Gutersloh: C. Bertelsmann, 1965, 360 pp.

Russian

Atlas Mira. Moscow, 1967, 250 pp.
Soviet World Atlas in English. 2d ed. Moscow, 1967, 250 pp., gazetteer and index, 1968, 1,021 pp., (distributed by Telberg Book Corporation, Sag Harbor, New York, $76.50).

[11] Richard W. Stephenson, "Published Sources of Information About Maps and Atlases," *Special Libraries,* February 1970, p. 87.

French

Atlas International Larousse Politique et Economique. Paris: Larousse, 1966, portfolio contains maps.

Italian

Touring Club Italiano. *Atlante Internazionale.* Milan, 1968, 173 pp., $80.

Because they have been published longer and receive greater attention to details, European atlases have been considered generally superior to American works. Using the evaluative scale, a European atlas or map in the equivalent price range of an American product will prove itself, almost without exception, equal if not superior. The gap, to be sure, is closing, and there are a number of American atlases that are at least equal to their European counterparts. Also, as noted, American publishers have used European maps in their own works.

> This is not to say that the atlases produced in the United States are carelessly done. On the whole, the long editorial experience of companies like Rand McNally and Hammond ensures against the substantive errors which accompany most new atlases. Rather, their tendency to produce for what must be an unsophisticated market gives us atlases which are visually dull, unbalanced in the amounts of space they allot to various parts of the world, or which are even meretricious.[12]

If the European works are so superior, why not use them in American libraries? The answer is that larger libraries do; and if "foreign" is expanded to include English atlases, *The Times Atlas* is as familiar a work in most libraries as the standard *Goode's World Atlas.* The major problem with the foreign atlas, as with any work issued abroad, is language and emphasis. Unfamiliar terms more than any other single feature cause students to abandon the study of foreign atlases and maps. Not only is the language different, but place names and symbols are confusing to an American who has difficulty ascertaining that Wien is Vienna or who cannot follow the metric system. Emphasis, too, tends to be more upon Europe with the larger scales used for European countries, the smaller for the remainder of the world.

The German atlas, in a slightly different form, has already been discussed, e.g., the McGraw-Hill *International Atlas.* If this atlas is to be purchased, it obviously would be best to buy the American version.

The Soviet atlas, also available in a translated edition, includes more than 215,000 place names in its 250 pages of oversized maps—average size 13 by 20 inches. The maps are superbly executed; but there is no

[12] Gomez-Ibanez, op. cit., p. 625.

English version of the index volume; and unless one has a knowledge of Russian, the Russian index is quite obviously limited. Furthermore, the place names on the map itself tend to be non-Western. Despite these drawbacks for Western readers, the Soviet atlas has many advantages: (1) There are no extraneous frills. (2) There is a large scale, i.e., the maximum scale is 1:7,500,000, while Europe is at 1:2,500,000 and Asia at 1:3,000,000. (3) There are numerous city maps and extremely detailed maps of major areas. (4) The balance between all parts of the world is among the best of any atlas. Equal care, according to experienced cartographers, is given to misrepresenting—if only slightly—the location of certain vital areas and cities in the Soviet Union. This is apparently an effort to confuse the military of other countries, but more likely to appease bureaucrats who control the cartographers in the Soviet.[13]

The Italian atlas should be purchased first among the foreign atlases listed here. The reason: It offers the largest place name index of any atlas—more than 250,000 names in a separate index volume. If anything, this may be almost too much detail for the average user, but it is a blessing for the specialist. The maps, on some 173 12- by 19-inch pages, are uniformly excellent; and there are superb thematic maps. The balance is a bit uneven, with most of the emphasis on Europe. This is the only major atlas which systematically gives linguistic, statistical, and cartographic sources used for the compilation.

While the French atlas is excellent, it has a major drawback for library use—the maps are on unbound sheets and anyone who has tried to fold a road map may surmise the difficulty of keeping everything in order in the library. The maps, some 75 of them, are good and the index includes place names in French, English, and Spanish. Of all the foreign atlases, this is probably the least desirable for "housekeeping" in libraries, yet among the best for larger collections.

THEMATIC MAPS AND ATLASES

Being a cartographic essay on a subject, the thematic map is as varied as man's knowledge. Almost every subject area can boast of at least one, if not several, atlases. Those listed here are but a cross section, indicative of the more popular types found in many libraries.

Thematic maps are used in regular atlases and are an integral part of any encyclopedia or basic reference text in a given subject area. The advantage of individual atlases is depth of coverage and the convenience of a single source. The distinct disadvantage is that many become rapidly

[13] Harry Steward, "Soviet Map Distortions," *Special Libraries. Geography and Map Division, Bulletin.* March 1970, pp. 45+.

dated; although, here one may argue that at least the basic materials in a historical, religious, or scientific atlas are always useful.

Thematic maps in an age of visual awareness are increasingly important. It seems much simpler to show the tides of economic or historical ebb and flow in a visual thematic map than in words. And anyone who even casually follows news magazines and newspapers will find such maps frequently employed. Aside from what is found in general atlases and encyclopedias, the average library user is almost unaware of what is available. The conscientious librarian would do well to bring some of these thematic atlases to the attention of users, and more particularly to teachers and students.

Historical

The New Cambridge Modern History. Atlas. (Vol. 14). New York: Cambridge University Press, 1970, 319 pp., $32.50.

Miller, Theodore. *Graphic History of the Americas.* New York: John Wiley & Sons, Inc., 1969, 59 pp., $3.95.

Gilbert, Martin. *Russian History Atlas.* New York: The Macmillan Company, 1972, 146 pp., $4.95.

Shepherd, William. *Historical Atlas.* 9th ed. New York: Barnes & Noble, Inc., 1964, 226 maps, $17.50.

The best single, relatively up-to-date historical atlas, the *New Cambridge Modern History Atlas,* includes 288 thematic maps which are primarily political and, as the title indicates, of the modern period—the Renaissance to the close of World War II. The maps are extremely well drawn, arranged in chronological groups, and reproduced on a scale which makes it possible to make meaningful comparisons. There is a good subject index. While the price is higher than for most titles of this type, it is well worth the expense for reference libraries.

On a narrower scale, the Miller work limits itself to historical developments of the Western Hemisphere. It covers all time periods, and there is a good balance between the Western Hemisphere and the United States and Canada. Unlike the Cambridge title, there is considerable emphasis on other than political changes; and the maps are useful for tracing variation in demographic, religious, and economic growth.

One of an ongoing series, the historical atlas of Russia contains 146 maps designed to give a survey of Russian history from the earliest times to the present day. The maps are admirably clear, carefully compiled, and of particular assistance for an area of the world that tends to be only superficially treated in more general historical atlases. There is an excellent index. Libraries in which the field of thematic historical atlases is a popular one should purchase others in this series, and librarians should read reviews of newer titles as they appear.

Historical maps are quite literally that; and for this reason, it is hardly necessary to have a totally up-to-date collection. If anything, some of the older, standard titles in this area will, and can, be used for many years to come. The average user is going to be more interested in the past than in the immediate future—hence a title with a copyright date in the 1960s, 1950s, or even earlier is not in any real reference sense out of date.

The Shepherd work has been standard for years and is considered one of the best. The last edition covers world history from about 2000 B.C. down to 1955. Outline maps prepared by Hammond indicate developments of commerce, war campaigns, adjustments of boundaries after wars, and countless other useful approaches to history. There is a full index of names. Despite its usefulness, the volume is relatively poor typographically and the colored maps tend to be somewhat out of register. One distinct advantage of Shepherd is that the work is frequently revised, normally with supplemental material.[14]

Economic and Commercial Atlases

Rand McNally Commercial Atlas and Marketing Guide. Chicago: Rand McNally & Company, 1876 to date, annual, $75.

Oxford Regional Economic Atlas: Western Europe. New York: Oxford University Press, 1971, 96 pp., $15.

As with historical thematic maps, many economic and commercial or business thematic maps will be found in subject handbooks, manuals, almanacs, and encyclopedias. The benefit of the specialized titles listed here is that they offer up-to-date, or relatively up-to-date, materials and are especially edited for the user seeking definite thematic-type information. They, also, serve other ready-reference purposes which should not be overlooked.

Many libraries justify the purchase of general atlases published by Rand McNally and Hammond in terms of their coverage of the United States—which is usually quite good. However, for the library which can afford to rent (it is rented not purchased) the *Rand McNally Commercial Atlas*, the problem of adequate United States coverage is not only solved, but solved in the best form possible.

Revised annually, the *Commercial Atlas*, accurately records changes on a year-by-year basis. All information is the most up to date of any single atlas or, for that matter, any reference work of this type. It is an excellent source for current statistic data, and the first 25 or so pages

---

[14] A revision is scheduled for the mid 1970s. Meanwhile, a useful supplementary work is Martin Gilbert's *Recent History Atlas: 1870 to the Present Day* (New York: The Macmillan Company, 1969, 121 pp., $4.95).

offers general information on everything from United States agriculture and communications to retail trade and transportation. The maps give basic demographic and business data for some 116,000 places in the United States.

Technically, the *Commercial Atlas* is not devoted entirely to the United States; but aside from a small number of world and foreign maps, the concentration is on the individual states. Each of the state maps, usually a double-page spread, places emphasis on the political-commercial aspects of the state. The maps are especially useful for indicating city and county boundaries. There is a wealth of statistical information (retail sales maps, analysis of business and manufacturers, and principal business centers) with each of the state sections. By far the finest atlas for detailed treatment of the individual states, the whole is tied together with a superb index.

The index serves as a fine ready-reference source for: (1) location of cities and towns by state and county; (2) the number and name of railroads and airlines serving the community; (3) estimated current population, including a separate figure for college and university students; (4) zip codes. (In fact, the publisher claims there are more than 60,000 zips not listed in the official post office *Zip Code Directory*.)

As both an atlas and a handy compilation of up-to-date statistics, the *Rand McNally Commercial Atlas* is unrivaled. Limited as it is for the most part to the United States, the encyclopedic information not only seems legitimate, but is a blessing.

The Oxford atlas is one of a series devoted to regional economics. Most of the titles are frequently revised and follow a standard pattern of giving basic information of a sort found in the *Rand McNally Commercial Atlas*. In this case, the data are limited to 17 European countries. Maps cover commodities, population, communication, production, and the like. The maps are, in the best British tradition, distinguished by their fine form.

Now somewhat dated, the *Oxford Economic Atlas of the World* (New York: Oxford University Press, 1965, 286 pp.) offers a similar approach for the world at large. Libraries would probably be better advised to buy individual titles in the series, at least until such time as the overall atlas is revised. Other titles cover Africa, Latin America, India, China, and Japan.

Other Thematic Atlases

The Atlas of the Universe. Chicago: Rand McNally & Company, 1970, 272 pp., $35.

U.S. Department of Agriculture. *Atlas of United States Trees.* Washington, D.C.: Government Printing Office, 1971, 310 pp., $16.75.

U.S. Environmental Science Services Administration. *Climatic Atlas of the United States.* Washington, D.C.: Government Printing Office, 1968, 80 pp., $4.25.

U.S. Department of the Army. *Official Table of Distances.* . . .Washington, D.C.: Government Printing Office, 1968, 1,200 pp., $1.25.

Almost every subject has its own thematic atlas, and the titles listed here can only give the reader a notion of what is available. New titles are issued each year. Older titles, found in Winchell and Walford, move from agriculture to congressional districts to literature.

Many of the general atlases now include at least a cursory glimpse at astronomical maps, but there are a number of specialized works of which the Rand McNally title is representative. This is considerably more than an atlas. In addition to maps, there are illustrations, photographs (most in full color), and essays on exploration of space, the solar system, and related topics. There is a good 10,000-entry index. The work is primarily geared for popular consumption, although it seems accurate enough. The price may be rather high for many libraries, particularly as a good deal of the essay information (not to mention the maps and photographs) can be found in a more limited way in general atlases and, since our moon adventures, in great detail in general encyclopedias.

A somewhat narrower, but considerably more scholarly, work is *The Times Atlas of the Moon* (London: Times Newspapers Ltd., 1970, 110 pp., $25). There are 60 maps from Bartholomew, based upon exploration of space up until 1969. More current, and in someways even better, is the *New Photographic Atlas of the Moon* (New York: Taplinger Publishing Co., Inc., 1971, 310 pp., $20) which includes excellent, recent space photographs. Also, the atlas offers a sound history of space and astronomy.

The United States government, as well as the United Nations and other countries, offers a number of thematic atlases. One example is the first volume in a proposed series which will cover all trees in America. The set begins with this title devoted to 300 maps of conifers and important hardwoods in the continental United States and Alaska. An interesting feature is the transparent overlays which show the correlation of forests with the environment, i.e., in relation to rivers, precipitation, climate, and so on.

The *Climatic Atlas* depicts the climate of the United States through a series of maps which show at almost a glance the differences between one region and another. This type of work is extremely useful in ready reference where someone may want to know variations in climate between, say, New York and Austin, Texas. Even the mean number of days of sunshine for each area is indicated.

While not a thematic atlas, the *Official Table of Distances* will save countless hours of consulting maps trying to arrive at the mileage between two points. (An effort often exerted for those who must verify distances in order to make claims for repayment on travel vouchers.) In tabular form, towns are listed in the United States with an average of some 900 distances given between them and other towns and cities in the United States, Hawaii, Alaska, Canada, Mexico, Puerto Rico, and Central America. The Army has a companion volume for distances between various foreign places.

GAZETTEERS

Columbia Lippincott Gazetteer of the World. New York: Columbia University Press, 1952 (supplements, 1962), 21,148 pp. + 32 pp., $75.

    Webster's New Geographical Dictionary. rev. ed. Springfield, Massachusetts: G. & C. Merriam Company, 1972, 1,408 pp., $14.95.

In one sense, the index in any atlas is a gazetteer, that is, it is a geographical dictionary or finding list of cities, mountains, rivers, population, and the features in the atlas. A separate gazetteer is precisely the same, usually without maps. Why then bother with a separate volume? There are three reasons: (1) the gazetteers tend to list more names; (2) the information is usually detailed; and (3) the advantage of a single easily managed volume is often welcomed. Having made these points, it can be argued, and with some justification, that a number of the atlases' indexes have more entries, are more up to date, and contain a larger amount of information. The wise librarian will first consider what is to be found in atlases before purchasing any gazetteer.

    Taken as separate entries, the number of gazetteers is somewhat limited. The obvious duplication between gazetteers and the indexes found in good atlases, the expense of preparation, and the limited sales probably account for the lack of interest by many publishers. The fact that most information sought by the layman can be found in even greater detail in a general or geographical encyclopedia does not increase the use of gazetteers. Their primary value is for locating places possibly overlooked by a standard atlas and as informal indexes.

    The two American gazetteers, found in almost every reference department, differ in two important respects. The *Columbia* work has some 130,000 entries as compared with about 48,000 for *Webster's,* while the price of the *Columbia* gazetteer is about nine times that of the *Webster's.* A minor difference which makes the *Webster's* more attractive for casual use is its comparatively compact size. The other title is heavy and bulky.

Aside from sheer volume, the *Columbia* gazetteer tends to give considerably more information about each place. For example, it devotes one and one-half long columns to Berlin, while *Webster's* dismisses the German capital in a few short paragraphs. Entries in both include pronunciation, location, area, population, geographical and physical description, and economic and historical data. There are adequate cross-references, and *Webster's* has 217 maps.

The element of time is against the *Columbia* volume, for despite the supplement which includes 1960 census figures, essentially the work is the same as the first edition in 1952. On the other hand, the revised *Webster's* includes the 1970 figures for America in the main text.

The difference in number of entries is dictated by selectivity. *Webster's*, while primarily geared to American users, does not list towns under 1,500 population in the United States and under 25,000 in Japan, China, and the U.S.S.R. The *Columbia* volume tends to include every town likely to be found on a map, incorporated or not. It also lists many more geographical features.

TRAVEL GUIDES

Neal, J. A. *Reference Guide for Travellers.* New York: R. R. Bowker Company, 1969, 674 pp., $18.95.

American Guide Series. Prepared by Federal Writer's Project, Works Progress Administration. Various publishers, 1937 to 1950; frequently reprinted and reissued by numerous publishers.

American Automobile Association. *Tour Book.* Washington, D.C.: American Automobile Association, various dates, free to members.

Hotel and Motel Red Book. New York: American Hotel and Motel Association Directory Corp., 1886 to date, annual, $12.50.

Frommer, Arthur. *Europe on $5 and $10 a Day.* New York: Simon & Schuster, Inc., 1957 to date, annual, $3.50.

Fodor's Europe. New York: David McKay Company, Inc., 1953 to date, annual, $8.95.

The Blue Guides. London: Ernest Benn, Ltd., 1918 to date, annual (distributed in United States by Rand McNally & Company) $6.95 to $13.95.

Fielding's Travel Guide to Europe. New York: William Morrow & Company, Inc., 1948 to date, annual, $8.95.

Guides Michelin. Paris: Service de Tourisme Michelin, 1905 to date, annual, various paging.

With lower air fares, greater income, more automobiles, and a distinct impression that travel is "fun," the average American sets aside at least two weeks to several months for touring his state, his country, or the world. Ready to assist him are countless travel guides—over 1,200 in the English language are listed in the Neal bibliography. While somewhat dated, this bibliography remains useful because most travel guides are annuals that change little except for updating the prices of hotel rooms and meals. And Neal provides some excellent annotations. The French *Avec Les Guides Bleus* (Paris: Librairie Hanchette, 1959) lists over 4,000 titles published only in France.

The purpose of the general guidebook is primarily to inform the traveler about what to see, where to stay, where to dine, and the best way of getting there. It is the type of book best carried in the car or in the hip pocket. Stay-at-home librarians frequently find these works useful for the vast amount of details about specific places. Atlases and gazetteers are specific enough about pinpointing location, yet rarely deal with the down-to-earth facts travelers require.

The travel agency or automobile club usually furnishes the traveler with much of what he needs in the way of immediate information. The American Automobile Association, for example, has a series of tour books covering the United States and North America which are "produced as an exclusive service for members," but do find their way into some library collections. There is a wealth of ready-reference material from average monthly temperatures for states and cities to historical data. Particularly useful are detailed, up-to-date maps of downtown areas of larger cities and even many smaller towns. The set runs from 15 to 16 volumes for the United States, with separate titles for Canada, Mexico, and Central America. The association also issues trip maps with up-to-the-minute information on the best roads, detours, and the like—again, only for members.

Good, indifferent, or bad, as the various privately published quides may be, the tourist usually wants more information than is normally found in such works. He may journey to the library simply to look over what is available before he makes a purchase, or he may want to reminisce over places he did see or wishes he had seen. More important, for reference purposes, many of the guides are annually revised and give current maps of cities and even small hamlets; describe the peculiar customs of the people; note the chief museums, libraries, hospitals, (and you-name-it kind of landmarks); list hotels, motels, resorts, sporting areas, and anything meant to entertain; and may go so far as to list flora and fauna. Usually there is a select group of drawings and photographs to entice the reader to this or that spot.

Other titles give historical background, but on the whole this is not always to be trusted. Editors normally have gleaned the material from standard reference works and, in the process, are not always accurate.

More trustworthy are figures dealing with distances, population figures, and conversion tables.

Another major drawback to many of the guidebooks is the lack of any consistent indexing. Usually a table of contents is deemed sufficient. In considering purchase, this should be a major check. Other evaluative measures for most reference books should be applied, but probably not too rigorously. The end result may be a library with few guidebooks. Publishers, after all, are generally more concerned with presenting a practical package than a reference tool for the librarian.

Not many years ago, the term "guidebook" was synonymous with Baedeker and Muirhead. In 1828, Karl Baedeker founded a Leipzig guidebook firm which published works for all the major countries of the world. They became famous, and rightly so, for their accuracy and their detailed maps and general background material. Today, many of these works are collector's items and a complete run not only gives a library an invaluable source of material and maps of early landmarks, but serves the social historian as a peculiar and wonderful guide to manners for the periods covered. Several generations later, in 1918, L. R. Muirhead began issuing the *Blue Guides*. These were equally well received and covered much the same territory.

Travel has increased considerably since Baedeker first started his series; and as a result, there are scores of guides which overlap, duplicate, and to a degree borrow one from the other. Each has peculiar features which it is hoped will make it a favorite, but only a representative few can be mentioned here.

Of all the guides listed here, the single most useful work for reference is unquestionably the *American Guide Series*. Originally produced during the Depression by writers for the Federal Writers' Project of the Work Progress Administration, the series includes over 150 different volumes.[15] Either private publishers or historical groups working within the various states have managed to update many of these works and keep them in print. The guides include basic, usually accurate, historical, social, and economic information for almost every place in the state from the smallest unmarked hamlet to the largest cities. Maps, illustrations, and highway distances add to their usefulness; and the majority also have excellent indexes. For the reference desk, they are particularly helpful for locating information on communities either entirely overlooked or only mentioned in standard reference books. Unfortunately, not all are up to date, but the basic information is valuable enough to

[15] Those in print are listed in *Subject Guide to Books in Print* under state name. The whole series is given in E. A. Baer's *Titles in Series* (Metuchen, New Jersey: Scarecrow Press, 1954, vol. 1, nos. 492 to 660, 2 vols., 1964).

warrant a complete collection in any medium-to-large reference depart-ment. Even the smallest library should have the guides for its own state and for surrounding communities. In addition to the basic guides, indi-vidual works were issued for some of the larger cities, countries, and regions.

Putting more emphasis on comfort than on courage, the *Mobil Travel Guides* (Chicago: Rand McNally & Company, 1958 to date, an-nual) are a typical example of annual guides organized to inform the traveler about the best motels, hotels, restaurants, or resorts. The work is divided into seven regional volumes, and each is divided by state and town. There are a number of city maps and the usual data on each place are covered. Some 21,000 different spots are graded with the star sys-tem—one for good, five for the best.

The technique is familiar to anyone who used the *Guides Michelin* (available in both French and English). There are a number of these, distinguished by color. The most famous are the red guides which pri-marily rate restaurants. Issued annually, they are watched with delight and fear by the French chefs whose very careers may depend upon the ratings. Not a few disappointed cooks have been known to commit sui-cide on the basis of a poor showing in the *Guides Michelin*. (There is no record of such an achievement for one-star holders in the *Mobil Guides*.) The Michelin green guides give detailed information on historical places to visit and dutifully star what is important for the conscientious tourist to see. *A Guide Michelin to New York City* was published in 1972; there were no restaurants listed for New York, however. The *Michelin* works are valuable in reference for the detailed town plans.

If the more adventuresome American traveler simply wants a listing of hotels and motels without ratings but including prices, the old stand-by is the *Hotel and Motel Red Book*. Revised annually, it is arranged by state and city and gives basic information about each accommodation. Since it is limited to association members, small towns are often not included. There are advertisements to further indicate features. Canada and some other countries are included in it and in Leahy's *Hotel-Motel Guide* (Chicago: America Hotel Register Co., 1876 to date). The latter work also lists lodgings in Mexico and has maps of each state as well as of major cities. *The Blue Guides* now cover most of Western Europe, but are particularly good for England, Scotland, Ireland, and Wales. One of the best general guide series, *Fodor's Modern Guides,* now covers most of Europe, Asia, and South America and puts more emphasis on detailed descriptions and illustrations than on maps. The information is geared to the modern, fast traveler who wants to see all he can in the least amount of time. It is particularly useful in reference work for the detailed data on what is needed to get from one place to another—official papers, shots, and the like.

A somewhat similar approach is offered by the numerous Fielding guides. While he and Fodor cover much the same material, many prefer the latter because of Fielding's overexcited prose and the great emphasis on shopping hints. As one critic pointed out, the Fielding guide to Italy has about two-thirds of the space devoted to hotels, shops, and night-clubs, with the rest given over to sightseeing features. A more charitable view of the enterprise and a fascinating article on how such guides are put together will be found in John McPhee's long article on Fielding.[16]

Based on the theory that the relatively poor as well as the middle classes and the rich can travel, the *5 Dollars a Day* series (now up to $10 and $15 a day) not only takes in Europe, but there are separate volumes for Mexico, the Caribbean, Greece, Israel, England, Japan, and a number of American cities. Each is prepared by the individual traveler who alleg-edly did it on $5 a day. It includes economic tips on the cheapest and most modest restaurants and hotels. Of more general interest are the comments on off-the-beaten-path attractions, from small towns to small beer gardens. Much of the advice is sound, but experience reveals that some guides are particularly uneven.[17]

SUGGESTED READING

Current, Charles E., "The Acquisition of Maps for School (and Other Small) Libraries" *Wilson Library Bulletin,* February 1971, pp. 578 +. General dis-cussion which ends with list of suppliers. *See also:* Bartz, Barbara, "Maps in the Classroom," *Journal of Geography,* January 1970, pp. 18 +. An all-media approach to collections for school libraries.

Drazniowky, Roman, "Need for Map Cataloguing," *Special Libraries,* May 1970, pp. 236-237. A brief discussion of cataloging maps. *See also:* Ristow, Walter, "Computerized Map Cataloguing Project," *Inspel,* July/October 1969, pp. 74 +.

Greenhood, David, *Mapping.* Chicago: The University of Chicago Press, 1964, 289 pp. The first section gives the background on maps and information for the layman on various aspects of map making. The second half tells the amateur how to do his own mapping. A more technical approach to the same basic material is included in T. W. Birch's *Maps, Topographical and Statistical* (New York: Oxford University Press, 1964, 249 pp.).

Hagen, C. B., "A Survey of the Usage of a Large Map Library," *Special Libraries, Geography and Map Division, Bulletin,* June 1970, pp. 27 +. Who uses maps and why. *See also:* Kiraldi, Louis, "Map Libraries in Michigan: A Survey,"

---

[16] "Profiles. Templex," *The New Yorker,* January 6, 1968, pp. 32-67.
[17] "At Home with John Wilcock," *The New York Times,* February 4, 1973 (Travel section), pp. 1 +. A witty interview with the man who wrote many of the $5-a-day guides. Inciden-tally, as of this writing, the deflated dollar is giving the editors pause. The guides may now go to $10 a day, or $15 a day.

Michigan Librarian, March 1969, pp. 4+. A survey, overview of map collecting and a good bibliography.

Lottman, Herbert, "Guidebooks as Christmas Presents," *The New York Times* (Travel section), December 12, 1971, pp. 1+. A critical, rewarding article on the best (and the worst) travel guides. An excellent buying guide for many libraries.

Skelton, R. A., *Maps: A Historical Study of Their Study and Collection.* Chicago: The University of Chicago Press, 1972. One of the most famous of all map librarians discusses the history and collecting of maps. Note: This is suggested for those who missed the section in the first edition of this text which discussed the history of maps. It was deleted to make room for other items.

Stevens, Stanley, "Planning a Map Library?" *Special Libraries,* April 1972, pp. 172+. Some useful suggestions for the beginner, applicable for any smaller collection.

White, R. C., "Map Librarianship," *Special Libraries,* May 1970, pp. 233+. A short discussion of the art.

CHAPTER TWELVE
GOVERNMENT DOCUMENTS[1]

The basic mystery for many beginning reference librarians is the government document. For some peculiar reason, the very term seems to frighten and confuse. Most of the cause can be attributed to a simple fact—too many libraries tend to forget that the purpose of a government publication is to inform, to answer questions, not to be an ignoble excuse for setting off hot discussion on organizational cataloging and administration.

Definition

A government document is any publication that is printed at government expense or published by authority of a governmental body. Documents may be considered in terms of issuing agencies: the congressional, judiciary, and executive branches, which include many departments. In terms of use, they may be classified as (1) records of government administration; (2) research documents for specialists, including a considerable number of statistics and data of value to science and business; and (3)

---

[1] In view of the nature of government publications, most accredited library schools offer one or more special documents courses. It is as complicated and as rewarding a study as any of the specialized subject areas. Throughout this text, various government publications are noted as part of units. This stems from a conviction that they should be an integral part of a reference collection and should not be treated as separate items.

popular sources of information. The physical form may be a book, pamphlet, magazine, report, monograph, or microform.

While this discussion mainly concerns federal documents, state, county, and municipal publications are also a major concern of any library.

Some of the mystery will be dispelled if one thinks of the average private publisher. He may well issue a record of government action, although normally it is in somewhat more felicitous prose and with editorial comments. He prides himself on publishing documents that may be considered useful for research, and he thrives on popular works.

What, then, is the difference between using the government document and the average work issued by one of the publishers whose items appear in *Books in Print?* The source, the organization, and the retrieval puzzle most people. An average patron does not know how to ask for a document, or if he does he may have difficulty finding it either in the library or through the catalog. He may think he knows the name, only to find that what he has is not the official title which appears in the standard lists.

Problems

In describing the problems with government documents, Margaret Hutchins observed:

> . . . nothing like 100 percent efficiency can be attained by any amount of reading about government publications unless what is read is immediately illustrated and applied in the actual handling of them.[2]

True enough, but the same statement might be made about all reference works. Too many librarians take solace from the fact that since they will not be "handling" government publications, they do not need to know about them. The extension of this line of reasoning is to avoid them whenever possible.

More specifically, the problems which arise in connection with government documents may be outlined as follows:

Source No private publisher can hope to rival the government (both at the federal and the local level) in the amount of paper issued each year. Approximately 27,000 separate publications are distributed by the Superintendent of Documents alone.

> No publisher in the world publishes 4,000 [new] titles a year nor deals with customers in terms of millions. The superintendent's office handles an average of 30,000 orders a day, spurting to 60,000 during peak periods

[2] Margaret Hutchins, *Introduction to Reference Work* (Chicago: American Library Association, 1944), p. 47.

at the start of the school year, the Christmas season, and income tax time. "Your Federal Income Tax" has sold over 14 million copies since 1947, topped only by "Infant Care," which has hit the 15 million mark after 20 years. The dollar value of sales has about doubled in the last 10 years, to $22 million.[3]

There are numerous departments, field offices, and agencies which publish items that may not emanate from the Superintendent of Documents; and the states, counties, cities, and other municipalities all have other methods of distributing their publications.

The major federal documents are printed by the Government Printing Office (GPO) in Washington, D.C. This printing plant was established in 1861, primarily in an effort to bring some order out of financial and political chaos. Up to that point, the government contracted with private printers. This proved a "fat" political contract, and the results frequently were that the publications were often neglected. Another by-product of this method was the lack of centralized control over collecting and distributing.

The Superintendent of Documents' office was established in 1895 to centralize the control and distribution of the documents. He is still working at it. Were all documents printed by the GPO, the problem might be simplified, but they are not. Consequently, they often do not come to the attention of the Superintendent, are not listed in standard bibliographies, and are found only with a great deal of effort.

Prior to 1895, the librarian attempting to build a collection of government documents had a major problem in locating them for purchase. It is still a headache but is made somewhat easier by present distribution methods. Where the early confusion if still noted is in retrospective searching of government publications and for work not distributed by the Superintendent of Documents.

Organization While no librarian would consider organizing a collection of books by publishers' names, many do this with governmental publications. Out of 26 large university libraries, nine have separate government documents collections, seven integrate the documents into the general collection, and ten combine the two systems.[4] Large public libraries follow a similar pattern.

---

[3] *The New York Times,* November 28, 1971, p. 95. The volume of filing, publication, and cost is summed up briefly by *The Wall Street Journal,* "The Paper Blizzard," August 31, 1972, p. 6.
[4] Jack E. Schultz, "Summary Report of Government Documents Questionnaire" (Amherst: University of Massachusetts Library, 1965) (Processed). A detailed discussion of the pros and cons of various ways of organizing government documents will be found in Ellen P. Jackson, *A Manual for the Administration of the Federal Document Collections in Libraries* (Chicago: American Library Association, 1955).

Here, for example, is a description of the collection of government documents in the library of Queens College, New York:

> Some government documents are treated as books and listed in the card catalog; others, the *Department of State Bulletin,* for example, are treated as periodicals. The majority, however, are classified separately according to a system of the U.S. Superintendent of Documents.[5]

The justification for separate collections is that the volume of publications swamps the library and necessitates special considerations of organization and classification. There are other reasons; but on the whole, it is a matter of the librarian's seeking to find the simplest and best method of making the documents available. Some argue that separation tends to limit use and try to compromise by separating the administrative and official works while integrating the more popular and highly specialized subject documents into the general collection.

A distinct disadvantage of a separate documents collection is that it isolates it from the main reference collection. The reference librarians are inclined to think of it as a thing apart and may answer questions with materials at hand rather than attempt to fathom the holdings of the documents department. Conversely, if patrons are referred to the documents librarian, he may attempt to answer questions that might be better handled by the reference librarian.

For most librarians, the matter of organization is not a problem, primarily because: (1) they do not have large enough government documents collections to warrant serious consideration of separate collections, and (2) more and more, they are coming to rely upon the large research and the depository library for help in answering questions which call for specialized documents.

This is to say that the two major factors which determine the selection and use of government documents are similar to those governing the selection and use of all forms of communication—the size of the library and its purpose. In terms of government documents, these libraries may be viewed as depository libraries. By the Printing Act of 1895, modified by the Depository Act of 1962, approximately 1,500 libraries are designated as depositories for government documents. They are entitled to receive publications free of charge from the Superintendent of Documents. The purpose is to have centers with relatively complete runs of government documents located throughout the country. These are likely to be state, regional, large city public libraries, and the major college and university libraries.

[5] Kenneth Freyer, *Paul Klapper Library Handbook* (Flushing, New York: Queens College of the City University of New York, 1965), p.47

In volume of title production, most of the depositories may receive about one-half the federal documents issued each year. Documents not issued by the Government Printing Office must be obtained elsewhere.

In most of the nondepository libraries, the responsibility for government documents rests with the reference staff. Here the reference librarian must not only be able to select judiciously, but must be aware of methods of borrowing documents from the larger libraries. A basic knowledge of the bibliographies that help in selection and location and verification are particularly necessary at this level.

Retrieval If there is no universally recognized method of organizing government documents, the manner of tracing them is equally varied. Without discussing the complicated field of cataloging and classifying government publications, a few general remarks are in order.

There are two general methods of retrieving government documents, both based on organization. If they are kept in a separate collection, the tendency is to follow the Superintendent of Documents classification system. This consists of a combination of letters and numbers assigned to documents. Unlike the systems known to librarians, the classification has no visible relationship to subject matter. It is related to the issuing agency.

The Superintendent of Documents classification system is used as a method of identification in all current Superintendent of Documents bibliographies and lists, as well as lists issued by various departments and agencies. Consequently, the lists serve the majority of libraries as a catalog, and the documents are organized and arranged on the shelves according to this system.

In smaller libraries, and in some larger ones, Library of Congress cards are used, and the Library of Congress or the Dewey classification scheme is used. Here the documents are classified as any book or periodical and treated as such in shelving.

An informal system, often used in special and small libraries, is to keep a separate file of the unusual publications but to classify and shelve the much-used reference works such as the *Statistical Abstract*. The separate file may be tapped either through a homemade subject file or through the librarian's memory.

Just as the separate collection tends to isolate the documents, so does the separate classification scheme. Since entries in the indexes and bibliographies are not normally repeated in the card catalog, the user may never know that a document concerning labor management exists and may be just what he needs. Some link has to be provided for the user to get him from the catalog to the necessary index, but even *see* and *see also* references are frequently insufficient.

Even when the documents are included, or hinted at in the card catalog, another problem occurs. Most government documents are listed under a corporate entry in the card catalog, rarely by title or by subject. A corporate entry is a listing under the name of the author, that is, the government body responsible for its issue. For example, a corporate governmental entry will be under the country (United States), state (New York), city (St. Paul), or other official unit that sponsored publication. Thus, someone requesting a publication about foreign affairs would probably first look under the U.S. Department of State.

Since there are a vast number of governmental agencies, it is frequently difficult to remember the proper point of entry. Until the new catalog code was approved, the custom was to compound confusion by entering a document under the higher rather than the subordinate agency. Thus, under old rules, one looking for a document issued by the U.S. Division of Coal Mine Inspection would first have to remember that the division was part of the U.S. Bureau of Mines. Although the new code has been adopted, it may be years before this change appears in catalogs; and until then, the higher agency must be consulted first.

Not only do the catalog rules change, but so do the names of the agencies, bureaus, and departments. Thus, when a bureau name is changed or a new one is added, there is another problem in retrieving the needed document. The *United States Government Organization Manual* is of help as is Andriot's *Guide to U.S. Government Serials and Periodicals* which gives background information on departments and agencies. The feature in both titles of listing agencies that have changed names or that have been abolished or transferred often will serve as the key to locating the proper author entry.

Too frequently, the subject headings employed by the Library of Congress, the Superintendent of Documents, and even the local library may be at variance. However, most libraries do follow the Superintendent of Documents procedure, primarily because of reliance on bibliographies issued by his office.

Still another problem is that an inquiry may come for a document in terms of its popular, rather than official, name. Hence, someone may ask for the Moynihan report or the Weinberg report. The latter is part of the President's Science Advisory Committee findings and is not easily found in standard bibliographies under the popular title of Weinberg. Of considerable help here is a list of select reports of United States executive, legislative, and judicial bodies published during the past 80 years. All are first listed by popular name and then by the full and official title. Although highly selective as a retrieval guide, this is an absolute must. Its official title is *Popular Names of U.S. Government Reports: A Catalog* (rev. ed. Washington, D.C.: Government Printing Office, 1970, 32 pp.).

From a user's viewpoint, all of this is academic. Whereas he may find most works himself by consulting the card catalog, he will almost always need help in the area of government documents. His principal question, stemming from the aforementioned variety of approaches to organization and cataloging, is simply "Where is it?" He rarely, for example, can go to the card catalog and hope to find government material under the subject heading he has become used to seeing in most indexes and card catalogs. He may think he knows the author's name but fail to penetrate the mystery of the corporate entry.

Another aspect of retrieval, and for that matter selection, is the failure of most trade and national bibliographies to list government documents. *Books in Print* and *Subject Guides to Books in Print* rarely concede there is such a thing as a government document, unless it has been reissued by a private publisher. Periodical indexes list some documents, but these are highly selective. Encyclopedias, biographical dictionaries, handbooks, yearbooks, and other forms of reference works rarely cite government documents in their bibliographies; even though they may draw heavily upon them for statistical and research materials.

Scope

Too much emphasis can be placed upon categorizing the various forms or types of government publications. The user, after all, is only interested in formation, not in whether this or that happens to be an executive document or a congressional work. The categorization is primarily useful as a mnemonic device for the librarian. For example, a question about current legislation will require one type of document; a statistical question, quite another. Recognizing the likely branch of the government dealing with the subject of the request helps to narrow the search.

Executive Publications This does not simply mean papers of the President; but all those issued by the ten departments and various agencies of the government prepared by the Department of State, Commerce, Agriculture, Defense, Labor, and the five other major departments are called executive documents. There are hundreds of independent agencies related to the main departments that also publish a variety of documents.

From a reference viewpoint, these documents are primarily of interest for the information given on subject material. Anyone doing research in such fields as economics, labor, industry, or education will inevitably need a number of executive publications.

They may be located through the various catalogs and indexes, particularly *The Monthly Catalog*. If the document is known to be the publication of a particular department or agency, there are a number of department lists and indexes that give fuller information than any of the general catalogs and indexes. Most of the departments issue current lists. There are given in some detail in both Boyd's and Schmeckebier's guides to government documents. A number of the documents of more general interest may be located through standard periodical indexes.

Congressional (Legislative) Publications Congressional publications are primarily a record of congressional activities from debates in Congress to committee hearings and reports. There are a number of aids—discussed in the section Current Indexes and Bibliographies—to help the librarian locate ongoing activities of Congress. The legislative history, though, may be traced through a number of publications, sometimes known as the "congressional set," which includes the vast number of congressional documents. The principal documents of Congress are:

1. *The Congressional Record* *The Congressional Record* is the daily record of the proceedings of Congress. There is an index every two weeks, and a cumulative index at the end of the session. Although this is supposed to be a verbatim report of activities, it is not. Congressmen reserve the right to add and to delete. Nor does the record usually contain the text of bills and resolutions.

2. *Laws* The process of passing a law is an involved, although not necessarily complicated, matter. It is fully explained in the often revised *How Our Laws are Made* (Washington, D.C.: Government Printing Office, 1971, 64 pp.). Briefly, the process begins with a "bill" which may originate in either the House or the Senate. A bill passed by either house goes to the other as a printed "act." Various forms of "resolutions" are similar to bills, and there is little real difference. If the bill is passed, it is printed in the form of an unbound broadside or pamphlet. The "slip law" may run from one to several hundred pages. Copies are available on an annual subscription basis from the Superintendent of Documents; and many are also printed in full, as are most of the bills, in the weekly *U.S. Code Congressional and Administrative News* described later. In order to provide a permanent collection of the slip laws, they are gathered and bound in the *Statutes at Large.* Each volume contains a complete index and a table of earlier laws affected. Finally, the *United States Code,* which is published every six years, is a codification and consolidation of the general and permanent laws of the nation. There is considerably more to the laws and Congress than indicated in this brief paragraph. A useful aid for librarians working with laws is Harry Bitner and Miles O. Price's *Effective Legal*

Research (3d ed. Boston: Little, Brown and Company, 1969) which thoroughly describes in clear, precise fashion the multiple legal reference aids.

3. *Hearings* The transcripts of testimony before a congressional committee or subcommittee are known as hearings. Where made public, the printed hearings may be indexed in the *Monthly Catalog, the Public Affairs Information Service Bulletin,* the *CIS/Index,* and the like. The hearings may or may not be in the "congressional set," depending upon whether the committee gave a serial designation to the publication. Occasionally, they are printed as parts of larger reports; and where published as separates, they are usually offered for sale by the Superintendent of Documents.

4. *Committee prints* Publications issued by the various committees, in addition to transcriptions of the hearings themselves, are called "committee prints." These are of major importance as they often are independent studies requested by the various committees, e.g., a 2-volume study ordered by the Committee on Foreign Relations of American foreign policy. These are indexed in the *CIS/Index* and are usually, though not always, sent to depository libraries, but may not appear in the *Monthly Catalog.*

5. *Miscellany* There are numerous other congressional publications from the "calendars" (the daily agenda of Congress) to the "legislative journals" (which include a history of legislation). Congress may order reports from many departments and agencies. Consequently, there is a given amount of duplication between congressional publications and executive publications. For example, the annual reports of the Atomic Energy Commission, the Interstate Commerce Commission, and the Secretary of the Treasury, to name but three, are published both as a part of the congressional set and as separate publications by the agencies. The *Monthly Catalog* indicates duplication in editions for current materials.

The importance of this duplication to a reference librarian is that if the library does not have the separate issue of the publication, it frequently will be found in the bound volumes of the congressional set.

Judicial Publications Judicial publications primarily consist of the published laws of the United States (i.e., as outlined above) but also include publications of the courts. In the latter category, the most important consist of the decisions of the Supreme Court. (While not technically judicial publications, the various regulations and decisions of the agencies and bureaus are more closely aligned with legal matters than with the average requests for an executive documents. They are treated here as part of the laws.)

Of all areas of government documents, judicial publications is the most highly specialized. It requires a considerable knowledge of governmental organization and, except for general questions, is probably best left to the special law library or legislative reference service. This is not to say that the reference librarian should not be aware of judicial publications or how to use them, but any use in depth is beyond the scope of the present text. (Of considerable help, even to the less than law-educated librarian, are the basic *Judicial Opinion Reporters* issued by the West Publishing Company. The publisher offers an informative booklet on their use, and they are described in many of the government document guides.)

In terms of subjects, perhaps 15 to 20 percent of all types of documents issued may be of enough general interest to warrant consideration as "popular" sources of information. The vast majority are for the expert in government or in a given subject area and, as such, are for reference work primarily in large libraries. The number of state and local documents which can be termed "popular" are even fewer.

Evaluation

When speaking of evaluating government materials, sources cite qualities rather than actual methods of evaluation.

Government publications, for the most part, can be considered from the following standpoints:

Authority   Authority applies particularly to the official source material which records a law, a hearing, a debate, or the like.

Cost   The cost is usually minimal, and no private publisher could hope to compete with the low prices of many documents. Frequently, the most useful are in the 25-cent and 50-cent range.

Timeliness   Timeliness is another valuable feature, particularly for the statistical reports and the present methods of keeping up with scientific and technological advancement. Many publications are issued on a daily or weekly basis.

Range of Interest   The range of interest is all encompassing. No publisher except the government has such a varied list.

Indexes and Bibliographies   Indexes and bibliographies are improving, not only in the documents themselves, but in works intended as finding devices for those documents.

Other aspects such as arrangement, treatment, and format may not be all that is desirable, but the reference librarian hardly has any choice. There is, after all, only one *Congressional Record;* and, evaluation is in terms of whether it can be used in a particular library, not in terms of its intrinsic value.

Acquisition

Once a document has been selected for purchase, its acquisition is no more difficult—indeed, often somewhat easier—then acquiring a book or periodical. Depository libraries do have a peculiar set of problems;[6] but for the average library, the process may be as follows:

1. Full information is given in the *Monthly Catalog* on methods of purchase from the Superintendent of Documents. Many of the more popular documents are now distributed by the Public Documents Distribution Center in Philadelphia and Pueblo, Colorado—an effort to speed up delivery by locating centers outside of the Government Printing Office in Washington, D.C. Payment is made in advance by purchase of coupons. In case of extensive purchases, deposit accounts may be established. Also, it should be noted that free material is often listed and may be acquired simply by request.

   The popular or much called for government documents may also be purchased at one of some 15 Government Printing Office book stores throughout the nation; and in Dayton, Ohio, a department store is experimenting with the sale of documents through its regular book department.

2. Some documents may be obtained free from members of Congress. However, as the supply of some documents is limited, the congressman should be warned in advance. It is particularly advisable to get on the congressman's regular mailing list to receive such publications as the *Yearbook of Agriculture.*

3. Issuing agencies often have a stock of publications which they will send free to libraries.

4. A growing number of private firms now publish government documents, i.e., the *CIS/Index* offers a complete collection of the working papers of Congress on microfiche. Efforts to arrive at guidelines on how the GPO and private publishers distribute government publications in microform is a matter of primary

[6] Depository libraries, and how they function, are clearly explained in most of the general guides to government documents. A short, still pertinent outline is provided by Thomas Shaw's "Distribution and Acquisition," *Library Trends,* July 1966, pp. 37+. *See also:* Clifton Brock, "Depository Libraries: the Out-Houses of the Government's Information Transfer System," *Library Resources and Technical Services,* Fall 1968, pp. 412+.

concern because of a conflict in interest between the firms and the government. At this writing, the GPO was working with the Information Industry Association (made up of the major microform publishers) to arrive at some equitable solution.[7]

For a variety of reasons, not all government documents may be acquired by libraries or by individuals. The controversy over the Pentagon Papers highlighted this problem for millions of Americans. Many papers are classified for good or for not so good reasons, e.g., there is a time lag of 20 years before the official documentary series, *Foreign Relations of the United States,* can be published. As of 1973, there were 298 volumes published in this set, but only through 1946. And the National Archives has some 4,000 cubic feet of secret documents, military and otherwise. A number of these, following the furor over the Pentagon Papers, are being declassified.[8]

A short piece in *The New York Times* (June 15, 1969, p. 54) may give reference librarians a key to finding information in the so-called "secret documents":

> Edward J. Cook, a Washington developer, was asked by Arundel County zoning officials to substantiate a contention that more housing was needed in the area of the security agency at Fort Meade, Maryland.
>
> Mr. Cook told the hearing that the agency employs about 2,000 persons. The developer then was asked whether he got the figure from security agency officials.
>
> "Oh, no," he replied. "I tried there first, but they wouldn't disclose it; so I called the Russian Embassy and they told me."

GENERAL GUIDES AND BIBLIOGRAPHIES

Schmeckebier, Laurence F. and Roy B. Easton. *Government Publications and Their Use.* 2d ed. Washington, D.C.: The Brookings Institute, 1969, $8.95.

Boyd, Anne, *United States Government Publications.* 3d ed. New York: The H. W. Wilson Company, 1949 (reprinted with corrections, 1952), 627 pp., $10. (Note: revision underway. No date of publication.)

Wynkoop, Sally, *Subject Guide to Government Reference Books.* Littleton, Colorado: Libraries Unlimited, 1970 to date, biennial, $11.50.

Body, Alexander, *Annotated Bibliography of Bibliographies on Selected Government Publications.* Kalamazoo, Michigan: Western Michigan University, 1967, 181 pp. Three supplements, 1968, 1970, 1972.

---

[7] "Govt. vs. Publisher," *Publishers' Weekly,* December 1, 1969, pp. 20+. This discusses the whole question of private versus government publication.

[8] "Now it Can Be Told," *The Wall Street Journal,* September 6, 1972, pp. 1+. A lengthy article on the problem of secret documents. *See also:* Joseph McDonald, "Rights in Conflict and Rights in Conflict," *RQ,* Winter 1969, pp. 124+.

Leidy, Philip, *A Popular Guide to Government Publications.* 3d rev. ed. New York: Columbia University Press, 1968, $12. (Note: publisher says 4th ed. to be published in late 1973 or 1974.)

There are two basic approaches to learning about United States government documents. Both are represented here. One is concerned with giving the reader an overview of the governmental process and the significance of government publications, i.e., Schmeckebier and Boyd; the other with listing and annotating some of the better, more general documents, e.g., Wynkoop. The guides serve to introduce librarians and laymen to the subject, as well as refresh the memory about a given point. The bibliographies are both a buying guide and an index which helps the librarian to locate materials in given subject areas.

At this writing, there were no completely up-to-date guides to government documents. The two standards listed here are infrequently revised. (The Boyd title will be reissued sometime in the mid 1970s. It is being revised and rewritten by F. J. O'Hara whose column on government documents appears regularly in the *Wilson Library Bulletin*.) In her introductory section, Wynkoop lists some 20 to 25 bibliographies and guides, but most of these are fairly specialized. The exception is John Mason's *Research Resources: Annotated Guide to the Social Sciences,* Volume Two (Santa Barbara, California: ABC/Clio Press, 1971, 273 pp.) which annotates and discusses the use of government documents in the social sciences. It is not entirely satisfactory, and although current, in no way replaces either Schmeckebier or Boyd.

Published shortly after Schmeckebier's death, the standard *Government Publications and Their Use* describes all aspects of documents from how they are produced to how they are used. It is particularly good in its description of the depository system. The two authors are sometimes difficult to follow; but on the whole, it is the best guide of its type available at this writing. Boyd's work was for many years the standard, and it goes into great and impressive detail about all aspects of the subject. It is still extremely useful for historical material and for broad, unchanging outlines of how laws are made and how bills are passed. But until it is revised, it is of limited use for beginners.

Serving as an annotated checklist of over 1,050 documents published during the previous two years, the Wynkoop title is arranged by broad subject and has a detailed index. In addition to relatively current documents, she includes series and serials, as well as basic titles which are necessary for almost all collections. Most of the annotations are descriptive rather than evaluative, but the evaluation reduces the 20,000 or so documents listed in the *Monthly Catalog* down to one-twentieth of that number for possible use and purchase by libraries. As a biennial guide, this is a first-rate work and should be found in all reference libraries, even those which may have few government documents. The publications, after all, can be borrowed on interlibrary loan or the patron may go to another library, or for that matter order them himself. (The author gives complete bibliographical details, including the "doc" number and the price.)

Body limits himself to government-published bibliographies which range from everything to air pollution and crime to public health and highway safety. In many ways, this is an ideal title to supplement the *Bibliographic Index*. It is not, and this should be emphasized, a general list of government documents as found in Wynkoop and other similar titles. Full bibliographical information is given and there are numerous indexes, including a subject approach. The annotations are lengthy, fully descriptive, and generally excellent. As a unique guide to bibliographical material, it should be better known; and it deserves a place in almost any library, even the one with limited government document service. The bibliographies will not only lead the researcher, the layman, and the student to useful, often unrecorded information but also indicate to the librarian the broad range of interests of all government documents.

A subject approach is offered by Ellen Jackson's *Subject Guide to Major United States Government Publications* (Chicago: American Library Association, 1968, 186 pp., $5.50). Emphasis is on documents of lasting value, both for the scholar and the layman. Arrangement is by subject and a concluding chapter covers guides, catalogs, and indexes. Documents are listed which the author believed to be of enough importance to compose a basic collection in any relatively large library. They range in time from the beginning of government publication through 1967; and in subject matter, they are of interest to almost anyone. Even libraries lacking the documents will find the guide helpful for interlibrary loan purposes.

While all of these guides and bibliographies are primarily for librarians and researchers, the Leidy title is prepared for popular consumption. Although now dated—a new edition is announced for 1973 or 1974—it remains a fine source for a subject approach to some 2,300 titles. In many ways, it is the best single work available for the nonspecialist and a checklist for purchase of works which otherwise might escape the librarian. Most of the titles were in print when the book was issued. Under such headings as Insects, Bees, Health, History, and other popular subjects, the author includes a vast variety of material. There is a detailed subject index and a number of sprightly cross-references. For example, the note under Insects sets the tone of the author's style: "The entries that follow deal with the pleasanter side of insects; for the other side of the coin see various headings under Pests." Some other items are also cleverly annotated. Obviously not for the expert, but a useful guide for the average user.

Other select lists are issued by many publishers and countless magazines. These are traced in most indexes and abstracting services, but more particularly the *Public Affairs Information Service Bulletin.* An excellent title is Sylvia Mechanic's *Annotated List of Selected United States Government Publications Available to Depository Libraries* (New York: The H. W. Wilson Company, 1971, 424 pp., $16). The author includes some 500 documents found in most libraries.

On a month-to-month basis, the best single source of annotated reviews is the aforementioned O'Hara column in the *Wilson Library Bulletin.* His "Selected Government Publications" usually includes some carefully chosen 25 to 35 titles. A broader, more discursive, and in some ways more satisfactory approach is offered by Joe Morehead's "A Mazeway Miscellany" in the quarterly *RQ.* He has a fine style, a quick eye for the unusual (and often the humorous), and, more important, tends to survey the whole field of government documents rather than one particular item.

CURRENT INDEXES AND BIBLIOGRAPHIES

Federal All issued by the Government Printing Office, Washington, D.C.

U.S. Superintendent of Documents. *Monthly Catalog of United States Government Publications,* 1895 to date, monthly, $7.

———— *Selected U.S. Government Publications,* 1928 to date, biweekly, free.

———— *Price Lists of Government Publications,* 1898 to date, irregular, free.

Federal All issued by private publishers.

Cumulative Subject Index of the Monthly Catalog of United States Government Publications. 1900-1971. Washington, D.C.: Carrollton Press, 1972, 14 vols., $965.

CIS/Index, i.e., *Congressional Information/Service Index to Publications of the United States Congress.* Washington, D.C.: Congressional Information Service, 1970 to date, monthly, service basis ($95 to $395).

In 1895, the office of the Superintendent of Documents was established; and in that same year, publication of the *Monthly Catalog* began. There have been several changes in the approach and the arrangement of the catalog; but from 1941 to date, it has been considered the basic record of government publications. It is roughly equivalent in purpose to *Books in Print.* It appears at the end of each month. Arrangement is alphabetical by publishing office. Prior to September 1947, the various smaller bureaus were subheads under the main government departments. Now they are primary listings.

Each entry includes title, date, pagination, price, classification number, Library of Congress card number, and a symbol showing where the publication may be purchased or whether it is sent to a depository library. Some of the 20,000 documents listed each year are for official use only, but 60 to 70 percent may be purchased directly from the Superintendent of Documents. None of the entries is annotated, the subject area being dependent upon the titles and the issuing department. This is not as confusing as it might seem, primarily because many of the titles are self-descriptive of content and the nature of the work may be assumed from the nature of the issuing agency.

Individual bills introduced in the House and Senate are included, but only by number. Titles of bills may be traced through the *CIS/ Index, Congressional Quarterly Weekly Reports,* the *Congressional Record, Facts on File,* and *The New York Times Index,* to name a few sources. In recent years, the sheet maps and charts formally recorded are no longer included; but they are listed in the sales catalogs of the Coast and Geodetic Survey and other agencies.

The February issue lists all government periodicals and subscription publications.

The *Monthly Catalog* as it is now constituted includes only about 50 percent of all government publications. Many administrative documents, research reports, and so-called "processed" reports (i.e., those duplicated by means other than printing such as mimeograph and xerox) are not listed. This has been a constant concern of librarians and also of the Superintendent of Documents, and studies continually are made to determine the feasibility of listing these works in the *Monthly Catalog* as well.

The uses of the *Monthly Catalog* may be summarized as follows:

1. It is the one single, close-to-comprehensive bibliographical guide for the identification and verification of government documents.
2. It is both an index and a subject guide which may be used by even the smallest library, not only for what may be in the collection, but for purposes of interlibrary loan.
3. For purposes of libraries that take the complete congressional set, the *Monthly Catalog* indicates reports and documents which are a part of the set. Given the House or Senate number of the item, it may be traced to its place in the set through the *Numerical List and Schedules of Volumes* (Washington, D.C.: Government Printing Office, 1928 to date). Information for each report or document, listed in numerical order, indicates the volume in which it may be found.
4. It can be used as a buying guide. This may appear formidable, but any librarian with a knowledge of his collection and the

subject needs of his users may scan an issue quickly for possible publications to acquire. For this purpose, it is as useful in the smallest library as in the large research library.

For reference purposes, the *Monthly Catalog* is of primary value to the nonspecialist because of the subject approach. Admittedly inadequate, it nevertheless is a tremendous aid in locating out-of-the-way types of information on a variety of topics from blueprint reading and part-time farming to (and these are actual titles of documents) "Geology of the Arabian Peninsula, Yemen" and "Proposed Large Scale Combination Nuclear Power-Desalting Project."

One of two other aids, which in no way replace the *Monthly Catalog*, is *Selected United States Government Publications*. There is a tendency among some librarians to feel this twice-monthly list is quite enough. It is not, particularly if the library is going to offer interlibrary loan service which may rely heavily on the *Monthly Catalog*. As a selection tool, it is favored by most public libraries serving populations under 50,000, a majority of school libraries, and some college libraries.

The selected list is published as a booklet and lists about sixty publications with full annotations as to content. Documents that are likely to be of more general interest and concern to the layman are selected from the *Monthly Catalog*. Unlike the *Monthly Catalog*, it frequently lists maps, as well as books, pamphlets, reports, and other types of publications. Usually four to eight items are especially featured in each issue, and these are given extensive annotations. The publication is offered free; and in each mailing, there usually are included special subject lists. These include current as well as retrospective materials.

Taken a step further, a particular subject is the theme about which each of the *Price Lists* is constructed. Some 50 of these are in print at any one time and must be ordered separately. Recent ones, for example, are entitled *Consumer Information* (No. 86) and *Radio and Electricity* (No. 82). As a subject concentration, they are particularly useful to students preparing papers. They have some value for the expert; but since they tend to be highly selective with a bias toward the popular, they usually serve the scholar only as a point of departure.

Given these basic current bibliographical aids, how does a user find what he is seeking? Each issue of the *Monthly Catalog* has its own index. There is an annual index in the December issue which includes subject headings; some, but not all, titles entries; and personal authors, with the exception of foreigners. Unfortunately, there are only two major government published cumulative issues: *Decennial Cumulative Index, 1941–50* (Washington, D.C.: Government Printing Office, 1953, 1,848 pp.); *Decennial Cumulative Index, 1951–60* (Washington, D.C.: Government Printing Office, 1968, 2 vols., $50).

Filling the gap, a private publisher has issued an index for the years 1900–1971. In a single alphabet, the 14-volume index includes subject entries from 81 different sources in the *Monthly Catalog* series. While government organizational author entries are included, the index does not list personal authors—the publisher says this is planned for another set.[9] The size of the index can be understood by the volume of indexing—over one million publications are analyzed. Although the price for the index is rather high, any library with a large documents collection will find it well worth it. (In conjunction with the index, the publisher offers the whole of the *Monthly Catalog* on microfilm, as well as the two decennial indexes; cost—$750 to $840.)

As valuable as the indexes to the *Monthly Catalog* are for all libraries, the primary index for all but the smallest library is the *CIS/Index*. Although the price can be high, it is more than worthwhile for reference work. Published in loose-leaf form, there are average additions of 100 to 200 pages per month. In an average year, the subscriber receives some 11,000 abstracts and over 60,000 index entries. The index provides abstracts of almost every document issued by the U.S. Congress during the previous month. This includes not only the obvious reports, but hearings and committee prints as well as nondepository and not-for-sale items.

The index is easy to use. The main section lists materials by subject, authors, witnesses in hearings, congressmen, popular names of bills, laws, and reports. Under each subject or author, there is a brief description of the material and an accession number which leads the reader to a document abstract in another section of the index. A full description is given of the document so it may be retrieved by the Superintendent of Documents number. Additional indexes cross-reference bills, public laws, reports and document numbers, as well as the names of committee and subcommittee chairmen. Also, for libraries who subscribe to the *CIS/Microfiche Library* collection, there is a key to where the document will be found on microfiche.[10]

Along with each monthly index is a newsletter, *CIS/Highlights*, which comes to subscribers a few days ahead of the index. This is by way of a current awareness service which announces particularly interesting documents to be indexed.

The index is cumulated quarterly, and there is an annual which contains all the abstracts and index references published the previous year. Furthermore, the annual makes an effort to summarize and in-

---

[9] Another publisher, Pierian Press of Ann Arbor, Michigan, offers the separate author index, but only for 1941–1965, in three volumes from $24.95 to $29.95 each. This is a valuable index because the *Monthly Catalog* did not include personal author entries from 1947 through 1962.

[10] Some half-million pages are available on microfiche. Subscribers receive these each month (at an added cost) with the index. Also, the microfiche may be ordered selectively for all House and Senate documents, Committee hearings, and so on.

cludes some material not found in the monthly version. Particularly valuable are the brief descriptions and legislative histories of all the laws enacted during the previous year.

Libraries which cannot afford, or do not need, the monthly index should try to purchase the annual volume which may be obtained separately ($160). In 2 volumes, it is the primary source of information on Congress and can be used by itself even without benefit of the documents.

Beyond the *Monthly Catalog* and the *CIS/Index*, there are numerous other aids for locating material. Most of these are used by larger libraries. In a survey of 36 depository libraries on how they locate documents, Simmons discovered:

1. Eighty-one percent answered that the *Monthly Catalog* was their chief source for retrieving documents.
2. Nineteen percent reported they compile separate subject indexes or catalogs for their documents. This is primarily for series and on works for which there is a high user demand. More than 90 percent however, did include cataloging for some documents in the full subject catalog in the library's main card catalog.
3. Other sources, cited more than once, included: (a) *Public Affairs Information Service Bulletin*. This leads the list because it not only indexes selectively government reports and documents, but indexes more than twenty-five government periodicals; (b) the *CIS/Index* was listed next—a second place which may be accounted for by the relatively new status of the index at the time of the survey; (c) various lists published by government agencies; (d) Andriot's *Guide to U.S. Government Serials and Periodicals;* (e) Leidy's *Guide;* (f) *CQ Weekly.* And several others were mentioned at least once from the *Education Index* and *Research in Education* (both of which include selected government periodicals and monographs) to standard guide books.[11]

With this admittedly far from complete, yet indicative survey in mind, the novice will probably be more than content to master the *Monthly Catalog,* a few of the guides, the basic indexes discussed in other chapters, and the *CIS/Index.* Still, there are other quite useful specific indexes. One example is the *Congressional Index* (Washington,

[11] Robert M. Simmons, "Documents Survey," *RQ.* See also: Dawn McCaghy and Gary Purcell. "Faculty Use of Government Publications," *College & Research Libraries,* January, 1972, pp. 7+. They found, much as Simmons, that faculty depend primarily on *The Monthly Catalog* and the library's own catalog which includes references to government documents.

D.C.: Commerce Clearing House, Inc., 1937 to date, weekly). This is in the familiar CCH binders which are so well known to business libraries. Weekly inserts keep information current on the status of House and Senate bills; and the service is particularly valuable for locating the subject matter or official name of a bill which is either pending or has passed. The *CIS/Index* covers much of the same material, but it is monthly. The weekly *Congressional Index* has the advantage of timeliness and concentrating primarily on bills and resolutions. (A somewhat similar approach is offered in the *U.S. Code Congressional and Administrative News,* discussed in the next section.)

REPORTS, SERVICES, AND PERIODICALS

Congressional Quarterly Service. Washington, D.C.: Congressional Quarterly, Inc., 1945 to date. A number of services which include: (1) *The Weekly Report,* 1945 to date, $144; (2) *The Quarterly Index to the Weekly Report,* 1945 to date, (included in the subscription price to *Weekly Report);* (3) *CQ Almanac,* 1945 to date, annual, $47.50.

    Congressional Digest. Washington, D.C.: Congressional Digest, 1921 to date, monthly, $12.50.

    National Journal. Washington, D.C.: Center for Political Research, 1969 to date, weekly, $200.

    U.S. Code Congressional and Administrative News. St. Paul, Minn.: West Publishing Company, 1939 to date, semimonthly.

    Andriot, John L., *Guide to U.S. Government Serials and Periodicals.* 1971 ed. McLean, Virginia: Documents Index, 1971, 4 vols. in 3, paperback, $60.

The general guides, bibliographies, and indexes assist the librarian to find specific documents; but beyond that there are some excellent—and rather expensive—services which provide weekly, monthly, and quarterly reports on government action. Several, too, print in part or in full the major bills pending before Congress, as well as other documents which are of current interest.

Probably the best known of these is provided by the Congressional Quarterly Service. The publisher issues a number of titles, all related to government and government documents. *The Weekly Report* provides summaries on bills before Congress, reports on coming activities, and details of major committee actions, as well as how congressmen vote. Full texts are provided when considered important. *The Quarterly Index* provides a name and subject index to the preceding issues of the weekly service. (Prior to the quarterly index, the librarian must depend upon the weekly table of contents for information; and the *Public Affairs Information Service Bulletin* which weekly indexes the reports.) The *CQ Al-*

manac is published in the spring and covers the previous year's activities as reported in the weekly title. However, it is rearranged and edited so the *Almanac* serves as both an index and summary volume. Where libraries cannot afford the weekly service, the *CQ Almanac* is a basic, much used reference aid. The annual can be used independently or with the weekly reports.

The firm publishes a number of other services and books, including the *Editorial Research Reports* (1923 to date, weekly), which select a major issue and assemble basic facts on all sides. The in-depth studies are cumulated semiannually.[12]

A former editor of the *CQ Weekly Report* began the *National Journal* in 1969; and in many ways, it is a competitor of the older work.[13] It differs in that there is more emphasis on the workings of federal agencies and the executive branch; and while Congress is covered almost as well as in the *CQ* title, its main purpose is not quite the same as its rival. There are four to five well-researched reports (somewhat similar to the treatment, if briefer, in the *Editorial Research Reports*) on current topics, and news of various governmental activities. It has one distinct advantage—there is a weekly personal name, private organization, and geographic index; and a quarterly index provides numerous entries into the weekly issues.

The *U.S. Code Congressional and Administrative News* differs from both the other weekly services in concentrating on publishing the text of all public laws, basic reports on congressional committees, administrative regulations, and the like. It is primarily, although not exclusively, a lawyer's and businessman's service; but because of the full texts, it is unquestionably of considerable aid to the larger reference library.

As good as these services are, many libraries cannot afford them. A useful aid, although in no way a substitute for the other titles, the *Congressional Digest* offers a brief summary of the previous month's activities in Congress. More important, though, it takes a current national topic and treats it in depth. Pro and con arguments are given; and the whole is written in a style ideal for the layman and, more particularly, for the student at the high school and college level. Parenthetically, the *Congressional Digest* is a commercial venture and should not be confused with the *Congressional Record.*

In addition to these services which record the activities of government, the government itself publishes over 4,000 serials and periodicals. Andriot's frequently revised guide is basic in this field. This, it should be

[12] Additional titles are noted in this text. For a summary of the better known works, see Joe Morehead's review of the *Congressional Quarterly Guide RQ,* Winter 1971, pp. 165 + . He discusses the *Guide* and other *CQ* publications. *See also,* the listing in Evelyn S. Meyer's "Reference Guides to Congressional Research," *RQ,* Fall 1972, pp. 32-33.

[13] "Battle of Capitol Hill," *Newsweek,* April 14, 1969, p. 100.

made clear, is a guide, not an index. The first section is an alphabetical listing of over 2,000 government agencies, committees, and the like— useful in no small part for the brief background and history he provides for each. The second volume lists the various publications which include not only magazines but also reports, releases, and even fugitive ephemeral materials. The third volume lists agencies which have been abolished or otherwise changed; and the last section is an agency and title index.[14] This is the standard guide in the field; but for libraries seeking a less complete listing, there are several substitutes: (1) Joe Morehead's selected annotated list of government magazines, which includes some foreign titles, in the author's *Magazines for Libraries* (2d ed. New York: R. R. Bowker Company, 1972); (2) The February issue of the *Monthly Catalog* which includes a directory of major government periodicals; (3) *Price List 36*, "Government Periodicals and Subscription Services," primarily the same list, with additions, found in the *Monthly Catalog.*

Retrospective Sources

Given the cumulative index to the *Monthly Catalog*, the researcher has a basic tool to locate government documents from 1900 to date. But how does one find documents prior to 1900? There are a number of sources, none of which is entirely satisfactory. Another problem with these aids is that they presuppose the library has the documents, which is rarely the case except for the better established series in larger research libraries.

Suffice to say for the beginner, retrospective aids do exist. These are explained in some detail in the basic guides such as Boyd and Schmeckebier or in Winchell.

STATE AND LOCAL DOCUMENTS

U.S. Library of Congress. *Monthly Checklist of State Publication,* 1910 to date, $8.

    Council of State Governments. *Legislative Research Checklist.* Lexington, Kentucky: The Council, 1970, quarterly, $5.

—— *Selected Bibliography on State Government,* 1959–1972. Lexington, Kentucky: The Council, 1972, 240 pp., paperback, $6.

    Index to Current Urban Documents. Westport, Connecticut: Greenwood Press, 1972 to date, quarterly, $75 (+ $30 for annual cumulative vol.).

If federal documents are little understood in many libraries, the state and local documents are even more in limbo. The reason is primar-

---

[14] For a descriptive, critical review *see: College & Research Libraries,* July 1972, pp. 333+.

ily twofold: (1) there is a lack of proper bibliographical control, although this is improving; (2) even with such control, the average librarian rarely thinks of state documents as a vital source of information. The reason for this latter assumption is that most states issue "blue books" which, as a manual, give answers to recurrent questions: Who is my representative? What is the address of X agency? Who is the head of Y agency? With the "blue books" or legislative manual at hand, most questions involving the state are readily answered. Furthermore, at a local level, the library tends to rely more on its own clipping file and possibly its own local newspaper index.

There is a need for a greater awareness of what state publications can do to help reference work. As Hernon puts it:

> State publications . . . provide data on a variety of subjects. Often they are the best or only access to state activities. . . .The trend seems to be for states to publish more, not less. Indeed, there is an information explosion, and it does not take long for reference sources on states to become dated or even obsolete. If the reference collection contains materials over five years old, librarians should consider their replacement, assuming later revisions are available. Fortunately, many of these reference tools are free or available at a nominal cost.
>
> By drawing upon these state materials, reference librarians can give patrons more in-depth guidance and at the same time refer them to current, pertinent sources. Part of the needed knowledge will come through the building of a versatile reference collection, and the rest will depend upon the reference librarian's better understanding of state publications, the problems in their distribution, and the inadequacies in governmental bibliographies.[15]

Where there is no concerted effort to collect state and local documents, the library should be aware of other libraries in the immediate area that have such collections. Usually the best single source of information about these collections, as well as the documents themselves, is the state library. By law, most state agencies must file copies of their various reports with the state library. The state library, in turn, will maintain its own collection and have some arrangement for distributing the excess documents to other libraries in the state, either on a systematic basis to state depository libraries (the system varies, but is somewhat the same as federal depositories) or on an informal basis to the smaller units.

At the state level, there is no entirely satisfactory bibliographical tool that lists the majority of publications. Of considerable help is the *Monthly Checklist of State Publications.* Issued once a month, prepared

---

[15] Peter Hernon, "State Publications," *Library Journal,* April 15, 1972, p. 1393. Other useful articles in this area: Philip Schwartz, "State and Local Document Retrieval," *RQ,* Spring 1972, pp. 250+; Margaret Lane, "Acquisition of State Documents," *Law Library Journal,* February 1970, pp. 92+; Jack Clarke, "State Manuals," *RQ,* Winter 1972, pp. 186+.

by the Library of Congress, it represents only those state publications received by the library. Arrangement is alphabetical by state and then, as in the *Monthly Catalog,* by issuing agency. Entries are usually complete enough for ordering purposes, although prices are not always given. There is an annual, but not a monthly, subject, and author index. The indexes are not cumulative. Since 1963, periodicals have been listed in the June and December numbers.

Beginning in 1973, the Greenwood Press offers a monthly service which includes microform copies of most of the documents listed in the *Monthly Checklist.* According to the firm, "it is estimated that approximately 15,000 documents or serial publications will be filmed" annually. Also, individual documents as selected by the librarian will be available in microform from the publisher.

The Council of State Governments is a nonprofit organization which was founded in 1925 to help governmental processes within the states. It issues a number of publications, including *The Book of the States* and the *Legislative Checklist.* The latter work is made up of three parts. The first section is a newsletter on developments in the legislatures; the second lists studies which are going to be made; and the third, and most important for reference work, lists reports completed by various state agencies and commissions. Entries in the third section are arranged by subject, then by state. Full bibliographical details are given for each document, but there are no annotations.

While the *Checklist* is not as complete as the *Monthly Checklist of State Publications,* it does cover a variety of material sometimes missing from the latter work. As such, it can be used to augment the basic monthly bibliography. In addition, there are various firms which offer microform copies of the 900 or so documents listed in the *Checklist,* and these may be ordered through the Council.[16]

From time to time, there are bibliographies of state documents issued; and the one mentioned here is representative. Also published by the Council, it is a computer produced index to over 1,000 state related titles. Most of the emphasis is on books and articles, but there are a number of state publications included. It is useful, as well, for a list of journals which report on state governments.

The total lack of any central control of city, county, and local documents may be solved by the *Index to Current Urban Documents.* "May be" is used advisedly because the service was too new at this writing to ascertain its ultimate success. Briefly, though, Greenwood promises to publish in microform all official public documents currently being issued by the 150 largest cities (i.e., with populations of 100,000 or more) and

---

[16] For a detailed description of the service and its problems, *see:* Charles Seal's "State Documents," *RQ,* Fall 1970, pp. 49+.

counties in the United States. The *Index* serves as the bibliographic control for the microform, but it is equally valuable to libraries who simply wish to identify the documents for possible order in the hard form. The alphabetical index is arranged by subject and area.

THE UNITED NATIONS AND FOREIGN GOVERNMENT PUBLICATIONS

Winston, Harry, *Publications of the United Nations Systems.* New York: R. R. Bowker Company, 1972, 192 pp., $10.95.

The majority of Western countries follow the basic pattern of publication and distribution of government documents employed by the United States. For example, the rough equivalent to the *Monthly Catalog* in Britain is the *Government Publications Monthly List,* which has an annual cumulation, i.e., *Catalogue of Government Publications.* Similar to our *Price Lists* is the *British Sectional Lists.* And in Canada, there is the *Canadian Government Publications Monthly Catalogue.* Beyond these basics, the patterns differ with each of the governments.

Unfortunately, though, there is no current guide which will take the novice through the terrain of foreign documents. A much cited work is the much dated *Study of Current Bibliographies of National Official Publications* (Paris: UNESCO, 1958, 260 pp.); and while this is of some help, it is far from the foreign equivalent to a Boyd or a Schmeckebier. The basic bibliographies and indexes are listed and briefly annotated in both Winchell and Walford. Still, without a proper guide, the listings may mean little to a beginner.

United Nations publications fare a bit better than the Winston title. The first section includes a listing of agencies, their aims, structure, and basic publications. The second part is an annotated list of useful publications under 29 general subject areas; and the final section lists and annotates some 300 periodicals. There is an index that, while helpful, is more of a bibliography than a guide.

Of considerable promise for keeping up with United Nations documents is the *International Bibliography, Information and Documentation* (New York: R. R. Bowker Company, 1973 to date, quarterly, $15). This quarterly magazine provides full bibliographic details and descriptive annotations for every new priced publication, including periodicals, of the various United Nations agencies.

Milton Mittleman writes an irregular column for *RQ,* which includes annotations of selected current United Nations publications. There is a brief description of the genre in several of the general guides to government documents—but on the whole the area is one which needs considerable development. That is a development and exploration which is beyond the current text. This brief entry can only serve to alert the beginner that government documents do not end with those issued by the United States.[17]

SUGGESTED READING

The best ongoing comments on government documents, as noted, are found in two columns: (1) Joe Morehead's "A Mazeway Miscellany," in *RQ,* quarterly; and (2) F. J. O'Hara's "Selected Government Publications," *Wilson Library Bulletin,* monthly.

Buckley, C. W., "Distribution of U.S. Government Publications," *Law Library Journal,* February 1970, pp. 100+. An outline of distribution methods.

Free, O. M., "Commercial Reprints of Federal Documents, Their Significance and Acquisition," *Special Libraries,* March 1969, pp. 125+. A discussion of private publishers and government document reprints.

Grossman, Julian A., "Putting Government Documents to Work," *RQ,* Fall 1971, pp. 42+. A short discussion of how one college uses government documents.

Hecht, Rachel, "Collecting and Keeping Federal Documents," *Law Library Journal,* February 1970, pp. 103+. A brief article on documents for law libraries.

Illinois Libraries, June 1971. Most of the issue is devoted to timely articles on "Federal Documents," and there is a good bibliography, pp. 418–425, covering current articles. *See also: Library Trends,* July 1966. The issue is given over to "Federal, State, and Local Government Publications." A bit dated, but useful.

Lester, Marilyn, "Federal and State Government Publications of Professional Interest to the School Librarian. . . ." Library School, University of Illinois, *Occasional Papers No. 100,* November 1971. A guide to and list of government publications for schools and educators.

Meyers, Evelyn, "Reference Guides to Congressional Research," *RQ,* Fall 1972, pp. 30+. A short annotated list of basic titles used in work with government documents.

Wagner, S., "Publishing on the Potomac," *Publishers' Weekly,* August 9, 16, 23, 1971, various paging. A well-written, easy-to-understand series on various aspects of government printing and publications.

---

[17] For an overview of the problem, as well as a brief list of some general and specific guides, *see:* James B. Childs, "Reference Use of Official Publications of National Governments," *Herald of Library Science,* October 1971, pp. 327+. A general article on the value of foreign documents is Eugenia Eaton's "A Collecting Policy for Foreign Documents," *RQ,* Fall 1970, pp. 59+.

INDEX